Mahbanoo Gandhi

POLITICS AND THE ECONOMY

POLITICS AND THE ECONOMY

James E. Anderson

University of Houston

Little, Brown and Company

Boston and Toronto

To My Parents

PREFACE

In the twentieth century the promotion and control of economic activity has become a highly important and pervasive governmental function. Few economic activities are not actively influenced by government in the United States. The modern regulatory state has replaced the comparatively passive and minimal nineteenth-century state.

This book is designed as an introduction to the national government's role in the American economy. It is not a comprehensive analysis because we have given limited attention to such topics as railroad regulation, natural resource policy, and financial regulation. Nonetheless, most areas of public economic policy are touched on at some point, and the reader should come away with a good view of both the development and scope of government's economic role.

The formation and implementation of public economic policy are examined, as well as its form and substance. Within the context of historical and economic environment, we concentrate on policy trends and patterns and the political factors—pressure groups, political parties, political culture, governmental structures, and the like—which affect policy. We have attempted, to put the matter somewhat differently, to combine discussions of the American political process and the economic regulatory process.

It is hoped that this volume will interest the general reader, the teacher, and the student with an interest (whatever its origin) in political-economic relationships. As a tool of instruction, it can be used in introductory courses dealing with public economic policy, whether offered in political science, economics, or business administration departments. As supplementary reading, or if properly supplemented, it can also be used in more advanced courses on government and the economy and public policy.

Many people have assisted me in preparing this book. Various colleagues, including Douglas S. Gatlin, Jivan R. Tabibian, Richard D. Sears, and Harold V. Rhodes, read portions of the manuscript and offered advice and encouragement. C. H. Richards, Jr., chairman of my department, provided a teaching schedule which facilitated my task and the Wake Forest Graduate Council chipped in with some useful financial assistance. Susan Keen Huffman, Mary June Merrill, and Emily G. Lincoln worked to convert my handwriting into a readable typed manuscript. David W. Lynch, of Little, Brown and Company, helped to improve the manuscript by his editing. My wife, Alberta, typed, read copy, sympathized, and in many other ways contributed to the book.

JAMES E. ANDERSON

WINSTON-SALEM, N.C.

CONTENTS

POLITICS AND THE ECONOMY

Chapter One

GOVERNMENT AND THE ECONOMY

The American experience has been characterized by distrust of government and the notion that politics and economics are properly separate and distinct spheres of social action. In actuality the two have always been intertwined—government has always intervened in the economy. The framers of the Constitution clearly did not intend separation of government and economy; rather, numerous powers to control and promote economic activity were granted to the national government. Only a few specific limitations were imposed on the power of either national or state governments to enact economic legislation. Since the adoption of the Constitution reliance on government—national, state, and local—for the solution of social and economic problems has greatly increased. Today there are no individuals or groups who do not depend in some way upon government for assistance in solving their problems, controlling their environment, or adjusting and settling their conflicts of interest.

The enactment of economic legislation is one of the major tasks of American legislative bodies. To verify this statement one need only compare the amount of attention the United States Congress or the "typical" state legislature devotes to legislation concerning economic activity with that involving religious, cultural, or family matters. Indeed, it is difficult to find fault with James Madison's statement in *Federalist No. 10* that "regulation of . . . diverse and interfering [economic] interests forms the principal task of modern legislation." Administrative agencies, and to a lesser extent the courts, are also deeply involved in public economic policy.

The hypothesis that government economic intervention increases as an economic system becomes more complex is the organizing principle for this chapter. The expansion of government economic activity in the

1

United States has been a function of economic growth and industrialization. To say this is not to subscribe to some form of blind economic determinism but is simply another way of saying that government and economy are related, that government, like any social institution, is affected by and responds to changes in its environment.

The following discussion of the development and present role of government in the American economy will move along several lines of analysis. (1) The economic system in the early nineteenth century, when government regulation was relatively minimal, will be compared with the economic system of today. (2) The historical evolution of public economic policy will be sketched, giving attention to some of the broad social and political forces affecting its growth. (3) Some of the underlying causes of the expansion of government economic activity which have resulted from alterations in the socio-economic environment will be discussed. (4) The role of government in our modern "mixed economy" will be considered.

THE AMERICAN ECONOMY: PAST AND PRESENT

In the early part of the nineteenth century the American economy was essentially agrarian, technologically primitive, and atomistic. The population of the United States in 1800 was less than five and a half million and was scattered over a territory ranging from Canada to Florida and from the Atlantic Ocean to the Mississippi River. Most of the population lived in rural areas—95 per cent in 1800 and 80 per cent as late as 1860. Agriculture was the chief source of livelihood for most of the people. Although many farms were small and self-sufficient, agriculture was the largest source of national income, surpassing such other sources as trade, shipping, and lumbering.

The Industrial Revolution, which was well under way in England, was only beginning in the new American nation during the early part of the nineteenth century. Most units of production were small and were in handicraft or domestic stages of production. In 1810, the largest manufacturing plant was worth less than $250,000. (The first *million* dollar corporation appeared in 1853.) The individual proprietorship and partnership forms of organization predominated. Only a few hundred corporations existed at the end of the eighteenth century. Although there were "merchant princes" and others of the sort, especially in the Northeast, the typical businessman was a storekeeper, peddler, or blacksmith. Big business was a post-Civil War phenomenon.

The economic and social systems were fluid; there were no rigid or sharply defined class structures to inhibit the mobility, upward or otherwise, of the population. Slavery, of course, was a notable exception. Natural resources, especially land, were abundant and individuals were free to acquire and exploit them. The "typical" American owned tangible property. All in all, the society conformed closely to the requisites of the agrarian democratic society envisaged by Thomas Jefferson, John Taylor, and others. It was an individualistic, competitive society in which most people neither needed nor desired much in the way of government control or promotion of the economy.

This small-scale, primarily agrarian economy was not to persist for long because another of its characteristics was expansion of all sorts—in technology, in communications and transportation, and in population. These, plus a favorable social and political environment for the budding entrepreneur, made for a dynamic and expanding rather than a static economy and society. In the 1840's, according to Walt W. Rostow, the American economy entered the "take off" stage which was to result in a mature, industrial, technologically modern economy in the early twentieth century and, ultimately, a high mass-consumption economy in the 1920's and after.[1] This transformation generated many sweeping and significant changes in our socio-economic system.

In sharp contrast to the early nineteenth century, the United States now has a remarkably complex, large-scale, business, corporate economy. Business enterprise has replaced agriculture as the principal source of livelihood for most citizens. Agriculture yielded only 3.9 per cent of the national income in 1960 as compared to 38 per cent in 1800 and 31 per cent in 1860. In 1960 less than 7 per cent of those gainfully employed were engaged in agriculture. The "typical" person is no longer an independent property owner but an employee of someone else, a wage or salary earner. Significant changes have also occurred in the residential location of the population. In 1920 for the first time the urban population outnumbered the rural population. Today more than two-thirds of the population of around 195,000,000 live in urban areas; over 63 per cent of the population lives in 212 metropolitan areas containing 50,000 or more inhabitants.

Notwithstanding several million individual proprietorships, partnerships, and farm units, the corporation is now the dominant form of economic organization in our economy. There are many small individually owned and operated businesses in the manufacturing sector

[1] See W. W. Rostow, *The Stages of Economic Growth* (London: Cambridge University Press, 1960).

of the economy, but they account for only a small part of the industrial output. In 1961 corporations received 95 per cent of the net income of all manufacturing enterprises.[2] In addition to manufacturing, corporations predominate in public utilities, transportation, communication, mining, and finance. More than half of the business in wholesale and retail trade is accounted for by corporations. There are some areas, however, in which the corporation does not predominate, including agriculture, some types of retail trade, service trades, and some relatively minor industries such as the women's clothing industry.[3] Thus it is more accurate to say that our economy is characterized by private *corporate* enterprise rather than private *individual* enterprise.

Within our corporate economy the concentration of economic activity has made the large corporation the center of economic gravity.

TABLE ONE–1

THE RELATIVE SHARE OF GIANT CORPORATIONS
IN VARIOUS SECTORS OF THE UNITED STATES ECONOMY
(1955)*

Sector	ALL CORPORATIONS		CORPORATIONS WITH ASSETS OF $250 MILLION OR MORE	
	Number	*Assets (billions)*	*Number*	*Percentage of all corporate assets*
Manufacturing	124,200	201.4	97	42
Mining[a]	9,700	13.3	(19)	(17)
Public utilities	4,800	62.9	56	72
Transportation	21,900	43.5	30	61
Finance	214,600	474.9	218	46

* From Edward S. Mason, ed., *The Corporation in Modern Society* (Cambridge: Harvard University Press, 1960), 87.

[a] The figures in parentheses show the number and share of corporations with assets of $100 million or more because of the small number of mining corporations in the $250 million classification.

In 1961, of the 1,190,282 corporations in *all* sectors of the economy that filed income tax returns, 2,632 corporations (less than 0.2 per cent), each of which had assets of over $50 million, owned 63 per cent of all corporate assets.[4]

[2] Derived from *Statistical Abstract of the United States, 1964*, p. 489.
[3] Robin Williams, *American Society*, 2nd ed. (New York: Alfred A. Knopf, 1961), 164.
[4] Derived from *Statistical Abstract of the United States, 1964*, p. 495.

4

These statistics show a substantial concentration of economic power in the economy, but they do not reveal the degree of concentration which exists in many industries. According to a report issued by the Federal Trade Commission in 1947, at least two-thirds of the assets of all corporations engaged in the production of motor vehicles, tin cans, copper, agricultural machinery, office machinery, cigarettes, liquor, meat, tires, aluminum, and plumbing equipment and supplies were controlled by the top four corporations in their respective fields. The top eight companies controlled more than two-thirds of the corporate assets in the steel, aircraft, glass, and chemical industries.[5] Thus a significant part of the American economy is characterized by oligopoly ("competition among the few") and not by competition among numerous independent firms. Many industries—steel, aluminum, and agricultural machinery are examples—are dominated by single firms (or leaders). In the early 1800's it is estimated that no single firm controlled as much as 10 per cent of the output in any manufacturing industry.[6]

As large corporations have developed, the nature of property has changed. Under the older forms of economic organization—the individual proprietorship and the partnership—the owner of property both controlled and managed its use and received its fruits. Adolf Berle has described this situation:

> Property . . . has two sets of attributes. On the one hand it can be a medium for creation and production and development. On the other, it offers possibility for reception, enjoyment and consumption. An old-fashioned farm or small business property held by a single owner or a small group of owners combined both groups of attributes in the same hands. The owner used his property to create, to produce, to improve. In a word, he used it as capital. He also used it to provide for his needs and for his enjoyment—in other words, for his consumption. Life was all in one piece, and the attributes were intertwined.[7]

This state of affairs does not apply to the large corporation with its multitude of owners (stockholders) often numbering hundreds of thousands and, occasionally, millions. In most large corporations, the bulk of stockholders are mere investors. Actual control and direction of the use of the corporation's property resides with management and "con-

[5] Federal Trade Commission, *The Concentration of Productive Facilities* (Washington, D.C.: Government Printing Office, 1949), 21.

[6] Robert S. Heilbroner, *The Making of Economic Society* (Englewood Cliffs, N.J.: Prentice-Hall, 1962), 118.

[7] Adolf A. Berle, *The 20th Century Capitalist Revolution* (New York: Harcourt, Brace & World, 1954), 29.

5

trol groups" or minority blocks. In 1930, for example, only 11 per cent of the 200 largest nonfinancial corporations were controlled by persons or groups owning a majority of the voting stock.[8] In other words, management and control have become separated from ownership and the nominal owner, the stockholder, is left with little but a claim on profits, the right to receive dividends. The power "to create, to produce, to develop" is no longer his and, as Edward S. Mason has commented, "it is a little difficult to see in the ownership of corporate securities the source of that invigorating moral, social, and political development that Jefferson saw in private property."[9] At the helm of the large corporation we find not the rugged individualist but the "smoothly efficient corporate executive" and the management team.

Since bigness and concentration are common in the economy today, is the trend in business organization toward ever greater concentration? The evidence is mixed but there appears to be no major trend in that direction. A Federal Trade Commission study concludes that "in 1935 the 200 largest manufacturing corporations accounted for 37.7 per cent of the total value of products of all manufacturing enterprises; by 1950 the proportion had risen to 40.5 per cent."[10] A more recent study shows that the proportion of total corporate assets in manufacturing, mining, and distribution held by the 100 largest firms did not increase significantly between 1935 and 1958 (28 per cent and 29.8 per cent, respectively).[11] If we look at specific industries, we find that concentration has increased in some and decreased in others. Between 1947 and 1954, the share of total industry shipments accounted for by the top four companies in the motor vehicle, tire, steel, and brewing industries rose; it declined in the petroleum refining, meat packing, and tobacco industries.[12] These figures indicate that there has been no marked increase in concentration in recent decades, but neither is there any obvious trend in the opposite direction or any likelihood that there will be one.

What effect has corporate concentration had on the competitive nature of our economy? Has it substituted monopoly for competition? A conclusive answer must await generally accepted definitions of

[8] Adolf A. Berle and Gardner C. Means, *The Modern Corporation and Private Property* (New York: Macmillan, 1934), 94.

[9] Mason, *op. cit.*, 15.

[10] Federal Trade Commission, *Changes in Manufacturing 1935 to 1947 and 1950* (Washington, D.C.: Government Printing Office, 1954), 17.

[11] Norman R. Collins and Lee E. Preston, "The Size Structure of the Largest Industrial Firms, 1909–1958," *American Economic Review*, LI (December, 1961), 989.

[12] *Statistical Abstract of the United States, 1961*, pp. 792–793.

"monopoly" and "competition." It is obvious, however, that concentration does mean that many industries are controlled, or dominated, by a very few firms. But competition is not necessarily absent in such industries; concentration and competition are not mutually exclusive economic phenomena. The automobile and cigarette industries, characterized as they are by extensive concentration, are vigorously competitive in advertising and innovation if not in prices. Although competition among the few does exist, as between General Motors, Ford, and Chrysler, it is far removed from the intense competition among numerous small economic units envisaged by Adam Smith. Some of the implications of concentration for competition and the economy generally are summed up here:

> Although concentration may not eliminate competition, it does endow corporate managers with substantial power over the market. They are in a position to influence prices, if not to control them, to a substantial degree. The existence of a high degree of control in some sectors of the economy and its absence in others tends to create serious maladjustments. Such disparities accentuate the effective bargaining of the organized sector of the economy as against the unorganized; they also inspire counter-organization among the unorganized and efforts to utilize the instrumentalities of government to strengthen the bargaining power of weaker economic interests.[13]

An important consequence of the growth of large corporate enterprise was the rise of strong labor unions. Prior to the Civil War, when business units were typically small, labor unions were of little import. Today, unions are still relatively unimportant in many sectors of the economy in which economic units are small. Agriculture and some types of retail trade are good illustrations. But in sectors marked by large economic aggregation, unions were, and are, necessary if workers are to bargain effectively with their corporate employers and to share more fully in their profits. Thus labor organization is largely a concomitant of large corporate organization, a means by which labor developed "countervailing power" to offset the power of big business.[14] The presence of Big Labor and its power is another of the important conditions confronting modern policy makers.

Measured by such common standards as gross national product and per capita national income, the American economy is the wealthiest and

---

[13] Merle Fainsod, Lincoln Gordon, and Joseph C. Palamountain, Jr., *Government and the American Economy,* 3rd ed. (New York: W. W. Norton, 1959), 17.

[14] See John Kenneth Galbraith, *American Capitalism,* rev. ed. (Boston: Houghton Mifflin, 1956), 114–117.

most productive, quantitatively, the world has ever seen. (The high productivity of large corporate enterprise has contributed significantly.) In dollars of constant purchasing power, gross national product increased from $30 billion in 1880 and $136 billion in 1920 to $504.4 billion in 1960. National income stood at $2,242 per capita in 1960. These figures show the overall "affluence" of our society but not how the fruits of the economy are distributed among the population. Has corporate concentration, for example, created a situation in which the rich are becoming richer and the poor poorer? The statistics in Table One-2 indicate that it has not.

TABLE ONE–2

PERCENTAGE OF MONEY INCOME RECEIVED BY EACH FIFTH AND THE TOP 5 PER CENT OF THE NATION'S FAMILIES AND UNATTACHED INDIVIDUALS*

	1935–36	1950	1960
Lowest fifth	4.1	4.8	4.5
Second fifth	9.2	10.9	11.0
Third fifth	14.1	16.1	16.3
Fourth fifth	20.9	22.1	22.6
Highest fifth	51.7	46.1	45.5
Top 5 per cent	26.5	21.4	20.0

* *Statistical Abstract of the United States, 1962*, p. 329.

The trend, though not great, is in the direction of equality, but there is still much inequality of income. Further, the ownership of wealth, apart from changes in income, is still highly concentrated. It is estimated that the top 1 per cent of "spending units" owns 65 per cent of the corporate stock.[15] Hence we can say that if ours is an affluent society some of its members are decidedly more affluent than others.

THE EXPANSION OF GOVERNMENT ECONOMIC ACTIVITY

The Constitution drafted in Philadelphia in the summer of 1787 provided the foundation for a legal order conducive to the development and expansion of economic enterprise. The founding fathers, desiring to create an environment favorable to business and property rights,

[15] Heilbroner, *op. cit.*, 173n.

gave the national government broad powers to protect and promote economic interests and at the same time limited the power of the states to control economic activity by prohibiting such practices as impairment of the obligations of contracts and the issuance of paper money. Under the influence of Alexander Hamilton and the Federalists, the national government followed a mercantilist policy of business promotionalism during the first decade of its existence. Operating on the Hamiltonian premise that government should stimulate and guide the growth of industry rather than leave it to a natural course of development, the national government enacted a protective tariff, established a national bank, funded the Continental and state debt to enhance the national credit, and in general adopted policies favorable to the propertied classes. These Hamiltonian policies benefited commercial, banking, and manufacturing interests but were of little advantage to small farmers, shopkeepers, and artisans. To the latter groups, Hamiltonianism meant higher taxes and higher prices for the goods they purchased.

With the expansion of suffrage which increased their political power, and under the leadership of Thomas Jefferson and James Madison, agrarian interests gained the ascendancy in the election of 1800 and continued to be the dominant force in politics until the Civil War. The years between 1800 and 1860 can be fairly referred to as the "age of agrarianism." Although agrarian interests generally opposed the use of national power to promote unduly industrial and commercial interests, they did not act to prevent or retard business expansion. Agrarianism was essentially anti-mercantilist rather than anti-business. Neither Jefferson nor Andrew Jackson, leaders of the agrarian interests, was willing to permit agriculture to be subordinated to industry or to allow government to be used primarily as an instrument for the care and nurture of business and industrial interests. Their position was summarized in the Jacksonian slogan, "Equal rights for all—special privileges for none."

Promotion of business by the national government continued during the age of agrarianism but in a more restrained manner than during the Federalist era. Thus tariff levels continued to rise until 1832 when at the insistence of southern interests the trend was halted. Also, throughout this period the national government continued to perform a core of functions which were essentially promotional: the maintenance of order and administration of justice, operation of the post office, aid for internal improvements, and provision of such facilities of commerce as a monetary system and a system of patents and copyrights. There were a few other promotional actions, such as the 1817 statute which gave American ships a monopoly of the coastwise trade. [Not until after the Civil War, however, was business again supported as strongly as it had been during the Federalist years.]

Agrarian dominance resulted in less frequent use of national power after 1800, but only because the agrarians preferred to deal with state and local governments and not because they accepted, in practice, laissez faire doctrines. The notion that the 1800–1860 era was an age of laissez faire has no standing in reality. Although very little national regulation of economic enterprise was undertaken, the national government continued to engage in promotional activity. The state governments were relied on for both promotion and regulation of economic activity. For example, the states were quite active in constructing internal improvements, including roads, canals, and railways. As one would expect in an agrarian age, internal improvement programs were supported mainly because they benefited farmers rather than business interests (although, in fact, the latter were helped as well).

To indicate more precisely the nature of state economic activity prior to the Civil War, let us briefly look at the experience of an older eastern state, Pennsylvania, and a newer western state, Missouri. In his study of economic policy in Pennsylvania between 1776 and 1860, Louis Hartz states that the objectives of economic policy "ramified into virtually every phase of business activity, were the constant preoccupation of politicians and entrepreneurs, and . . . evoked interest struggles of the first magnitude. Government assumed the job of shaping decisively the contours of economic life."[16] In the promotional area, Pennsylvania granted corporate charters, constructed and operated public works, and participated in mixed companies in such fields as banking and internal improvements. Regulatory activity included regulation of creditor-debtor relations, inspection and licensing programs, control of liquor traffic, regulation of banks and insurance companies, and labor legislation. Public economic policy in Missouri involved the granting of corporate charters, promotions of internal improvements, participation in mixed enterprise, licensing of doctors, lawyers, and peddlers, legislation (especially inspection laws) to promote agricultural interests, and labor legislation. James Primm concludes:

> In Missouri, as in Massachusetts, Pennsylvania, and New Jersey, the state took an active, positive role in the economic affairs of its citizens during the period before the Civil War, and was not hampered appreciably in this course by laissez-faire or non-interven-

[16] Louis Hartz, *Economic Policy and Democratic Thought: Pennsylvania, 1776–1860* (Cambridge: Harvard University Press, 1948), 289.

tion theories. Insofar as negative ideas found expression, they tended to be directed at federal, rather than state economic activity. Even then, professed opponents of federal participation in the economy were often pleaders for some special type of intervention.[17]

The broad picture of prewar America that emerges from the above discussion is certainly not that of a laissez faire utopia. Although the state governments were more active in the economic sphere than the national government, both did intervene in a significant manner. Promotion of economic interests, not regulation, was the major attribute of public policy.

United under the banner of the Democratic Party, the alliance of western and southern agrarian interests had been able to hold commercial and industrial interests in check. As conflicts over the issues of slavery and the disposal of public lands in the West increased in intensity, however, the agrarian interests began to divide along sectional lines and then were split asunder by the Civil War. The victory of the new Republican Party in the election of 1860 marked the beginning of a realignment of forces in American politics. The labor-agrarian alliance that brought about Lincoln's election was not to endure, however. What finally emerged was a combination of eastern business interests and western agrarian interests with the former as the dominant members of the "partnership."

Public policy in the second half of the nineteenth century reflected the efforts of the Republican Party to hold these divergent groupings together. Though the party was most responsive to business and industrial interests, many benefits were given to the agrarian wing. The Homestead Act (1862) permitted farmers to acquire free lands in the West, and the Morrill Act (1862) provided support for the creation and operation of state land grant colleges. The Department of Agriculture was also established in 1862 to provide services to farmers. Internal improvement programs, especially assistance for railroad construction, were intended to attract and hold western agrarian support. Later programs (in the 1880's) included support for agricultural research and promotion of dairy interests by the taxation of colored oleomargarine.

Agrarian interests benefited from these policies, but aid to business interests was more extensive, direct, and significant. The protective tariff, increased to unprecedented levels during the Civil War, was

[17] James Neal Primm, *Economic Policy in the Development of a Western State: Missouri 1820–1860* (Cambridge: Harvard University Press, 1954), 125.

raised still further after the end of the war. "Hard money" and regressive taxation policies were also of much value to the business community. Railroad corporations were assisted by land and monetary grants and other means. Industrial and commercial interests, given an impetus by the economic demands of the Civil War, and aided by such public policies, found themselves in a highly favorable economic position. Accepting government promotion as their due, they began to proclaim a new-found faith in laissez faire in their attempt to forestall government interference (i.e., regulation) with the unrestricted pursuit of wealth.

The first significant demand for government regulation of business arose in the 1870's. The Granger movement was basically an agrarian response to the agricultural depression of the late 1860's and 1870's, (although the movement also received support, perhaps extensive, from small merchants and businessmen).[18] Farmers found themselves confronted simultaneously with falling farm prices and high prices for the goods and services they had to buy. Especially was their ire directed at the railroads, whose rates were often considered excessively high or extortionate. The Grangers turned to the state legislatures for redress of their grievances and the result was the famous "granger laws." Illinois, for example, established a Railroad and Warehouse Commission in 1871 and two years later gave the Commission power to regulate rates and prevent undesirable practices. Similar legislation was enacted in other states, especially in the Midwest. The Granger movement marks the beginning of a shift in public policy from promotionalism to regulation. And, as Solon J. Buck has written: "it is not too much to say that the fundamental principles upon which American regulation of railroads by legislation has developed were first worked out in the Granger states of the Northwest during the decade of the seventies."[19]

The Granger movement waned and ceased to be of importance by the end of the 1870's, but demands for governmental control of the new industrialism did not fade. During the 1880's farmers, small businessmen, and the general public demonstrated growing concern over the power of big business. The development of monopolies and the use of trusts, pools and similar devices by business to control various sectors of the economy caused many to fear the disappearance of a com-

[18] See Lee Benson, *Merchants, Farmers and Railroads* (Cambridge: Harvard University Press, 1955).
[19] Solon J. Buck, *The Granger Movement* (Cambridge: Harvard University Press, 1913), 215.

petitive economy and "traditional American democracy." Spurred on by improved means of transportation, communication, technology, and organization, business became nationwide in its scope and operations. It appeared that only the national government possessed adequate power and jurisdiction to effectively control large corporations and the railroads. The result was a shift in emphasis from state action to national action. In response to the demands of farmers and small businessmen for railroad regulation, Congress passed the Interstate Commerce Act (1887), and, for the first time, made significant positive use of its power to regulate interstate commerce. The Sherman Antitrust Act (1890) was also enacted with strong support from the agrarian-small business alliance. These two statutes were the climax of the first important movement for national regulation; they also marked the end of it. Not until after the turn of the century was the drive for national action successfully resumed.

Agrarian demands and discontent were given expression by the Populists and the Democratic Party under William Jennings Bryan's leadership during the 1890's. So far as the exercise of national regulatory power was concerned, however, these were years of quiescence. The leadership of the conservative Republican and Democratic administrations in office during the decade were disinclined to place additional controls on the business community. In fact, some of the recent gains were lost, at least temporarily, as the effectiveness of both the Sherman and Interstate Commerce acts was impaired by adverse decisions emanating from an unsympathetic Supreme Court. The generally conservative economic policy of the 1890's was characterized by hard money, high tariffs, and noninterference with the affairs of big business.

With the accession of Theodore Roosevelt to the Presidency in 1901, a second successful movement for the expansion of national power got under way. The Progressive movement, drawing support from agrarian, labor, small-business, and urban middle-class interests, was a response to the growing industrialization and urbanization of American society. Progressivism was concerned with social and political as well as economic reform, but it is the latter which is of interest here. During Roosevelt's administration new national regulatory activities were started and some existing ones were expanded. Effective railroad rate regulation dates from the Hepburn Act (1906), which gave the Interstate Commerce Commission power to set maximum rates. Forty-three antitrust proceedings were started by the Roosevelt administration in an effort to restore vigor to the Sherman Act and a Bureau of Corporations was established to assist in antitrust enforcement. The Hours of Service Act (1907) and the Employers' Liability Act (1908), although limited to interstate railroad workers, were a significant step in the development of national labor legislation. The need to protect the interests of consumers was recognized by the Pure Food and Drug Act (1906) and the Meat Inspection Act (1906). Conservation of national resources received serious attention and support in the form of both legislation and executive action.

If the expansion of federal regulatory power slowed down during the Taft administration, it certainly did not stop. The power of the Interstate Commerce Commission over railroad rates was further strengthened by the Mann-Elkins Act (1910); and the Valuation Act (1913) was intended to provide a scientific basis for setting rates. Twice as many antitrust proceedings were started in the Taft administration as in that of Roosevelt. Significant accomplishments in conservation were obscured by the Pinchot-Ballinger dispute. The income tax amendment was proposed and became part of the Constitution in 1913. Other activity included mine and railroad safety legislation, abolition of white phosphorous matches by use of the taxing power, and a law providing the eight-hour day for government workers.

Under the leadership of Woodrow Wilson and the banner of the "New Freedom," the progressive forces stepped up the rate of expansion of national power. The Federal Reserve Act (1913) revamped the nation's monetary and banking system. The Federal Trade Commission (1914) and Clayton (1914) acts were designed to strengthen the effort to maintain a competitive economy. The Tariff Commission and the Shipping Board were established. A variety of promotional farm legislation was enacted, including the Smith-Lever Act (1914), the Federal Farm Loan Act (1916), the Grain Standards Act (1916), and the Smith-Hughes Act (1917). Nor were the interests of labor neglected by the New Freedom. The Clayton Act attempted to free labor from the antitrust laws and the labor injunction. The Newlands Act provided for the voluntary arbitration of railway labor disputes, and the Adamson Act established the eight-hour day for railroad workers. Child labor laws were passed in 1916 and 1919, although both were later declared unconstitutional by the Supreme Court.

World War I brought with it extensive governmental control and direction of the economy, but most of these wartime emergency measures were eliminated with the cessation of hostilities. United States participation in the war marked the effective end of the Progressive

14

movement. Except for the Transportation Act (1920), which greatly increased national control of the railroads, and the creation of the Federal Power Commission, there was little extension of national power during the remainder of Wilson's term of office. An era which saw the adoption of many of our basic regulatory commitments and policies thus came to a close.

The business-oriented Republican regimes of the 1920's were predisposed to follow the slogan of "less government in business and more business in government." The decade of the 'twenties returned to "normalcy" with Harding and kept cool with Coolidge. Nonetheless, the trend toward greater government intervention in the economy was only slowed again. Pressures for government action, though operating in an environment less favorable than that of the Progressive era, registered some successes. Agricultural interests, unhappy about the depressed condition of agriculture and operating through the Farm Bloc in Congress, won a number of victories. Agricultural legislation included the Futures Trading Act (1921), the Packers and Stockyards Act (1921), the Capper-Volstead Act (1922), the Intermediate Credit Act (1923), the Co-operative Marketing Act (1926), and the Agricultural Marketing Act (1929). Efforts to get government support of farm prices, however, were unsuccessful. The McNary-Haugen bill was passed twice by Congress only to be vetoed each time by Coolidge. Technological changes created pressures resulting in the Air Commerce Act (1926) and the Federal Radio Act (1927). The Federal Power Commission, formerly a cabinet committee, was reorganized as an independent regulatory commission in 1930. The Railway Labor Act (1926), which contained the first federal guarantee of labor's right to bargain collectively, is still the basic law in its field. These actions were neither spectacular nor of vital importance to the functioning of the economy. They are symptomatic of continuing pressure for the exercise of federal power.

Herbert Hoover's inauguration as President was followed in a few months by the stock market crash of 1929 and the beginning of the Great Depression. The demand for reform, fed by unemployment, insecurity, economic instability, and abuses of private economic power, became irresistible. The result was the enactment of a vast body of federal economic legislation, most of it during the New Deal years. Before 1929, government intervention had been concerned primarily with problems and conflicts arising in an essentially healthy society and economy and, as George Steiner states, with some exceptions federal

15

legislation was "within the scope of a liberal interpretation of the limited-government doctrine."[20] After 1929 government was confronted with the necessity of dealing with the broader problems of economic stability and prosperity as well as the more "traditional" problems. Where formerly government had functioned as an "impartial arbiter" between conflicting economic forces, it now became actively and positively interventionist, assuming far-reaching responsibility for directing and regulating the economy. Contributing to this change in the role of government was a shift in the sources of political power. The Republican administrations of the 1920's were based on the upper and upper-middle classes—on bankers, industrialists, larger businessmen. The New Deal, however, derived the bulk of its support from an urban-rural coalition of wage and salary earners, small businessmen, and small farmers; and it was most responsive to these groups.

Efforts to combat the depression were begun by the Hoover administration, although these were essentially emergency measures, designed to alleviate immediate distress and dislocation. Policies to expand the availability of credit were adopted by the Federal Reserve Board. The Federal Farm Board, created by the Agricultural Marketing Act (1929), tried unsuccessfully to support the price of some farm commodities. The Reconstruction Finance Corporation was established to make loans to banks and other financial institutions, insurance companies, railroads, and other businesses in danger of bankruptcy. A program of public works was started. Some relief activities were undertaken, especially as it became obvious that state and local governments and private organizations could not handle the burden of relief. The Federal Home Loan Act of 1932 was designed to provide help to homeowners in danger of mortgage foreclosure. In retrospect, although the activities of the Hoover administration were inadequate, it assumed greater responsibility for combating economic crisis than any previous administration.

The approach of the New Deal to the problems presented by the depression was much more energetic and more extensive than that of the Hoover administration. The lending activity of the Reconstruction Finance Corporation was stepped up and expanded. Government lending programs were established to prevent foreclosures on homes and farms. Public programs for the relief of the needy, the destitute, and the unemployed, and public spending or public works were greatly expanded. Among the notable depression agencies set up were the Federal Emergency Relief Administration, the Civil Works Adminis-

[20] George A. Steiner, *Government's Role in Economic Life* (New York: McGraw-Hill, 1953), 87.

16

tration, the Works Progress Administration, and the Civilian Conservation Corps. In 1935 Congress passed the Social Security Act, which put the federal government in the welfare field on a systematic and permanent basis. The act provided old age insurance, public assistance, and unemployment compensation programs to deal with some of the major economic hazards of life. Deficit spending, or "pump-priming," was also resorted to in order to stimulate the economy and restore prosperity. By the late 1930's a new theory of fiscal and monetary policy had emerged which stressed the use of government tax, credit, and expenditure policies to stabilize the economy, to maintain full employment, and to equalize the distribution of wealth.

The New Deal was highly responsive to the interests of labor and agriculture. A large amount of legislation, most of it promotional in design, was enacted in these two areas. Section 7a of the National Industrial Recovery Act (declared unconstitutional in 1935) and the National Labor Relations Act (1935), provided protection of the right to organize and bargain collectively, and helped to create a favorable environment for union organization and activity. The Walsh-Healey (1936) and Fair Labor Standards (1938) acts were designed to improve the working conditions and wages of workers. The Wagner-Peyser Act (1933) provided federal funds to aid the states in establishing employment offices. In agriculture, the most significant statutes were the Agriculture Adjustment Act (1933) (declared unconstitutional in 1935), the Soil Conservation and Domestic Allotment Act (1936), and the Agriculture Adjustment Act (1938), enacted for the purpose of supporting farm commodity prices. Farm credit institutions were expanded and strengthened. The Resettlement Administration and its successor, the Farm Security Administration, were organized to provide financial and other assistance to the poorer, marginal farmers, including tenants and sharecroppers.

In the area of business regulation, governmental controls were extended into new areas and expanded in existing fields of regulation. The Securities and Exchange Commission was formed to regulate the stock markets in order to protect investors. Interstate domestic water transport and motor carriers were placed under the control of the Interstate Commerce Commission. The authority of the Federal Power Commission was extended to cover the interstate activities of electric and natural gas companies. The Federal Communications Commission, set up in place of the Federal Radio Commission, acquired jurisdiction over interstate telephone and telegraph communications. The Connally "Hot-Oil" Act of 1935 helped implement state oil proration laws by

17

prohibiting interstate shipment of oil produced in violation of state laws. An extensive system of controls was placed on the bituminous coal industry, with price fixing as its major objective.

After a period of indecision following the failure of the National Recovery Administration experiment in business "self-regulation" (or cartellization) the Roosevelt administration launched a vigorous effort to enforce the antitrust laws. The Robinson-Patman Act (1936), which strengthened the Clayton Act prohibition against price discrimination, was enacted at the insistence of wholesalers and small retailers who wanted protection against chain stores, discount houses, and other large retail organizations. The Miller-Tydings Act (1937) gave support to state "fair trade" (or resale price-maintenance) laws. These were another aspect of the campaign by small retailers to offset the advantages of their larger competitors, as were the taxes on chain stores enacted by many states. The Food, Drug and Cosmetic Controls Act (1938) provided additional protection for consumers. Controls over railroads, foreign commerce, and the banking system were extended. Regulation of the airlines was strengthened and a Civil Aeronautics Board was created to administer the new controls. The Public Utility Holding Company Act (1935) gave the SEC "life-or-death" power over public utility holding companies, including authority to simplify their corporate structures.

The New Deal years also witnessed broad expansion of conservation activities and spectacular growth in the number and variety of public enterprises. Many public works agencies, such as the CCC and the WPA, had conservation as a primary objective. The Taylor Grazing Act (1934) was passed to protect the public domain against unwise use. Activities in the areas of soil conservation, flood control, irrigation, and reclamation were expanded. The Tennessee Valley Authority, a government corporation, was established to control and develop the waters and resources of the Tennessee Valley area in cooperation with state and local governments and other federal agencies. Public enterprises, usually organized as government corporations, were most significant in electric power production, credit and banking, and housing. Among the federal enterprises established were the Federal Deposit Insurance Corporation, the Rural Electrification Administration, the Export-Import Bank, the Commodity Credit Corporation, and the Home Owners Loan Corporation.

Mobilization of the civilian economy by the government during World War II involved far greater governmental control and direction than it did during World War I. Price controls, rationing of con-

18

sumer goods, and allocation of manpower and materials were administered by a plethora of wartime agencies as the productive endeavors of the nation were united in support of military victory. The process of "decontrol" started before the war in Europe was over and most of the wartime controls were abandoned soon after the surrender in the Pacific.

The years since 1945 can be broadly characterized as a time of general prosperity and complacency on the domestic economic scene. Although government regulatory activity has continued to expand, there have been few significant innovations or departures from past policies. The Eisenhower administration (1953–1961), the first Republican regime in twenty years, produced no major redirection of public policy. Rather, the New Deal-Fair Deal policies were generally accepted (rhetoric aside) and in some cases extended—for example, welfare and minimum wage programs. Some of the more significant developments since the close of World War II can be mentioned here. The Employment Act of 1946 committed the national government to maintaining "maximum employment, production, and purchasing power" and can be regarded as a formal recognition of the role of government in ensuring economic stability and growth. The Atomic Energy acts of 1946 and 1954 laid down government policy in this new and highly important field. The Taft-Hartley Act (1947) and the Labor Reform Act (1959) placed a number of controls on labor unions and constituted a modification of New Deal labor policy. In agriculture, price support programs were continued along the patterns established in the 1930's. Active enforcement of the antitrust laws was the rule under both Democratic and Republican administrations, and the laws have been strengthened by legislation such as the Celler Anti-Merger Act (1950). Government activity in conservation continued to follow existing models (though applied with less enthusiasm by the Eisenhower administration) and was extended into the increasingly important area of water pollution control. Some additional legislation for the protection of consumers was also adopted. In the early 1960's a variety of programs to combat poverty and unemployment were adopted.

Developments and events in the international arena after World War II led to greater participation in international affairs and produced great concern for national defense and security, which, in turn, had important economic consequences. Government spending increased greatly: in fiscal year 1963 for the first time the national budget approximated $100 billion. The largest portion (around two-thirds) was accounted for by defense spending and related activities. Economic and military aid programs and strong support for international economic organizations and institutions were a manifestation of heightened international involvement and responsibility. Significant efforts to reduce international trade barriers included the Trade Expansion Act of 1962.

This historical survey amply illustrates the continued close relationship between government and the economy. It also indicates that the long-range trend is continual though uneven expansion of government economic activity. Thus in the twentieth century, we have had two periods of vigorous expansion, the Progressive and New Deal eras, and two periods of lessened expansion, the 1920's and the post-World War II years. Though the movement of the regulatory clock has sometimes been slowed, it has never really been turned back.

CAUSES OF EXPANDING GOVERNMENT ECONOMIC ACTIVITY

The framework for the expansion of government activity has been provided by technological development, economic growth, and the evolution of the United States from a rural, agrarian society to a complex urban, industrial society.[21] As a society becomes more complex and industrial, and people become more interdependent and less self-sufficient, the needs, conflicts, and demands which give rise to government action multiply. As Robert MacIver states:

> Wherever technology advances, wherever private business extends its range, wherever the cultural life becomes more complex, new tasks are imposed on government. This happens apart from, or in spite of, the particular philosophies that governments cherish. . . . In the longer run the tasks undertaken by governments are dictated by changing conditions, and governments on the whole are more responsive than creative in fulfilling them.[22]

In a rural agrarian society people either produce most of their own

[21] In this discussion we draw generally on the following sources: Solomon Fabricant, *The Trend of Government Activity in the United States since 1900* (New York: National Bureau of Economic Research, 1952), ch. 7; Marshall A. Robinson, Herbert C. Morton, and James D. Calderwood, *An Introduction to Economic Reasoning* (Washington, D.C.: The Brookings Institution, 1956), ch. 10; and Steiner, *op. cit.,* ch. 6.

[22] Robert MacIver, *The Web of Government* (New York: Macmillan, 1947), 314–315.

food or buy it from those with whom they are fairly well acquainted. There is little likelihood of producer-consumer conflict and the prevention of fraud or other undesirable practices in the sale of food is hardly a problem. In contrast, in an urban, industrial society most people are dependent upon a vast and impersonal system of production and distribution for their food supply. They typically lack time, ability, or means to determine whether the food and meat they buy are pure, disease-free, and sold as represented. The result has been the development of pure food and drug laws, meat inspection laws, anti-misrepresentation laws, and other legislation to protect the consumer.

The impact of technological change on government is demonstrated by the invention, development, and expanded use of the automobile, which has contributed, directly and indirectly, to the development of numerous government activities. We now have a federal Bureau of Public Roads, a highway commission or department in every state, and county and city road and street departments. A system of federal grants-in-aid to the states and state assistance to local governments for road construction and maintenance has emerged. New techniques for controlling and facilitating the movement of traffic have become necessary, as well as the licensing of both vehicles and drivers. Problems of balancing the interests of automobiles and motor carriers with other forms of transportation have appeared and have necessitated both increases and changes in government policies. Automobiles are expensive and the common practice of buying them on credit has produced new regulations on installment buying. The development of large corporations for the manufacture of automobiles has contributed to such problems as monopoly and labor-management relations. Government intervention has resulted because of conflicts between automobile manufacturers and dealers and between dealers and purchasers. There is scarcely a facet of American life which has not been affected by the invention and proliferation of the automobile.

The need to resolve and adjust group conflicts has been a significant factor in the expansion of government activity. With growing complexity and specialization, the number of groups increases and conflicts between groups become more frequent and more intense. Conflicts between the industrial and agrarian sectors of the economy, labor and management, and small and large businesses have given rise to a variety of governmental programs, which attempt to resolve disputes and often to alter the relative economic power of the groups involved. At the same time, and because of the widespread acceptance of such middle-class values as "fair play" and humanitarianism, government has acted to protect the economically weak against the economically strong. Professor Steiner comments that this "has always been a function of government in the American code of political morality."[23] Protection of the economically weak is exemplified by child labor and wage and hour laws, and workmen's compensation legislation. Conflicts between the interests of particular groups and the public have also helped generate government activity. Public utility regulation, natural resource conservation, and, in recent years, government intervention in labor-management disputes which threaten the "national health or safety" are illustrative.

Changing public attitudes on the use of government to provide security against some of the economic risks of life are another significant contributor to the growth of government activity. The use of government in an extended and positive fashion to provide personal security is a twentieth-century development. A number of factors have contributed to the changed conception of the proper role of government in this area, including the risk of depression, growing industrialization job specialization, increasing urbanization, and a rising proportion of old people. Only government possesses enough power to deal adequately with the problems of depression and economic fluctuation. In addition to unemployment, other economic hazards—accident, old age, death of the family breadwinner—are intensified by the factors mentioned above and they, too, often cannot be met adequately by the individual. Government is consequently called upon to provide solutions. Fiscal and monetary policies are used to maintain employment and to prevent depression. Unemployment compensation, workmen's compensation, old age insurance, and public assistance are employed to reduce personal risks and to provide people with a minimum standard of existence.

The desire and ability of groups to shift some of their economic risks to government, and thereby "socialize" them, has also furthered the growth of government activity. Two related causes are operative here. One is the idea that promotion of the interests of given economic groups, industries, or sectors of the economy is a proper function of government because it contributes to the general welfare. Second, economic groups are often unwilling to accept the risks, hazards, or results of the operation of the economic system and have sought government protection for their interests. Consequently, farmers have crop insurance and price supports; businessmen have protective tariffs and

[23] Steiner, *op. cit.*, 136.

22

resale price maintenance laws to protect them from some of the risks of competition; securities purchasers have the Securities and Exchange Commission; depositors in banks and savings and loan associations have deposit insurance; lenders have insurance for housing loans; the petroleum industry has depletion allowances; and labor unions have protection of the right to organize and bargain collectively. Few significant groups have not obtained some governmental aid or protection. Whether all the programs for the protection and promotion of group interests are necessary is not our present concern. The point we wish to make is that they make manifest the high value which Americans place on economic security and their willingness to use governmental action to realize it.

Population trends have both directly and indirectly stimulated the expansion of governmental activity. Between 1900 and 1965, the population more than doubled, increasing from 76,000,000 to approximately 192,000,000. There has been a simultaneous, massive movement of the population into urban and suburban areas. These developments have necessitated an expansion of governmental services: schools, health and sanitation facilities, police and fire protection, recreational facilities, roads and streets, and urban transportation systems. Many of these services are either not required by a rural society or can be provided easily by the family itself. Or, if needed in a rural society and beyond private action, they can be provided by a lower scale of government effort.

These population trends and the concurrent economic growth have brought rising incomes and standards of living, contributing to the demand for more and better governmental services. At the same time, people are able, through taxes, to pay for expanded services. Improved highway systems are necessary as people drive more, bigger, and faster cars. Better schools and better health and recreational facilities are demanded as standards of living rise.

War, the threat of war, and the requirements of national defense and security, especially since the 1930's, also have expanded government economic activity. As war becomes more complex, the equipment and weaponry required become more costly. Training and equipping the modern soldier is now much more expensive than it was for his nineteenth-century and early twentieth-century counterparts. Spending on international affairs and defense-related activities has also increased. These developments are reflected in national administrative budget expenditures, which totaled nearly $98 billion for fiscal 1964. (See Table One-3.)

TABLE ONE–3

NATIONAL BUDGET EXPENDITURES, FISCAL YEAR 1964*

(millions of dollars)

National defense	$54,181
International affairs	3,687
Space programs	4,171
Agriculture	5,560
Natural resources	2,478
Commerce and transportation	3,002
Housing and community development	+80
Health, labor, and welfare	5,475
Education	1,339
Veterans benefits and services	5,492
General government	2,280
Interest on national debt	10,765
Total	$97,481

* From Bureau of the Budget, *The Budget in Brief, 1966* (Washington, D.C.: Government Printing Office, 1965), 70–71. Budget expenditures exclude some spending, as from the Social Security trust fund.

Around three-quarters of the total is accounted for by national defense and defense-related expenditures, including the costs of past wars (international affairs, veterans programs, interest on the war debt, and so on). The total budget expenditures amounted to 16.2 per cent of the gross national product, which was $604 billion in fiscal 1964. A substantial portion of the national income is thus channeled through the national government. The way in which this money is raised and expended has a significant impact on the overall operation of the economy. Moreover, certain regions and industries (southern California and the aerospace industry are illustrative) have come to depend heavily upon national expenditures, especially for defense, for their economic growth and well-being.[24] Other government expenditures have also grown in recent decades, but their rise has not been as spectacular as those involving defense activities.

Finally, changes in political thought and practice have helped create an environment favorable to increased governmental control and guidance of the economy. Such nineteenth- and early twentieth-century developments as gradual extension of the suffrage, emergence of well-

[24] See, for example, James L. Clayton, "Defense Spending; Key to California's Growth," *Western Political Quarterly,* XV (June, 1962), 280–293.

organized and active political parties and interest groups, transformation of the electoral college to provide (in effect) for direct election of the president, and direct election of senators created a more direct relationship between citizens and public officials. Government has become more sensitive and responsive to popular and group needs and demands, especially those emanating from the lower classes. There also has been a change in the general conception of the proper role of government. Attitudes against government "paternalism" and "interference" have given way to a view of government as an instrument properly to be used in meeting public needs and problems. The old negative "police" state has been replaced by the positive service (or welfare) state. Further, as the individual increasingly encountered economic and social circumstances beyond his control, the negative definition of liberty as the absence of governmental restraint withered. Substituted for it was a belief that government could and should act positively to increase the freedom of the individual by equalizing opportunity and by removing economic and social barriers to the full exercise of his faculties and capacities. The Hamiltonian conception of a strong national government was thus made consistent with the Jeffersonian belief in individual freedom.

GOVERNMENT AND THE MIXED ECONOMY

The growth of government economic activity in the United States over the last century and three-quarters has resulted in an economic system best described as a "mixed economy." To depict our modern economy in terms of such grand alternatives as capitalism or socialism, freedom or regimentation, market economy or planned economy, is to confuse rather than to enlighten. Our economy stands somewhere between the poles of each of these dichotomies and, at the same time, it represents a combination of all of them. It is a complex and sometimes perplexing combination of private enterprise, government controls and promotion, competition and monopoly, together with a sprinkling of cooperative enterprise.[25]

The role of government in our mixed economy is extensive and pervasive. Though all economic activity is affected in some way by governmental action, it is not possible to state with any precision the degree and extent to which economic activity is determined or con-

[25] Cf. Robert A. Dahl and Charles E. Lindblom, *Politics, Economics, and Welfare* (New York: Harper & Row, 1953). Also Heilbroner, *op. cit.*

trolled by government. We can, however, indicate the various ways in which government affects economic processes and decisions.[26]

First, government prescribes rules (or norms) of economic behavior in many important areas of the economy. There is a tendency for the rules to increase in number and detail as economic relationships become more complex, but within the established framework of rules, individuals and groups are left free to act as their interests dictate. Among the areas in which government prescribes "rules of the game," as they can be called, are labor-management relations, the sale of securities and grain futures, advertising and product labeling, and competition. In competition, the businessman is free to decide, to act, to conduct his business as he chooses so long as he does not violate the laws against unfair competition and monopolistic behavior.

Second, government directly participates in the management of private enterprises, going beyond establishing rules of behavior to determination of the detailed actions of the controlled enterprises. Public utility regulation as applied to railroads and airlines, electricity and gas companies, and gas pipeline companies typifies this type of government activity. Also affected may be such enterprises as stockyards, securities exchanges, financial institutions, and agriculture. The degree of governmental control varies from one enterprise to another, involving such actions as determination of rates to be charged, services to be rendered, accounting procedures to be followed, or amount of crops to be grown.

Third, government owns and operates a wide variety of enterprises which produce goods and services. Prominent here are the post office, power production facilities, arsenals and other defense department enterprises, atomic energy installations, and credit and insurance institutions. Although public enterprise has increased greatly in the United States over the last few decades, it is not nearly as significant here as in many of the Western European countries where, for example, public ownership of transportation and communication facilities is quite common. Only a minor portion of the national income and the total value of goods and services produced in the United States are accounted for by public enterprise.[27]

Fourth, government directly or indirectly exerts control over prices or rates in a number of sectors of the economy. With the exception of public utility regulation, there was almost no government price control in the nineteenth century. Today government controls or influences such subjects as interest rates, wages, agricultural commodity prices,

[26] The following discussion borrows from Steiner, *op. cit.*, ch. 9.
[27] *Statistical Abstract of the United States, 1964*, pp. 321, 327.

and foreign exchange rates as well as public utility rates. Some attempts are also made to influence the prices of industrial commodities (as in the steel industry) although there are no direct controls in this area.

Fifth, public economic policies affect the distribution of the goods and services produced by the economic system. A variety of welfare programs—old age and survivor's insurance, public assistance, etc.,—guarantees minimum access to the products of the economy to large numbers of people. Low-income groups receive more direct benefits from public spending on education, hospitals, health centers, and so on, than do high-income groups. Though the graduated income tax brings about some equalization of income and public expenditures do redistribute personal income and produce some transfer from high to low income groups, it is difficult to say precisely how much.[28]

Sixth, the portion of the national income channeled through government is large and, as measured by some standards, is increasing. (See Table One-4.)

TABLE ONE–4

GROWTH IN GOVERNMENT EXPENDITURES*

(*billions of dollars*)

	National government	% GNP	All governments	% GNP
1950	$ 43.1	15.2	$ 61.5	21.7
1963	113.8	19.5	162.7	27.8

* Derived from *Statistical Abstract of the United States, 1964*, pp. 321–323, 389.

To reiterate a point made previously, the ways in which these sums are raised and expended have an important impact on the structure and operation of the economy and national welfare.

Seventh, fiscal, monetary, and credit policies are employed by the national government in an attempt to promote maximum employment, production, and purchasing power. These macroeconomic policies can strongly affect the operation of the economy and the nation's economic health depends substantially upon their wise use.

Finally, to include a catch-all category, government influences economic activity through policies designed to promote, to protect, and to guide or influence the economic activities of individuals and groups. A wide range of government policies is included here. Examples are

[28] See Donald S. Watson, *Economic Policy* (Boston: Houghton Mifflin, 1960), ch. 23.

promotion of airlines by operating subsidies, protection of bank depositors by deposit insurance, and encouragement of industrial plant modernization by favorable tax amortization policies.

Although government is deeply involved, the economy is still essentially private (non-governmental). The economy is not centrally planned or directed; rather it is characterized by a large measure of decentralization in decision making. Agriculture, business, labor, and government all share in the power and responsibility for economic decisions. While governmental controls have grown, so has the economy and the resultant opportunity for private decision. Contentions that government action has destroyed economic freedom and private enterprise are clearly exaggerations. Within the present structure of government controls, what remains for individual and group action and initiative? Most of our economic goods and services are produced and distributed by business organizations which are neither managed nor owned by government. Millions of individuals, groups, labor unions, proprietorships, and corporations are relatively free to make economic choices. By far the largest portion of the national income is spent by individuals or business firms with relatively little restriction. Property, in all forms, is for the most part under private control. There is a minimum of governmental restraint on the right of people to choose and change occupations. In short, within the framework of governmental controls, most economic decisions are privately made. Moreover, many governmental programs—the array of services provided by the Department of Commerce is illustrative—are designed to strengthen or facilitate private decision making, not to restrict it.

As a consequence of such factors as the modern scientific and technological revolution, growth in the size and importance of private economic organizations, and increased national defense activities, the line between public and private economic action, public and private enterprise, is becoming ever more blurred.[29] Government is making increased use of private organizations to carry out public programs and policies, as in scientific research. Private enterprise often calls upon government for support and assistance, as when government underwrites operating losses of airline companies. Further, many decisions of large private organizations have broad public significance; a decision by the steel companies to raise their prices, for instance. The blurring of the line between public and private action is both private and governmental in origin. The end result is more "mix" in the mixed economy.

[29] A. H. Raskin, "Our Economy: Mixed and Mixed-Up," *The Reporter,* XXVIII (October 11, 1962), 27–31.

Also, the old distinction between public enterprise and private enterprise is breaking down. In numerous instances it is not possible to categorically state whether an enterprise is public or private. How, for example, does one classify the aerospace industry? The aerospace companies depend primarily upon government contracts for their business. Government officials specify the volume, character, and priority of the product and closely supervise its production. The companies are privately owned, but is this really private enterprise? Or how does one classify the new Telstar communications satellite corporation? Public investment in the development of the satellite was substantial. The voting stock of the corporation established by Congress to handle the satellite program was sold, half to the public and half to the existing communications companies. The fifteen-man board of directors of the corporation is drawn from four sources: the American Telephone and Telegraph Company, other communications companies, the non-communications investors, and the public. To further complicate the matter, the corporation's rates will be regulated by the Federal Communications Commission. In any negotiations on a global communications system, the corporation supposedly will accept advice and guidance from the State Department and the President. Is the satellite corporation public, private, or what? Many other examples of the blending of public and private economic action could be cited.

New, dynamic, and subtle relationships between government and the economy are evolving to meet the needs and demands of our urban, industrial society. Only by examining these new relationships can we adequately understand the role of government in our modern mixed economy.

Chapter Two

THE MAKING OF PUBLIC ECONOMIC POLICY

THE CULTURAL CONTEXT: A PERSPECTIVE

In political science, as in any of the social or behavioral sciences, the basic unit of analysis is the individual in a group context. With respect to government decision making in the economic policy area, which is our central concern, we want to know why individuals, or groups, behave as they do. Why are certain decisions made and not others? Why are certain goals of action selected? Why are certain means or procedures employed?

One of the important factors shaping the behavior of individuals and groups in government decision making, as in other aspects of social life, is the culture of the particular society within which decision making occurs. While individuals are unique, each being somewhat different from all others, they also have much in common. Those who live in a particular society share in the various common values and beliefs which constitute part of its culture. Culture is transmitted from one generation to another by a "socialization" process in which, by "thousands of specific experiences with specific persons [parents, friends, school teachers, political leaders] in specific situations," the individual learns the values, norms, and beliefs of the society. Culture, then, is acquired by the individual, becomes a part of his psychological makeup, and is manifested in his behavior.[1]

One segment of the "general" culture of a society can be designated as "political culture."[2] Political culture consists of widely shared values

[1] Robin M. Williams, Jr., *American Society*, 2nd ed. (New York: Alfred A. Knopf, 1960), 22–25.
[2] See the discussions of political culture in Gabriel A. Almond, "Comparative Political Systems," *Journal of Politics*, XVIII (August, 1956), 391–409;

and beliefs relating to the nature and exercise of political power and the purposes for which it is employed. Because of different patterns of development, environmental conditions, and historical factors, political culture will vary from one national society to another. Differences in public economic policy and policy making in various countries can be explained (at least partially) by examining their political cultures. Public medical care programs have been more numerous and extensive in Western European countries than in the United States because, in Western Europe, there has been greater public acceptance *and expectation* of government action for that purpose.

A definitive statement of American political culture will not be attempted here, if indeed such is presently possible. More modestly, we will indicate and illustrate some of the implications and significance of political culture for economic policy making.

Values are the criteria or standards by which people evaluate the goodness or badness, desirability or undesirability, of actions, goals, and objects. The fundamental values of a society, although somewhat imprecise and subject to differing interpretations, serve as general motives and guides for behavior. A well-known sociologist, Professor Robin M. Williams, has described a number of "major-value orientations" in American society, some of which are briefly noted here.[3]

Individual freedom is a widespread and persistently affirmed value, often designated as the greatest benefit of "the American way of life." In the nineteenth century there was a strong tendency to equate freedom with the absence of governmental restraint. Now freedom is often held to mean the absence of barriers—whether social, economic, or political—to the exercise of the individual's faculties and capacities to the fullest extent consistent with the rights of others and social order. But however defined in a given era, our cultural bias has been toward individual freedom and governmental action which will increase that freedom.

Equality is another major-value orientation and it takes various forms. Men are viewed as deserving at least a minimum of respect and consideration because of their intrinsic worth as human beings, creatures of God, etc. Equality is also held to mean equality of legal rights— "equal protection of the laws"—for all citizens. In the economic realm

---

Samuel H. Beer and Adam B. Ulam, eds., *Patterns of Government: The Major Political Systems of Europe,* 2nd ed., (New York: Random House, 1962), ch. 3; and William C. Mitchell, *The American Polity* (New York: The Free Press, 1962), ch. 5.

[3] The following discussion is based on Williams, *op. cit.,* ch. XI.

it generally takes the form of equality of opportunity, not equality in social and economic rewards (substantive equality). A deep-set and persistent stress on equality has been a peculiarly American trait.

Progress is a third major-value orientation. Progress, and the belief in it, have been central features of the American experience. Progress entails optimism, emphasis on the future rather than the past, openness to change, and technological innovation. Further, progress frequently comes to mean bigness as well, because of the tendency of the average American to equate bigness with "betterness."

Efficiency and *practicality* constitute a value orientation which indicates a concern for technical efficiency, better methods, the "one best way," empiricism rather than abstract thought. To be technically efficient, to do a good job, tends to become an end in itself. To label something as "impractical," "inefficient," or "backward" is to derogate it. In contrast, efficient," "up-to-date," "modern," and "practical" carry favorable connotations in our society. This orientation is also reflected in American philosophy, with its strong strains of empiricism and pragmatism.

Value orientations such as these clearly have significance for economic policy making, as do such other values as democracy, individualism, humanitarianism, and material achievement and success. Democracy is held to mean, at a minimum, public participation in and control of government along with governmental responsiveness to recognized needs of the population. The general approach of Americans to economic regulation has been practical, or pragmatic, emphasizing particular solutions to present problems rather than systematic long-range planning or doctrinal purity. Concern with individual freedom has created a general presumption against governmental restriction of private economic activity in favor of the fullest possible scope for private action. Restriction of the freedom of some individuals, through antitrust laws, labor relations legislation, or whatever, is generally considered justifiable only if it is necessary to protect or increase the freedom or opportunity of others. Our stress on individualism is manifested in several ways. One is in the assumption that most problems can be solved by individual action. Another is the often-expressed notion that a person should be generally free to use his property as he sees fit. A third is in our approval of legislators who refuse to be "dictated" to by party leaders but rather "vote their conscience" or act in the interests of their constituents.

Beliefs are statements about what *is,* what "actually" exists, which are used to describe our environment. They are "pictures of reality" which we carry in our minds and which help determine our actions.

Widely shared beliefs about the actual nature and operation of the economic system help shape the interests which groups try to protect or promote through government action. In the nineteenth and early twentieth centuries the belief that the economy was governed by natural economic laws, and that a policy of laissez faire was therefore both wise and beneficent, certainly slowed the growth of government regulation. Antitrust policy is handicapped today by the belief that big business is more efficient than small business. The belief that government is less efficient than private enterprise has contributed to the minimal role of government enterprise in American society. On the other hand, the beliefs that government is subject to popular control and that social and economic problems can be solved by government action have contributed to the growth of government economic activity.[4]

Social beliefs, however, do not remain constant. As they change, for example, matters once viewed as beyond the power or ability of government to control may come to be thought of as amenable to governmental action. The nineteenth-century belief that the business cycle was beyond governmental control has given way to the view that government can effectively act to maintain economic activity. The latter belief greatly increases the likelihood of some kind of political action in this area.

Within the "consensus of belief" which may exist on a given matter, such as the need for public education, social security, or action to maintain competition, there remains much room for disagreement. Although the widespread belief in the necessity and desirability of social security programs makes their abandonment quite unlikely, there is continuing controversy on such matters as the forms and amounts of benefits. Again, the belief that citizen access to the policy-making process is necessary for democratic government to exist is not accompanied by agreement as to what arrangements are necessary to provide access. Beliefs and values, to be widely shared, must be general; but this does not deprive them of meaning and significance for political action.[5]

The struggle over the formation of economic policy takes place within the context provided by a nation's political culture.[6] Widely

[4] Cf. the discussion of the significance of "belief patterns" in commercial air transport regulation by Emmette S. Redford, "The Significance of Belief Patterns in Economic Regulation," *Western Political Quarterly,* XIV (September, 1961), 13–25.

[5] V. O. Key, Jr., *Public Opinion and American Democracy* (New York: Alfred A. Knopf, 1961), 29–32.

[6] James W. Prothro and Charles M. Gregg, "Fundamental Principles of Democracy: Bases of Agreement and Disagreement," *Journal of Politics,* XXII (May, 1960), 276–294.

shared values and beliefs place limits on governmental action and further, within these limits, help determine what is actually done. To illustrate, because of general agreement on the desirability of private property and the belief that government control of the prices charged by "private" business is undesirable and unnecessary, we can rather safely predict that any proposals for control of the steel industry involving nationalization or formal price regulation would have little chance of success at the present time. Indeed, they are not even likely to be seriously proposed. On the other hand, much room remains for action or inaction with respect to regulation of the steel industry. But within the range of the permissible, the decisions made will be affected by our political culture—such as beliefs favoring free enterprise, fair government procedures, and competition.

In sum, common values and beliefs inform, guide, and limit the behavior of political decision makers. These values and beliefs also serve as the basis for verbal formulations by which the actions of public officials can be explained or rationalized—as, say, "democratic," "practical," or "in behalf of individual freedom"—so as to gain greater public acceptance of them.[7]

THE INSTITUTIONAL FRAMEWORK FOR POLICY MAKING

The formal governmental institutions of a political system significantly affect the formation, substance, and implementation of public economic policy. These institutions—patterns of regularized, habitual, or stable behavior which have developed with the passage of time—lend continuity and stability, and sometimes rigidity, to the processes of policy making and administration. If one wants to comprehend these processes, he must concern himself with more than the motives, interests, and attitudes of particular individuals and groups. He must consider also their institutional context, within which they act. As Eulau states: ". . . current behavior is necessarily circumscribed and directed by the past pattern we call institutions."[8] Much of the activity involved in the regulatory process can be explained by institutional norms or

[7] Richard C. Snyder, "A Decision-Making Approach to the Study of Political Phenomena," in Roland Young, ed., *Approaches to the Study of Politics* (Evanston: Northwestern University Press, 1958), 36. Also Robert E. Lane, *The Regulation of Businessmen* (New Haven: Yale University Press, 1954), 42–43.

[8] Heinz Eulau, *The Behavioral Persuasion in Politics* (New York: Random House, 1963), 18.

prescriptions. The congressional norms supporting committee consideration of legislation and deference to committee action help explain the importance of committees in legislative policy making. Congressional-executive conflict over policy becomes more understandable as one considers the institution of separation of powers and the relevant norms and values.

In this section we will discuss some of the fundamental institutions of our governmental system—federalism, the separation of powers, and the Supreme Court—as they relate to and affect the policy-making and administrative processes. Among the three branches of government, the Supreme Court is singled out for extended treatment here in order to emphasize its role in the policy process and because it receives less attention than Congress and the President elsewhere in the book.

Federalism

Let us begin with a few basic facts. Government power in the American federal system is constitutionally divided between the national government and the several state governments. The Constitution delegates to the national government such powers as those to regulate interstate and foreign commerce, tax and spend for the general welfare, establish post offices and post roads, coin money and regulate its value, grant patents and copyrights, and raise and support armies and navies. The national government is also delegated all powers "necessary and proper for carrying into execution the foregoing powers." Then, in the words of the Tenth Amendment, "All powers not delegated to the United States by the Constitution, nor prohibited by it to the States, are reserved to the states respectively, or to the people." The governmental powers reserved to the states are not specified by the Constitution but the powers of the states can be put under four headings: the police power—power to protect and promote the public health, safety, welfare, and morals; the power to tax and spend; eminent domain—the power to take private property for public use upon payment of just compensation; proprietary power—power to own and operate economic enterprises. Under the doctrine of national supremacy, conflicts between state laws and constitutional provisions and Congressional enactments are resolved in favor of the national government if its actions are in pursuance of its delegated powers.

The *formal* constitutional division of power between the national government and the states is about the same today as it was in 1789. The only amendment to the Constitution dealing specifically with economic activity is the Sixteenth, which gave the national government power to levy income taxes. What has changed markedly since 1789 is the *real* allocation of power. Within the rather vague and general language of the Constitution, and in response to changing political, economic, and social conditions, the control of economic activity by the national government has increased greatly, especially from the 1880's onward. Today, national regulatory activity is more important, if not more pervasive, than that of the states.

A number of factors have contributed to the trend toward national regulation. (1) Probably the most important cause of expanding national action is that, with the development of a national economy, many matters can be dealt with effectively only by the national government. Many economic problems are beyond the ability and legal power of the states. Into this category fall problems in such areas as inflation, unemployment, agricultural prices and surpluses, industrial monopoly, foreign trade, collective bargaining, and flood control. Governmental action, to be effective, must be as broad in scope as the problems with which it is concerned. (2) In some cases uniform national action is necessary if regulation is to be effective. Laws relating to the grading of commodities, the labeling of products, and standards of quality for drugs are examples. (3) Supreme Court decisions sometimes have been the proximate cause of national action by denying the states' power to act in a given area. The Wabash Rate Case in 1886 necessitated national railroad regulation by holding that the states could not regulate interstate railroad rates, even in the absence of national action. (4) National action has been demanded occasionally to make state regulation effective. This was the primary reason for national "fair trade" (resale price maintenance) legislation. Without it, the effectiveness of state "fair trade" laws would be greatly reduced. (5) The failure of the states to take action, or to act adequately, has led to national action in such areas as welfare, conservation of natural resources, and child labor legislation. Various reasons are given for the lack or inadequacy of state action, including lack of financial resources, rural domination of state legislatures, and poor administrative machinery. Also interstate competition may retard or prevent state action. A state may hesitate to enact legislation —higher taxes, unemployment compensation, minimum wage legislation—which may place its businesses at a disadvantage in competing with those in states having milder legislation (or none). Interstate competition has a tendency to drive all down to the level of the lowest.

The constitutional basis for the expansion of national regulatory activity generated by these and other factors derives primarily from expanded interpretation of the powers to regulate interstate and foreign commerce and to tax and spend for the general welfare. Rather than discuss the historical evolution of the commerce and tax clauses at this point, we will focus on their meaning and import for regulatory activity today.

The nature of the commerce clause, and the extent of Congressional power under it can be illustrated by two Supreme Court cases. The definition of the clause followed today is essentially that given it by Chief Justice Marshall in *Gibbons v. Ogden* (1824).[9] "Commerce" was broadly defined as including not only the buying, selling, and interchange of commodities but all means by which "commercial intercourse between nations, and parts of nations, in all its branches" was carried on, including transportation. Interstate commerce, "commerce among the several states," was that which *affected* more states than one. Marshall also made a distinction between what is now called interstate and intrastate commerce. Commerce was intrastate, and a matter for the states to control, when it was "completely internal" and did not "extend to or affect other states."

Marshall's definition gives Congress broad power to regulate interstate commerce. Any activity or subject, even if located in a single state, can be regulated by Congress if it has an impact beyond the borders of that state. The case of *Wickard v. Filburn* (1942)[10] illustrates the extent, or "reach," of Congressional power. The case involved the Agricultural Adjustment Act of 1938, under which marketing quotas could be imposed on farmers in order to stabilize the price of wheat. Anyone growing wheat in excess of his quota was subject to penalties. Roscoe Filburn, an Ohio farmer, sowed 11.9 acres and harvested 239 bushels of wheat in excess of his assigned quota, and was penalized therefor. Filburn contended that since the wheat was not intended for interstate commerce (in fact, it was all used or consumed on his farm) the national government's power under the commerce clause did not extend to his production. (A few years before the Supreme Court had held that agricultural production was a matter for the states to regulate.) His contention was rejected by the Supreme Court. Justice Jackson, for the Court, held that "even if [an] activity be local and though it not be regarded as commerce, it may still, whatever its nature, be reached by Congress if it exerts a substantial economic effect on interstate com-

[9] 9 Wheaton 1 (1824).
[10] 317 U.S. 111 (1942).

merce. . . ." He went on to explain how Filburn's home consumption of wheat affected interstate commerce:

> The power to regulate commerce includes the power to regulate the prices at which commodities in that commerce are dealt in and practices affecting such prices. One of the primary purposes of the Act in question was to increase the market price of wheat and to that end to limit the volume thereof that could affect the market. It can hardly be denied that a factor of such volume and variability as home-consumed wheat would have a substantial effect on price and market conditions. This may arise because being in marketable condition such wheat overhangs the market and if induced by rising prices tends to flow into the market and check price increases. But if we assume that it is never marketed, it supplies a need of the man who grew it that would otherwise be reflected by purchases in the open market. Home-grown wheat in this sense competes with wheat in commerce. . . . This record leaves us in no doubt that Congress may properly have considered that wheat consumed on the farm where grown, if wholly outside the scheme of regulation, would have a substantial effect in defeating and obstructing its purpose to stimulate trade therein at increased prices.

On the basis of *Wickard v. Filburn* it is apparent that Congressional power over commerce is quite sweeping. Indeed, as the commerce clause is now interpreted Congressional power is almost without limit. But if there is little formal constitutional limitation on its power, it does not follow that Congress is not limited in other ways. Possession of a given power and ability or willingness to exercise it are not synonymous. To illustrate: If Congress can regulate agricultural production, and if it can regulate the wages and hours of workers in industrial production, as it can under the commerce clause, there would seem to be no constitutional barrier to Congressional enactment of a minimum wage law for farm workers. But Congress has not done so. Why? Because there is sufficient political opposition from within and without Congress to prevent it. On this issue the balance of political power is tilted in favor of the opponents of agricultural wage legislation. The absence of formal constitutional limitations on the exercise of power thus does not mean the absence of all limitations. There are also important political limitations, although they are often neglected because of our concern with the meaning of formal constitutional provisions.

We turn now to the power of Congress to tax and spend. Although the primary purpose of taxation is to raise revenue to finance governmental activities, and though it has been used mainly for that purpose,

Congress has also used the taxing power to regulate economic activity. The protective tariff is perhaps the best illustration. Taxation has also been used to handicap the sale of colored oleomargarine, to eliminate the manufacture of white phosphorus matches, and to regulate gambling and traffic in narcotics. With the exception of some cases decided during the 1930's,[11] the Supreme Court has sustained the use of the taxing power for regulatory purposes in all cases brought before it. The power of Congress to tax for regulatory purposes is generally considered to be as broad as its power to regulate commerce.

Concerning the power of Congress to spend money, conflict developed early in our national history, with the major contending positions being set forth by Madison and Hamilton. Madison contended that Congress could spend only in support of those powers enumerated in the Constitution. Hamilton, in contrast, asserted that Congress could spend for any purpose, whether enumerated in the Constitution or not, so long as it was beneficial to the general welfare of the United States as contrasted with private welfare. Hamilton's position, which gives extensive power to the national government, is the one which has prevailed. In *United States v. Butler* (1936),[12] the Court accepted the Hamiltonian viewpoint and stated that the only limitation on the power to tax and spend was that, in order to meet the general welfare standard, it must be used for "matters of national, as distinguished from local, welfare." In the following year, in the course of sustaining the Old Age and Survivors Insurance program of the Social Security Act, the Court said that the discretion to decide whether use of the taxing and spending power was for the general welfare "belongs to Congress, unless the choice is clearly wrong, a display of arbitrary power, not an exercise of judgment. . . . Nor is the concept of the general welfare static. Needs that were narrow or parochial a century ago may be interwoven in our day with the well-being of the nation."[13]

Federal funds have been expended for a variety of purposes and programs, often in cooperation with the states, which have little relation to the other powers of Congress enumerated in the Constitution. Agricultural research, urban renewal, aid to education, maternity and child welfare services, medical research, and public housing are only a few examples. Congress has taken a broad view of the general welfare

[11] Most notably, *Bailey v. Drexel Furniture Co.,* 259 U.S. 20 (1922), and *United States v. Butler,* 297 U.S. 1 (1936). The decisions in these cases, which struck down taxes on products made with child labor and the processing of agricultural commodities respectively, are no longer binding.

[12] 297 U.S. 1 (1936).

[13] *Helvering v. Davis,* 301 U.S. 619 (1937).

in its exercise of the taxing and spending power and has moved into many areas once thought reserved to the states.

Notwithstanding the great expansion of both national constitutional power and economic activity, the states continue to play an important role in the economic policy area, with respect to both their own policies and activities and those of the national government. In many areas the states continue to be the primary policy-makers. Among these are the definition of the rights of property ownership, the regulation of trades and professions, the provision of educational and welfare facilities, the construction and maintenance of highways, and the regulation of local aspects of business and labor. Many fields of regulation—banking, transportation, communications, pure foods and drugs—are shared by the national and state governments. Typically, when the national government enters a field in which the states are already acting, national action supplements rather than replaces state action. Indeed, it is difficult to find any governmental activities which do not in some way involve both the national and state governments.

Although the balance of power within our political system has been tilted toward the national government in recent decades, there still remains a real diffusion of power among the national government and the states. Let us look now at some of the ways in which federalism appears to affect the formation, substance, and administration of economic policy, especially national policy.

First, federalism affects the access of groups to government and, consequently, their opportunities to exert influence on the policy process. Some groups may have more access at the national level, others at the state level. Groups that are rather weak or uncertain of their influence at the national level "may hold advantageous positions in the state governments and will be vigorous in their insistence upon the existing distribution of powers between state and nation."[14] In their campaign for state control of the offshore oil deposits under the ocean (the "tidelands"), the oil companies invoked the doctrine of states' rights in behalf of their position. But, as Robert Harris commented:

> The solicitude of the oil companies for states' rights is hardly based on convictions derived from political theory but rather from fears that Federal ownership may result in the cancellation or modification of state leases favorable to their interests, their knowledge that they can

[14] David B. Truman, *The Governmental Process* (New York: Alfred A. Knopf, 1951), 323.

successfully cope with state oil regulatory agencies, and uncertainty concerning their ability to control a Federal agency.[15]

Labor groups, in contrast, have found the national government to be more responsive to their interests than the states and so have often favored national action. In turn, the states are sometimes characterized by labor as dominated by "special interests" and "selfish groups." Over time, groups may switch their allegiance from one level of government to another. Business groups supported national action in the early decades of the nineteenth century when it was mostly promotional. Since the Civil War, however, they have often been proponents of states' rights in their effort to avoid regulation by the national government. At any given time the position of most groups on federal-state relations will be affected more by considerations of relative advantage than by the "rights" of the state or national governments.

In formulating national policy Congress is often quite sensitive to state and local interests, governmental and nongovernmental, and appears generally reluctant to infringe on state powers and functions in any drastic way. Congress, an English scholar has remarked, "is composed of a number of individuals who are, at one and the same time, national statesmen and local politicians, although perhaps some members rarely achieve the former status even temporarily."[16] Congress is receptive to state and local claims for consideration whether these are made by genuine local interests, national pressure groups, or a combination of the two. Many instances demonstrate the impact of "localism" on national policy, but the unemployment compensation program will serve as a representative example. When this program was set up in 1935 such factors as the nationwide consequences of unemployment, the poor financial and administrative conditions of the states, and powerful support from within the executive branch, pointed toward a solely national program. The controlling factor, however, was Congressional concern for state and local interests. Congress was unwilling to bypass the states and so a federal-state cooperative program was established.[17] The effect of federalism is further demonstrated by the fact that the unemployment compensation programs in the various states show wide diversity in such matters as eligibility requirements,

[15] Robert J. Harris, "States' Rights and Vested Interests," *Journal of Politics,* XV (November, 1954), 467.

[16] M. J. C. Vile, *The Structure of American Federalism* (London: Oxford University Press, 1961), 90.

[17] Morton Grodzins, "American Political Parties and the American System," *Western Political Quarterly,* XIII (December, 1960), 978–980.

and duration and amounts of payment. Again, when Congress repealed the national tax on colored oleomargarine in 1950, the repealing legislation left the individual states with full power to regulate the use of oleomargarine within their borders. This was done at the insistence of dairy interests and dairy-state Congressmen and in the name of local needs and control.

Third, though the American federal system is characterized more by national-state cooperation than by conflict, it is possible for the national and state governments, in the use of their respective powers, and in response to different sets of interests, to adopt inconsistent or contradictory policies. This has happened in the area of antitrust policy. National efforts to maintain competition in the economy have been hampered by state action in the form of highly permissive incorporation laws (often giving corporations almost unlimited powers), resale price maintenance legislation, and restrictive occupational licensing laws. (National policy in the antitrust area, of course, has not been the picture of consistency.) Contradictions may also develop in the area of economic stability policy, as during the 1930's. While the national government was trying to stimulate economic activity by deficit spending the states collectively were realizing budget surpluses. The result of this action by the states was to partially reduce the impact of national spending on the economy. Problems of this sort, which are unlikely to arise in a unitary system, complicate the policy process and reduce the effectiveness of policy.

Finally, the administration of national policies is deeply affected by federalism, particularly in grant-in-aid programs in such fields as welfare, highway construction, and agriculture extension, where the programs are actually administered by state and local officials in accordance with national standards. Cooperation between the national and state agencies concerned with such programs is necessary if national policy is to be effective, and such cooperation may be forthcoming only at a "price." Much latitude may be permitted the states in the administration of these programs. Moreover, rules, regulations, and program changes usually are not made by national officials without consultation of or participation by state or local officials.[18] Political realities may cause the adoption or retention of practices that national administrative officials consider administratively or otherwise undesirable. Attempts to "dictate" to state or local officials may produce a

[18] Edward W. Weidner, "Decision-Making in a Federal System" in Arthur W. Macmahon, ed., *Federalism Mature and Emergent* (Garden City: Doubleday, 1955), 377–380.

Congressional reaction. The refusal of national welfare officials to permit state officials to disclose the names of public assistance recipients in 1951 led within a matter of months to Congressional legislation authorizing such action.

State and local interests and officials do not confine their efforts to influence national administration to grant-in-aid programs. Rather, they attempt to influence federal administrative structure, personnel selection, and policy in all areas of national action. Thus, local livestock interests have strong impact on the way in which federal grazing control programs are administered in the western United States. Many of the national antipoverty programs discussed in Chapter Eight depend heavily on state and local governments for their implementation, giving local interests and officials an opportunity to exert influence on the selection of local program personnel and antipoverty projects. Although the impact of "localism" on national administration and policy cannot be attributed solely to the existence of "semi-independent" state and local governments, their existence certainly contributes to the political power and influence of local interests.

The Separation of Powers

A second basic feature of our governmental system is the separation of powers among legislative, executive, and judicial branches. This institutional arrangement functions to increase the points of access through which groups can attempt to exert influence on policy. A group which fails to realize its goals through Congressional action may seek favorable executive or judicial action. Thus, a group unable to prevent Congressional enactment of a law may seek a Presidential veto. Failing in this, the law may be challenged in the courts. Even if it is not declared unconstitutional the law may be interpreted in a way favorable to the group's interests. But let us assume that the group fails here also. It can still attempt to influence the agency entrusted with administration of the law to act in a favorable manner.

The separation of powers would seem to work to the advantage of groups attempting to prevent the enactment of legislation, especially when we take into account the organization of Congress. Congressional power is divided not only between the House of Representatives and the Senate but within each house it is scattered among a number of points—leaders, influential members, committees. In other words, Congressional power is dispersed, not concentrated. A group trying to prevent action may succeed if it can gain the support of one of these centers of power. The support of the committee (or perhaps just its chairman) considering the measure objected to by the group may be sufficient to kill it. On the other hand, this dispersion of power works to the disadvantage of groups supporting the enactment of legislation because it greatly multiplies the points at which the legislation may be blocked. Even if passed by Congress a bill may be substantially changed or watered down as a condition for its passage.

Because of the differences in the manner of their election, the President and Congress tend to represent, or "over-represent," different interests.[19] The President, because of the workings of the electoral college, tends to "over-represent" interests located in populous, urban, two-party states. In contrast, Congress tends to "over-represent" interests situated in small, rural, one-party states. This difference in the "effective constituencies" of the two branches may lead to Presidential-Congressional disagreement or conflict in policy making, even when both branches are controlled by the same political party. The possibility of conflict or disagreement is further increased by institutional loyalties which have developed over time. Congress especially is often quite concerned to protect its prerogatives against executive "encroachment." This set of conditions has significant implications for policy making since most important policy decisions require approval or action by both President and Congress. Consequently, in order to avoid stalemate or inaction, bargaining and compromise will be necessary. Important policies generally will be established only after extensive deliberation and consideration of a broad range of affected interests. The separation of powers may also mean that adopted policies will be vague or ambiguous or that action will be slow in coming.

Together the separation of powers and federalism have discouraged the development of political parties able to act with unity at the national level. Federalism has produced a decentralized party system in which the primary bases of political strength are in state and local party organizations. The separation of powers has helped prevent the development of party cohesion within Congress or between President and Congress, even when both are controlled by the same party. This situation has resulted from constitutional provisions which provide the President, House, and Senate with different election constituencies, which we have already commented on in part; which provide for staggered terms of election; and which assign different powers to the various branches of government. The absence of cohesive, policy oriented par-

[19] The following discussion draws on Lewis A. Froman, Jr., *People and Politics* (Englewood Cliffs, N.J.: Prentice-Hall, 1962), 80–89.

ties has strengthened the position of interest groups in the making of policy and they undoubtedly have more impact here than in countries with strong, disciplined parties. "Because the legislator's tenure in office depends on no overarching party organization, he is accessible to whatever influences are outstanding in his local constituency almost regardless of more inclusive claims."[20] National issues are often viewed and acted upon according to their meaning for state and local interests. The party system only partially bridges the gap between President and Congress created by the separation of powers; much room is left for the play of interest groups in policy making.

The Role of the Supreme Court

The Supreme Court is a political as well as a legal institution, a law-making as well as a law-judging body. In the exercise of its powers of judicial review and statutory interpretation, the Court goes beyond the performance of a purely judicial function. When the Court declares a legislative act unconstitutional, or gives a particular interpretation to a statute, or holds an administrative action illegal, it is making decisions which help shape, often quite significantly, the nature and substance of public policy.[21] Issues are brought before the Supreme Court, and the other courts, because some individual or group is dissatisfied with a legislative enactment or its application by administrative officials. The courts thus serve as an alternative arena for conflicts over policy and the interests favored by the courts may not be the same as those favored in legislative or administrative bodies. In recent decades the Supreme Court has been less responsive to interests favoring the restriction of competition than have many legislatures.

Although the nature of its role has varied from one era to another, the Supreme Court has always been a participant in the economic policy area. Between 1890 and the middle 1930's the Court was one of the major barriers to economic regulation, using the doctrine of substantive due process of law and a narrow view of the national government's delegated power to strike down economic legislation disliked by conservative and business interests. However, since the "constitutional revolution" of 1937, the Court has followed a course of judicial self-restraint in economic policy. The necessity and wisdom of regula-

[20] Truman, *op. cit.,* 325.
[21] Cf. Jack Peltason, *Federal Courts in the Political Process* (New York: Random House, 1955); and Victor Rosenblum, *Law as a Political Instrument* (New York: Random House, 1955).

tory measures are viewed by the Court as matters for determination through the political processes in the legislative and executive branches. No Congressional statute involving economic activity has been declared unconstitutional in the last twenty-five years. State regulatory laws are also generally left alone except when they conflict with national policy. In following this course of self-restraint, the Court, whatever its motives, acts to the benefit of interests favoring positive governmental action and regulation.

Although the Court no longer acts as a "super-legislature" in the economic policy area, it has by no means entirely left the field. The impact of the Court is still felt through the functions it performs in such matters as statutory interpretation, national-state relations, and the control of administrative agencies.

The Court frequently is called upon to interpret statutes in deciding cases brought before it; and many statutes—the Sherman Antitrust Act and the Clayton Act are illustrative—derive much of their "operational" meaning from judicial interpretations. If the Court does not seek this task neither can it be avoided. Many laws enacted by Congress are quite general or ambiguous, permitting a number of differing interpretations, because Congress is frequently unable to make a precise settlement among the affected interests. Consequently the courts and administrative agencies, which enforce and implement the law, are left with the tasks of filling in the details and giving the statute more definite meaning and, in so doing, adjusting or reconciling the interests in conflict. Though the Court may explain its interpretation of a statute according to the "intent of Congress" or the "plain words of the statute," these plain words and intent are often neither clear nor self-evident. In exercising its discretion here, in giving a statute one interpretation rather than another, the Court, regardless of its intentions, must of necessity favor some interests over others. If there were no conflict over the meaning of a statute as enacted, if different interests did not seek to give it different interpretations, the matter would not come before the Court for determination.

Secondly, the Court's decisions concerning national-state relations often have a bearing on economic policy. Both the nature of policy and the level of government at which policy can be made will be affected by the Court's action. Some decisions concern the broad allocation of power between the nation and the states and will touch off interest conflicts of the first magnitude. An example is the Court's highly controversial decision in 1950 that ownership and control of the offshore oil deposits rest, under the Constitution, with the national government and not the state governments, which had been exercising jurisdiction over this subject.[22] The Court's decision, for a policy of national control, was partially reversed when Congress, by the Submerged Lands Act of 1953, gave the states control over offshore oil deposits to the extent of their "historic boundaries." Cases of this importance are relatively rare, however.

The Court is more deeply and consistently involved in another, less spectacular aspect of national-state relations. Within the broad constitutional division of power as it now exists, Congressional action essentially determines how a given field of activity will be divided up between the national and state governments. In many instances, however, it is not clear how much jurisdiction Congress intended to take and how much is left to the states. Conflicts between national and state policy arise, many of which come to the Supreme Court for settlement. The regulation of labor-management relations, handled concurrently by both levels of government, is an example. The problems confronting the Court in this area, which have undoubtedly become more complex since the Labor Reform Act of 1959, were described by Justice Frankfurter in 1955:

> By the Taft-Hartley Act Congress did not exhaust the full sweep of legislative power over industrial relations given by the Commerce Clause. Congress formulated a code whereby it outlawed some aspects of labor activities and left others free for the operation of economic forces. As to both categories, the areas that have been preempted by Federal authority and thereby withdrawn from State power are not susceptible of delimitation by fixed metes and bounds. Obvious conflict, actual or potential, leads to easy exclusion of State action. Such was the situation in *Garner v. Teamsters, C. and H. Local Union.* . . . But as the opinion in that case recalled, the Labor Management Relations Act "leaves much to the States, though Congress has refrained from telling us how much." . . . This penumbral area can be rendered progressively clear only by the course of litigation.[23]

The Court's decisions will do more than merely determine whether the States can regulate a given matter. To hold that, in the absence of positive national policy, the states can regulate may be to leave the door open for restrictive state legislation where previously matters were left to the private parties concerned.

[22] Lucius J. Barker, "The Supreme Court as Policy-Maker: The Tidelands Oil Controversy," *Journal of Politics,* XXIV (May, 1962), 350–360.
[23] *Weber v. Anheuser-Busch,* 348 U.S. 468, 480–481 (1955).

Third, the Court can exercise control over the activities of administrative agencies and, since 1937, judicial review of administration has had more importance for the regulatory process than review of substantive legislative policies. The powers to make rules or policy (legislation) and to apply policies to particular individuals or cases (adjudication) have been increasingly delegated to administrative agencies by Congress in the twentieth century. The Supreme Court and the other federal courts are called upon to help ensure that administrative agencies act fairly and within the scope of their legal authority in performing their tasks.

Those who consider themselves to be adversely or improperly treated by administrative agencies frequently seek judicial redress of their grievances. (The discussion here is broadened to apply to the courts generally.) Agencies are expected to follow fair procedures and to stay within their legal authority when taking action but they may depart from one or both of these expectations, which have legal and constitutional bases. The scope of judicial review here can be summarized conveniently in the form of three sets of questions which concern the courts when reviewing administrative action. (1) Were the proceedings "regularly conducted"? That is, did the agency use fair procedures? Were the affected parties given adequate notice and opportunity to be heard before the agency acted? (2) Was there error in the interpretation or application of the law? Did the agency have legal authority to act? Did it give the proper meaning to the law and its duties thereunder? (3) Was there adequate basis in fact for the agency's decision? Was the decision or action of the agency based on the record of proceedings and supported by "substantial evidence"? Agency actions which do not meet these standards may be overruled and declared null and void. The Supreme Court has accorded considerable freedom of action to administrative agencies in recent decades, however, and upholds their actions more often than not when challenged.[24]

Even if the courts are willing to review administrative action, it should be observed that a number of factors may limit the ability or desire of those adversely affected by an agency to challenge it judicially.[25] Many agency actions will be accepted as a matter of course, as being necessary, inevitable, or just, or as not warranting the time and

[24] See Joseph Tanenhaus, "Supreme Court Attitudes Toward Federal Administrative Agencies," *Journal of Politics,* XXII (August, 1960), 502–524.

[25] Emmette S. Redford, *Administration of National Economics Control* (New York: Macmillan, 1952), 337–338; and Tanenhaus, *op. cit.,* 504–507.

expense involved in judicial appeal. A related point is that administrative action, when considered undesirable or improper, will often be contested in the political arena—before higher administrative officials or in Congress—rather than in the courts. Again, much of the work of administrative agencies is handled through informal procedures, by compromise or negotiation between an agency and the affected party, and is thus beyond the reach of the courts. Finally, some administrative actions, even highly important ones which generate much conflict or controversy, do not involve justiciable issues of the sort handled by the courts. Examples are a Federal Reserve Board decision to raise or lower the rediscount rate, a policy of lax enforcement of the antitrust laws, or a presidential decision not to enter into certain types of reciprocal trade agreements. Many administrative activities are thus simply beyond the reach of the courts, regardless of their importance or impact.

The Supreme Court has played and continues to play an important role in the regulatory process. Who supports and who opposes particular decisions of the Court depends to a considerable extent upon whose ox is gored. Those who object to the policy-making aspects of Court action may gain partial comfort from the fact that "the policy views dominant on the Court are never for long out of line with the policy views dominant among the lawmaking majorities of the United States."[26] Moreover, most of the Court's decisions relating to national economic policy are based on statutory interpretations and can be rather readily overcome by a "determined majority" in Congress.

AN APPROACH TO THE
POLICY-MAKING PROCESS

Policy has been referred to as the "nucleus of politics."[27] People engage in political activity—voting, electioneering, communicating with public officials, holding office—because they hope to affect public policy in some way. The possibility of other motives for political participation

[26] Robert A. Dahl, "Policy-Making in a Democracy: The Supreme Court as a National Policy Maker," *Journal of Public Law,* VI (Fall, 1957), 285. Dahl argues that FDR's "difficulties with the Court [in the 1930's] were truly exceptional," primarily because he had to wait more than four years before making any appointments to the Court. Through his power to appoint its members, the President can significantly influence the decisions made by the Court.

[27] Marian D. Irish and James W. Prothro, *The Politics of American Democracy,* 2nd ed. (Englewood Cliffs, N.J.: Prentice-Hall, 1962), ch. 16.

is, of course, not excluded. The study of politics, by and large, can be viewed as the study of the various factors which, directly and indirectly, now or in the future, affect public policy making. But what is policy? A policy can briefly be defined as a course of action followed by an actor or group of actors on a given subject. A common-sense definition of a *public* policy is one made by government officials or agencies. Building on these definitions, a public economic policy is a course of action followed by government with respect to some aspect of economic activity—for example, antitrust policy or agricultural price support policy. Defined as a course of action, a public policy is more than a decision or a series of decisions that something shall be done or not done; it also includes the action undertaken to implement the decision(s). Policy includes not only what is *supposed* to be done but also what is *actually* done. There may be a divergence, for example, between the intent of Congress in enacting an antitrust law and what in reality happens in the application of the law. Both aspects are a part of antitrust policy.

Public policies can be usefully viewed as arising out of conflicts or disagreements between groups of people, both private and official, possessing different interests or desires.[28] One of the prime sources of conflict in our society is economic activity. Because of their differing interests or desires, conflicts may occur between big business and small business, employers and employees, creditors and debtors, retailers and wholesalers, chain stores and independents, consumers and sellers, farmers and the purchasers of farm commodities, and so on. Conflicts thus may occur between groups within the same sector of the economy as well as groups in different sectors. Groups which are underprivileged or dissatisfied in their relationships with other groups in the operation of the economy may seek to improve their position by calling upon government for assistance. Thus farmers may demand price supports, employees minimum wages, and consumers pure food and drug legislation. It is usually the weaker or disadvantaged (in a relative sense) group or groups in a "private" conflict, as between employers and employees over wages, which looks to government for assistance. The dominant group, the one able to achieve its goals satisfactorily in the absence of governmental action, has no desire to bring government into the matter. To state the proposition in bald terms, in the absence of conflicts or disagreements between groups of citizens,

[28] See E. E. Schattschneider, *The Semi-Sovereign People* (New York: Holt, Rinehart and Winston, 1960), ch. 1.

and without the unwillingness of some groups to abide by the results of "private" conflicts, there would be few demands for governmental action and consequently little public action.

Because they arise out of group conflicts, public policies have the effect of favoring some groups and their interests over others. Some groups will be benefited and others disadvantaged by a given policy such as minimum wage legislation or progressive income taxation. This statement should not be taken to mean that public policies are products of the actions of "selfish groups" or "special interests." Rather, it simply describes a result, the practical effect of a policy, without passing judgment on its goodness or badness, desirability or undesirability. Nor should our comments be interpreted as stating that public policies can be accounted for solely in terms of interest group activity. That other factors are also operative should be made clear as our discussion proceeds.

Before turning to our model of the policy process, it seems advisable to clarify the meaning of some words, (or concepts), such as "interest" and "interest group," which appear throughout this study. There are *interests* in such matters as higher wages, fair competitive practices, lower income taxes, water pollution control, and soil conservation services. These interests are manifested by the activity or behavior— writing, speaking, bargaining, lobbying, voting—of people who favor or support them. Thus we say that people who support fair competition have an interest in it. All of those who seek to influence government in behalf of a given interest, say higher minimum wages, constitute an *interest group*. Alternatively, we can say they are part of the *group interest* in such wages. The same individual may simultaneously belong to several interest groups. He may be a member of the interest groups supporting lower taxes and pure food legislation as well as higher minimum wages.

People who have common interests often form organizations in order to better promote or protect their interests. An organization which supports a given interest or set of interests by political activity can be referred to as either an *organized interest group* or a *pressure group*. A distinction is thus drawn between an interest group and an organized interest (or pressure) group. For example, the AFL-CIO acts as a pressure group when it exerts "pressure" on Congress in behalf of higher minimum wages. But other organizations and individuals may also support this interest, and, along with the AFL-CIO, they constitute the interest group supporting higher minimum wages.

On the other hand, members of the AFL-CIO who do not support higher minimum wages are not part of this interest group. The various concepts discussed in these two paragraphs are used here for descriptive rather than evaluative purposes. They are simply means of describing and relating diverse actions and events. Our primary concern will be with organized interest groups.

A "Model" of the Policy Process

The making of public policy in the United States is a highly complex (and sometimes confusing) process. All branches and all levels of government make, or participate in the making of, public policy. In addition to government agencies and officials, a variety of other factors and forces help shape or condition the formulation of policy. In his study of the Employment Act of 1946, which involved *legislative* policy making, Professor Bailey concluded:

> Legislative policy-making appears to be the result of a confluence of factors streaming from an almost endless number of tributaries: national experience, the contributions of social theorists, the clash of powerful economic interests, the quality of Presidential leadership, other institutional and personal ambitions and administrative arrangements in the Executive Branch, the initiative, effort, and ambitions of individual legislators and their governmental and non-governmental staffs, the policy commitments of the political parties, and the predominant culture symbols in the minds both of leaders and followers in Congress.[29]

If this description were broadened to include policy making by the other branches of national government and the state and local governments, as well as the relationships among the various levels of government in policy making, one would have some notion of the total complexity of the policy-making process.

The "model" diagrammed below is an oversimplification of the policy process at the national level. Only some of the many factors and relationships which could be included in the policy process are indicated by it. It does not, for example, indicate the relationships and interactions among the different branches of the national government, the influence of federalism, or the role of personal values and beliefs of

[29] Stephen K. Bailey, *Congress Makes a Law* (New York: Columbia University Press, 1950), 236.

government officials in the policy process.[30] Our purpose, however, is not to catalog all of the factors which may affect the formulation of policies but only to indicate some of the important variables common to the making of most policies—especially economic policies. Our discussion here is based on the previously stated premise that public policies (at least those of any general significance or impact) originate in the conflict of group interests. The various aspects of the "model" can be viewed as factors which shape, condition, or affect the translation of group demands or interests into public policy.

FIGURE ONE-1
THE POLICY-MAKING PROCESS: A MODEL

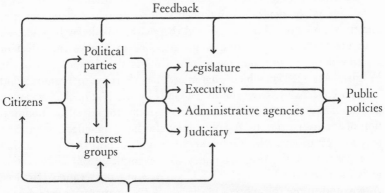

Government agencies and officials can be pictured as standing in the middle of the policy process in this fashion: inputs → government → outputs. Government officials function as the authoritative decision-makers for a society. As Milbrath states: "The very designation 'official' is a formal recognition by all the members of a civil society that a designated individual, or set of individuals, has the right and the power to make and enforce authoritative decisions that are binding on the entire society."[31] Demands (inputs) for action are made on government officials in their role as authoritative decision makers

---

[30] For a statement of the multiplicity of variables affecting policy making see Snyder, *op. cit.*

[31] Lester W. Milbrath, *The Washington Lobbyists* (Chicago: Rand McNally, 1963), 183.

by interest groups, political parties, individuals, and other government officials. Governmental action on these inputs results in outputs—policies or decisions—in the form of legislative statutes, executive orders, administrative decisions, judicial orders and decrees. But one should not conclude, that public policy making is merely a process of "the pressure goes in here and the results come out there." Government officials do respond to the needs and demands of interest groups and others in their desire to win votes at the next election, build a "good record," promote their conception of the public interest, or maintain the support of other government officials. However, numerous factors, some of which will be noted later, will affect the chances of a particular group in achieving some or all of its goals.

Two other aspects of our "model" merit brief attention. The "feedback" line in the diagram is intended to indicate that policies made at one time, and experiences associated therewith, will have an effect on later policy-making activities. A given policy may have the effect of creating new demands on government. Congressional enactment of the Wagner Act (1935), which guaranteed labor's right to organize and bargain collectively, gave rise to demands by the National Association of Manufacturers and other conservative groups for repeal or modification of the initial statute. A policy may also have the effect of creating new interest groups which often organize and support the continuation or expansion of the original policy. An example is soil conservation legislation and the National Association of Soil Conservation Districts. Again, and to use the concept of "feedback" a bit more conventionally, knowledge and experience gained in connection with the making and implementation of policies may serve to guide, modify, or condition future decision making. Loopholes or shortcomings in a given law, revealed in the course of its application, may result in demands for supplemental or corrective action being fed back to the legislature by administrative officials.

The environment of a society, particularly its economic system and political culture, significantly affect the making and substance of public economic policy. The demands made on economic policy makers, and their responses to these demands, will in part be determined by the nature of the economic system and the political culture of the society. For example, the demands for economic policy arising in a complex, urban industrial society will differ from those arising in a rural, agrarian society. What is done in the way of welfare activity will be affected by the availability of economic resources and beliefs about the proper role of government.

The Role of Pressure Groups

Public policies, as stated, arise out of the conflicts of group interests. Before policy making can occur, however, these conflicting group interests must be translated into demands for governmental action or inaction. Pressure groups, or organized interest groups, serve as the voice (or at least one of the voices) of interest groups, as a connecting link between interest groups and governmental decision makers. It is in the form of pressure groups that interest groups contend for power and attempt to influence policy in our political system. Although proposals for policy stem from a variety of sources, pressure groups are a prime source of demands for the adoption, modification, or rejection of policies, particularly if the concept of pressure group is expanded to include administrative agencies when they seek to influence the action of other government officials or agencies.[32] Although the political parties may also act as policy initiators and shapers, their loose, undisciplined nature and their emphasis on political campaign activities combine to make them less influential in initiating and shaping policy than are the more disciplined, programmatic parties in Great Britain. "A striking feature of American politics is the extent to which political parties are supplemented by private associations formed to influence public policy."[33] But the political parties still have much significance, as will be made clear in later chapters, for such matters as Congressional voting behavior.

Interest groups as phenomena of political significance have long been present in our society. This is evidenced by James Madison's statement in *The Federalist Papers,* No. 10:

> Those who hold and those who are without property have ever formed distinct interests in society. Those who are creditors, and those who are debtors, fall under a like discrimination. A landed interest, a manufacturing interest, a mercantile interest, with many lesser interests, grow up of necessity in civilized nations, and divide them into different classes, actuated by different sentiments and views. The regulation of these various and interfering interests forms the principal task of modern legislation, and involves the spirit of party and faction in the necessary and ordinary operations of government.

[32] See J. Leiper Freeman, "The Bureaucracy in Pressure Politics," *The Annals of the American Academy of Political and Social Science,* CCCIXX (September, 1958), 10–19.

[33] V. O. Key, Jr., *Politics, Parties and Pressure Groups,* 4th ed. (New York: Thomas Y. Crowell, 1958), 23.

Organized interest groups, although not nonexistent in the nineteenth century, have greatly proliferated and increased in diversity in the twentieth century. Today it appears that there is scarcely an interest of any importance in our society which is not represented by at least one organized group. Although we are concerned here with economic pressure groups, it is well to keep in mind that by no means all pressure groups are concerned with economic matters. There are also groups supporting such goals as equal rights for minorities, "good government," anti-vivisection laws, curbs on the sale of alcoholic beverages, and a stronger navy.

The growth in number of organized interest groups is in part a consequence of the growing complexity of our economic and social systems. As our economy has developed, it has come more and more to be characterized by specialization in the production of goods and services, which, as we noted in the first chapter, has led to increases both in group conflicts and in governmental action to control relations among groups. Governmental intervention, or the threat of it, "stimulates the formation of organized groups by those who begin to sense a shared interest. This chain reaction may be set in motion not so much by government itself as by the formation of one organization to press its claims, through the government, upon other groups which in turn organize in self-defense. . . . Organization begets counterorganization."[34] A second factor conducive to the formation of pressure groups is a permissive political environment. Freedom of association and the right to petition government for redress of grievances are cherished components of the "American way of life" and are protected against undue governmental limitation by the Bill of Rights. Also, the structure of our governmental system probably has affected both the number of pressure groups and their activity. Federalism, the separation of powers, and bicameralism have created numerous points at which organized groups can attempt to influence the making of policy. The result is a standing invitation to group participation in policymaking. Organized groups have not declined the invitation and a variety of groups is clustered around each of these points of access.

Pressure groups operate on all levels of government—national, state, and local—and strive to influence the policy-making activities of all branches of government. They use a variety of methods attempting to secure their policy goals. These include lobbying, the manipulation of public opinion or, if one prefers, public relations activities, alliance building and log-rolling, electioneering, participation on advisory

[34] *Ibid.*, 143.

56

committees to governmental agencies, and letter-writing campaigns. The nature of a group will help determine the particular forms of activity which it stresses in seeking its goals. Groups with large memberships, such as the AFL-CIO, are more likely to use political campaign activities in promoting their interests than are groups with small memberships and, consequently, small voting impact. The latter may stress lobbying techniques or log-rolling and alliance-building. Groups with limited financial resources are more apt to resort to lobbying than to public relations campaigns. Well-financed, high status groups, as the National Association of Manufacturers and the American Medical Association, will probably use lobbying and public relations techniques more than electioneering, endorsing candidates, ringing doorbells, getting out the vote, and the like, in influencing policy. But whatever the group, and whatever the methods used, the goal is the same: promotion of the group's interests by obtaining favorable and preventing unfavorable governmental action.

In discussing the efforts of pressure groups to promote their particular interests we should not lose sight of the useful functions they perform in our political system. The spokesmen for organized groups are an important source of information on public needs and issues for government officials. Much of this information is specialized or technical and would not otherwise be available. In turn, the leadership of organized groups act to keep their memberships informed on what the government is doing and how they may be affected thereby. In a broad sense, organized groups provide a form of functional representation for social and economic interests which are only imperfectly represented by our system of geographical representation. The individual legislator cannot be expected adequately to speak for or appreciate the myriad interests present in his own district or state, let alone those which spread across broader areas. Finally, organized groups may perform a psychological function. Through their activities individual group members may gain a feeling of access to government, a feeling that they have some influence on policy making, which strengthens their sense of "belonging" and security. It may also increase the acceptability of public policies.

Pressure Groups: What Impact on Policy?

We now come to a particularly sticky question: How effective are pressure groups in attaining their policy goals and in shaping the course of governmental action? How much influence do they really have in the policy process? Here we must resist the temptation to assume that, for example, because pressure group A supports policy alternative X, the adoption of policy alternative X is the direct result of A's activities. Perhaps it is the case, but then perhaps it is not, because X might have been adopted had group A not even been in action. We often cannot be certain because of the numerous factors which affect the adoption or rejection of a given policy proposal, especially one of major importance.

Several recent studies pertaining to the influence of pressure groups and lobbies in Congressional policy making lead to the general conclusion that organized interest groups are less powerful in promoting their interests at this point than is sometimes assumed (especially on the basis of popular and journalistic exposés of lobbying).[35] In their study of reciprocal trade legislation, Bauer and his associates state:

> This story of partial success demonstrates the limitations and also the potential lobbying. The major effect of the lobby is seldom that which gives it its name. It is seldom successful in buttonholing Congressmen, in persuading, in working behind the scenes, and in buying or bullying votes. In the instances we cited, as indeed in most cases, the major effect achieved by small activist groups was in building a series of fronts through which they could speak. Since such fronts came to be regarded by the general public and Congress alike as the representatives of important interests, those who controlled what these groups said controlled thereby the accepted image of what the issues were and how the major interests felt about them.
> . . . The power of the pressure organization seems to be that it is recognized as the voice of its supporters. Thus, what it says is endowed with a kind of canonical authority as the expression of their point of view. Its power lies in that slight aura of legitimacy, not in having any capability for persuasion or coercion.[36]

On the other hand, evidence also indicates that public policy is sometimes largely the result of pressure group activity. Some statutes in reality are the legislative ratifications of agreements reached by the organized groups concerned with particular issues. Thus Steiner and Gove report that "the long-standing Illinois legislative tradition . . . limits the enactment of labor legislation to bills agreed upon by organized labor and organized management. . . ."[37] Further, instances can

[35] See Donald R. Matthews, *U.S. Senators and Their World* (Chapel Hill: University of North Carolina Press, 1960), ch. VIII; Raymond A. Bauer, Ithiel de Sola Pool, and Lewis A. Dexter, *American Business and Public Policy* (New York: Atherton Press, 1963); and Milbrath, *op. cit.*, ch. XVII.

[36] Bauer, *op. cit.*, 372, 374.

[37] Gilbert Y. Steiner and Samuel K. Gove, *Legislative Politics in Illinois* (Urbana: University of Illinois Press, 1960), 19.

be cited in which state occupational licensing laws apparently were enacted primarily at the insistence of, and are essentially administered by, the licensed groups or their representatives.

With our present knowledge of pressure groups, it is not possible to provide a definitive answer to the question of what impact pressure groups have on policy making. Their influence, or impact, obviously varies substantially from one situation to another and the success of an organized group in achieving its goals, in exerting influence, will be affected by a number of factors. These include the group's organization, membership size, leadership, resources, and status in the community; the presence or absence of conflicting and supporting groups; the level and branch of government involved; the role of political parties and leaders; the "political philosophies" and interest group affiliations of public officials; the economic environment; and political culture. Also, it should be noted that interest groups may have weight in policy making without being formally organized. Political decision makers may act in behalf of the interests of such groups as home owners, urban dwellers, or the inhabitants of a particular area.

Much empirical research remains to be done before we can make accurate and supportable generalizations about the extent to which public policies generally are the result of organized interest group activity. In the meantime we should approach statements such as "It is true that the action of Congress and of all the state legislatures is largely determined by the pressure of organized groups . . ." with a healthy skepticism and a call for evidence.[38]

A CASE STUDY: NATURAL GAS

The regulation of the natural gas industry, especially the conflict over exemption of independent producers from price regulation, presents an instructive example of the policy-making process. It illustrates many of the points at which interest groups can exert influence, the clash of interests in policy making, and the way an interest group may move from one point to another seeking a favorable decision. It also demonstrates that policy making is a continuing process, that all branches and levels of government may become involved in a given area of policy, and that there is conflict within government as well as among interest groups in making policy. Further, it epitomizes the political nature of policy making.

[38] Harvey Ferguson, *People and Power*. Quoted in Arnold A. Rogow, ed., *Government and Politics: A Reader* (New York: Thomas Y. Crowell, 1961), 185.

The natural gas industry encompasses three basic economic functions: the producing and gathering of gas in the field, transportation to the market area, and distribution to the ultimate consumers.[39] A series of Supreme Court decisions have placed the first and third functions within the scope of state regulatory power. Most of the transportation of gas, however, takes place in interstate commerce and therefore falls under the jurisdiction of the national government. State utility commissions could regulate the prices charged to local consumers but not the wholesale prices at which gas was sold to local distributing companies by interstate pipeline companies. The lack of power to regulate these wholesale rates greatly handicapped the states in their efforts to regulate the prices charged to ultimate consumers.

This jurisdictional gap was filled when Congress enacted the Natural Gas Act of 1938, partly because of abuses in the operation of interstate pipeline companies. The Act empowered the Federal Power Commission to regulate the transportation of natural gas in interstate commerce. Production and gathering of gas, direct sales to industrial users, and the local distribution of gas were exempted from control by the Commission. A problem soon arose, however, because the Act was not clear as to whether field prices of gas—the prices charged by processors and gatherers to pipeline companies—were sales in interstate commerce and thus subject to regulation by the Federal Power Commission.

At first the FPC held that it did not have jurisdiction over the field prices of gas. Then, in 1943, the Commission reversed itself and held that it did have such jurisdiction. The Supreme Court upheld the Commission, and ruled, in effect, that all sales to interstate pipeline companies were sales in interstate commerce and within the jurisdiction of the FPC. The Court declined to accept the contention that such sales were part of the processing and gathering function and thus exempt from national regulation. To say the least, the Court's interpretation of the Natural Gas Act differed greatly from that of the gas interests and their supporters.

Even before the Supreme Court issued its 1947 decision, a move started in Congress, led by members from the south and southwest and supported by oil and gas interests, to amend the Natural Gas Act. One bill, introduced by Representative Rizley of Oklahoma, would have

[39] See Ralph K. Huitt, "National Regulation of the Natural-Gas Industry," in Emmette S. Redford, ed., *Public Administration and Policy Formation* (Austin: University of Texas Press, 1958), 53–116, for an excellent discussion of natural gas regulation. Also Cornelius P. Cotter, *Government and Private Enterprise* (New York: Holt, Rinehart and Winston, 1960), ch. 12, and Robert Engler, *The Politics of Oil* (New York: Macmillan, 1961), *passim*.

exempted sales by both integrated and independent producers from FPC regulation. (An integrated producer is one having its own pipelines or affiliated with a pipeline company. An "independent" is the value-laden title given to a company, regardless of size, which does not control its own pipelines.) The FPC opposed the Rizley Bill but gave its support to another bill designed to exempt only independent producers. Further, by a 4 to 1 decision in 1947, the FPC issued its Order No. 139, by which it interpreted the Natural Gas Act as denying it power to regulate prices charged by independent producers. This, however, did not abate the Congressional effort to amend the Act. Moreover, by 1949 the position of the Commission had shifted again and three members now opposed exemption of independents. Leland Olds, the FPC chairman, was especially strong in his opposition.

Activity now began to pick up in Congress. In 1949, Senator Kerr of Oklahoma introduced a bill to exempt sales by independent producers. The House had passed a similar bill by a 183 to 131 vote. At first the Senate Committee on Interstate and Foreign Commerce, partly because of the strong opposition of Chairman Olds, refused to report out the Kerr Bill. About this time, Olds' term on the Commission expired and his name came before the Senate for renomination. A bitter attack against his renomination was launched by oil and gas interests and Senate supporters of exemption. Over the protests of some Senators from gas-consuming states and consumer interests, Olds' renomination was rejected by a 51 to 15 vote. With Olds out of the way, the Senate turned its attention to the Kerr Bill and passed it by a vote of 44 to 38. Most of the opposition came from the gas-consuming states in the North and East. Former Senator Mon Wallgren, who had been appointed to take Olds' place on the FPC, now joined with two "consumer-minded" incumbent commissioners to recommend a presidential veto. Following President Truman's veto of the Kerr Bill, the Commission repealed its Order No. 139.

The FPC now became the primary locus of the regulatory struggle. While the Court had held the Commission was authorized to regulate independent producers, it had not said the Commission was required to do so. In 1951, in the Phillips Petroleum Company case, the Commission again changed its mind. By a 4 to 1 decision it decided that the exemption of production and gathering from regulation included the sale of gas by independents to pipeline companies. The Commission's action was challenged judicially and in 1954 the case came before the Supreme Court. Allied in support of the Commission's position were the FPC itself, the Phillips Petroleum Company, and the State of

Texas. In opposition were the State of Wisconsin and several cities, acting in support of consumers' interests. The Court reversed the FPC decision and directed the Commission to regulate independent producers' prices.[40] The Court said this was consistent with the legislative history of the 1938 Act, even though the FPC had relied heavily on the same history in reaching the opposite conclusion. The effect of the Court's action was to increase the responsibility of a reluctant Commission for the balancing of consumer and producer interests through regulation.

To back-track for a moment, it is noteworthy that Commissioner Buchanan, the sole dissenter from the 1951 FPC decision, failed to gain senatorial approval of his renomination in 1952. President Eisenhower appointed an "industry-minded" commissioner to take his place in 1953. In such manner Buchanan, like Olds, was "punished" for his opposition to the gas industry viewpoint. "Thus are independent commissions made responsive to political change."[41]

Following the Court's 1954 decision the struggle over exemption of independents shifted back to Congress. Much pressure was exerted on Congress by oil and gas interests to amend the 1938 Act to exempt independents. An intensive public relations campaign was started to convince the public that exemption was necessary to free independents from regulation and to ensure adequate supplies of gas at reasonable prices for consumers. Thousands of gas producers gave their support to the campaign. Further support came from President Eisenhower, who favored exemption of independents from national regulation as a means of reducing excessive centralization in government. The American Farm Bureau Federation also entered the fray on the side of the gas interests, an action which accorded with its generally conservative position on economic regulation. Strong opposition to exemption came from cities in the North and East, labor groups, gas consumers, and local utility companies (who feared exemption would increase the prices they paid for gas). Coal interests also opposed exemption in an attempt to protect their competitive position vis-a-vis the gas industry.

Identical bills to exempt independents from national regulation were introduced in the House and Senate by two Arkansas Democrats, Representative Harris and Senator Fulbright. The House passed the bill toward the end of 1955 by a 209 to 203 vote, which is indicative of the closeness and intensity of the struggle over the bill. The next

[40] *Phillips Petroleum Company v. State of Wisconsin*, 347 U.S. 672 (1954).
[41] Huitt, *op. cit.*, 101.

February the bill came before the Senate for consideration. During the Senate debate, Senator Case (Rep., S.D.) announced that he would vote against the bill, although he previously had favored it. In explanation he announced that an oil company lawyer had offered him a $2500 campaign contribution with the condition that he vote for the measure. The Senate was undeterred by the publicity and controversy which this disclosure touched off and subsequently passed the bill by a 53 to 38 vote. Voting in both houses on the bill was based on regional and economic considerations rather than party lines. In the House, for example, representatives from gas-producing states tended to favor it whereas representatives from northern, gas-consuming areas tended to oppose it, regardless of their party affiliation.

This legislative effort came to naught when President Eisenhower, who had favored the bill, vetoed it because of the "Case incident." In his veto message the President stated:

> Since the passage of this bill a body of evidence has accumulated indicating that private persons, representing only a very small segment of a great and vital industry, have been seeking to further their own interests by highly questionable activities. These include efforts I deem to be so arrogant and so in defiance of acceptable standards of propriety as to risk creating doubt among the American people concerning the integrity of governmental process.[42]

In other words, those involved in the "Case incident" had violated the basic "rules of the game" governing the political struggle. The exertion of pressure is one thing, bribery quite another.

To add another dimension to our study, we should mention that the gas interests also attempted to overcome the 1954 decision by state action. In the fall of that year, the Oklahoma Corporation Commission began to set minimum field prices for national gas. This move, if constitutional, would have prevented the FPC from fixing lower prices. A somewhat similar ploy was attempted in Texas, in the hallowed name of conservation. This stratagem failed when the Supreme Court declared that it was unconstitutional for Oklahoma to regulate field prices of gas moving in interstate commerce. The Court thus invoked the Constitution on the consumer side of the conflict.

Some efforts have been made in Congress since 1956 to amend the Natural Gas Act but they have been unsuccessful. Most bills have not gotten out of committee. In 1958 a bill to exempt several thousand

[42] *Congressional Record*, CII, 2793.

small independent gas producers from price regulation never really got off the ground, although it was sponsored by Senators from both gas-producing and gas-consuming states. This bill was unappealing to the large gas companies who wanted something more than exemption for the "little fellow." At present, legislative exemption of gas producers appears to be a dormant if not a dead issue, although it is possible the conflict could be renewed in the future.

Since 1954 the task of reconciling producer and consumer interests through the medium of regulation has rested with the Federal Power Commission. With assistance from the Supreme Court and a couple of presidential vetoes, the FPC has emerged (or should we say remained?), however reluctantly, as the primary policy maker in this area of public policy. What, now, has the Commission done with its rate authority? Partly because of the complexity of the problem, the large and varied number of gas producers involved (more than 18,000), and its lethargy during the Eisenhower years, the FPC is still confronted with the basic task of how to determine just and reasonable rates to be charged for natural gas. Having given up on the traditional individual company cost-of-service methods used in public utility regulation, the Commission is now trying to set gas prices on an area basis for each of twenty-three gas producing regions. In August, 1965, agency action in the first area rate case—that involving the Permian Basin of western Texas-eastern New Mexico—was completed.[43]

The Commission's decision represented a victory for consumer interests after a decade of waiting. Ceilings of 16½ and 15½ cents per 1,000 cubic feet were set for gas produced in Texas and New Mexico, respectively. Gas producers had argued for a 20 cent ceiling, with the going market price being from 17 to 18 cents a 1,000 cubic feet. The gas companies expressed dissatisfaction with the FPC decision and began to plan an appeal to the federal courts. It could be months or years before the new rates go into effect and the consumer derives something more than symbolic benefits from natural gas regulation.

[43] *The New York Times,* Aug. 6, 1965, pp. 1, 24.

Chapter Three

PUBLIC ADMINISTRATION AND
ECONOMIC POLICY

It is often remarked that the execution of a law may be as important as the law itself. To understand fully the nature and import of public economic policies one must go beyond the enactment of statutes by legislative bodies. One must also consider the way in which legislation is implemented—how it is interpreted and applied by those involved with its execution. As we indicated earlier, there may be extensive disparities or differences between public economic policies as statutes in the law books and the form and meaning given them in the course of day-to-day application. Much of the responsibility for the administration of public economic policies, as with other public policies, now rests with administrative agencies.

In the past it was assumed that "politics," or policy making, and administration were separate and distinct spheres of governmental activity. According to this assumption, "politics" terminates with the enactment of legislation and the legislature's mandates are then implemented more or less automatically and without alteration by administrative agencies (or the "administrative process"). This assumption has been discarded as unrealistic. Rather, we find that no absolute lines can be drawn between policy making and administration. They are related and interwoven parts of the public policy process. As Professor Friedrich has commented:

> The concrete patterns of public policy formation and execution reveal that politics and administration are not two mutually exclusive boxes, or absolute distinctions, but that they are two closely linked aspects of the same process. Public policy, to put it flatly, is a continuous process, the formation of which is inseparable from its execution. Public policy is being formed as it is being executed, and it is likewise

being executed as it is being formed. Politics and administration play a continuous role in both formation and execution, though there is probably more politics in the formation of policy, more administration in the execution of it.[1]

THE GROWTH OF ADMINISTRATION

Along with the expansion of government economic activity discussed in Chapter One has come a great increase in public administrative activity. This growth in administration has been especially rapid in the twentieth century. In area after area of economic activity, administrative agencies possessing extensive powers to promote, regulate, or operate economic enterprise have been established. In 1963 the executive branch of the national government comprised more than seventy separate departments and agencies employing approximately two and a half million persons. Roughly half of these people worked for one department, the Department of Defense; nonetheless, most departments and agencies and several hundred thousand federal employees are involved in some way in the administration of economic policies and programs. Some conception of the size and complexity of the federal administrative organization is given by the current edition of the *United States Government Organization Manual.*

In the area of economic regulation, for example, over the past several decades a marked shift from judicial regulation to administrative regulation has taken place. In the nineteenth century the "typical" approach to a problem was legislative enactment of a law, which was then enforceable by government attorneys or private persons acting through the regular judicial courts. (A significant exception to this pattern was railroad regulation in the latter part of the nineteenth century.) The courts have not dropped out of the picture, but they now play a decidedly smaller role in the implementation of regulatory policies than they formerly did. Today, primary responsibility for the enforcement of a new regulatory act is ordinarily given to an administrative agency, either one newly established for the purpose or an already existing agency. Exceptions are more likely to occur at the state than at the national level.

The question arises, why has this growth in administration occurred? Why the increased resort to the administrative process for implement-

[1] Carl J. Friedrich, "Public Policy and the Nature of Administrative Responsibility," in Friedrich and Mason, eds., *Public Policy* (Cambridge: Harvard University Press, 1940), 6.

ing economic policies? A complete answer would require examination of the many factors contributing to the growth of administration in all areas of activity. Our discussion, however, will be confined to some of the broad, general causes for expanding administrative activity.[2]

A major cause of administrative growth is the fact that, as public economic policy has expanded, government has taken on many tasks and responsibilities not of the sort normally handled by legislatures and courts. A few examples are the payment of social security and other welfare benefits, lending money to small businesses, open-market operations of the Federal Reserve Board, inspection of meat, grading of grain, examination of banks, operation of power production facilities, and management of public lands. Such activities are beyond the scope of the legislative and judicial processes and as a matter of course have been entrusted to administrative agencies. Indeed, the only alternative to administration for the performance of such functions is the elimination of the functions themselves.

In many cases, however, legislative and judicial functions have been delegated to administrative agencies. Here the real or alleged inadequacies and limitations of legislatures and courts have clearly contributed to the growth of administration. Because of such factors as the lack of time to deal adequately with both details and broad policy matters, the technicality and complexity of many problems and the resulting need for specialized information, the need for experimentation, and the necessity for continual adaptation of policy to changing circumstances, Congress has often found it necessary to enact general legislation and to leave sub-legislation, the filling in of the details, to administrative agencies. There is a large element of truth in the second Hoover Commission's statement: "The administrative process has been developed and utilized by Congress primarily because regulatory action requires attention to a multitude of details and situations which cannot be met by statutory enactments. Congress declares policy, prescribes standards defining agency action, and entrusts to the agencies of the executive branch the function of completing the process of control."[3]

[2] The following discussion draws on Emmette S. Redford, *The Administration of National Economic Control* (New York: Macmillan, 1952), ch. III; Walter Gellhorn, *Federal Administrative Proceedings* (Baltimore: Johns Hopkins Press, 1941), 1–14; and Kenneth C. Davis, *Handbook on Administrative Law* (St. Paul: West Publishing Co., 1951), 4–17.

[3] Commission on Organization of the Executive Branch of the Government, *Legal Services and Procedures* (Washington, D.C.: Government Printing Office, 1955), 53–54.

The administrative process has also been utilized to avoid the shortcomings of courts in implementing policy. Consequently, many agencies have been empowered to perform judicial (or adjudicatory) functions. Administration has offered a means of escape from slow, cumbersome, and expensive judicial procedure and, at the same time, an opportunity to dispose of large numbers of routine cases by quick "informal" procedures, such as bargaining, consultation, conferences, and correspondence. Administration permits avoidance of the lack of uniformity which results when a number of courts exercise initial jurisdiction in a complex policy area. Further, although courts are normally tribunals of general jurisdiction handling a variety of cases, administrative agencies can be given specialized jurisdictions, and therefore they are able to develop "expertise" in particular policy areas. Finally, administration offers escape from the conservative bias against policy changes and the emphasis on private or particular interests over social interests which is said to be often characteristic of judicial behavior.[4] Whether or not one considers these charges against the courts to be valid, they have contributed to increased reliance on administration.

However, the growth of administration cannot be explained adequately by citing only the development of activities outside the scope of the legislative and judicial processes and the shortcomings of courts and legislatures as policy implementors. The positive aspects or advantages of the administrative process for implementing policy must be added.

In most areas of public economic policy, continuous and organized institutional action is required if policy goals are to be effectively realized. Continuous, day-to-day supervision and action are necessary for the adaptation of policy to changing needs and circumstances. Because positive action is often needed in order to effectuate policy, it is not sufficient to enact a law and leave its enforcement to individual action after the law has been violated. Much legislation is now "preventive," requiring an agency which has explicit responsibility for enforcement and which can take action to prevent violations of the law. How else but through the administrative process could such policies as safety regulation of airlines, control of agricultural production, or regulation of minimum wages be effectively implemented?

Administration is also a "flexible and evolving process" which has provided a variety of methods for implementing numerous and diverse

[4] See Davis, *op. cit.,* 14–15.

public policies. Among these methods are inspection, examination of books, licensing, publicity, conference techniques, negotiation and bargaining, mediation and conciliation, rule making and adjudication. Administration also has provided a variety of organizational forms: departments, government corporations, and independent regulatory commissions for the performance of policy functions. The legislature thus has a number of alternatives, both in enforcement techniques and in forms of organization, and can choose those considered most suitable (or politically acceptable) for the administration of a given policy.

Finally, the large size of many governmental programs is another cause of administrative expansion. It takes a large organization to administer such extensive undertakings as agricultural price support programs, the provision of veterans' benefits, the operation of social security programs, the collection of taxes, and the conservation and control of natural resources. Agencies often have to decide or otherwise dispose of huge numbers of cases. In 1960, for example, the National Labor Relations Board closed more than 11,000 unfair labor practice cases, the Federal Communications Commission processed 329,000 license applications for commercial radio operators, and the Veterans Administration adjudicated approximately 2.5 million benefit claims.[5] Vast amounts of paper work are required and countless records must be maintained. Again, important and complex decisions, such as some of the Interstate Commerce Commission's rate-making proceedings, may occupy the attention of sizable staffs for a long time. Large administrative organizations are a logical result of the activities mentioned here.

The growth of administration has thus followed the expansion of governmental activity. It has appeared as the best alternative for carrying forward the public business.

ORGANIZATION FOR POLICY IMPLEMENTATION

A bewildering variety of agencies have evolved for the administration of economic policies and programs. Although each agency is unique, there are four general types of organizations—departments, independent agencies, government corporations, and independent regulatory commissions. Especial attention in our discussion will be given to the independent regulatory commissions because of their great importance in the conduct of economic regulatory programs.

[5] Peter Woll, *Administrative Law: The Informal Process* (Berkeley: University of California Press, 1963), 127, 160–161.

The Departments

Eleven federal agencies are currently designated as executive departments. They are established by Congress and are headed by officials usually called secretaries (the Postmaster General and the Attorney General are the exceptions) who are members of the President's cabinet. The present departments, in the order of their establishment, are State, Treasury, Interior, Justice, Post Office, Agriculture, Commerce, Labor, Defense (including the three service departments, Army, Navy, and Air Force), Health, Education, and Welfare, and Housing and Urban Development.

The departmental secretary is a political appointee who stands in the presidential chain of command and is accountable to the President for his actions. He is consequently expected to carry out presidential policy as it relates to his department. In addition, the secretary is the operating head of his department; he engages in departmental policy making and supervises and coordinates the activities of the various units in the department. The secretary also acts to protect and represent the interests of his department before the President, Congressional committees, other executive departments and agencies, and the public. To assist him in performing his duties there are a number of under secretaries, assistant secretaries, and staff sides for such matters as policy making, personnel, budgeting, and legal services.

Prior to the 1870's, most of the government's activities were handled by the departments. When new functions were assumed, they were assigned to a unit, either existing or newly created, in one of the departments. Now, many functions are handled by independent regulatory commissions and other agencies "outside" the departments. Nonetheless, the department can still be fairly regarded as the basic unit of organization in our national administrative framework. Most of the work of government is still performed by the departments and their sub-units, including much economic regulatory activity. It has been said of one of the departments: "The Department of Agriculture is one of the largest regulatory agencies in the Federal Government. It administers the greatest number of regulatory acts of any Federal agency—acts which vary widely in subject matter and in administrative enforcement procedures—and has had long experience in the regulatory field."[6] The Department also has many promotional and price-

[6] Commission on Organization of the Executive Branch of the Government (First Hoover Commission), *Task Force Report on Agriculture Activities* (Washington, D.C.: Government Printing Office, 1949), 52.

support programs. Other departments with significant regulatory and other responsibilities in the economic policy area include Labor, Commerce, Treasury, Interior, Justice, Post Office, and Health, Education, and Welfare.

The departments are often classified as either integrated or of the holding company type. Integrated departments, such as Agriculture and Post Office, consist of numerous units performing the same or similar functions. The holding company department, in contrast, has within it units performing a variety of distantly related functions. An example is the Department of Health, Education, and Welfare, which includes agencies dealing with education, old age and survivors insurance, and food and drug regulation. In either case, however, the departments are large organizations with tens of thousands of employees (or more) and many major operating (or "line") subdivisions, variously called bureaus, administrations, services, or offices. A partial listing of the major units of the Department of Interior includes the following: Fish and Wildlife Service, Bureau of Mines, Office of Oil and Gas, Bureau of Indian Affairs, Bureau of Land Management, Bureau of Reclamation, The Alaska Railroad (a bureau), and the Bonneville, Southeastern, and Southwestern Administrations.

The top-level leadership of the departments is often hard put to coordinate and control the various bureaus. Unity in a department is sometimes more a goal than a reality (bureaus may enjoy considerable autonomy in their operations.) This stems partly from the large size and diversity of the departments, but other factors may contribute. Competition between bureaus for power and appropriations or conflicting bureau purposes and policy viewpoints may work against departmental unity. An example is the conflict between the Soil Conservation Service and the Extension Service in the Department of Agriculture over conservation policy.[7] Some bureaus may have sufficient pressure-group and congressional support to free them somewhat from departmental control or direction, e.g., the Corps of Army Engineers. The strong support it receives from the National Rivers and Harbors Congress and congressmen interested in river and harbor ("pork-barrel") projects enables it to maintain partial independence from control by the Secretary of Defense and even the President.[8] Again, traditions of bureau autonomy may militate against departmental control. Such a tradition has impeded Interior Department direction over the National Park Service. A departmental official recently felt constrained to re-

[7] Charles M. Hardin, *The Politics of Agriculture* (New York: The Free Press, 1952).

[8] Arthur Maass, *Muddy Waters* (Cambridge: Harvard University Press, 1951).

mind the Park Service that it was part of the Interior Department and not "an autonomous agency that could bypass departmental administration."[9]

Much of the work of the departments, and of other administrative organizations, is done not in Washington but in the "field" where the people served and the industries aided or regulated are located. Approximately 90 per cent of the federal civil personnel are *not* located in Washington. Agencies and bureaus usually have a number of regional and district offices scattered throughout the country. The field offices are responsible for the day-to-day implementation of policy and the central (or Washington) office has policy-making and supervisory functions. The Wage and Hour and Public Contract Divisions of the Department of Labor, which administers federal wage and hour legislation, operates through eleven regional offices. Although field organizations, are necessary for public convenience and effective policy implementation, they do complicate the administrative process. Also, they may produce situations in which, because of communications problems and the pressure of local interest groups, policy as actually applied varies from one area to another or differs from that laid down in Washington.

The Independent Agencies

By independent agencies we mean administrative agencies outside of the departments which do not fit into the categories of government corporations and independent regulatory commissions. They are responsible to the President but may have some independence from executive control because of their location. Among the independent agencies are the Veterans Administration, Atomic Energy Commission, Federal Aviation Agency, Small Business Administration, Federal Mediation and Conciliation Service, and the Railroad Retirement Board. These agencies have significant functions in the economic policy area; but others, such as the National Aeronautics and Space Administration and the National Science Foundation, clearly do not.

Some independent agencies are quite large. The Veterans Administration has about 190,000 employees, more than most departments, and is really a department in all but name and formal status. Others, the Railroad Retirement Board for instance, are small. Some agencies are headed by single administrators; others have multiple heads: the FAA and the AEC respectively. It is not exaggerating much to say that independent agencies come in all sizes, shapes, and forms.

[9] *The New York Times,* Oct. 17, 1963, p. 22.

Independent agencies are sometimes set up to deal with problems created by emergencies such as depressions and wars. Many disappear once the emergency passes but a few remain. Some can be attributed to the action of organized interest groups. Others were established to handle new or unique programs which did not appear to fit into the departments: the AEC and NASA. The desire to keep new programs out of the hands of hostile or unfriendly departments, e.g., the Small Business Administration, is also a factor. Moreover, once an agency has been in existence for a time, strong support for the continuation of its independent status usually develops, preventing its integration into a department.

Government Corporations

The corporate device has been used by government primarily for the operation of economic enterprises or commercial activities—lending money, insuring bank deposits, operating power production facilities, purchasing and selling farm commodities, and so on. Although the history of the government corporation at the national level goes back to the First Bank of the United States in 1791, little use was made of it until the twentieth century. Many corporations were established to meet needs arising from the two World Wars and the depression of the 1930's; in 1945 approximately 100 separate corporations existed. This number has declined to around 80 at the present time because for various reasons some have been liquidated. Prominent government corporations today include the Tennessee Valley Authority, the Commodity Credit Corporation, the Federal Deposit Insurance Corporation, the Export-Import Bank of Washington, the Federal National Mortgage Association, and the Saint Lawrence Seaway Development Corporation.

Organized along lines somewhat similar to those of private business corporations, government corporations were intended to provide more flexibility and freedom from overhead legislative and executive controls in the performance of business or commercial activities than was possible under the departmental form of organization. In 1937 a presidential committee said the advantages of government corporations included "freedom of operation, flexibility, business efficiency, and opportunity for experimentation."[10] During the early 1930's the typical government corporation was chartered by Congress, or sometimes by the chief executive on the basis of existing legislation. Given capital to

[10] President's Committee on Administrative Management, *Report with Special Studies* (Washington, D.C.: Government Printing Office, 1937), 44.

carry on its activities, the corporation was run by a board of publicly appointed directors and a manager. It was free from many of the budgeting, accounting, and personnel controls applicable to the departments and was authorized to borrow money, to buy and sell commodities, and to sue and be sued.

However, criticism of the corporations' freedom from executive and legislative controls and their failure to integrate their policies with overall government policy, led to a gradual extension of controls over them. This culminated in the Corporation Control Act of 1945, which authorized the General Accounting Office to conduct "business type" audits of their activities and directed them to submit their budgets for presidential and congressional review. The Act also required specific congressional authorization of capital expenditures and prohibited the establishment of corporations except by congressional action.[11] With the notable exception of TVA, other legislation has given the Civil Service Commission jurisdiction over corporation personnel policies.

Most of the government corporations are now located within executive departments and agencies. The Commodity Credit Corporation in the Department of Agriculture and the Federal Housing Administration in the Department of Housing and Urban Development are illustrative. Others such as the TVA and FDIC have remained independent (outside other agencies). Although government corporations as they now exist generally have less autonomy of action than formerly, they are nonetheless probably more free of legislative and executive controls than are most other government agencies (especially those which have retained their independent status). For example, they still are normally governed by boards, can sue and be sued, submit non-detailed budgets for legislative and executive review, and can often take action, as in the use of their "profits," without specific legislative authorization or control.

The government corporation remains as an important and useful organizational device for the administration of "commercial" activities requiring a measure of operating freedom and flexibility.[12] Future expansion of government enterprises would probably bring with it increased use of this form of organization.

[11] C. Herman Pritchett, "The Government Corporation Control Act of 1945," *American Political Science Review*, XL (June, 1946), 495ff.
[12] Cf. Harold Seidman, "The Theory of the Autonomous Government Corporation: A Critical Appraisal," *Public Administration Review, XII* (Spring, 1952) 89–96.

The Independent Regulatory Commissions

The national administrative organizations designated as independent regulatory commissions have a number of common characteristics. They are headed by boards or commissions having from five to eleven members. They are engaged in the regulation of private economic activity. They are independent both in the sense of having a measure of freedom from presidential supervision and in being outside of the departments. Also, they possess what are called quasi-legislative and quasi-judicial powers and have both policy-making and implementation functions.

The first national independent regulatory commission, the Interstate Commerce Commission, was established by Congress in 1887. Since then the use of the independent regulatory commission has expanded, and it has become the most important administrative instrument for the regulation of economic activity. Nine agencies are now generally considered to come within this category. Together with their dates of establishment and areas of jurisdiction, they are:

Interstate Commerce Commission (1887): railroads, motor carriers, domestic water carriers, and pipelines

Federal Reserve Board (1913): money, credit, and commercial banks belonging to the Federal Reserve System

Federal Trade Commission (1914): unfair or deceptive trade practices

Federal Power Commission (1920): electricity and natural gas

Federal Communications Commission (1933): telephone, telegraph, radio, and television

Securities and Exchange Commission (1934): stock exchanges, sale of stocks and bonds, investment bankers, trusts, and advisers, holding companies

National Labor Relations Board (1935): labor-management relations (unfair labor practices and collective bargaining)

Civil Aeronautics Board (1938): air carriers

Federal Maritime Commission (1962):[13] water carriers in foreign commerce

The regulatory commissions perform a variety of functions and no two of them use the same set of methods or form of organization. We can, however, make some generalizations about the nature of commission activities. Most commissions are concerned with the en-

[13] The ancestors of the Federal Maritime Commission date back to the Shipping Board of 1916.

forcement of laws, including preliminary investigation, prosecution, informal settlement of cases, and administrative adjudication. The National Labor Relations Board and the Federal Trade Commission, for example, give much time to the enforcement of labor and unfair trade legislation. Second, many of the commissions make rules and formulate broad policies. The Securities and Exchange Commission makes rules governing the stock exchanges and the Federal Reserve Board makes major policy in the area of credit and money supply. Third, some of the commissions engage in such activities as rate regulation and licensing for particular industries. The Interstate Commerce Commission and the Federal Power Commission regulate railroad and natural gas rates respectively. The Federal Communications Commission licenses radio and television broadcasters. Fourth, along with their regulatory responsibilities some commissions also have promotional and executive functions. Thus, the Civil Aeronautics Board is enjoined to promote the development of a national air transportation system, in part by the granting of operating subsidies. Both the ICC and the CAB perform essentially executive functions with respect to railroad safety and the investigation of airline accidents.

These functions are also often performed by departments and independent agencies having regulatory duties. Commission regulation is distinctive, however, because of the broad grants of authority given the commissions and their particular form of organization. The commissions, as noted above, are plural-headed. The members are appointed by the President for fixed, staggered terms of office, ranging from five to fourteen years, and are removable only for stated causes (e.g., malfeasance in office). Both political parties must be represented on all except the NLRB and FRB. Their organization, and the legislation creating them, gives them greater freedom from executive control and supervision than the other administrative organizations have.

Many factors have contributed to the establishment (and retention) of the independent commission form of organization for regulatory activity. Previous state experience with the independent regulatory commission device clearly contributed to the establishment of the Interstate Commerce Commission. Experience with the ICC in turn influenced decisions to establish additional commissions when new regulatory functions were undertaken. The need for experimentation and flexibility of action in new areas of regulation could best be met by new and independent agencies. When regional representation was desired in making policy it could be provided by plural commissions. The independent commission was also said to provide for expertness, impartiality, group deliberation and decision making, and continuity in regulatory activity. By setting up an independent commission and providing for bipartisan representation on it, it was thought that regulation could be "taken out of politics." There was also a conviction that since the commissions exercised legislative and judicial powers they should be somewhat independent of the chief executive. Finally, an important element in the choice of the commission form "has undoubtedly been the desire to find a system of control which would be palatable to the regulated interests. Commissions appeared to these interests to be a safer repository of powers of intervention; and congressional adoption of commission regulation was a kind of compromise between private ownership and public control."[14]

But too much emphasis should not be given to the "independence" of the regulatory commissions. The President can exert influence on them by means of his power to appoint commissioners and his managerial controls over the commissions' budgets, staff personnel, and legislative proposals. Congress can conduct investigations of the commissions, and can restrict, modify, or even abolish them. The courts can review commission actions, when challenged, to determine whether or not they meet the requirements of administrative due process or are acting within the scope of the power delegated to them by Congress. Moreover, the commissions are not "independent" of politics. Commission regulation is a highly political process, as is indicated by the role of the Federal Power Commission in the case study of natural gas regulation in Chapter Two. Pressure groups; Congress, its committees, or individual members; the President or other executive officials; all may attempt to influence important commission decisions.[15]

Numerous criticisms have been aimed at the regulatory commissions in recent years. An impression of their scope and tenor can be conveyed by a quick listing of some of the major criticisms.[16] First, commission decisions are often delayed because of inadequate budgets and staffs, large numbers of cases, the slowness inherent in group decision making, and so on. Second, commission procedures have become highly formal and judicialized and have further reduced the expedition of action. Third, the commission system impedes coordination of economic

[14] Emmette S. Redford, *The President and the Regulatory Commissions,* a report for the President's Advisory Committee on Government Organization (Washington, D.C.: 1960, multilith), 5.

[15] See Bernard Schwartz, *The Professor and the Commissions* (New York: Alfred A. Knopf, 1959).

[16] Elaboration of these and other criticisms can be found in James M. Landis, *Report on Regulatory Commissions to the President Elect,* Senate Committee on the Judiciary (Committee Print), 86th Cong., 2nd Sess. (1960); and Redford, *Administration of National Economic Control,* ch. X.

policies between commissions and other agencies. Conflicts have occurred, for example, between the FRB and the Treasury Department regarding monetary policy. (See Chapter Four.) Fourth, the commissions have failed to develop policy adequately, as with the FCC and UHF television broadcasting. Fifth, commission personnel have not been of uniformly high caliber. Some have little knowledge of the industry they are to regulate. Others have accepted gifts, loans, and other favors from those doing business with the commissions. A member of the FCC was forced to resign for this reason in 1959. Sixth, the commissions have become too closely identified with the interests of the regulated. It has often been alleged that the ICC is a "captive" of the railroads. Finally, the extent to which the commissions are responsible to the President and Congress has not been appropriately defined. Taken together these criticisms constitute a serious indictment of the commissions.

Many students of administration have become convinced that the regulatory commissions are in poor shape and that remedial action is required. There has not, however, been agreement on the direction reform should take. Two general positions have developed. Louis J. Hector, a former member of the Civil Aeronautics Board, has described the two positions: "The issue is between those who feel the commissions are basically sound and need only some better men or improved procedures or new codes of ethics, and those . . . who feel that the problems of the agencies arise out of basic and inescapable contradictions of their structures."[17] Hector, who takes the latter position, believes the commissions are unable to plan or make regulatory policy effectively because they are faced with the incompatible and time-consuming task of handling a mass of quasi-judicial proceedings. He advocates transference of their policy-making functions to the executive departments. The first position, as stated by Hector, has been taken, among others, by James Landis and the House Subcommittee on Legislative Oversight, which investigated the commissions during 1957–1961.[18] They favor retaining the present independent commissions but with improvements in their personnel, procedures, and ethics.

Much attention was given to commission reform during the first year or two of its existence by the Kennedy administration. Changes in the internal organization and procedures of some of the commissions were effected, and President Kennedy tried to appoint more able and

[17] *The New York Times,* Jan. 3, 1961, p. 4.
[18] See Landis, *op. cit.,* 84–87; and Subcommittee on Legislative Oversight of the House Committee on Interstate and Foreign Commerce, *Independent Regulatory Commissions,* House Report 2238, 86th Cong., 2nd Sess. (1961).

qualified people for the commissions. The appointment of Newton W. Minow as chairman of the FCC, for example, injected new life into that agency. Minow created quite a stir by characterizing television programming as a "vast wasteland" and urging improvement. FCC policy, however, has apparently not undergone any drastic change.

The economic and political forces supporting the commissions in their present form, together with the tradition of independence surrounding them, have been and continue to be strong enough to prevent any "drastic" changes in the commissions. The interests regulated by the commissions like them as they are and have opposed attempts to effect major alterations. Congress has taken a dim view of any effort to tamper with the independent status of the commissions and open them to greater presidential control. As a result, proposals for major change, such as that urged by Hector or in the form of strong presidential control of the commissions, have come to naught. The regulatory commissions remain basically unchanged and, with the subsiding of the fervor for reform, have once more dropped from the public eye. Like old man river, they "just keep moving along."

Some Policy Implications of Administrative Organization

There is a long-existent belief that decisions on administrative organization, including the allocation of functions among agencies, may have important policy consequences. Pressure groups and others seeking to influence public economic policy often manifest much concern over the particular agency, or type of agency, which is to administer a given policy. The political struggle over issues of administrative organization may be as intense as the struggle over substantive policy itself. Our purpose here is to suggest some possible implications of administrative organization for administrative policy making and administration.

It is thought that a change in the location of an agency in the executive branch will affect the ability of interest groups to influence policy as administered by the agency. Whatever the case may be *in fact,* this belief is widely accepted and acted upon and thereby serves as a motive for action. Groups generally satisfied with their relationships with an existing agency fear that a change in its location, or form, through reorganization, may adversely affect their capacity to influence agency action. They consequently resist attempts at reorganization. Thus the railroads, who find their relationships with the Interstate Commerce Commission satisfactory, are decidedly opposed to the establishment of a Department of Transportation. Strong and successful resistance to reorganization affecting the Corps of Army Engineers has come from the

National Rivers and Harbors Congress.[19] It is of great importance in these and related situations "that the groups opposing reorganization may reasonably feel that they are confronted with the prospect of exchanging a known situation, in which their capacity to influence policy has been proven, for an unknown situation, in which there exists at least some risk that previous patterns of power may no longer prevail."[20]

Administrative agencies often develop "a tradition, an outlook, and a policy inclination of their own."[21] These agency behavior patterns are transmitted from one "generation" of agency personnel to another and are an important factor influencing the decisions made by members of the agency.[22] The Department of Commerce, for example, has developed a general orientation toward the welfare of business and conservatism in economic policy. In 1961 administration of the Area Redevelopment Act, which provided assistance for depressed areas, was entrusted to the Department of Commerce. Many conservatives supported this move, apparently assuming that the Commerce Department would act conservatively in administering the Act. This was opposed by liberals and labor groups, however, who said the Commerce Department was too "business-minded" to effectively administer a program dealing with unemployment problems. They favored assigning the program either to the Department of Labor or a newly created agency.[23] Those concerned with a policy or program thus want it administered by an agency with a policy favorable to their interests or viewpoint, a further indication that administrative organization is not neutral in its consequences for policy.

Again, those supporting an existing program may try to have it transferred from one agency to another to escape unfavorable or hostile handling of it. This was the reason for the transfer of administration of the national forests from the General Land Office in the Department of Interior to the Department of Agriculture during the Theodore Roosevelt Administration. "The national forest idea ran counter to the whole tradition of the Interior Department," according to Gifford

[19] David B. Truman, *The Governmental Process* (New York: Alfred A. Knopf, 1951), 410–415.

[20] Francis E. Rourke, "The Politics of Administrative Organization: A Case History," *Journal of Politics,* XIX (August, 1957), 478.

[21] V. O. Key, Jr., *Politics, Parties, and Pressure Groups,* 4th ed. (New York: Thomas Y. Crowell, 1958), 743. See also Herbert A. Simon, Donald W. Smithburg, and Victor A. Thompson, *Public Administration* (New York: Alfred A. Knopf, 1950), 42–43.

[22] Cf. Herbert Kaufman, *The Forest Ranger: A Study in Administrative Behavior* (Baltimore: Johns Hopkins Press, 1960).

[23] *Congressional Quarterly Weekly Report,* XIX (Feb. 10, 1961), 242.

Pinchot. "Bred into its marrow, bone, and fiber, was the idea of disposing of the public lands to private owners."[24]

Congressional establishment of independent agencies outside the executive departments to administer new or expanded programs may have long-term policy consequences. Independent agencies and regulatory commissions in time tend to become identified with the industry or interests they are set up to regulate or serve. Of independent regulatory commissions established to regulate single industries, it has been said: "Deprived of the influences on policy that flow from the give-and-take of other departments and from the directions of the chief executive, the independent commission gravitates toward an industry point of view."[25] To gain the political support needed to survive (and cooperation to facilitate performance of its functions), the regulatory commission seeks the confidence and support of the regulated interests. Should the agency antagonize these interests, it may have difficulty in obtaining needed funds, legislation, and appointments from Congress.

Further, the interests supporting enactment of a given policy often advocate the establishment of an independent agency to administer it. They believe they will be most likely to make their viewpoint prevail, or at least that it will be given careful consideration, if an independent agency handles the new program. This belief contributed to the establishment of the Small Business Administration as an independent agency rather than as part of the Commerce Department.[26]

Finally, the internal organization of an agency also may have an impact on policy. Congress may prescribe in some detail the internal structure of an agency which is to administer a particular policy. One way of allocating functions and responsibility within the agency may produce different results from another. Agency organization, as Professor Scher states, "is a tool designed by men to achieve particular results."[27] This is illustrated by the revamping of the National Labor Relations Board by Congress in 1947:

> The conversion in 1947 of the National Labor Relations Board from a multimember board of three who had all responsibility for

[24] Key, *op. cit.*, 747n.

[25] V. O. Key, Jr., "Legislative Control," in Fritz Morstein Marx, ed., *Elements of Public Administration,* 2nd ed. (Englewood Cliffs, N.J.: Prentice-Hall, 1959), 321. Also note Truman, *op. cit.*, 418–421.

[26] Harmon Zeigler, *The Politics of Small Business* (Washington: Public Affairs Press, 1961), 104–111.

[27] Seymour Scher, "The Politics of Agency Organization," *Western Political Quarterly,* XV (June, 1962), 328. The quotation below is also from this source.

enforcing the Wagner Act into an agency with two separate and generally independent branches—a five-member board and a General Counsel—was achieved by particular men in order to produce particular results. Congress in 1947 saw a need to alter the basic labor law [the Wagner Act, which protected labor's right to organize and bargain collectively] to include restrictions on union behavior. But it was not satisfied to leave the agency that would apply the restrictions with the same men or administrative machinery that had come, since 1935, to be considered "pro-labor," the organizing agent of unions," "infected with the Wagner-Act mentality," etc. A congressional majority at the time of the passage of the Taft-Hartley Act saw a need to provide safeguards against administrative sabotage of the new law. A drastic change in agency structure was one means devised to curb some tendencies and promote others in the administration of the law.

The supporters of the Taft-Hartley Act thus believed that changing the structure of the NLRB would contribute to the administration of the law in conformity to their policy beliefs.

POLITICS, POLICY MAKING, AND ADMINISTRATION

So far in this chapter we have been concerned primarily with the growth and organization of administration. In this section we shift our focus to administrative agencies as active participants in the policy-making process. The role of administrative agencies as policy makers, some factors which affect administrative policy making, and administrative involvement in legislative policy making will be taken up in that order.

Agencies as Policy Makers

It has been said that the administration of a statute is "an extension of the legislative process."[28] Because of the discretion they have in implementing legislation, administrative agencies clearly are more than mere executory instruments for carrying the legislative will into effect. As we have seen, agencies are also much involved in the interpretation and determination of law—that is, in the formation of

---

[28] Truman, *op. cit.*, 439.

policy. Much of the actual substance and "operational" meaning of economic policy is a product of the administrative process.

The important role played by administrative agencies in the formation of economic policy is an outgrowth of the generality characteristic of much economic legislation. Many statutes are really general statements of objectives or policy and authorizations to administrative agencies to effectuate these goals. Thus, to cite some examples, the Interstate Commerce Commission is directed to set "just and reasonable" rates for rail and motor carriers; the Secretary of Agriculture is authorized to establish "standard grades" for agricultural commodities; the Securities and Exchange Commission is empowered to make certain rules "as it deems necessary in the public interest or for the protection of investors"; and the Small Business is authorized to "establish general policies . . . which shall govern the granting and denial of applications for assistance by the Administration." The general nature of these grants of authority means that the agencies will have broad discretion in their implementation and enforcement activities.

In addition to those noted earlier, an important factor contributing to generality in legislation is the inability or unwillingness of the legislature to directly settle conflicts of group interests, which may produce statutes that are general or ambiguous. The possible cause and effect of this situation are described here:

> ambiguities may be an inevitable product of conflict in the legislature. Where compromise in the legislative stage is the alternative to temporary failure and where the imperative of compromise is accepted by some participants as a means of avoiding the open frustration of expectations widely held in the community, the terms of legislative settlement are bound to be ambiguous. Such compromises are in the nature of postponements. The administrator is called upon to resolve the difficulties that were too thorny for the legislature to solve, and he must do so in the face of the very forces that were acting in the legislature, though their relative strength may have changed.[29]

But whatever the cause, general statutes and grants of authority lead to policy making—the adjustment and compromise of conflicting interests and demands—by administrative agencies.

That administrative agencies make policy by exercising their rule-making powers should now be apparent. In addition, agencies may

[29] *Ibid.*, 443.

sometimes develop policy by case-to-case decision making (adjudication). This has been true of the Federal Trade Commission and the prohibition of unfair methods of competition. Policy here has been marked out in decisions in particular cases rather than by general rule-making. Another example can be found in motor carrier regulation by the ICC. In 1958–1959 the ICC was concerned with a recent amendment to the law which dealt with conversion of motor carriers from contract to common carrier status. Since this change was to the advantage of carriers, numerous applications were screened and ten were picked for decision before any of the others because they appeared to present all important questions likely to arise over the new provision. Much attention was given to policy matters in deciding the ten cases and as a result fairly definite policy guidelines for the ICC and the carriers were developed.[30] Policy was thus developed through adjudication.

Agencies may also make policy by their general enforcement activities. A statute may be enforced vigorously, in a lax manner, or not at all. It may be applied to some situations and not to others. The Hepburn Act of 1906 authorized the ICC to regulate pipeline rates. The ICC, however, took no action whatsoever on this matter prior to 1934 and not until 1948 did it complete a pipeline rate proceeding, and then no effective action resulted.[31] A congressionally prescribed policy of pipeline rate regulations was thus nullified by the ICC and what actually existed was a policy of no regulation. Policy may also be redirected by administrative action. During the 1920's a conservative Federal Trade Commission substituted a policy of "helping business help itself" for the original policy of preventing unfair competition by the use of cease and desist orders. In sum, when policy is viewed as a course of action, as a continuous flow of activity set in motion by legislative enactments, as realistically it must be, administrative enforcement activities will significantly determine the "real" substance of policy.

To illustrate more fully the policy-making role of administrative agencies, and to tie together some of these generalizations, we will use a brief case study of administrative policy-making under the Taylor Grazing Act.

In 1934, at the urging of conservation interests and over the strong opposition of western livestock interests, Congress enacted the Taylor

[30] David M. Welborn, *The Certification of Motor Common Carriers of Property: A Study in National Regulatory Administration* (Doctoral dissertation: University of Texas, 1962), 371.

[31] Davis, *op. cit.,* 165–167, provides a fuller account of this matter.

Grazing Act to provide for regulation of government-owned grazing lands in the western states.[32] The purposes of the Act, as stated in its preamble, are "To stop injury to the public grazing lands by preventing over-grazing and soil deterioration, to provide for their orderly use, improvement, and development, to stabilize the livestock industry dependent upon the public lands. . . ." To accomplish these purposes, the Secretary of the Interior was authorized to establish grazing districts on lands which, in his opinion, were valuable chiefly for livestock grazing. The Secretary was further authorized "To make rules and regulations . . . enter into such cooperative agreements, and to do any and all things necessary to accomplish the purposes of this Act and to insure the objects of such grazing districts." The Secretary was also directed to provide for cooperation with "local associations of stockmen, State land officials and official State agencies engaged in conservation . . . of wildlife."

Actual administration of the Taylor Act was handled first by a Grazing Division, next by a Grazing Service, and now by the Bureau of Land Management in the Interior Department. Range regulation has taken the form of control of the volume and conditions of grazing and the levying of fees for the use of the public lands by private stock raisers. Within the framework provided by the directives stated above and others in the Act, a considerable body of administrative rules and regulations governing grazing has been developed. These comprise a Federal Range Code which is implemented by a relatively informal process of individual decisions by officials at the "grass roots" level. The stockmen and their supporters have had a much larger voice in the development and application of the Federal Range Code than have conservation interests.

The regulatory program has lessened but not prevented overgrazing and soil deterioration. Little "improvement and development" of the public range has occurred, partly because of the low fees charged for range use. The objective most emphasized and most successfully carried out is stabilization of "the livestock industry dependent upon the public range." This has been the goal supported by the stockmen. What we have here is a regulatory program which, in its actual operation and impact, has produced a policy significantly different from that favored by the proponents of the Taylor Act and stated in its preamble. In the implementation of the Act, some interests have clearly been favored over others. The conflict between conservation and livestock interests,

[32] This account is derived from Phillip O. Foss, *Politics and Grass* (Seattle: University of Washington Press, 1960).

which gave rise to the Taylor Act, and which was not settled by the Act (note its multiple objectives), has been resolved to the advantage of the livestock interests through the administrative process.

The Political Environment of Agencies

Although administrative agencies may have wide discretion in the performance of their legislatively authorized functions, they are by no means unlimited and uncontrolled in the exercise of this discretion. Agencies exist and operate not in a vacuum but in a highly political environment in which many "forces" may, at one time or another and in differing forms and degrees, exert influence on their actions.[33] The forces which influence the policy-making and implementation activities of agencies may include any of the following:

1. RELEVANT LAWS, RULES AND REGULATIONS, ACCEPTED CUSTOMS AND MODES OF PROCEDURE, CONCEPTS OF "FAIR PLAY." These can be called the basic "rules of the game" which help inform and guide official behavior and to which officials are generally expected to conform. These "rules of the game" will be supported by potential or unorganized interest groups, among others.[34]

2. THE CHIEF EXECUTIVE. Administrative agencies are either located in the presidential chain of command or are otherwise subject to presidential control and direction. Even the independent regulatory commissions, as noted previously, are subject to the president's managerial controls and can be influenced by them.

3. THE CONGRESSIONAL SYSTEM OF SUPERVISION. This includes the congressional committees, their staffs, committee chairmen, and influential congressmen who are concerned with the activities of particular agencies. Here it is well to note that congressional supervision and influence is fragmented rather than monolithic, emanating usually from parts of Congress, not Congress as a whole.

4. THE COURTS. Through their power of judicial review and statute interpretation, or the possibility of such, the courts may influence or control agency action. The role played by the courts will vary from agency to agency. The Federal Trade Commission has been significantly affected in its operations by judicial action while the Federal Reserve Board has been unaffected thereby.

---

[33] The following discussion is partly based on a lecture given by Professor Wallace Sayre of Columbia University at the University of Texas during the spring semester, 1958.

[34] For further discussion of the "rules of the game" and support for them, see Truman, *op. cit.,* 446–450.

5. OTHER ADMINISTRATIVE AGENCIES AND DEPARTMENTS. Agencies with competing or overlapping jurisdictions may exert influence, as does the Department of Agriculture on the fixing of shipping rates for agricultural commodities by the ICC. The FTC and the Antitrust Division of the Justice Department share jurisdiction in antitrust enforcement. One agency may aspire to absorb some of the functions of another. The Department of Commerce would like to take over some of the promotional functions of the Civil Aeronautics Board.

6. OTHER GOVERNMENTS. The state governments, municipal or local governments, or associations of state or local officials may attempt to influence agency decisions. The associations of state highway officials and state welfare officials apply "pressure" on the Bureau of Public Roads and the Welfare Administration, respectively.

7. THE POLITICAL PARTY ORGANIZATIONS. Their role has declined but, at times, they may be a factor of importance. Appointments to administrative positions or administrative decisions may be influenced by party welfare considerations. President Eisenhower's directive to his Secretary of Agriculture to raise the support price levels for some agricultural commodities prior to the fall elections in 1956 was intended to promote the political welfare of the Republican Party.

8. INTEREST GROUPS. Organized interest groups are much concerned with the activities of administrative agencies, trying to obtain favorable and prevent unfavorable action toward group interests. The American Farm Bureau Federation and the Farmers Union often are influential in the Department of Agriculture (although usually not at the same time), as are the AFL-CIO and the American Legion in the Department of Labor and Veteran's Administration, respectively. Groups may be brought directly into the administrative process by the use of advisory boards or the appointment of their members to agency positions.

9. COMMUNICATIONS MEDIA. The media of mass communication, radio, television, and the press have a role beyond their use by pressure groups and others. The communications media may be important in shaping public opinion toward an agency by revealing or publicizing agency action, favorably or unfavorably. This may affect public and, in turn, congressional support for an agency. Agencies often exhibit much concern with maintaining a "good press."

Each of the forces listed here is multiple rather than monolithic. A variety of pressure groups, administrative agencies, or sources of congressional supervision may be concerned with the activities of a particular agency. Moreover, conflicting viewpoints or positions may be held both by the members of the same category and by members of different categories. The typical agency is the focus of conflicting forces, pushing and pulling against one another with varying degrees of intensity. The forces operating on an agency may cancel out or balance one another, leaving the agency with freedom of action. The National Labor Relations Board, for example, is the focus of two broad sets of forces, one favorable to it and the other critical of it. As a result, the Board seems to have considerable leeway of action.

The field of forces surrounding an agency will be drawn from among the above categories and it will form the "constituency" of the agency, "those groups, both governmental and non-governmental, which the agency must take into account" in performing its functions.[35] The concept of "constituency" is broader than the related concept of "clientele." An agency's clientele is comprised of groups and individuals which it directly serves or regulates, whereas its constituency is all those who are in some way concerned or involved in its operations. Thus, rail, water, and motor carriers form the clientele of the Interstate Commerce Commission, but its constituency includes congressional committees, shippers, and other administrative agencies as well.

The constituency of an agency is dynamic rather than static in nature. Some groups, or forces, may be only occasionally concerned with the agency as particular issues arise or are settled. Other groups, or forces, will be more or less continually concerned or involved and will constitute the "stable core" of the agency's constituency. The "stable core" of the Civil Aeronautics Board consists of the air carriers, the congressional commerce committees, and the congressional appropriations committees. The chief executive, the Department of Commerce, and the congressional small business committees are intermittently involved with the CAB.[36] Constituency elements manifesting continuous concern appear to have the most likelihood of success in affecting general patterns of agency action.

The relationship of an agency to one element in its constituency will depend upon its relationships with the other elements. An agency which has strong presidential support tends to be less responsive to pressure groups than an agency without such support. In contrast, strong congressional and interest group support for an agency may lessen presidential influence (recall the case of the Corps of Army Engineers). Again, strong public support, garnered by many tech-

[35] The quoted clause is from Peter Woll, *American Bureaucracy* (New York: W. W. Norton, 1963), 53–54.

[36] Richard E. Caves, *Air Transport and Its Regulation* (Cambridge: Harvard University Press, 1962), ch. 12, discusses the political environment of the Civil Aeronautics Board and its effect on Board decisions.

niques, has enabled the Forest Service to resist pressures from lumber and livestock interests. In general, we can say that agency policy-making and implementation activities will reflect the interests supported by the dominant elements in its constituency. But, in any case, agency decisions are shaped by the interaction of the agency and its constituency.

Why, now, do agencies respond to elements in their constituencies in making decisions? We can suggest a number of possibilities. First, in order to survive and carry on their activities, agencies need to maintain "a favorable balance of political support over political opposition."

> Few, indeed, are the administrative agencies that have all friends and no enemies. There is almost certain to be some hostility towards any administrative agency and its program. To survive with any given program of activities, an agency must find friendly groups whose political support is strong enough to overcome the opposition of hostile groups. To preserve its friends, it must to some degree adapt its program to their interests. To neutralize its enemies, it must sometimes sacrifice elements in its program that attract the most effective political opposition. Hence, organizations are in a continual process of adjustment to the political environment that surrounds them—an adjustment that seeks to keep a favorable balance of political support over political opposition.[37]

Usually support from both private groups and government officials is needed as there is unlikely to be significant governmental support in the absence of private support.

Agencies may also find it necessary to consider and respond to private group interests in order to gain their cooperation in carrying out agency functions. In the area of regulation, the greater the degree of detailed and technical government control the greater is the need for "consent and active participation" by the regulated interests if the regulation is to be effective.[38] Noncooperation by the railroads would greatly hamper or frustrate railroad rate regulation by the ICC.

Third, agency personnel may hold, or come to hold, the same values and policy viewpoints as those affected or regulated by the agency's program perhaps because the regulators and the regulated have similar social and career backgrounds. Also, continued association with the regulated groups or industries, especially in the absence of much

---

[37] Simon, *op. cit.,* 338–339.
[38] E. Pendleton Herring, *Public Administration and the Public Interest* (New York: McGraw-Hill, 1936), 192.

contact with competing interests or sources of information, may lead to identity of outlook between agency and industry personnel.

Fourth, our "business culture" sensitizes administrative officials to business interests, to the businessman's side of things. As Robert Lane has commented: "the bureaucrat is operating in a business culture which permits the denigration of bureaucrats by businessmen but discourages the abuse of businessmen by bureaucrats. Therefore some of this sensitivity to the businessman's point of view is culturally enforced, a product of outside pressure on the bureaucracy."[39]

Last, an agency's response to its constituency may stem from statutory mandates or directives. Lines of control may be established by statute to the chief executive, the courts, Congress, or other administrative agencies. Judicial review of agency decisions may be provided, or the chief executive may be authorized to review or participate in certain agency actions (as in the awarding of international air routes by the CAB). Whatever specific form such participation takes, the agency must consider the possible reactions of other officials or agencies when making decisions. To ignore them may mean loss of political support or the rejection of agency decisions. Statutory mandates may also lead to responsiveness to private group interests or needs, as when the CAB is directed to promote the development of an adequate air transport system or the Grazing Service is directed to stabilize the livestock industry dependent upon public grazing lands.

Agency decision-making cannot be explained solely in terms of external pressures and influence. We must also consider such internal factors as the values and beliefs which agency personnel bring to their jobs, their estimate of the balance of competing interests in policy matters, their view of the intent of Congress in passing the statutes they administer, and the degree of their identification with the goals and well-being of their agency. Our purpose here, however, was primarily to indicate the political nature of administrative decision making —that the political struggle to influence policy does not end when a bill becomes a law.

Administrative Participation in the Legislative Process

The policy-making activities of administrative agencies are not limited to the implementation of legislation. Agencies also play an important role in the legislative process, in the adoption or rejection of proposed

[39] Robert E. Lane, *The Regulation of Businessmen* (New Haven: Yale University Press, 1954), 75–76.

legislation by the legislature. Much of the legislation passed by Congress traces its origin to the executive branch and the administrative agencies. The initiative in the legislative process, the development of proposals for action, now rests more with the executive branch than with Congress. According to one observer: "The executive branch, because of its superior information, is in a preferred position for identifying social and political problems. Thus, it can structure the agenda for the total decision process, including the agenda of the legislative branch."[40] The President's annual and special messages to Congress, for example, contain numerous proposals for legislation, most of which have come up from the various agencies and departments.[41] Here, however, the focus will be on agency-Congressional rather than Presidential-Congressional relationships.

Administrative participation and initiative in the legislative process is a consequence of the technicality and complexity of much legislation and the context from which it arises. A large proportion of legislation takes the form of expansion, improvement, or other modification of existing policies and programs. Because of their continued activity and involvement in particular policy areas, administrative agencies and officials possess the experience and information needed for the effective formulation of policy changes and additions. Congress does not normally possess adequate information of its own, and so must rely on agencies for advice and assistance when legislating, if it is to act intelligently.

Agencies are generally expected to make policy recommendations in their respective areas of jurisdiction and are sometimes given this duty by statutory provision. Their annual reports of the independent regulatory commissions customarily include a number of policy recommendations. Moreover, as a matter of routine, Congress requests the views of affected administrative agencies on pending legislation, whatever its source or origin. Agency officials are also widely called upon to testify at committee hearings and to present information on bills.

Congress, of course, does not always follow the advice and recommendations of agencies, but it does do so in many instances. Much of the railroad legislation enacted by Congress since the establishment of the Interstate Commerce Commission has evolved out of the recommendations of that body. Because agency support or opposition appears

[40] James A. Robinson, *Congress and Foreign Policy-Making* (Homewood, Ill.: The Dorsey Press, 1962), 8.
[41] See Richard E. Neustadt, "Planning the President's Program," *American Political Science Review*, XLIX (December, 1955), 980–1021.

to significantly affect the enactment of legislation, pressure groups often try to take policy positions favorable to group interests.

In supporting or opposing proposed legislation, agencies frequently act as representatives or spokesmen for the groups which constitute their clienteles. Indeed, agencies and pressure groups often contend that it is the proper duty of an agency to protect and promote the interests it serves when making legislative recommendations. Business groups expect the Department of Commerce to serve as their spokesman, agricultural groups expect similar treatment from the Department of Agriculture, and so on. Many agencies owe their existence to the groups they serve and may need group support in order to survive or maintain their programs against hostile attack, further encouraging the agencies to act as group spokesmen. An agency subjected to conflicting group pressures may be relatively free in devising policy recommendations, but an agency dependent on a single interest group, as is the Veterans Administration on the veterans, may find it exceedingly difficult to act against that group's interests.

The techniques employed by agencies in their efforts to influence legislative action are various. Most agencies maintain legislative liaison offices to deal with congressional problems and requests for information, hoping for congressional goodwill and support for the agency when needed. The testimony presented at committee hearings is usually so phrased as to support the agency's position. Attempts may be made to withhold information which is unfavorable to the agency. The assistance of private pressure groups may be sought to bolster the agency's position. The Department of Labor, for example, may plan its legislative strategy in cooperation with labor union officials or representatives or other favorably inclined groups. The support of the chief executive, high-level executive officials, or prestigious private citizens can often be used to advantage. Agencies may also attempt to mobilize public opinion in their behalf, as Secretary of Agriculture Freeman did (although unsuccessfully) in attempting to win congressional approval of the Kennedy administration's agriculture policy proposals in 1962.

Administrative participation in the legislative process often neither originates in nor produces controversy. Some matters are quite controversial, as administrative proposals for major policy changes or proposals which pose serious threats to existing agency programs. Here agencies can generally be counted on to support their positions with all the means at their disposal. Much legislation, however, is a matter of routine and is intended "to accomplish objectives that, by common consent, are wise and necessary for the conduct of public business." Then the role of the agency is "not so much one of advocacy as of consultation with [congressional] committeemen who have a responsible concern about the administrative operation in question."[42]

PUBLIC ECONOMIC POLICY: THE PROBLEM OF COMPLIANCE

Viewed in broad terms, all public economic policies are "regulatory," although they may be individually described as promotional, facilitative, restrictive, or prescriptive. The broad purpose of public economic policies is to get people to follow lines of conduct that are in accord with governmentally determined goals and standards. Policies are intended to secure or maintain desired courses of action and to prevent those which are undesired, e.g., to maintain competition and prevent monopolistic activity. To this end, policies prescribe new standards or patterns of economic behavior and seek to maintain or reinforce existing behavior patterns which, though desired, might be abandoned in the absence of policy. Policies are thus intended to produce changes in economic behavior.

The literature dealing with public economic policy typically gives little consideration to the problem of compliance, of why people obey law, except for discussion of enforcement techniques and sanctions for violators. Perhaps the reason for this is our traditional legalistic approach to government with its assumption that people have "an absolute duty to obey the government." The correlative assumption is that governmental decisions will be more or less automatically obeyed. This is not necessarily the case at all. Many laws on the statute books are more disregarded than followed; Sunday "blue laws" are an example.

The burden of achieving compliance with public economic policies rests, so far as official responsibility is concerned, primarily with administrative agencies. A lesser role is played by the courts. Achieving compliance with policy is the central purpose of the various forms of administrative action. But administrative enforcement activities and the application of sanctions are not adequate by themselves to ensure compliance with policy.

[42] Key, *Politics, Parties, and Pressure Groups,* 750–751.

Why Do People Comply with Policy?

Although the degree of compliance with policy varies with the law in question, the situation, and the people involved, apparently most of the people obey most of the laws most of the time. How can we account for this condition?

There is much respect for authority in our society, including authority as expressed in the decisions of governmental agencies and officials. Statements to the effect that Americans are a "lawless people" overstate reality and should not be permitted to obscure this fact. Respect or deference to authority is inculcated into our personality make-up by a process of socialization. We are trained from birth to defer to the authority of parents, knowledge, status, "the law," especially if these forms of authority are "reasonable" in nature. It is consequently believed morally right or proper to obey the law. Disobedience of the law will often lead to feelings of guilt or shame. The tendency of most people is to conform to the law because of prior conditioning and force of habit unless it conflicts with strongly held beliefs and values.

Possible individual violators of policy prescriptions may be deterred from noncompliance by a desire to avoid community disapproval, to avoid being stigmatized as a lawbreaker. Because of group pressures for conformity, if the groups to which a person belongs and with which he has frequent contact support compliance, his tendency to comply will be further strengthened. The desire of individuals to gain or retain community and group acceptance, respect, and esteem leads them to conform to accepted behavioral norms and patterns—in this case compliance with law.[43]

Compliance with policy may be furthered by the conviction that the policy in question is necessary, just, or reasonable, even where it conflicts with the immediate self-interest of individuals. Most people undoubtedly would rather not pay taxes and many people try to avoid or evade taxes. But if people believe that the tax laws are reasonable or just, or that taxation is necessary to provide needed governmental services, this in all likelihood will contribute to compliance with tax policies.

[43] On the matter of group pressure for conformity see Muzafer Sherif, "Conformity-Deviation, Norms, and Group Behavior," in Irwin A. Berg and Bernard M. Bass, eds., *Conformity and Deviation* (New York: Harper & Row, 1961), ch. 5.

A related factor is the belief that a governmental decision or policy should be obeyed because it is "legitimate" in the sense that it is "constitutional," or was made by officials with proper authority to act, or that proper procedures were followed in making it. People would be much less likely to accept judicial decisions as legitimate if, in making decisions, the courts followed procedures similar to those used in legislative decision making. Again, some people in the South are willing to comply with the Supreme Court's school desegregation decision of 1954 because they regard it as legitimate, as within the scope of the Court's competence, even though they may not agree with its substance.

Considerations of self-interest may also contribute to policy compliance. Individuals and groups may directly benefit from acceptance of policy standards. Farmers will comply with acreage allotments on agricultural production (which are voluntary in nature) if they believe it is to their advantage to qualify for price supports and benefit payments by so doing. Securities regulation is accepted by the responsible members of the securities business as a means of protecting themselves against the unethical practices of some securities dealers. Milk price control laws are sought and complied with by dairymen and dairy companies as a means of promoting their interests. Compliance by those regulated or affected by economic policies may thus result because private interests and policy prescriptions are in harmony rather than conflict, as is too often assumed.

The possibility of punishment in the form of fines, imprisonment, and other sanctions for those who violate the law also works for compliance. The threat or imposition of legal sanctions by themselves, however, are not sufficient to induce compliance. "The strong disposition in this country to believe that any behavior can be controlled by threatening punishment has filled American statute books with hundreds of unenforced and unenforceable laws."[44] Sanctions are inadequate to bring about compliance in the face of widespread or mass violations, as in the case of national prohibition in the 1920's.

Although in some cases compliance may stem largely from the fear of punishment, the main function of sanctions is to supplement and reinforce other causes of compliance. If people who normally comply with policy see others obtaining advantages through non-compliance, they themselves may become violators. Here sanctions can be effective

[44] Simon, *op. cit.,* 479. For some of the limitations on coercive enforcement see Charles E. Merriam, *Political Power* (New York: McGraw-Hill, 1934), ch. VI.

in gaining compliance. Moreover, in many instances sanctions are effective more because of the desire of people to avoid being stigmatized as lawbreakers than because of the legal penalties involved. In many instances, the penalties actually imposed for violations of economic legislation are quite nominal. The average fine imposed for antitrust violations through criminal proceedings from 1946 to 1954 was $2,600, although in some cases fines were much higher (e.g., $175,000 for the A & P).[45] The real deterrent here is the adverse publicity which accompanies such proceedings and not the actual fine, which usually represents only a tiny fraction of the earnings of the companies involved. In other situations, of course, the sanctions imposed may be more severe and have a stronger deterrent effect.

Finally, acceptance of a policy tends to increase with the passage of time, during what may be called its "period of continuation." The policy becomes a part of the accepted state of things, one of the "conditions of doing business." New individuals will come under the policy who have no direct experience with the 'pre-policy situation. And, "since freedom (in part) is a state of mind, such men feel the restrictions to rest more lightly upon them."[46] Compliance with policy, unless it is made obsolete by social or political change, may thus be greater during the period of continuation than during the period immediately following its adoption.

Causes of Noncompliance

Although there are a number of causal factors for policy compliance, it is readily apparent to even the casual observer that all those affected by economic policies do not comply with them.[47] Statistical information on numbers of violations detected can be obtained from the reports of government agencies. Many other violations go undetected or unreported. What causes people to violate or fail to comply with laws and regulations? Why do some people, or many people in some situations, deviate from officially prescribed norms of behavior? As in the case of compliance, the causes of noncompliance are multiple.

Noncompliance may be the product of laws which conflict too sharply with the prevailing values, mores, or beliefs of the people

[45]Clair Wilcox, *Public Policies Toward Business,* rev. ed. (Homewood, Ill.: Richard D. Irwin, 1960), 110.

[46] Lane, *op. cit.,* 69–70.

[47] See Edwin H. Sutherland, *White Collar Crime* (New York: The Dryden Press, 1949), *passim,* for some illustrative data.

generally, or with those of particular groups such as businessmen and labor union officials. Widespread violations of national prohibition during the 1920's and price and rationing controls during World War II are in considerable measure attributable to this factor, as is much of the noncompliance in the South with the school desegregation decision of 1954. In such instances the general disposition to obey the law is overcome by the attachment to particular values and practices. Noncompliance results because the law is in advance of strongly held values or, as we say, "public sentiment."

A closely related cause of noncompliance is called "selective disobedience of the law."[48] Some laws are not regarded as binding as others. Those who strongly support and obey "criminal" laws may have a more relaxed or permissive attitude toward economic legislation and regulations. Thus many businessmen apparently believe that laws relating to such matters as banking operations, trade practices, taxation, and labor-management relations are not as binding on the individual as laws prohibiting robbery and burglary. Laws regulating economic activity generally developed later in this country than "criminal" laws and they often run counter to notions of nonintervention by government in the economy. Nor is the same stigma attached to the violation of economic legislation as to criminal laws. As Clinard comments: "This selective obedience to the laws rests upon the principle that what the person is doing is illegal, perhaps even unethical, but certainly not criminal."

Further, just as one's associations and group memberships may support compliance, so may they under different conditions lead to noncompliance. Association with men and ideas disrespectful of government and public economic policies, or with groups which violate the law, may cause the individual to acquire antisocial norms which dispose him to violate the law. Or, the individual may learn specific techniques or practices for violating the law. Professor Lane's research indicates that there are higher rates of labor legislation violations among the companies located in some communities than in others.[49] Although this line of analysis will help explain why some individuals or their companies engage in noncompliance, unfortunately it does not explain why the original patterns of noncompliance originated.

Violations may also occur because of the desire to make a "fast buck." This is often cited as a cause of noncompliance and certainly it would

---

[48] Marshall B. Clinard, *Sociology of Deviant Behavior* (New York: Holt, Rinehart and Winston, 1957), 168–171.
[49] Lane, *op. cit.,* ch. 5.

seem to operate in many cases of misrepresentation, such as passing one product off for another, short-weighting, and the use of deceptive containers. It is difficult to say, however, how widespread this is as a motive for noncompliance. By itself it is clearly inadequate. Thus, if two companies have similar opportunities to profit through law violations, and one does and the other does not, why? It may be, as Professor Lane suggests, that "urgency of need" rather than merely the opportunity to violate is an important factor. His findings indicate that less profitable or declining firms are more apt to violate the law, in an attempt to survive, than are more profitable firms.[50] Care must be exercised, then, in attributing violations to monetary motives. In many cases, such as labor-management relations, violations of the law may have little if any relation to financial matters.

Our cultural emphasis on individual achievement and success, especially insofar as it is measured by material standards, may also be a causative factor in noncompliance. In some individuals this may produce attitudes of "anything goes," so long as it aids in the attainment of desired goals. In other words, individuals with an excessively strong "success-orientation" may not accept and follow those laws which hamper or reduce goal attainment.

Again, violations may result from ambiguities in the law, from lack of clarity, or from conflicting purposes or provisions. A businessman may not believe that a given practice is prohibited by the law, only to find later, upon prosecution, that it is. This situation may also arise because businessmen and government officials may have different "frames of reference" and thus interpret the law in different ways. Ignorance of the law is sometimes a factor in noncompliance. Violators may be unaware of given laws or rules. In still other instances, it is possible that violations result from difficulties in complying with the law. Adequate time may not be given for filing complicated forms or for making required adjustments in existing practices. Violations thus may stem from "structural" defects in the law rather than from disagreement with its substance.

Finally, if those who violate a law are respectable enough, and numerous enough, they will tend to make all violations acceptable. This may further lead to erosion of the general social disapproval of law violations and violators. Administrative agencies, in the course of implementing and enforcing policy, can do much to prevent this sort of situation.

[50] *Ibid.*

98

Administration and Compliance

Public economic policies, as stated earlier, are intended to influence economic behavior in desired ways. For our discussion, it is assumed that there are essentially two ways in which administrative agencies can influence people to behave in the desired ways—to comply with policy. First, agencies, through educational and persuasional activities, can seek to alter the values or criteria employed by people in making economic choices so they will choose to act in the desired ways. Second, agencies can seek to limit the acceptable alternatives of choice available to people by attaching sanctions or penalties to undesired alternatives and rewards or benefits to desired alternatives.[51]

Administrative agencies engage in a wide range of educational and persuasional activities intended to convince those directly affected, and the public generally, that given policies are reasonable, necessary, just, or legitimate. Much of the effectiveness of policies depends upon the ability of agencies to gain understanding of and consent for them and thereby minimize violations and the need for sanctions. The educational approach to securing compliance can be illustrated by an educational campaign undertaken by the Wage and Hour and Public Contract Divisions of the U.S. Department of Labor.[52]

In 1961, Congress enacted amendments to the Fair Labor Standards Act which broadened the coverage of the Act and increased the required minimum wage from a dollar to a dollar-and-a-quarter an hour. An intensive campaign was undertaken by the Divisions, which administer the Act, to acquaint the public, and especially the affected employers and employees, with the new provisions. Various bulletins, pamphlets, reference guides, and posters concerning them were prepared. Information explaining the meaning and significance of the new legislation was sent to employers well in advance of its effective date. Explanatory announcements were made on radio and television and news stories were released to the press. Representatives from the Divisions outlined the amended Act and official interpretations of it before hundreds of national, regional, state, and local meetings, conferences, and conventions. Various forms of individual contact were also utilized, including mailings, telephone calls, and personal inter-views. Cooperative programs were developed with state and local offi-

[51] Simon, *op. cit.,* 453.
[52] The following discussion is based on U.S. Department of Labor, *Annual Report, 1962* (Washington, D.C.: Government Printing Office, 1962), 222–223.

cials and local school officials concerning the child labor provisions of the Act. After the amendments became effective, press releases and other devices were used to inform employees and the public of the Divisions enforcement activities and judicial interpretations of the Act.

Administrative agencies also use propaganda appeals in attempting to induce compliance with policy. The word "propaganda" is used here not in a pejorative sense but rather to denote efforts to gain acceptance of policies by identifying them with widely accepted societal values and mores. During World War II efforts were made to induce compliance with rationing and price controls through appeals to patriotism. Controls were described as necessary to "win the war" and as a way of "helping out the boys at the front." Again, antitrust programs may be described as necessary to maintain "our system of free competitive enterprise." Agricultural price support programs have been depicted as necessary to secure "equality for agriculture" and to preserve the "family farm." This method of securing compliance can be viewed either as an effort to reduce the "moral costs" of adapting to a new policy or an attempt to attach positive values to it.[53]

In the course of administering a policy, changes or modifications may be made by the enforcement agency which will contribute to compliance. Inequities or ambiguities in the law may be reduced or eliminated. Simplified procedures for compliance may be developed, as in the case of federal income tax returns for lower income groups. Administrative personnel may develop knowledge and skill in enforcing the law so as to reduce objections and misunderstandings. Also, the law may be interpreted or applied in such a manner as to make it more acceptable to those directly affected, as by lessening its forces or restrictiveness.

Sanctions will be used by administrative agencies when the various factors in society supporting obedience and the other methods available to agencies are inadequate to bring about compliance with policy. Sanctions are penalties or deprivations imposed upon those who do not behave in officially prescribed ways. Their effectiveness rests upon the desires of people to avoid disadvantages and to obtain advantages.

Sanctions may be classified as either administrative or judicial, depending upon whether they are imposed by administrative or judicial agencies. Common types of judicial sanctions are fines, imprisonment, and writs of injunction. Here concern is with administrative sanctions. They are used much more frequently in enforcing economic legislation than are judicial sanctions because of their greater variety, flexi-

[53] See Simon, *op. cit.,* 457.

100

bility, and promptness of impact. Among the various types of sanctions which may be employed by administrative agencies are the following:

1. Threat of prosecution
2. Fines or pecuniary penalties which have the effect of fines
3. Power to remit or mitigate statutory penalties
4. Awards or benefits for approved conduct [or their withdrawal or denial in cases of unapproved conduct] . . .
5. Publicity, either favorable or unfavorable
6. Revocation, annulment, modification, suspension, failure to renew licenses
7. Summary seizure or destruction of goods
8. Award of damages.[54]

To be most effective, the degree of severity of sanctions must be geared to the violations at which they are directed. If sanctions are too mild their effectiveness as deterrents may be weak. On the other hand, if the sanctions available for a violation are too severe in their impact, there will be a tendency not to use them. For example, until 1933 the only sanctions available to the Comptroller of the Currency for banking law violations were the powers to appoint a receiver for the offending bank and to initiate court proceedings to dissolve a banking association. These were too drastic for dealing with minor banking violations and were largely unused. The development of appropriate and effective sanctions for non-compliance is a major task of administrative agencies.

Effective agency action in securing compliance will necessitate the coordinated use of all the methods discussed here. In addition, compliance must be the concern of the entire agency—those who formulate agency procedures and plans, those who deal with the public, those who gather information, etc., as well as those formally given enforcement functions. Each aspect of the agency's operations will affect in some way its ability to gain compliance with the policies it administers. However, just as the use of sanctions alone is not adequate to secure compliance, neither are agency operations as a whole. Much will depend upon the attitudes of the public and, especially, those directly involved with given policies. In a democracy the effectiveness of government and public policy ultimately depends upon the consent, explicit or tacit, of the governed.

[54] Redford, *Administration of National Economic Control,* 166–167.

Chapter Four

FISCAL AND MONETARY POLICY

Government control of economic activity takes two general forms: the regulation, promotion, and control of specific activities through such means as antitrust policy, agricultural price supports, and government ownership of enterprise; and the control of over-all levels of economic activity through macroeconomic policies. The second form of control, which is the main concern of this chapter, involves the use of fiscal and monetary policy to maintain economic stability. Fiscal policies relate to government taxation and expenditure; monetary policies have to do with money, credit, interest rates, and management of the public debt.

After a discussion of economic stability and economic stabilization policy, the federal budgetary and taxation processes will be examined. Although these are the main instruments of fiscal policy, they have specific as well as aggregative effects on economic activity. Thus, federal taxation affects the income of specific individuals and groups as well as the total demand for goods and services in the economy. Taxing and spending also have significance for other economic policies, as will be seen later.

ECONOMIC STABILITY POLICY

Introduction

What is economic stability? A variety of responses are possible. Economic stability may be defined as meaning the absence of fluctuations in the business cycle, stability in the price level, stable growth in economic output and employment; full employment in the economy; economic growth without inflation; and so on.[1] These possibilities, in turn, are subject to varying definitions and various combinations of them can be used as definitions. Conflicts over stability policy may arise in part because of disagreement as to the meaning of economic stability, and, consequently, the causes of instability which policy is to remedy. Although we recognize the shortcomings of general definitions, economic stability will be viewed here as a rising national income under conditions which provide full employment and general price stability.

Why, now, is it desirable to maintain economic stability? To answer, we must keep in mind the effects of economic instability on economic welfare, social stability, and political stability, which are widely shared interests in American society. The following comments are suggestive rather than definitive. Economic instability, in deflationary form, causes losses in national income and production. Goods and services that could be produced are not because the economy is operating below capacity. Inflation causes losses in real income as the purchasing power of the dollar declines. This bears down especially hard on groups with relatively fixed incomes—school teachers, government employees, pensioners, bond holders—whose incomes do not change with the price level. Both inflation and deflation redistribute income between debtors and creditors, and between fixed and flexible income groups. This process produces inequities, or greater inequities, as the case may be, in the distribution of income among groups and individuals.

Economic instability may produce political instability. (The causation may also be in the opposite direction. "Galloping" inflation, as in Germany after World War I and China after World War II, usually occurs in societies characterized by severe political instability.) Economic instability intensifies conflict in society, as when depression threatens such vital interests as security, social status, and predictability of the future. People are threatened with downward mobility, with a loss of social status, economic position, self-respect. Eric Hoffer has written: ". . . with the widespread diffusion of a high standard of living, depressions and the unemployment they bring assumed a new aspect. The present-day workingman in the Western world feels unemployment as a degradation. He sees himself disinherited and injured by an unjust order of things, and is willing to listen to those who call for a new

[1] Donald S. Watson, *Economic Policy: Business and Government* (Boston: Houghton Mifflin, 1960), 529–539.

103

deal."[2] What Hoffer says applies to the white-collar worker, the small businessman, and others who may feel equally threatened.

When conflict intensifies, the resolution of conflict tends to become more authoritarian and to spill over into violence or civil disorders as the consensus necessary for deliberative (democratic) government and decision making is weakened. In the United States, hostility and resentment caused by falling prices and incomes have often led to civil disorder. In Iowa in the early 1930's, farmers, discontented with depressed agricultural conditions, acted forcibly to prevent sales of farm commodities, stopped eviction sales, and attacked law-enforcement officials.[3] Many people were attracted to radical, authoritarian, and extremist movements which promised solutions for their problems. In Germany the frustration, resentment, and insecurity created by the depression, especially among the members of the middle class, was an important factor in the rise to power of Hitler and the Nazi movement.

During periods of prosperity, when prices are stable, incomes are rising, and employment is high, economically stimulated conflict is less bitter and intense, and the political system is more stable. Extremist and authoritarian movements lose their appeal. Compare the significance of such movements in the 1930's and the far more prosperous 1950's.

Economic instability also affects social stability. In the United States, for example, social stability means not static social conditions, but rather a larger degree of mobility—opportunity for social groups to change, for individuals to improve their status, for mobility between social classes. When unemployment is serious, people are frozen in their jobs. They hesitate to change jobs or engage in new ventures because of the risks involved. During times of prosperity and high employment greater opportunities exist for social mobility and change. Again, we can note that family life is affected by economic conditions. Birth rates in the United States have increased during periods of prosperity and dropped off during periods of depression. Other things being equal, we can assume the existence of a causal relationship here.

The foregoing discussion indicates that the maintenance of economic stability is not an end in itself, nor only economic in its consequences. The discussion also illustrates the essential interrelatedness of the economic and political systems, which was commented on in Chapter One.

[2] Eric Hoffer, *The True Believer* (New York: Mentor Books, 1958), 32.
[3] Arthur M. Schlesinger, Jr., *The Coming of the New Deal* (Boston: Houghton Mifflin, 1956), 42–44, 65–66.

Development of Government Responsibility

Only in recent decades, and especially since World War II, has the national government assumed explicit and active responsibility for the maintenance of economic stability. This is probably the most important development in public economic policy in the postwar period.

It was once thought that government could do little to control fluctuations in the business cycle (even though they appeared to be an intrinsic feature of a capitalistic, industrial economy). The operation of the business cycle supposedly was governed by "natural" economic laws which made governmental action unnecessary and undesirable. Depressions, for example, were thought to be self-correcting. Did not Say's Law, a main feature of classical economic theory, state that supply creates its own demand, and that continued unemployment or underconsumption is thus impossible? The best thing government could do was to balance the budget, by cutting expenditures and increasing taxes, lest business conditions be worsened by a lack of public confidence in the government's financial condition.

Acceptance of governmental responsibility for economic stabilization resulted from the combined influences of: (1) the Great Depression, which began in 1929 and was the most severe the nation had ever known; (2) the persistence of large-scale unemployment throughout the 1930's; the development of new and more effective tools of economic measurement and analysis; and (3) the economic impact of World War II, which brought a tremendous increase in government spending.[4] Also of great importance were the ideas of the famed English economist, John Maynard Keynes. In his *General Theory of Employment, Interest, and Money* (1936) and other writings, Keynes argued that deficit spending by government could add to the total demand for economic goods and services, offsetting a decrease in private demand, and thus help to maintain a high level of demand, output, and employment. His ideas came to be widely accepted and constituted a rationale for the use of fiscal policy by government to maintain economic stability.

The New Deal, partly on the basis of Keynesian ideas, used deficit spending in an effort to stimulate the economy and bring recovery. This technique was often referred to as "pump-priming" and "com-

[4] Merle Fainsod, Lincoln Gordon, and Joseph C. Palamountain, Jr., *Government and the American Economy*, 3rd ed. (New York: W. W. Norton, 1959), 798.

105

pensatory spending." The deficit spending activities of the New Deal, though they were regarded by many as highly radical, were really quite moderate (at least in retrospect). Indeed, it has been argued that the reason for the persistence of unemployment during the 1930's was that the deficits incurred by the Roosevelt administration were insufficient to compensate for the large drop in private spending.[5]

What the deficits of the 1930's failed to do was accomplished by the huge deficits ($46 billion in 1943) which resulted from the government's spending for the war effort of the 1940's. Stimulated by these large deficits, the economy expanded, production rose sharply, and unemployment almost disappeared. This experience led to a general feeling that if large-scale government activity could expand production and maintain employment in wartime it could also do so in peacetime.

The Employment Act of 1946 formally committed the national government to act to maintain economic stability. The act reflected the belief, based on wartime experience, that government could act effectively, through the use of its fiscal and monetary powers, to stabilize the economy. Also contributing to the passage of the act was the fear, supported by the predictions of many economists, that the changeover from a wartime to a peacetime economy would be accompanied by a depression.[6]

Much conflict attended the passage of the Employment Act. Truman administration leaders and liberal and labor groups wanted to commit the government to full use of fiscal policy to ensure full employment. In opposition, business and conservative groups argued that extensive use of fiscal policy to maintain full employment would lead to high labor costs, budget deficits, inflation, and excessive government intervention in the economy. They emphasized the capacity of the private economy to provide jobs. Also, they placed more faith in the ability of monetary policy to stabilize the economy. (Monetary policy—the use of controls over credit and interest to maintain stability—had not prevented the depression and had consequently lost favor, especially with liberals and fiscal policy proponents.)

The Employment Act in its final form was passed by overwhelming majorities in Congress. However, because of the resistance to it, espe-

[5] Francis M. Bator, "Money and Government," *The Atlantic*, CCIX (April, 1962), 116–117.
[6] An excellent discussion of the enactment of the Act is Stephen K. Bailey, *Congress Makes a Law: The Story Behind the Employment Act of 1946* (New York: Columbia University Press, 1950).

cially in the House, it was much altered from the original bill introduced by Senator Murray of Montana. For example, the Murray bill had specifically provided for the use of public works and favorable loans to maintain employment. This provision was replaced by a commitment to use "all practicable means." The goal of "full employment" in the Murray bill became "maximum employment" in the final version. Such compromises were part of the cost of passage. It does, however, represent a large amount of agreement and a general course for public policy to follow. The act's declaration of policy states:

> it is the continuing policy and responsibility of the Federal Government to use all practicable means consistent with its needs and obligations and other essential considerations of national policy, with the assistance and cooperation of industry, agriculture, labor, and State and local governments, to coordinate and utilize all of its plans, functions, and resources for the purpose of creating and maintaining, in a manner calculated to foster and promote free competitive enterprise and the general welfare, conditions under which there will be afforded useful employment opportunities, including self-employment, for those able, willing, and seeking to work, and to promote maximum employment, production, and purchasing power.

The act established some machinery to help carry out the declared policy. A Council of Economic Advisers, consisting of three members, was created. The Council has the duties of collecting and analyzing data on current and future economic trends and preparing them for the President's use. It also advises on how new and existing programs can be used to effectuate the Employment Act's policy statement. The Council played a large role in formulating, and persuading President Kennedy to make to Congress, the tax cut proposal which resulted in the Revenue Act of 1964.[7]

The Employment Act also provides that the President shall deliver an Economic Report to Congress at the start of each session. In it the President is to analyze current economic trends and conditions and present "a program for carrying out the policy declared in Section 2, together with such recommendations for legislation as he may deem necessary or advisable." Within Congress, the act provided for a Joint Economic Committee (as it is now called) to consider the President's Economic Report and advise the two Houses concerning the President's recommendations. In general, the Council and the Joint Eco-

[7] *The New York Times,* Feb. 27, 1964, p. 18.

nomic Committee are intended to direct attention to, and contribute to understanding of, the over-all operation of the economy and the role of government in relation thereto.

Economic Stability Policy: The Instruments

A variety of fiscal and monetary techniques are available to government decision makers in their efforts to maintain economic stability. The use of another possible set of techniques—direct controls, e.g., over prices—is culturally proscribed except during wartime. At other times, and even to some extent during wartime, direct controls run counter to accepted notions of the proper role of government in the economy.

The fiscal and monetary instruments discussed here are considered primarily as means for preventing inflationary and deflationary movements in the economy or, alternatively, as instruments of counter-cyclical policy. Further, attention is focused on the problems of inflation and deflation caused by imbalances between aggregate supply and demand. Other possible causes of instability will be indicated at later points.

To set the scene for what follows, and to provide some "feel" for the discussion, let us suppose the economy is faced with the possibility of an "inflationary gap." This is a situation in which demand is in excess of supply—"too many dollars are chasing too few goods," and prices are rising. What can government do to reduce demand, bringing supply and demand into better balance and restraining the rise in prices? The Federal Reserve Board can restrict the credit supply to discourage investment spending. The President and Congress can work for a budget surplus, so the government will take in more money than it spends and thus reduce the funds available for private spending. In case of a "deflationary gap"—demand is inadequate to clear the market of available goods and services—the problem and government action required are the reverse of the above.

Monetary Policy

Most of the instruments of monetary policy are under the control of the Board of Governors of the Federal Reserve System (Federal Reserve Board). They involve control of the supply of money and credit and the interest rate. The Federal Reserve Board has primary responsibility for the implementation of monetary policy because of its authority over the credit-creating activities of the commercial banks of the

108

country. Changes in the nation's money supply result largely from changes in the volume of commercial bank credit. The Federal Reserve System was established by Congress in 1913, primarily for the purpose of adjusting the money supply to the fluctuating needs of commerce and industry. "Nothing in the [Federal Reserve] Act relates the monetary authority to the function of national economic stabilization; yet this is its prime task today."[8]

The Federal Reserve System has been aptly described by Professor Reagan "as a pyramid having a private base, a mixed middle, and a public apex."[9] At the top is the Board of Governors, whose seven members are appointed by the President, with senatorial consent, for fourteen-year, overlapping terms. Members are removable by the President for cause, but none ever has been. In the middle of the pyramid is the Federal Open Market Committee, comprised of the seven Federal Reserve Board members and five of the twelve Federal Reserve Bank presidents. At the bottom of the pyramid are the twelve district Federal Reserve Banks. These are "banker's banks," formally owned by the national and state chartered banks in each district which belong to the System. All national banks must belong and state banks may if they meet System requirements. The banks belonging to the Federal Reserve System account for about 85 per cent of the commercial bank reserves of the country.

The primary instruments of monetary policy employed by the Federal Reserve System in maintaining economic stability are the setting of reserve requirements for member banks, control of the discount rate, and open market operations. Formally, these three functions are allocated to the Federal Reserve Board, the Federal Reserve Bank Boards of Directors, and the Federal Open Market Committee, respectively. In actuality, the exercise of all three is controlled by the FRB, which, in turn, at least in recent years, has been dominated by its chairman. Since the real substance of monetary policy depends upon the manner in which the various policy instruments are used, the nature of monetary policy at a particular time will be affected by the economic philosophy and conception of the proper role of the FRB held by the Board Chairman. It should be remarked here that, although the FRB is legally independent of the President, there has been extensive cooperation and identity of viewpoint between them in recent

[8] Michael D. Reagan, "The Political Structure of the Federal Reserve System," *American Political Science Review*, LV (March, 1961), 65.
[9] *Ibid.*, 64.

years. A brief examination of the Federal Reserve Board's monetary policy instruments is now in order.[10]

OPEN-MARKET OPERATIONS. The FRB can buy and sell government securities through the Federal Reserve Banks in the open market, i.e., the place where government securities are regularly bought and sold. When the Banks sell securities the ultimate effect is a reduction in member banks' reserves and consequently in the amount of loans they can make. The opposite effect occurs when the Federal Reserve Banks buy government securities. This instrument is regarded as the most effective one the FRB has for increasing or decreasing the supply of credit.

THE DISCOUNT RATE. This is the rate of interest charged by the Reserve Banks to member commercial banks desiring to borrow money from them to finance lending activities. Raising the discount rate is intended to discourage borrowing by banks for the purpose of making loans, and lowering the discount rate is expected to achieve the reverse effect. Changes in the discount rate are usually moderate and are seldom sufficient by themselves to encourage or discourage bank borrowing. But, whatever their other impact, such changes are a means by which the FRB can signal its view of the economy to the banks. If they encounter higher discount rates the banks know the FRB believes credit is expanding too rapidly and that they can expect further action to contract credit if expansion continues.

RESERVE REQUIREMENTS. Although the FRB uses this method sparingly, it can alter the ratio of reserves to deposits (or loans) which must be maintained by member banks. If the reserve requirement is 20 per cent, banks can make five dollars in loans for each dollar of reserves they have. By raising or lowering reserve requirements the FRB can decrease or increase the amount of loans banks can make, thus contracting or expanding the supply of credit.

Two other instruments used by the FRB are *moral suasion* and *selective credit controls*. Moral suasion refers to the efforts of the Board to influence bank actions by suggestion, exhortation, and informal agreements. Selective credit controls are exercised over particular groups of borrowers. The Board now regulates margin requirements for stock purchases—the minimum down payment that must be made by purchasers of stock. If the margin requirement is 80 per cent, only 20 per cent of the purchase price of stock can be borrowed. During the

[10] For a fuller discussion of these instruments, see Board of Governors of the Federal Reserve System, *The Federal Reserve System: Purpose and Functions,* 4th ed. (Washington, D.C.: Government Printing Office, 1961).

Korean War the Board was empowered to regulate down payments for real estate and consumers' durable goods, but this power ended in 1952.

Two other monetary instruments which may be used for economic stabilization are management of the national debt and federal lending activities. The national debt was $309 billion in 1963. The Department of the Treasury, which handles the debt, is constantly refinancing it, even in periods when there are neither budget surpluses nor deficits. Previously issued securities come due and are paid off; new securities are issued to replace them. The way in which the debt is financed will affect credit supply and interest rates. Long-term securities, for example, carry higher rates of interest than short-term securities. In either case, the rate of interest paid on government securities will affect private interest rates and, consequently, private borrowing and investment. Again, during deflationary periods the supply of credit can be increased if debt financing takes the form of borrowing by the sale of short-term securities to commercial banks. This will enlarge their reserves and thus increase their capacity to make loans.

Government lending and loan guarantee programs, set up to aid particular groups or sectors of the economy, may be used for stabilization by encouraging or discouraging borrowing and investment. A number of such actions were taken during the 1957-1958 recession to stimulate investment. The housing credit rules of the Federal Housing Administration and the Veterans Administration were liberalized, and the processing of FHA loan applications was stepped up. The rules for obtaining Farmers Home Administration loans were also liberalized.[11] Similarly, in an inflationary period changes could be made to discourage borrowing.

In deflationary periods it is expected that the FRB will act to stimulate the economy by following an "easy money" policy—expanding the supply of credit and lowering interest rates to encourage investment. This was the policy adopted by the Board during the 1953-1954 recession as soon as the decline in spending and employment became apparent. Conversely, during an inflationary period, the FRB typically acts to contract credit and raise interest rates to discourage borrowing. This is referred to as a "tight money" policy and was followed during much of the 1950's.

[11] Wilfred Lewis, Jr., *Federal Fiscal Policy in the Postwar Recessions* (Washington, D.C.: The Brookings Institution, 1962), 221-222. This book contains good short discussions of government actions taken to combat recession after 1945, with emphasis, as the title indicates, on fiscal policy.

The proponents of monetary policy argue that it is more useful than fiscal policy for stabilization because it is more rapid and more flexible. Decisions on monetary policy are made by an administrative agency (the FRB) which can respond quickly to changes in the level of economic activity. Fiscal policy, in contrast, is often slower in application because of the need for Congressional action on taxation and expenditures.[12]

The proponents of monetary policy also argue that it is a "good" policy because it is indirect and impersonal in its working. The government, in using monetary policy, does not directly control or prescribe individual actions and decisions but rather acts to change the environment in which individuals act and make economic decisions. Thus, the proponents conclude, monetary policy involves less government intervention in private economic activity than does fiscal policy.

Although the Federal Reserve Board occupies the central position in the area of monetary policy, its actions may not be well coordinated with those of agencies concerned with agricultural, housing, and veteran's loan programs, all of which affect the over-all supply of credit. They were, after all, set up to serve particular interests and purposes. The FRB may also be limited in effectiveness by demands that it facilitate the Treasury Department's debt management task. During the late 1940's the Board was prevented from following an anti-inflationary policy by its agreement to help maintain low interest rates on government securities. In 1951 an "accord" was negotiated between the Board, which had strong Congressional support, and the Treasury, which had presidential support. The "accord" committed the Board to maintain an "orderly" market for government securities but otherwise left it free to use monetary policy for countercyclical purposes. Divided responsibility and conflicting interests within the executive branch are thus productive of conflict over monetary policy, which may reduce its effectiveness.

Fiscal Policy

Fiscal policy involves the use of the national government's taxing and spending powers to influence the level of income, employment, and growth in the economy, i.e., to maintain economic stability. When federal spending was small, the opportunity of the national govern-

[12] This paragraph and the one following are based on Marshall A. Robinson, Herbert C. Morton, and James D. Calderwood, *An Introduction to Economic Reasoning* (Washington: The Brookings Institution, 1962), ch. 7.

ment to influence the economy through fiscal policy was slight. With the national government's greatly increased spending in recent decades, this situation has changed. In fiscal 1964 the national government purchased approximately 11 per cent of the gross national product; total cash payments by the national government accounted for a little over 20 per cent of the gross national product (explained below). This volume of spending gives the national government significant ability to affect the over-all operation of the economy, depending on how it is spent and obtained. Indeed, government spending will have fiscal policy *effects* even if not used intentionally to promote economic stability.

Fiscal policy affects the aggregate (or total) volume of spending for goods and services in the economy. Simply stated, fiscal policy for stabilization is based on the assumption that at some level of gross national product (GNP), the economy will operate at a "full" employment level. (Gross national product is the sum of consumption spending plus investment spending plus government spending or, in equation form, $GNP = C + I + G$.) According to fiscal theory, if private spending for investment and consumption (plus "normal" government spending) is inadequate and results in insufficient demand to clear the market of the available supply, government can act to increase aggregate demand by spending more than it receives in taxes. Conversely, if an excess of demand is causing inflationary pressures, government can act to reduce aggregate demand by spending less than its tax take, thereby reducing aggregate demand. The most powerful instruments of fiscal policy are budget surpluses or deficits.

There are two general ways by which budget surpluses or deficits for stabilization can be achieved: the operation of "automatic stabilizers" and the use of discretionary fiscal policy.

Some automatic stabilizing devices have, intentionally or unintentionally, been built into the economy, and they help to counteract economic fluctuations without positive action by government decision makers. The federal personal and corporate income taxes and social security taxes all have automatic stabilizing effects. Without any change in their rates they bring in more revenue when national income rises and less revenue when national income falls. Moreover, as is well known, the personal income tax rates are progressively graduated and consequently rise faster in proportion than does income and, conversely, fall faster than income when the latter declines. With respect to spending, social security, unemployment compensation, and agricultural price support payments tend to increase in times of recession or decline and to decrease in prosperous times. In combination, these various programs decrease federal revenues and increase federal spending in deflationary periods so as to produce budget deficits. When national income rises, they produce budget surpluses.

The automatic stabilizers played an important role in controlling the recession of 1957–1958. While some argued for a vigorous program of government spending to counteract the recession (by adding to aggregate demand), the Eisenhower administration, without any essentially new spending programs, and without fully intending to, ran a budget deficit of some $12 billion in fiscal 1959. This deficit resulted mostly from the automatic drop in tax revenues and the increase in social security and unemployment compensation payments caused by declining income. (Stepped-up spending under authorized programs and an expansionary monetary policy also helped.) The automatic stabilizers clearly contributed to keeping the recession milder than had been predicted by many economists.

Most economists agree that the automatic stabilizers by themselves are not adequate to maintain full stability. They lessen, but do not fully control, upward and downward fluctuations in the economy. Unemployment compensation benefits, for example, do not fully compensate for the loss of consumer spending caused by unemployment. With the reduction of the federal income tax rates by the Revenue Act of 1964, it may be that the effectiveness of the income tax as a stabilizer will be lessened. In any case, there is still a need for discretionary fiscal action.

Discretionary fiscal policy involves deliberate changes by political decision makers (the President and Congress) in taxing and spending policies to achieve budget surpluses or deficits. These changes can be made in a number of ways: (1) tax rates can be held constant and the volume of spending varied; (2) the volume of spending can be held constant and taxes may be increased or decreased; and (3) some combination of changes in both tax rates and volume of spending can be used. Which alternative to use, if any, is often a cause of sharp political conflict.

To counter a recession or stimulate the economy, the government could increase spending, reduce taxes, or both, to inject more money into the economy. If tax rates were cut and spending were maintained, more money would be left in the hands of consumers. Assuming "normal" consumer behavior, most of this money would be spent, thereby adding to aggregate demand. If tax rates were left alone and government spending were increased, this too would increase aggregate demand. One may now ask, what difference would it make whether a budget deficit (or in the opposite case, a budget surplus) is achieved

114

by changing tax rates or spending volume, so long as it is achieved. The answer is, quite a bit. In the first case (a tax cut), private individuals would determine how the additional funds would be spent; in the second, additional spending would be for governmentally determined purposes. From a "free-enterprise" perspective, the first alternative is more conservative because it involves less direct intervention by government in the economy. It will thus probably be more acceptable to economic conservatives, although some still may oppose it because of the resulting deficit, since deficits tend to violate their concept of "sound" public finance. Those who see a need for more government spending for public works and facilities will be inclined to favor the increased spending route. Ideological differences may therefore lead to conflict here.

At the urging of the Kennedy-Johnson administration, Congress passed the Revenue Act of 1964 to stimulate aggregate demand and thereby create more jobs and economic growth by cutting taxes. The act provided for an $11.5 billion reduction in personal and corporate income taxes over a period of two years. It was accompanied by only a modest decrease in government spending; the result was an estimated budget deficit of $5 billion for fiscal 1965. The 1964 tax cut was unique in that this was the first time an administration had planned a tax cut to stimulate employment and economic growth during a period of economic expansion. The use of more conservative approach of cutting taxes rather than increased spending to achieve a deficit, plus some gestures toward "fiscal frugality" by President Johnson, undoubtedly facilitated passage of the fiscal proposals.

In June, 1965, Congress passed another tax cut law, this time providing for a $4.6 billion reduction of federal excise taxes on a wide variety of consumer goods. Over a four-year period most sales or excise taxes will be eliminated except those on tobacco products and alcoholic beverages and those levied to finance highway and airport construction (e.g., taxes on gasoline and air travel tickets) or to regulate gambling and narcotics traffic. In January, 1965, the Johnson administration had announced that later in the year it would propose a reduction in federal excise taxes. This decision was prompted by business appeals for changes in the excise tax structure and growing Congressional responsiveness to these pleas. The administration had been hard put to prevent Congress from attaching a big excise tax cut to the 1964 income tax reduction bill. In May, 1965, when President Johnson submitted his tax cut proposal other factors had contributed to its shape. These were the desires to offset the "drag" on the economy from a planned increase of several

115

billion dollars in Social Security taxes and to help maintain the existing period of business expansion, then in its fifty-first month and in danger of dying of old age. Tax cuts are now more than simply tax cuts. They have become basic instruments of national economic policy, designed to alter the course of business activity or to keep it on a desired course from which it might otherwise depart.[13]

Economic Stability Policy: Some Limitations

It is generally accepted that fiscal and monetary policies can go far in controlling fluctuations in the business cycle and in encouraging economic growth. Nonetheless, they are not without limitations or defects of an economic nature. These must be taken into consideration by policy makers if the solutions they devise for instability problems are to be most effective.

A major problem in economic stability policy is the difficulty in accurately analyzing and predicting trends in the economy. Although the tools of economic analysis have been greatly improved in recent years, precise indicators of changes in the flow of national income are still lacking. This is the result of such factors as the complexity of our economic system and shortcomings in statistical data. Some sectors or industries in the economy may be prospering while others are in stagnation or decline. Relationships between elements in the economy, as between the levels of consumer income and spending, may be changing. Some economic data may be available only at quarterly, yearly, or longer intervals. Several months may elapse before analysts can say with certainty that a boom is ended or that recovery is under way. Proper choice and timing of stability policies are necessary if they are to be most effective, but such decisions must be made on less than full information, leaving room for error. Too, in the absence of clear-cut indicators of future trends in the economy, officials tend to "wait and see," to let matters work themselves out. Uncertainty may produce inaction here as it often does elsewhere.

Another related problem is limited knowledge of the full impact of particular policies. It is not known, for example, how much stabilizing action results from the operation of the automatic stabilizers. It is consequently difficult to know when and to what extent to make use of discretionary stability policies. Nor can it be said with certainty what effect a given fiscal or monetary action will have on, say, consumer

[13] See *The New York Times,* May 16, 1965, pp. Fl, 12; and President Johnson's message on excise tax reduction, *The New York Times,* May 18, 1965, p. 26.

spending. Problems of this sort are most important when moderate economic fluctuations are in question. In a severe recession or inflation, there is less immediate need to be precise in the timing and degree of stabilizing action. What is most needed is strong counteraction until a measure of stability has been achieved.

Both monetary and fiscal policy are inadequate for dealing with inflation caused by a wage-price spiral. In such a situation prices and wages are not simply the result of interaction of supply and demand. Rather a price increase leads to a wage increase, and a wage increase to another price increase, and so on upward because large corporations and unions possessing substantial economic power are able to "administer," i.e., set, prices and wages. Monetary and fiscal policies, as we have seen, work by producing changes in aggregate demand. But administered prices and wages may move upward even when demand is less than supply or is falling, as steel prices did in the 1950's. To control inflation caused by a price-wage spiral, or by administered prices, might require fiscal and monetary policies so restrictive as to touch off a recessionary movement before they affected the groups causing the wage-price spiral. In this case, fiscal and monetary policies are too blunt in their impact to be effective. Other courses of action are possible,[14] as President Kennedy demonstrated with respect to the proposed steel price increase in 1962. His sharp criticism of the proposed price increase, which he regarded as inflationary, led to its withdrawal by the steel companies without resort to legal action. The power of corporations to administer prices may also reduce the effectiveness of fiscal policy in combating recession. During the depression of the 1930's some of the impact of New Deal deficit spending to stimulate the economy was siphoned off into price increases rather than additional employment.

Both fiscal and monetary policy have shortcomings when unemployment or economic decline is concentrated in particular industries or geographical areas. Here a broad fiscal and/or monetary program to increase aggregate demand may lead to inflationary effects before the expansionary program produces much benefit for the distressed industries or areas. Fiscal and monetary policies are again too broad in their impact; the need is for more precise instruments. An example is the Area Redevelopment Act of 1961, which was directed to the needs of communities and regions having unemployment problems. The act

[14] For a discussion of possibilities and problems of government action to combat wage-price spirals (or cost-push inflation) see Emmette S. Redford, *Potential Public Policies to Deal with Inflation Caused by Market Power*, Study Paper No. 10, prepared for the Joint Economic Committee, 86th Cong., 1st Sess. (1959).

provided funds for business loans, urban renewal, and community facilities to provide an economic stimulus for particular distressed areas. Another example, broad in range but intended to deal with particular problems, is the "War on Poverty" launched by the Johnson administration in 1964.

By itself, monetary policy appears ineffective in initiating recovery from severe economic depression, as during the 1930's. Lowering interest rates and expanding the available supply of credit are not sufficient by themselves to stimulate increased borrowing and investment. If potential investors have a pessimistic view of future economic conditions, as they did in the 1930's, cheaper and easier credit is unlikely to be sufficient to induce them to borrow and invest. Nor are statements to the effect that "prosperity is just around the corner" likely to be sufficient to cause people to take an optimistic view of future economic conditions. Positive and effective action, to provide an "objective" basis for favorable future expectations, would seem to be required.

To digress for a moment, it is well to keep in mind that stability policy, like all economic policy, is concerned with influencing human behavior. Economic theory holds that, other things being equal, people will be influenced in borrowing and investing by the rate of interest. Among the "other things," however, are the psychological attitudes and expectations of people (and these are not always "equal"). If these include a pessimistic evaluation of the economic future, they may well overweigh such material factors as lower interest rates in individual decision making. Here, as elsewhere in social life, individuals do make a difference, and they cannot be assumed to act always as the "economic man" of classical economics.

The use of monetary policy to combat inflation may also have some unintended effects. Restrictions on credit may bear down more heavily on small businesses than on large businesses. When the Federal Reserve Board tightens credit, commercial banks are apt to restrict credit first to small businesses because of the larger risk in such lending. Further, large corporations may meet their financial needs out of retained earnings and depreciation reserves. Or they may have access to such sources of credit as insurance companies, pension trusts, and investment banks, which are beyond the reach of the FRB. Monetary policy, in its actual impact, is somewhat less impartial than its proponents sometimes contend.[15] Supporters of small business have criticized monetary policy on this ground.

[15] John Kenneth Galbraith, *The Affluent Society* (Boston: Houghton Mifflin, 1958), 226–238.

Fiscal policy, by itself, is unlikely to be adequate for preventing inflation. Thus, budget surpluses in 1947 and 1948 did not prevent inflationary price movements. One reason was that, at the same time, the FRB was following an expansionary credit policy which made money easy to borrow, thus offsetting the contractionary effect of budget surpluses.

Politics and Stability Policy

The formation and implementation of stability policy is not a mere "technical" task performed in a vacuum. Rather, it occurs in a highly political environment populated with individuals and groups, official and unofficial, having conflicting values, expectations, and interests concerning desirable stability policy. Conflict and struggle take place over what means to use, to what extent, and at what time. Is there a need for positive action? Should monetary or fiscal policy be stressed? Should a budget deficit be achieved by increasing spending or cutting taxes? These are some questions which may arise. What is done in the way of policy action will be affected by the structure of our governmental system, our political processes, and political behavior.

Turning first to governmental structure, the semi-independence of the state and local governments in our federal system may hamper the efforts of the national government to maintain economic stability.[16] Although government spending is an important countercyclical instrument, the national government has little control over the spending activities of state and local governments. State and local revenues and spending tend to fluctuate with changes in the business cycle, increasing in good times and decreasing in bad times—the reverse of what should occur according to the dictates of countercyclical policy. This tendency is reinforced by the legal limitations imposed on deficit spending by many state and local governments. Consequently, national policy to maintain stability may be partially offset by contradictory state and local action based on a different conception of "proper" public policy. In an earlier chapter it was noted that the stimulative effect of deficit spending by the national government during the 1930's was reduced by retrenchment in spending at the state level.

If larger national expenditures are used to counter recession or stagnation in the economy the way in which they are used can affect the structure of the federal system. Channeling them through the state and

[16] Fainsod, *op. cit.,* 814–817. The ensuing discussion draws in part on this source.

local governments, via grant-in-aid programs, will strengthen those levels of government. Conversely, the power of the national government will be increased if the expenditures are used for exclusively national programs. The scene is thus set for conflict between proponents of national interests and state and local interests as to where and how additional funds should be expended by the national government.

The formation and implementation of stability policy is also affected by the separation of powers, especially when fiscal action is involved. Authority over taxation and expenditures is divided between the President and Congress. The traditional rivalry between the two branches is here intensified by the zealousness of Congress in protecting its financial powers against "executive encroachment." It may be further intensified by divided party control of the two branches. To be most effective for countercyclical purposes, broad flexibility in the use of taxation and expenditures would be required. A proposal in this direction was made by President Kennedy in 1962 when he recommended that the President be given authority "to make temporary countercyclical adjustments in the first bracket rate of the personal income tax." This proposal, which would have required Congress to surrender some of its authority over taxes, was never seriously considered. Though the development of the executive budget has strengthened the ability of the President to plan expenditures for stabilization purposes, the need to gain Congressional approval remains.

One consequence of Congressional consideration of stability proposals is delay. More than a year elapsed before the tax cut proposed by President Kennedy was enacted into law as the Revenue Act of 1964. Another consequence of Congressional consideration is that the influence of group and sectional pressures, operating through Congress, will be fully felt on stability proposals. Here it should be noted that every fiscal policy measure, because it involves taxes or expenditures, will have other policy implications. It will affect not only the over-all operation of the economy but also the interests and well-being of particular groups and individuals. Pressure groups can generally be counted upon to resist changes in taxes and expenditures which they consider adverse to their interests, especially if changes come in the form of increased taxes or reduced expenditures. In general, group pressures make it more difficult to counteract inflation than deflation. But if we assume that taxes are to be cut to stimulate the economy, there remains the question of *whose* taxes are going to be cut—those of individuals or businesses, high or low income groups, etc.? Or, assuming that expenditures will be increased, how will they be used? For military, welfare, or general government spending? For public works? For aid to distressed areas? In any case, various groups and interests will struggle for preferment. Congressional action on stability measures will reflect compromises and adjustments of the demands of conflicting group, sectional, and local interests as well as the requirements of stability policy.

The general policy commitments of the political parties is another factor which may affect stability policy. Though it is often said that the parties differ little, if any, on policy matters, there is significant evidence to the contrary, especially when party leaders are concerned.[17] It seems fair to differentiate the parties in this way: The Republican Party is more concerned with preventing inflation and maintaining a "sound dollar." They favor the use of monetary policy over fiscal policy and are decidedly opposed to direct controls. The Democratic Party is more concerned with combating recession and stagnation and with maintaining a high level of employment. They favor the use of fiscal policy over monetary policy and want stronger Presidential control over the Federal Reserve Board. The Republican Party strongly supports the independence of the FRB as, not surprisingly, does the Board itself. (Since the early 1950's the FRB has been especially concerned with preventing inflation.) What we have depicted here, it must be emphasized, are tendencies rather than hard-and-fast differences. Professor Seymour Harris offers the following comment on these tendencies:

> Though this is no black and white matter, Democrats tend to stress fiscal policy more and monetary policy less; the [Republican] administration, monetary policy more and fiscal policy less. In part, this difference of emphasis is based on the theory that fiscal policy means Government activity and intervention through debt policy, through variations of the amount and structure of taxes and expenditures. Hence Republicans tend to look with disfavor on the use of these weapons. They prefer monetary policy because to them this reflects the operations of the free market.[18]

These tendencies are revealed in the different approaches to stability policy followed by the Eisenhower and Kennedy administrations.

[17] See Herbert McClosky, Paul J. Hoffman, and Rosemary O'Hara, "Issue Conflict and Consensus Among Party Leaders and Followers," *American Political Science Review*, LIV (June, 1960), 406–427.
[18] *Hearings on the January, 1957 Economic Report of the President,* Joint Committee on the Economic Report, 85th Cong., 1st Sess (1957), 484.

Concern over balanced budgets has acted as a restraint on the use of fiscal policy. Despite the wide acceptance of Keynesian economics and experience with unbalanced budgets, apparently there is still strong sentiment for a balanced budget. To conservatives in either political party, budget deficits are a symbol of greater government intervention in the economy. There is also a persistent belief that governments, like families, cannot wisely spend beyond their means. In 1963, the "average voter" apparently was more interested in a balanced budget than a tax cut. Dr. Walter W. Heller, chairman of the President's Council of Economic Advisers, characterized this as a "quite remarkable" manifestation of "the basic Puritan ethic of the American people."[19] To counteract this attitude, President Kennedy agreed to hold down spending, although liberal Democrats had wanted increased spending plus a tax cut. The same tack was followed by President Johnson after his succession to the Presidency.

The President may be limited in his ability to propose or take countercyclical actions by policy positions taken publicly at some earlier time. In 1953–1954 it would have been politically difficult for the Eisenhower administration, which came into office pledged to reduce spending and balance the budget, to recommend increased spending as a countercyclical measure (apart from Republican disfavor of fiscal policy). Again, it would have been difficult for President Kennedy, in the spring of 1961, to propose a tax cut as a counter-recessionary measure. One of his early advisers, Professor Paul A. Samuelson, later commented: "whatever the economic merits of the tax cut, it seemed politically out of the question. The President had run on a platform that asked sacrifices of the American people. How then could he begin by giving them what many would regard as a 'handout'?"[20] President Kennedy later did propose a tax cut, which indicates that political commitments, like professions of affection, do not necessarily last forever.

Government action to maintain economic stability is now generally accepted, and expected. The President and party who fail to take effective action to deal with severe economic fluctuations are likely to receive harsh treatment at the polls, as the election of 1932 illustrates. Currently it appears unlikely that either party would fail to take action. The monetary and fiscal means at the disposal of the government, make remote the chance that either severe depression or runaway in-

[19] *The New York Times*, Sept. 22, 1963, p. 4E.
[20] Paul A. Samuelson, "Economic Policy for 1962," *Review of Economics and Statistics,* XLI (February, 1962), 3.

flation will develop. But when inflation and recession, especially the former, are "mild," there will undoubtedly continue to be considerable disagreement as to what discretionary action, if any, should be taken by the government.

THE BUDGETARY PROCESS

Prior to 1921, the President had little control over the expenditures of the various executive departments and agencies. The federal budget was prepared by the Treasury Department, which was merely authorized to receive, index, print, and transmit agency requests to Congress. There was no attempt to eliminate overlap, duplication, or extravagance in agency requests. In Congress a number of committees acted on appropriations requests in an uncoordinated manner. Little effort was made to balance expenditures with revenues (in the latter part of the nineteenth century, the government was often confronted with the need to dispose of surplus revenues), or to compare the relative merits of different appropriations. The situation was indeed fragmented and chaotic. Even had there been the desire to do so, the budget could not have been used as a fiscal policy instrument.

Change came with the Budget and Accounting Act of 1921, which authorized an executive budget system. The Act provided that the President should prepare and submit to Congress an annual budget covering the various agencies for its guidance in making decisions on expenditures and taxes. The Bureau of the Budget, initially located in the Treasury Department and now in the Executive Office of the President, was established to assist the President in discharging his responsibility. The Bureau has authority to "assemble, correlate, revise, reduce, or increase the estimates of the several departments and establishments" (including government corporations). The Act also created a General Accounting Office, which acts as "arm of Congress" in auditing agency expenditures.

The executive budget system today is regarded as an instrument essential to policy development and execution and to responsible financial administration. In support of the executive budget, Professor Mosher has written:

> It is the only device invented in democratic governments [for policy development] *which does, or can do*, all of the following things: (1) Bring about a regular, periodic reconsideration and reevaluation of government purposes and objectives; (2) Facilitate a comparative

valuation of different programs and purposes in relation to each other and in relation to their total costs; (3) Provide a basis for examining the total role of government and its cost in relation to the private sector of the economy, and thus for tailoring the governmental program to the society and the economy as a whole; (4) Provide a periodic link among the administrative organizations, the Executive, Congress, and segments of the public, and thus an important basis of information and discussion and of democratic control of governmental activities.[21]

The budget submitted by the President to Congress in January of each year is for a single fiscal year, extending from July 1 of the year in which the budget is submitted to June 30 of the following year. The period from July 1, 1965 to June 30, 1966 is known as fiscal year 1966 since it takes its name from the calendar year in which it ends. Although the budget is for a twelve-month period, the total budgetary process, from the time work on the budget begins in the executive branch to the end of the fiscal year, covers a span of more than two years.

The total national budgetary process can be divided into four stages.

(1) PREPARATION OF THE BUDGET. This is handled by the executive branch, under the direction of the President and the Bureau of the Budget.

(2) AUTHORIZATION OF THE BUDGET. This is the responsibility of Congress. The Constitution provides that "no money shall be drawn from the Treasury, except in consequence of appropriations made by law."

(3) EXECUTION OF THE BUDGET. This stage involves the actual expenditure of money appropriated by Congress. Control here is mainly with the executive branch.

(4) THE AUDIT. The General Accounting Office, which is responsible to Congress, performs this activity. The ensuing discussion of the budgetary process will emphasize its meaning and implications for economic policy.[22]

[21] Frederick C. Mosher, *Program Budgeting: Theory and Practice* (Chicago: Public Administration Service, 1954), 5–6. My italics.

[22] Much more extensive discussions of the budgetary process can be found in Arthur Smithies, *The Budgetary Process in the United States* (New York: McGraw-Hill, 1955); and Jesse Burkhead, *Government Budgeting* (New York: John Wiley and Sons, 1956). Some of the political aspects of budgeting are well discussed in Aaron Wildavsky, *The Politics of the Budgetary Process* (Boston: Little, Brown, 1964); and Robert Ash Wallace, *Congressional Control of Federal Spending* (Detroit: Wayne State University Press, 1960).

The President and the Bureau of the Budget have the major roles in preparing the budget. The latter is in charge of day-to-day activity. Other participants in budgetary planning may include the Treasury and Commerce departments, the Cabinet, the Council of Economic Advisers, and the Federal Reserve Board. These provide advice and information (not always in harmony) on such matters as future revenues, the state of the economy, and policy and political implications of the budget. Basic decisions on budgetary policy are made by the President. Included here are decisions on such fiscal policy issues as the total size of the budget, the balance between civil and military expenditures, whether the budget will be balanced, the size of the surplus or deficit, and whether spending in excess of revenues will be financed by borrowing or additional taxes.

Although the Bureau of the Budget is in charge of budget preparation, it also serves as an important means for continuing Presidential control and direction of the policy activities of the departments and agencies. Additionally, it is concerned with achieving economy and efficiency in government. The Bureau is organized into several offices and divisions for the performance of its various duties. The Office of Budget Review coordinates the preparation of the budget and also exercises control over agency spending once funds are appropriated by Congress. The Office of Legislative Reference functions as a "clearing house" for agency proposals for legislation and executive requests to ensure their conformity with "the program of the President."[23] Studies and other activities to improve agency and government-wide organization and management practices and procedures are undertaken by the Office of Management and Organization. The Office of Statistical Standards supervises and coordinates federal statistical services and activities. The Office of Accounting works with other government agencies to improve their financial management practices and procedures. The Bureau also includes a number of divisions: Commerce and Finance, International, Labor and Welfare, Military, and Resources and Works. Each of these divisions is concerned with the budget requests, spending practices, and general operation of the agencies within its own program area.

[23] On this matter, see Richard E. Neustadt, "Presidency and Legislation: The Growth of Central Clearance," *American Political Science Review*, XLVIII (September, 1954), 641–671.

The Bureau of the Budget and the executive branch began work on the budget early in the year preceding the January in which it is submitted to Congress. Budgetary planning begins in March at the chief executive's level and probably prior to then down in the departments and agencies.[24] In May or June general budgetary policy is developed by the Bureau and the President. By the end of June tentative budget ceilings are formulated and transmitted to the agencies, along with a call for agency estimates and a policy letter setting forth the major assumptions governing the proposed budget. On the basis of the tentative ceilings the agencies prepare and submit detailed budget requests to the Bureau by the middle of September. From then until the end of November agency requests are reviewed by Bureau examiners and hearings are held at which the agencies justify their requests (which may exceed the tentative ceilings). On the basis of these reviews and hearings Bureau officials make recommendations to the Director of the Bureau. He then reviews the recommendations and may modify them. Finally, agencies which are dissatisfied with Bureau action on their requests, and which have access to the President (such as the Defense Department), may appeal to him to restore cuts from their requests made by the Bureau. Or he may make further cuts in the budget, in the fashion of President Johnson. Early in January the budget, along with the President's annual budget message, is delivered to Congress.

The budget presented by the President to Congress represents a temporary balance between two different but related sets of conflicting forces. First, there are forces for and against spending. There is internal pressure within the executive branch from agencies, usually supported by external pressure groups, for larger appropriations. Agency officials often believe they need more funds for their agencies to perform effectively or for the expansion of their programs. Pressure for more spending may also come from Congress. In the fall of 1960 some liberal Democratic congressmen wanted the administration to propose larger expenditures to combat unemployment and related problems. Bureau of the Budget officials may oppose increased spending in order to promote economy. They are sometimes depicted as having an "economizing orientation."[25] The President may favor less spending in order to reduce the total size of the budget to make it more acceptable to Congress and the public; or reduced spending may be in line with his "political philosophy." President Johnson reduced the size of the budget

---

[24] The dates listed are approximate. The time schedule may vary from year to year and from one department to another.

[25] Burkhead, *op. cit.,* 301, and sources cited there.

he submitted to Congress in 1964 to gain support from conservative Congressmen for a proposed tax cut. And, in his early years in office, President Johnson made $100 billion his personal limit on the size of the budget, apparently believing there would be adverse political reactions if it went beyond this sum.

Second, the President's budget represents a balance between conflicting expenditure groups within the executive branch. Although the national budget is of vast size, funds are still not sufficient for every agency to get all the money it would like. Consequently, within the limits set by the total budget figure, the needs and interests of different agencies must be weighed, balanced, and decided upon. Awareness of the relative political strength of the agencies is one of the factors affecting such budgetary decisions. Agencies having strong public or pressure group support for their programs and policies are likely to fare better than agencies lacking such support. The policy views of the President will also be a factor, as will those of Budget Bureau officials. One President may favor more defense spending, another more welfare spending.[26]

The discretion of the President and budgetary officials in deciding on the budget is limited by the fact that many expenditures are relatively "uncontrollable," at least in the short run. They represent continuing obligations or commitments—examples are appropriations for interest on the national debt, veteran's benefits, grant-in-aid payments to the states, and agricultural price supports. Further, as long as our present commitments for national defense remain, major changes in defense expenditures (especially downward) are foreclosed. These items account for a substantial portion of the total budget. Moreover, and generally, the government's various policy commitments represent responses to political and economic pressures and interests. As long as the group or groups favoring a policy continue to support it, budget decision makers in both the executive and legislative branches are unlikely to make any drastic changes in the appropriations required for implementation of the policy.

Congressional Authorization

The budget comes to Congress in the form of a comprehensive statement of recommended expenditures, but it is considered by Congress in piecemeal fashion. For purposes of Congressional enactment the budget is usually divided into fourteen or fifteen appropriations bills, which are passed one at a time over a period of several months. At no

[26] See Wildavsky, *op. cit.,* 35–47.

place in Congress is there any real consideration of the budget as a whole. Nor is there any joint consideration of it by the House and Senate appropriations and revenue committees. The Legislative Reorganization Act of 1946 provided that these four committees meet jointly and set ceilings on appropriations to guide Congress in considering the budget. This was tried once and abandoned, as was the attempt to enact a single comprehensive (or "omnibus") appropriations bill. Traditional and accepted patterns of action have prevailed.

By custom, consideration of the budget begins in the House. There it is referred to the Appropriations Committee, which is divided into a number of subcommittees (agriculture, foreign aid, public works, etc.). Each subcommittee handles one or two of the appropriations bills. Hearings are held at which agency officials (who have the main burden of defending agency requests), pressure group representatives, individual citizens, and others may present testimony and answer questions. Following the hearings, the subcommittee meets in executive session to determine its recommendations to the full Appropriations Committee. These are customarily accepted by the full committee with little or no change, and its recommendations in turn are usually accepted by the House with few if any amendments and often little debate.[27] (Foreign aid appropriations have been a significant exception.) Subcommittee dominance in the Congressional authorization process stems from tradition, Congressional deference to the knowledge and expertness of the subcommittees, and the lack of time and information on the part of individual Congressmen.

Once passed by the House, appropriations bills move on to the Senate. Consideration there begins with a subcommittee of the Senate Appropriations Committee and proceeds in much the same fashion as in the House. The Senate, however, tends to act as an appellate body to which agencies can appeal for restoration of cuts made in their requests by the House (which often reduces agency requests for larger appropriations than they currently have). The Senate usually responds positively to such pleas, restoring at least part of the House cuts. Possibly the longer terms of office of Senators, and the fact that urban interests favoring increased spending for some purposes are better represented in the Senate, are among the factors making the Senate more liberal on spending.

Differences in the House and Senate versions of an appropriations bill are resolved by a conference committee. The compromise reached by this means, and then accepted by the two houses, will be somewhere between the extremes in the original House and Senate bills. The sum

[27] *Ibid.*, 54–55.

authorized by Congress is usually close to the figure initially recommended by the President in his budget.

In its consideration of budget requests, Congress is motivated by two conflicting desires. As a whole, Congress is economy-minded and much is said about the need for greater economy and reduced spending by the government. At the same time, individual Congressmen are sensitive to pressures and demands for spending emanating from their states or districts, or from particular groups and interests to whom they are sympathetic or responsive. The resultant conflicting attitudes are well illustrated by the perceptions of the tasks of the House Appropriations Committee held by its members. There is a consensus among the committee members that their tasks include guarding the Federal Treasury against ill-advised expenditures and, relatedly, cutting whatever budget estimates are submitted because agencies nearly always ask for more funds than they need. But no committee member "is expected to commit electoral suicide" by being unresponsive to demands of benefit to interests in his district.[28] Taking Congress as a whole, the general desire for economy tends to break down in the face of a multitude of particular pressures for increased spending. It is noteworthy that the only two bills enacted by Congress over President Eisenhower's veto involved the spending of money: the authorization of a pay raise for postal workers and an appropriation bill for rivers and harbors projects. Both are traditional "vote-getters."

It should be emphasized that the initiative in the budgetary process rests with the chief executive, partly because of the greater sources of information available to him. Congressional committees in turn are handicapped by a lack of information sufficient to "provide them with a reasonable basis for differing from the President on major items."[29] In our society there is a general cultural expectation that decision makers will act "rationally"—on the basis of facts and knowledge of alternatives and their consequences. Those with the best sources of information are therefore in a stronger position. But beyond this, the budget is prepared with possible Congressional reactions in mind.

Congress retains ultimate constitutional authority over appropriations, but its influence is felt primarily on particular items and not on the over-all size of the budget. The requests of some agencies may be reduced, perhaps substantially, but a 5 per cent cut in the total budget, even by a hostile Congress, is the exception rather than the rule.[30]

[28] Richard F. Fenno, Jr., "The House Appropriations Committee as a Political System: The Problem of Integration," *American Political Science Review,* LVI (June, 1962), 310–324.

[29] Smithies, *op. cit.,* 141.

[30] *Ibid.,* 140.

129

Execution of the Budget

The departments and agencies are not free to spend as they see fit, within the framework of appropriations legislation, once Congress has acted. Formerly, an appropriation was held to be not merely an authorization but an imperative order to the executive to expend the funds provided. The newer concept, which leaves more to executive discretion, is that appropriated funds will be spent only if necessary. Thus, Presidents Truman and Eisenhower refused to spend money for the Air Force and the Marine Corps, respectively, which they had not requested from Congress. Irritating though this was to some members of Congress, there was little they could do about it. It is quite improbable, however, that a President would refuse to expend funds needed to carry on an established and accepted program because of the political repercussions such an act would set off. Imagine the reaction if a President refused to spend funds appropriated for veterans benefits or farm price supports.

Controls over spending are also exercised by the Bureau of the Budget. The principal means of Bureau control is apportionment. After appropriations bills become law, each agency develops a spending program on the basis of funds available and submits it to the Bureau for approval and authorization of quarterly apportionments. The Bureau's apportionment provides that an agency can spend no more than a specific amount of its funds in any quarter of the fiscal year. This limitation is intended in part to prevent agencies from running out of money and then having to request "deficiency appropriations" from Congress or else curtail their operations. The Bureau may also require agencies to set aside reserves, perhaps 5 per cent of their appropriations, for use in emergencies or for economizing or budget balancing.

Congress is not content merely to make funds available to agencies, but attempts to influence or control spending in a number of ways. Detailed appropriations bills limiting the discretion of agency officials may be enacted. Or some specific directives or prohibitions may be written into appropriations laws. The following restriction, which was also an expression of policy, appeared in the Interior Department Appropriation Act for 1952:

> *Provided further,* That no part of this or prior appropriations shall be used for construction, nor for further commitments to construction of Moorhead Dam and Reservoir, Montana, or any feature thereof

until a definite plan thereon has been completed, reviewed by the States of Montana and Wyoming, and approved by the Congress.[31]

Less formally, hearings and committee reports may be used as media for exerting control. Agreements may be made between agency officials and subcommittee members during hearings as to how funds will be used. Committee reports which accompany appropriations bills often contain suggestions and directives which administrators are expected to follow, even though they are not law as such. Agencies neglect such agreements or directives at their own peril. Agency officials may be criticized or rebuked when subcommittee hearings are held in the following year or, more seriously, the agencies' funds may be cut.[32] By such means Congress strives to influence agency spending and policy. But the attempt to influence comes primarily not from Congress as a whole but from individual Congressmen and groups of Congressmen.

The Audit

The audit stage of the budgetary process as discussed here involves review of agency expenditures after they are made (often called a post-audit). This audit is performed by the General Accounting Office, headed by the Comptroller General. He is appointed by the President, with the consent of the Senate, for a fifteen-year term and can be removed only upon a joint resolution of Congress. The agency continually stresses that it is an "arm of Congress."

The GAO conducts spot-checks and investigations of agency expenditures to determine whether waste, extravagance, or illegality were involved. It reports its findings and makes recommendations thereon to Congress or to particular committees, which then decide what use to make of the information presented. The GAO may also exhort agencies and departments to mend their ways and improve their spending practices and procedures.

The Budget and Economic Policy

The national budget is much more than a financial statement—a statement of estimated receipts and proposed expenditures, as one definition has it. As proposed and adopted, the budget is also a policy statement

[31] Quoted in Roland Young, *The American Congress* (New York: Harper & Row, 1958), 230.
[32] Arthur W. Macmahon, "Congressional Oversight of Administration: The Power of the Purse," *Political Science Quarterly*, LVIII (June, 1943), 380–414.

131

or, more precisely, a statement of the various policies which will be pursued by the government during the budget year. (And beyond. Agencies are often authorized to incur "obligations" in pursuance of policies that will be paid in future years.) It has been well described as "a compilation of public policy decisions of great complexity and of far-reaching effect upon the national welfare in terms of total outlay, in terms of the . . . allocation of that outlay among various activities, and in terms of the amount available for any one particular endeavor."[33] The policy nature of the budget has become more evident in recent years with the growing emphasis upon program budgeting. The program budget stresses the purposes for which funds will be used—soil conservation, antitrust enforcement, agricultural research—rather than specific objects of expenditure like automobiles, office equipment, pencils, and paper.

The budget conveys a picture of the government's total policy program for the year. It will provide answers, not necessarily satisfactory, for such policy issues as the balance between public (federal) and private spending, the balance between military and civilian spending, more or less welfare spending, more or fewer public works programs, more or less antitrust and other regulatory enforcement activity. The budgetary process, by which the budget is formulated and adopted, is thus a means for making choices among competing social values and allocating resources to achieve them. It is a highly political process.

It is important to realize that the total impact of national government spending is not revealed by the "administrative" budget which the President submits annually to Congress. Many billions of dollars of funds spent by government agencies—now more than $30 billion annually—are not included in the administrative budget. They are instead drawn from separate trust funds, with by far the largest expenditures coming from the Old Age, Survivors, and Disability Insurance Trust Fund. Administrative budget and trust fund expenditures together comprise the "cash" budget of the national government. It is the cash budget which reveals most fully the total volume of national revenues and expenditures and, thus, their total fiscal impact on the economy.

Leaving fiscal policy aside, the importance of public economic policies cannot be measured solely by the money expended in their support. For example, expenditures for veteran's benefits are now more than $5 billion a year, whereas no money is appropriated in the budget for the Federal Reserve Board. The earnings of the Federal Reserve Banks

[33] John D. Millett, *Government and Public Administration* (New York: McGraw-Hill, 1959), 358.

more than pay the operating costs of the entire Federal Reserve System. But surely the impact and long-range effects on the economy of FRB monetary policy are greater than those of veteran's benefit programs.

However, the nature and effectiveness of public economic policies do depend in an essential way upon the amount of funds appropriated to carry them out. Antitrust policy will serve as an example. What is done in the way of antitrust enforcement, and consequently the substance of antitrust policy, will depend significantly upon funds provided for the Antitrust Division to hire lawyers, investigators, clerical help, and to meet other expenses. The more funds the Antitrust Division has the more vigorous it can be in uncovering and prosecuting antitrust violations. Its interpretation of the antitrust laws will probably be more liberal because it will be better able to prosecute cases that are doubtful, marginal, or difficult to prove. In short, whether antitrust policy is lax or vigorous, broad or narrow in scope, will be affected by appropriations.

Conflicts between the President and Congress, or more accurately, between particular agencies and appropriations subcommittees, over the amount of funds to be appropriated are in reality often conflicts over policy. An agency whose policy activities have aroused the antagonism of strong economic interests and their Congressional supporters may find itself the "victim" of an appropriations cut. In the late 1940's control of the public grazing lands in the West by the Grazing Service and its successor was greatly reduced in effectiveness by an appropriations cut.[34] This was not a simple "economy" move but part of the campaign of western livestockmen and their Congressional supporters to reduce or eliminate regulation of the public range, which they obviously did not like. Conversely, agencies carrying on programs that are well supported, or that are popular with some of the Congressmen, may find Congress willing to grant more funds than they have requested.

The budget and the process by which it is adopted thus provide the President and Congress with an opportunity to review periodically the various economic policies and programs of the government (with the exception of those financed outside the administrative budget). All the policies and programs of all the agencies, however, are not considered in detail every year. The attention of Congress is exercised somewhat selectively. In any particular year intensive consideration will be given primarily to policies and programs involving large in-

[34] Phillip O. Foss, *Politics and Grass* (Seattle: University of Washington Press, 1960), 171–193.

creases or decreases in requested appropriations and to those which for some other reason have aroused the interest of pressure groups, executive officials, or members of Congress. Over the course of a number of years most economic policies will be given relatively full consideration through this procedure.

In sum, the budget is a policy statement and the budgetary process a means by which conflicts over public economic policies can be adjusted or settled. Further, it is a means by which the President and Congress can control or influence the nature and direction of public economic policies as carried on by administrative agencies.

NATIONAL TAXATION AND THE TAXING PROCESS

The expenditures of governments in the United States have increased greatly in the twentieth century. In 1962 national, state, and local expenditures totaled $168.5 billion as compared to $2.5 billion in 1913. In the earlier year, approximately three-fourths of all government expenditures were accounted for by the state and local governments; now the national government accounts for about two-thirds of the total. Thus, all government spending has increased, but that of the national government has risen most spectacularly. The increase in government spending is the result of such factors as the high cost of national defense; the great expansion of welfare programs; growing expenditures for highways and education; and, especially at the state and local levels, increased spending for police and fire protection, health and sanitation, recreation, and other services and activities required by an increasingly urbanized population.

The growth in governmental services and functions has vastly increased the revenue needs of government. This is the broad causal force which has led to higher taxes and the constant quest for new sources of revenue, whether from taxation or otherwise. Although the most important source of government revenue is taxation, governments do derive a portion of their revenues from non-tax sources. For the national government these include the following: commercial receipts from government enterprises, such as the Post Office and electric power production facilities; the sale of public lands and property; fees for government services; fines and penalties; grants and gifts (a few people actually give money to the national government); and borrowing through the sale of bonds and securities. The following chart indicates some of the various revenue sources of the national, state, and local governments and the extent to which they rely on each.

GOVERNMENTAL REVENUE
BY SELECTED SOURCES, 1961*
(*billions of dollars*)

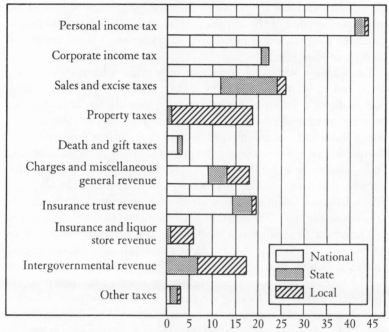

* *Statistical Abstract of the United States, 1963*, p. 417.

As the chart illustrates, there is a rough division of revenue sources among the three levels of government. The national government relies primarily on income taxes, the state governments on sales and excise taxes (which fall ultimately on the consumer), and local governments on property taxes. The national government still makes use of some excise taxes, and grants-in-aid are an important source of revenue for both state and local governments.

Nature and Objectives of Taxes

Taxes are compulsory levies or charges imposed on persons, according to some criterion such as income or property ownership, for the support of government. One has no choice when it comes to paying taxes. Taxes may also be viewed as a means of allocating the financial costs of government among individuals and groups within the community. That taxes serve this function does not necessarily make people any happier when the tax collector cometh. Few people like to pay taxes, Justice Holmes and his statement "I like to pay taxes. With them I buy civilization," notwithstanding. This is especially the case if people do not directly benefit from the activities financed by taxes or if they object to the performance of the activities themselves. Much political effort is expended by groups and individuals in trying to shift the burden of taxes to someone else.

Taxes take a variety of forms—income taxes, sales taxes, property taxes, poll taxes, inheritance taxes, customs duties. They can be classified as direct or indirect. Direct taxes fall directly on the persons or property taxed and provide little opportunity to shift the burden elsewhere. Indirect taxes are imposed at some stage of the production and distribution processes—taxes on the manufacture of alcoholic beverages and on sales are examples—and can readily be passed on to others, namely, consumers, in the final selling price. This twofold classification is based on the matter of *incidence:* on whom does the burden of taxation finally rest? The initial payee, or someone else?

The power of taxation is a multi-purpose instrument which can be and is put to a variety of uses. Most commonly and importantly, of course, it is used to raise revenue. But, in conjunction with the raising of revenue, and sometimes well apart from it, the power to tax has been utilized in achieving a number of other objectives. (For the use of taxation to maintain economic stability by affecting aggregate demand in the economy, see pp. 113–16). Several others may be analytically distinguished although in practice they overlap and blend together.

Taxation has long been used as a means of promoting the economic well-being of groups and industries. The protective tariff was initially designed to protect the development of "infant" industries and still remains as a way of protecting American businesses against some of the rigors of foreign competition. Although the tariff was once the main source of national revenue, this purpose is now clearly secondary to its protective aspect. Within the existing national tax structure favorable provisions serve to promote some companies or industries by reducing their taxes below the level paid by other enterprises. A good example is the depletion allowance given to many mining industries. Mining companies can make deductions from their gross income, ranging from 5 per cent for coal and sand to 27½ per cent for oil and gas before computing their taxes. This allowance has much reduced their tax liability, as compared to companies in other industries, under the corporate income tax.

Somewhat similarly, favorable tax provisions can be used to encourage certain kinds of investment. The exemption of interest on state and local government bonds from federal income taxation has made such bonds attractive to investors, especially those in high income brackets, even though such bonds carry lower rates of interest than do most other bonds.

Taxation is also often used for regulatory purposes—to restrict, control, or prohibit economic activity. State bank notes were taxed out of existence by a tax levied on them in the 1860's by the national government. The manufacture of matches using white phosphorus (a noxious substance) was purposely eliminated by the White Phosphorus Match Act of 1911. A tax on them made their cost higher than that of matches made with other materials. In 1949 Congress imposed a federal tax on persons engaged in the business of placing or accepting wagers. The purpose was not to raise revenue but to assist state and local governments in controlling illegal gambling (assuming that state and local officials desire to do so) by aiding in the disclosure of persons engaged in such activity.

Taxes have sometimes been levied, at least in part, to influence the buying habits of consumers. Those who regard the use of tobacco and alcoholic beverages as evil or immoral have sometimes urged that they be taxed at high rates so as to discourage their use, and, in fact, tobacco and liquor products are taxed at high rates in most states. The high taxes, however, have most likely come about because such taxes are good revenue producers, since demand for these products seems not to be much affected by higher prices caused by high taxes. Nonetheless, the fact that many people regard liquor and tobacco as evil, or undesirable, or as "luxuries," has made it easier to levy higher taxes on them. Think of the conflict that would be caused by a serious proposal to tax milk at the same rate as whiskey. Again, during World War II taxes were levied by the national government on telephone service and rail transportation to discourage their use by civilians. As often happens, these taxes remained as sources of revenue long after the end of the war.

Taxation may also be used to equalize or otherwise influence the distribution of income. The federal graduated income tax is supported by many people, and opposed by others, because of its supposed effect in reducing disparities between high and low income groups by taxing away larger portions of the income of the former. The income tax is a symbol of greater economic equality and thus produces ideological conflict between the proponents of greater and lesser equality. In actuality, it appears that less income equalization results from the income tax than is usually imagined. "Loopholes" in the tax laws often enable high-income groups to avoid paying the higher rates. Also, evasion of the tax occurs, as through the failure to report much taxable income from interest and dividend payments. The divergence here between symbol and reality illustrates the fact that it is what people perceive to be "real," rather than reality itself, that shapes their attitudes on policy issues.[35] Another example of taxation intended to influence income distribution is the excess profits tax placed on corporations during World War II. This tax was designed to prevent "profiteering" from the war effort through "abnormal" profits. Such action during wartime is normally viewed as unfair, inequitable, and unpatriotic.

The Formation of Tax Policy

The existing tax structure provides the framework within which conflict over tax policy occurs. Because of its direct impact on the economic interests and well-being of individuals and groups, tax policy is especially productive of political conflict. The conflict between individuals and groups, official and non-official, can be viewed analytically as having three principal sources:[36] conflicts between private interests, between differing conceptions of the public interest, and between differing economic analyses and beliefs concerning the impact of taxes and changes in tax policy. In practice it is difficult to separate these sources of conflict but, for analysis this conceptualization should be helpful in explaining and understanding tax conflict.

Conflicts among private interests, arising out of differences among people in wealth, income, expenditure patterns, and so on, are probably the most important source of controversy over taxes. The question of who will bear the burden of tax increases or derive the advantage of tax decreases is most frequently answered according to personal and group interests. Blough's examination of tax proposals made to Congress in 1942 and 1947 revealed that most individuals and groups made proposals on only one or a few specific points. Almost unani-

[35] See Murray Edleman, "Symbols and Political Quiescence," *American Political Science Review,* LIV (September, 1960), 695–705.
[36] The following discussion draws on Roy Blough, *The Federal Taxing Process* (Englewood Cliffs, N.J.: Prentice-Hall, 1952), 4–11.

mously they wanted a decrease, or at least not an increase, in their specific tax loads.[37] While most major interest groups favored President Kennedy's proposal in 1963 for tax reduction, each had its own view as to how the reduction should be distributed. Labor wanted more and quicker reductions for low-income persons than were proposed by the President. Business groups advocated larger cuts in the upper income brackets to "promote investment." Conflicts among private interests are likely to be more intense when incomes are falling than when they are rising because people are especially anxious to prevent declines in their standards of living and "status."

Conflicts on tax policy also arise out of differences over what will best promote the public interest. The "public interest" may be defined by persons or groups as what is best for their own material interests, but it will also be given broader, more universal definitions. We should not fall into the error of assuming that the individual is always motivated solely by direct, material interests. Thus some people may oppose a tax cut, even though they would personally benefit from it, because it might result in a (larger) budget deficit which they regard as contrary to the public interest. Others may support a tax cut, apart from their own interests, as in the public interest because it will promote economic growth or improve the economic position of low income groups. Many taxpayers in 1963 were apparently opposed to the Kennedy administration's tax cut proposal because it would mean only a few extra dollars in take-home pay and might lead to larger budget deficits. Consequently, the strategy of the administration in supporting the tax cut was "keyed more to the national interest than to the selfish interest of individual taxpayers." The tax cut was stressed as necessary to promote economic growth and employment and thus as in the national (or public) interest.

A third source of conflict is differences in economic analyses and beliefs—for example, differing opinions about who will actually bear the burden of a particular tax and what will be the future effect of the tax on economic activity. Such differences may arise from inadequate knowledge of taxes and tax policy and also because of imperfections in the tools of economic analysis. Economics is not an exact science and so does not yield absolute and conclusive answers for tax problems. Differences also may arise because people have different values. Two individuals with different sets of values may look at the same set of objective data and come away with decidedly different conclusions. They may agree that taxes should be anti-inflationary but disagree as

[37] *Ibid.*, 32–35.

to what taxes and tax rates will actually be anti-inflationary. Further, one may find analysts and observers who select only those data from the total available which support their preconceptions on, say, whether the graduated income tax reduces economic incentives.

Authoritative decisions on tax policy at the national level are made, under the Constitution, by the Congress and, to a lesser extent, the President. Congress can enact tax legislation over the President's veto but the President cannot secure changes in the tax laws (except as there is room for administrative interpretation) without the concurrence of Congress. Within Congress the primary centers of decision on tax matters are the House Ways and Means and the Senate Finance Committees. These committees, which tend to be moderate to conservative in their policy orientations, are among the most powerful, prestigious, and respected of the Congressional committees. Their power is enhanced by the complexity of the federal tax laws (the Tax Code) which has been described as "a remarkable essay in sustained obscurity."[38] The knowledge and understanding of the tax laws which the members of the revenue committees gain from specialization and continued experience in tax matters gives them a significant advantage over the rest of the members of Congress. Moreover, in the House major tax bills are considered under a closed rule which either prohibits all amendments or permits only those acceptable to the Ways and Means Committee, which, in practice, means its chairman.

The Constitution provides that tax bills shall originate in the House. The Senate, however, has complete freedom to make changes in tax bills sent to it by the House and it often does amend them. Senate amendments, however, frequently perish in the conference committee used to resolve differences in the House and Senate versions of a tax bill. In the tax bill which became the Revenue Act of 1964, the conference committee dropped seven principal provisions which had been passed by the Senate but not the House. Only three provisions passed by the House alone were dropped from the final bill.[39]

Recommendations and demands for changes in tax policy usually find their source outside of Congress, coming from the administration, organized interest groups, business companies, and individual taxpayers. Proposals for tax increases and tax reform, which often increase taxes for specific individuals or groups by eliminating or tightening loopholes, usually originate with the administration. Congress is much

[38] Louis Eisenstein, *The Ideologies of Taxation* (New York: The Ronald Press, 1961), 215.
[39] *Congressional Quarterly Weekly Report,* XXII (February 28, 1964), 388.

more willing to initiate tax decreases, acting in response to individual and group pressures. Though the President has the final word on the administration's tax proposals, the Treasury Department carries the major burden in formulating the proposed changes and in explaining and defending them before Congress. In its dealings with the tax committees the Treasury will, in effect, be one group among many seeking to influence the course of committee action and will come into conflict with private groups seeking to gain or preserve advantages for themselves. The Treasury is somewhat handicapped in this group struggle because, unlike other departments such as Labor and Agriculture, it does not have a well organized and responsive clientele from which it can draw support.

It is impossible for the administration in proposing tax reform to avoid arousing the antagonism of pressure groups. Behind practically every loophole in the tax laws there will be at least one interest group that benefits from it, that feels intensely about it, and that is ready to act to retain it. In 1962 the Kennedy administration proposed, in an effort to plug one loophole, the withholding of taxes on dividends and interest. Such income had long been subject to taxation but much of it had gone unreported. A massive letter-writing campaign against the proposal, stimulated by the U.S. Savings and Loan League (a trade association), is credited with its defeat in Congress.[40] Support for the proposal, outside the administration, was diffuse and inarticulate. Also, most of the reform proposals in the comprehensive tax program submitted to Congress by President Kennedy in 1963 failed of enactment into law because of group opposition to them. The Treasury was the principal voice for reform—a multitude of voices spoke against reform. For example, after the Secretary of the Treasury presented the administration's recommendations on the oil depletion allowance to the Ways and Means Committee, sixty-seven other witnesses were heard on the matter. All were opposed to reform affecting the depletion allowance. Congress took no action. The difficulty in obtaining tax reform has been explained by a reform-minded member of the Ways and Means Committee in this vein: "The average American doesn't mind other people having their own loopholes—he only cares about getting his. So you shouldn't blame Congress or the committees for what the American people don't want. If we don't vote tax reform, it's simply because there's no pressure for it."[41]

[40] Philip M. Stern, "The Slow, Quiet Murder of Tax Reform," *Harper's*, CCXXVII (December, 1963), 68.
[41] *Ibid.*, 68. See also Eisenstein, *op. cit.*, 199–223.

Although the broad outlines of the federal tax structure have remained relatively stable since the early 1940's, within this framework there has been constant change. In a typical year Congress enacts a dozen or so amendments to the tax laws. Some are for the benefit of particular individuals, groups, and companies; others are to correct defects and inequities which have been revealed during the administration of the tax laws. "Major" tax legislation comes much less frequently; three such statutes, in 1954, 1964, and 1965, were enacted in the last decade. Piecemeal or "minor" changes in the tax structure may take such forms as the modification of a particular tax rate, the adoption of a new excise tax, the tightening or loosening of tax exemptions or permissible deductions, or the alteration of tax collection procedures. Such changes, even though they may be highly technical or specific, may have much significance for the income or wealth of those affected. Some may attract much attention and controversy. Others will be passed by Congress without hearings, with little, sometimes no debate, and with such innocuous titles as "A bill to amend Part III of Subchapter O of the Internal Revenue Code of 1954." This bill provided substantial retroactive tax relief to the Hilton Hotel chain. Whether the tax legislation is considered "major" or "minor," it has the related effects of changing the allocation of the costs of government and of distributing advantages and disadvantages (lower or higher taxes) among the populace.

Changes in the tax structure also may be made by administrative and judicial interpretation of existing tax provisions. One cause of particular administrative interpretations, or reinterpretations, of tax provisions is rather interesting. By threatening to enact amendments to the tax laws, Congress or, more precisely, influential members thereof, may induce the Treasury Department to give interpretations of tax provisions favorable to particular private interests. In 1959, Representative Byrnes (R., Wis.), the third-ranking minority member of the Ways and Means Committee, used this strategy to obtain a favorable ruling for a Milwaukee investment company. It is estimated that two to a dozen such cases occur annually.[42] Such instances can be thought of as conflicts between particular special interests and the Treasury Department in its role of guardian of the public interest (or, at least, its conception of the public interest). Many such attempts fail, however, as do many efforts of individuals or groups to get favorable (to them) legislation from Congress.

[42] *The New York Times,* Nov. 18, 1963, p. 6.

Chapter Five

GOVERNMENT AND BUSINESS

A large portion of the current complex of economic legislation, regulations, and decisions is concerned with business, with the mediation and control of relationships between different business groups and between business and other economic groups, such as labor and agriculture. This complex of laws and decisions is characterized by variety, diversity, and sometimes inconsistency.

No attempt will be made here to discuss the total spectrum of public policies toward business. Nothing, for example, will be said directly about the regulation of banks and other financial institutions. Rather this chapter will be concerned with four general patterns of national policy toward business activity: promotion of business; regulation of business to maintain competition and prevent monopoly; public utility type regulation; and government ownership and operation of economic enterprise. In the order in which they are listed, these patterns of policy can be viewed as arranged along a continuum from the least control to the most (or complete) control in the case of government ownership. They represent four general alternative courses of action available to government decision-makers in dealing with business problems. Government ownership also can be considered an alternative to the first three, which involve varying degrees of public control or intervention in private business activity.

Before we turn to these policy patterns, some remarks on the politics of business are in order. Business groups have long been concerned with government intervention in the economy and, unsurprisingly, public policy is reflective of this concern and the involvement of business in politics which has risen from it.

143

THE BUSINESS COMMUNITY:
DIVERSITY, UNITY, POLITICS

The word "businessmen" encompasses an exceptionally heterogeneous assortment of people. The large corporation executive, the investment banker, the Wall Street broker, the chain-store president, the general store owner, the real estate agent, the service station operator, the barber, the florist, the motion picture magnate, the textile manufacturer, and the corner drugstore and poolroom owners are all businessmen.

The heterogeneity of businessmen is matched by that of business organizations and trade associations which have been established to promote and protect their interests. It is estimated that there are around 13,000 national, regional, state, and local trade associations, 5,000 local chambers of commerce, and several hundred national business organizations. Practically every line of industrial and commercial activity has a national trade association. Thus we find such associations as the American Iron and Steel Institute, the American Bankers Association, the Automobile Manufacturers Association, the American Meat Institute, the National Association of Retail Druggists, the American Federation of Retail Kosher Butchers, the Portland Cement Association, and the Institute of Makers of Explosives. Also, there are such well-known general business organizations, or "peak associations," as the National Association of Manufacturers and the Chamber of Commerce of the United States. Organizations that claim to speak generally for "small business" include the National Small Business Men's Association and the Conference of American Small Business Organizations.

The numerous spokesmen for the business community tend to expound an ideology which stresses free enterprise, free competition, and nonintervention by government lest it disrupt the natural workings of the economy.[1] But, as Professor Bernstein has observed: "While the businessman describes the operation of the economy in terms of absolute laissez-faire concepts, he himself does not rely exclusively on these natural forces to preserve his position in society. Instead he seeks to utilize the coercive authority of government to enhance his interests."[2] Business likes to be left alone by government except when it (or some

---

[1] Francis X. Sutton, Seymour E. Harris, Carl Kaysen, and James Tobin, *The American Business Creed* (New York: Schocken Books, 1962), ch. 8.
[2] Marver H. Bernstein, "Political Ideas of Selected American Business Journals," *Public Opinion Quarterly*, XVIII (Summer, 1953), 258–267.

segment of business) needs the help of government in securing advantages or meeting needs. In this regard business behavior is not unlike that of other economic groups. The late Senator Robert A. Taft, expressing general opposition to legislation of the sort represented by the Investment Company Act of 1940, was moved to aver: "I may say that one of the great difficulties of Congress in attempting to avoid the detailed regulation of business, with indefinite power in a Federal bureau, is the fact that in many cases the businessmen themselves seem to want that kind of regulation. It is so in this case, and so has it been in other cases."[3]

Business organizations and associations are established to perform a variety of functions but nearly all of them, at one time or another, engage in efforts to influence the direction and substance of public economic policy. Some business organizations, the NAM and the Chamber of Commerce are examples, are continually involved in political activities; others, whose interests are narrower, are only occasionally involved. The recourse of business groups to government "results both from the need of these groups for help in furthering their aims and from the closely related need of protection from their economic and political rivals."[4] In the first instance they want such things from government as subsidies, research and technical services, aid in controlling intra-group competition, and other forms of direct assistance. In the second instance the objectives of business groups may involve either opposition to demands for regulation of business or insistence that the activities of rival economic groups be regulated, whether these are other business groups, labor unions, or whatever. In either case, the motivation behind the political activity of business groups is the desire for protection and security against "hazards" in the form of disruptive economic changes, "unfair" practices of rival economic groups, unwanted government regulation, and so on.

Business groups are clearly not always united in their stands on public policy issues. Because of the complexity and diversity of our economy there are many conflicts of interest and purpose among different segments of the business community. Conflict and competition occur within and between industries. Small business contends for advantage with big business; depressed industries seek government assis-

[3] *Congressional Record,* LXXVII, 10070. Taft, however, did not oppose the act itself, since it had been agreed to as acceptable by the Investment Trust Association.

[4] David B. Truman, *The Governmental Process* (New York: Alfred A. Knopf, 1951), 79.

tance, which is opposed by more prosperous industries; importers are opposed to the pleas of domestic manufacturers for tariff protection; domestic oil and coal producers differ with the refiners of imported oil over oil import quotas; independent retailers and wholesalers want protection against the chain stores and other large distributors; railroads compete for advantage with motor carriers and other forms of transportation; regional economic interests compete for advantage in the form of wage and transportation rate differentials; "responsible" stock brokers want protection against unethical practices by less responsible members of the industry. A large portion of the legislation relating to business in the statute books is the product of conflicts between business groups. It would indeed be erroneous to assume that business always speaks with a single voice and that there is a single monolithic "business interest." Neither, however, should it be assumed that there is no unity among business groups.

Notwithstanding the clashes and conflicts which occur among business interests, there does appear to be a measure of unity within the business community. Key has commented on this matter:

> Conflicts among business groups are commonplace, yet a network of common interest pulls the business community together on major issues when its security is threatened. Party lines, sectional lines, religious lines divide businessmen when their common interests are in peril. Within the business community powerful factors operate to bring conformity to the predominant views. Unanimity is rare, but a predominant business sentiment usually crystallizes and makes itself heard on major issues affecting the group as a whole.[5]

Most businessmen would probably take a common position on such items as opposition to business tax increases, the need for restriction of "big labor," the protection of business against foreign competition, and the general enhancement and promotion of business. When united, the business community is a potent political force. Contrarily, many important business regulatory programs have been instituted at times when business interests were divided. Much support for the Interstate Commerce Act and the Sherman Antitrust Act, for example, came from small businessmen and others arrayed against "big business."

Some of the factors which contribute to unity in the business community, and thus to the enhancement of its political influence, can be mentioned here. Business organizations, like other human groups,

[5] V. O. Key, Jr., *Politics, Parties, and Pressure Groups,* 4th ed. (New York: Thomas Y. Crowell, 1958), 83.

develop norms of conduct and common interests to which their members are expected to adhere. Group social pressures operate to encourage the individual's adherence to them, or at least to discourage open deviation from them. Financial relationships among business units may also provide the basis for unity or the discouragement of dissent. A manufacturer who expresses "unbusinesslike" views may find his customers taking their business elsewhere. Newspapers may hesitate to editorialize against business interests for fear of losing advertising revenues. Further, business associations, interlocking and overlapping corporate directorates, corporate hierarchies, and the dominance of many industries by a few large firms to help tie the business community together through a web of relationships. These, together with modern means of transportation and communication, permit the ready transmission of the views of business leaders throughout the country and facilitate the mobilization of business for unified political action on broad policy questions.

Two organizations which claim to speak for business as a whole are the National Association of Manufacturers and the Chamber of Commerce. Assuming that they really do, a brief look at their views should provide us with "a microcosmic indicator of the common values of American business."[6] The Chamber of Commerce is a federation of more than 3,000 state and local chambers of commerce, trade associations, and other business organizations. Its major function is to speak for American business on public policy issues, especially those which concern business generally and not just particular business groups. Because of the broad and diverse constituency which it represents, the Chamber's policy views and pronouncements are often general.

The Chamber strongly favors "free enterprise in preference to public enterprise." Although it does not oppose all government intervention in the economy, the Chamber generally favors the reduction of existing controls and opposes the imposition of new controls. Some of its stands on more specific policy issues include: advocacy of voluntary health insurance and opposition to compulsory government health insurance and medical care; support for exemption of natural gas producers from rate regulation; demands for more restrictions on labor unions; opposition to the extension of credit by federal agencies; and the desire for greater trade opportunities with Communist countries. In general, the Chamber favors state action over national action when there is a need for governmental activity.

[6] Harmon Zeigler, *Interest Groups in American Society* (Englewood Cliffs, N.J.: Prentice-Hall, 1964), 110–111.

147

The National Association of Manufacturers was established in 1895 to promote trade and commerce by securing favorable government legislation and other means. It did not become really significant until 1903, when it became involved in labor questions, especially the defense of American business against the "assaults" of labor unions. The NAM has long been noted for its antipathy toward organized labor and, though this antipathy has moderated in recent years, it has been a major factor contributing to NAM's cohesiveness. Reorganized in 1933, the NAM has been dominated by representatives of big business and deeply involved in political activity. It is regarded as a strongly conservative organization and its main objectives have been:

> (1) reduction of the bargaining position of organized labor, both with respect to direct employer-employee relations and to indirect governmental sources of union power. (2) minimization of the tax burden on industrial profits and managerial compensation; (3) elimination, modification, and prevention of public regulation or government participation in industrial functions and processes; and (4) encouragement of direct and indirect public aid to industry if not in conflict with other objectives.[7]

Spokesmen for the NAM express preferences for free enterprise, individualism, and the American way rather than "socialistic" government controls and big government. In recent years the NAM has expended much money and effort to educate the American people on the virtues of the free enterprise system.[8]

In seeking to influence public economic policies, business groups use a variety of strategies. One is persuasion, which may involve activities ranging from threats of injury or retaliation for unwanted conduct, to lobbying before legislative and administrative bodies, to efforts to shape public opinion. In recent decades business groups have devoted much time, effort, and attention to the development, through public relations activities, of a favorable climate of opinion for free competitive enterprise. The old "public be damned" attitude expressed by William K. Vanderbilt is a thing of the past. Rather, by using the mass media and other means of communication, business groups strive to

[7] Alfred S. Cleveland, "NAM: Spokesman for Industry," *Harvard Business Review,* XXVI (May, 1948).

[8] Richard W. Gable, "Interest Groups as Policy Shapers," *Annals of the American Academy of Political and Social Science,* CCCXIX (September, 1958), 88–89.

148

convince the public of the virtues, achievements, and benefits of private business and a free enterprise economy. Business advertising is concerned with the merchandising of ideas as well as the sale of products and, together with other public relations activities, is employed to win supporters for specific policy proposals favored by business and to create opponents for those it opposes. But, as V. O. Key has observed: "of more fundamental importance is the continuing propaganda calculated to shape public attitudes favorably towards the business system as a whole or toward particular types of business. The assiduous dedication of effort to the capture of public favor lays a foundation of good will on which business groups may build in their efforts to obtain particular legislation or to obstruct undesired governmental actions."[9]

Business groups may also use concession and compromise in pursuing their goals. "Farsighted and realistic business leadership has recognized the advantage of placating the opposition, and, on occasion, has followed the Bismarckian and 'Tory Socialist' tactic of controlling or limiting reform by annexing or sponsoring it."[10] Mild regulation may be proposed or accepted as a means of staving off more severe regulation. The New York Stock Exchange has used this strategy in trying to prevent the promulgation of more severe rules governing stock trading by the Securities and Exchange Commission. Concessions may be made to other groups as a means of gaining their support or reducing their opposition. A good example of concession and compromise is revealed in the position taken on labor relations legislation by the NAM after 1939. It abandoned its attempts to eliminate legislation protecting labor's right to organize and bargain collectively, which had gained general public acceptance, in favor of a position of limited approval for such legislation. The NAM then set to work to bring about changes in the Wagner Act favorable to management and it was instrumental in securing the adoption of the Taft-Hartley Act in 1947.

A third method involves efforts to secure the selection of administrative officials who are sympathetic to business interests and viewpoints for policy-making positions. In some instances, as with some occupational licensing boards, officials are literally selected by the regulated groups. In other cases, business influence may be less direct. During the Eisenhower administration, which was responsive to business interests, changes in labor-management relations policy favorable to

[9] Key, op. cit., 103.
[10] Merle Fainsod, et. al., Government and the American Economy (New York: W. W. Norton, 1959), 28.

business were secured by the appointment of business-oriented members to the National Labor Relations Board.[11] In still other cases, continued association by regulatory officials with businessmen, together with limited contacts with other groups, may cause the officials to take on business viewpoints. This is one reason why business groups (or other economic groups, for that matter) want separate agencies to handle programs with which they are concerned. Professor Edleman has commented: "Probably the most effective way to make a public official act as an interest wishes him to do is to insure by institutional means that he will become thoroughly acquainted with its problems as the adherents of the interest see them."[12]

If business groups are unable to prevent the enactment of undesired legislation they may follow a fourth strategy, that of attempting to discredit, delay, or otherwise frustrate its implementation. Litigation has sometimes been used for this purpose. In the late nineteenth and early twentieth centuries, especially, public utility concerns often resorted to the courts in combating administrative regulation of their rates. The effectiveness of the Interstate Commerce Commission was greatly reduced until 1906 by railroad-instigated judicial limitations. During the 1930's business groups launched an all-out judicial attack on New Deal legislation and succeeded, prior to 1937, in getting several important statutes declared unconstitutional. Though there is nothing improper about challenging the constitutionality or legality of governmental actions, such challenges may become so numerous (and their obstructional intent so obvious) as to constitute a form of not-so-covert warfare against government action. Actual or threatened noncooperation by those affected by legislation may also be used to slow down or prevent its implementation.

In recent years business groups have begun to place increased reliance on another strategy for affecting the nature of public economic policy: direct participation in party and electoral politics, including politics at the "grass roots" level. Individual businessmen, in addition to their organized group activities, are being urged to take an active personal part in party politics. Thus, a former president of the U.S. Chamber of Commerce encouraged businessmen to "get into politics" in order to counter the political power of organized labor. Businessmen,

[11] Seymour Scher, "Regulatory Agency Control Through Appointment: The Case of the Eisenhower Administration and the NLRB," *Journal of Politics,* XXIII (November, 1961), 667–688.

[12] Murray Edleman, "Governmental Organization and Public Policy," *Public Administration Review,* XII (Autumn, 1952), 279.

he said, should "Get to work at the precinct and ward levels where political decisions are made and office holders chosen." He pointed out the importance for business of bringing about the selection of favorably-oriented public officials instead of trying to influence officials "already elected and already committed to a political philosophy hostile to business."[13] The Chamber of Commerce has sold tens of thousands of copies of an instruction pamphlet entitled "Action Course in Practical Politics." Courses in "practical politics" utilizing this pamphlet, or similar materials, have been sponsored by many corporations and local chambers of commerce. Whatever the actual impact of this strategy on public policy, it has undoubtedly gotten many businessmen and management personnel involved in direct political activity.

There is no precise way of determining the impact of business groups and the business community on the substance and implementation of public economic policy. Their effectiveness in this endeavor will be affected, at any given time, by such factors as the amount of cohesiveness and consensus among business groups, the strength and cohesiveness of opposing groups, the prestige of the business community, the degree of public acceptability of business ideas and viewpoints, the administration in power (e.g., whether Republican or Democratic), and the policy issues in controversy. But so long as the business community and its component groups retain major control over the economic assets of the nation, they will represent a force, or set of forces, of much political potency. The control of wealth, and the economic power that goes with it, is an important source of political power and influence.

PROMOTION OF BUSINESS ACTIVITY

Government promotion of business takes the form of positive aid, assistance, and encouragement to particular business groups, industries, or sectors of the economy. It is intended to help those aided in the attainment of their goals, which would certainly include survival and profits, by protecting them from, or helping them overcome, some of the risks and uncertainties of economic life. Promotion of business, like regulation of business, is based on the broad assumption that it will further the general welfare.

Business has always depended upon government for the performance of such functions as maintenance of law and order, protection of prop-

[13] *The New York Times,* Sept. 20, 1958, p. 40.

151

erty rights, enforcement of contracts, provision of a monetary system, provision of corporate charters, issuance of patents and copyrights, and legislation to lessen the pain of bankruptcy. Without this framework of activities and services, as we suggested earlier, our system of private enterprise would be unable to exist. In a broad sense these services and activities may be considered forms of business promotionalism. They are, however, indivisible and indiscriminate in nature and they benefit not only businesses but workers, farmers, consumers, and citizens generally. Our discussion will be focused on more direct and positive forms of assistance to the business community or to particular segments of it: subsidies, provision of services, loans, and the like.

Government promotional activity involves minimal control of business activity in the sense of regulation or restriction. The businessman is typically not required to make use of available assistance or benefits. No sanctions are imposed for his failure to do so, except as the businessman may perceive the loss of an available benefit as a deprivation. But to say, as we did, that promotion involves minimal control is not to say that it involves no control of business behavior. The businessman may be required to assume certain duties or obligations, or to modify his behavior in certain ways, in order to qualify for assistance or benefits. He will have to do so, for example, if he wants to secure tax concessions for industrial plant modernization, or to obtain a Small Business Administration loan to expand his operations, or to receive a subsidy for operating a merchant ship. Government assistance is not necessarily given without "strings" attached.

Promotion and regulation of business activity are also intermingled in another way. Some measures undertaken to assist one group in the attainment of its goals may involve regulation of the activity of other groups. The well-being of small retailers may be promoted by resale price maintenance legislation which restricts the pricing policies of other businesses. The railroads have sometimes sought to promote their interests by supporting regulation of the activities of competing forms of transportation, such as motor carriers. Whether a given policy is considered promotional or regulatory will frequently depend upon whose ox is being gored.

The Politics of Promotion

Businessmen and business groups, despite their numerous protestations against government intervention in the economy, have long sought and obtained governmental aid and encouragement for their economic endeavors. It is often remarked that the second statute enacted by the government under the Constitution provided for a protective tariff. Under the nurture and guidance of Hamilton and the Federalists business promotionalism became a firmly established national policy by the end of the eighteenth century. Throughout the nineteenth century the dominant policy of the national government toward business was promotionalism rather than regulation. While business interests in the latter part of the nineteenth century proclaimed the virtues of a policy of laissez faire in their efforts to ward off regulation of their activities that was demanded by agrarian and other groups, they found such governmental policies as protective tariffs, subsidies and land grants for railroad construction, and lax incorporation laws much to their liking. The business community, in its political activities, was motivated and guided by practical considerations, by the desire to secure positive advantages and to avoid disadvantages, and not by the desire to be ideologically consistent or pure. A similar situation prevails today.

Within the business community harmony does not always reign on the matter of promotion. Because of the divergence of interests among various business groups, actual or proposed promotional programs may give rise to intra-business conflict. Business groups desire benefits for themselves, but they are apt to take a jaundiced view of assistance for their competitors. The railroads, for example, have manifested little enthusiasm for rivers and harbors improvements or for the payment of subsidies to airlines. Private electric utility companies have been outspoken in their opposition to government aid through low interest loans to electrical cooperatives but have shown little reluctance to avail themselves of the opportunity to exploit public waterpower sites. Acquisition for themselves or denial to others, as the case may be, of governmental assistance is one of the tactics used by business groups in their struggle with one another for economic advantage.

The claims of business groups for governmental aid and assistance are advanced and supported in a number of ways. Quite typically, it is contended that by promoting the interest of a given group the government will contribute to the general welfare, or alternatively, promote the public interest. "Throughout American history particular sections or groups . . . hoping to validate the claims of their interests, have capitalized on the popular acceptance accorded to the public interest."[14] Another tactic is to stress the benefits which will flow to groups other than the one directly aided. Protective tariffs have been

[14] Frank J. Sorauf, "The Public Interest Reconsidered," *Journal of Politics,* XIX (November, 1957), 620.

defended on the ground they support the interests not only of manufacturers but of farmers and workers as well. Construction subsidies to railroads in the nineteenth century were defended by suggesting the economic benefits and advantages which would accrue to the regions served by the railroads. Assistance to a particular industry may also be defended as necessary or vital to the national security. Thus it is contended that subsidies for the construction and operation of American merchant ships are needed to ensure an adequate merchant fleet in the event of war. This argument (and belief) has apparently been important in gaining congressional support for these subsidy programs.[15]

Again, and especially in recent years, particular promotional programs have been supported as contributing to greater economic growth. This argument is appealing because of the present emphasis on the need for greater economic growth if the United States is to "keep up with the Russians," or reduce unemployment, and so on. Tax concessions for industrial plant modernization have been advocated and defended on this ground, as have programs benefiting industries in depressed areas. Finally, promotion of one group may lead to demands for assistance by others, supposedly to offset unfair advantages conferred on their competitors. Some spokesmen for the railroads have argued for government assistance as a means of offsetting the advantages of their "subsidized" competitor carriers. Other spokesmen see as a solution to the railroads' problems more regulation of competing carriers, especially those motor and other carriers exempt from regulation by the Interstate Commerce Commission.[16] There is thus more than one way to promote a railroad, a fact which has led to intra- as well as inter-industry conflict.

Patterns of Promotion

Because of the vast number and variety of promotional programs, no attempt will be made to enumerate or discuss all of them.[17] Rather, we will set forth a number of categories under which promotional programs can be grouped and provide some examples in each category. The categories are credit and loan guarantees, subsidies, construction of facilities, technical and informational services, and taxation (see Chapter Four for the use of taxation for promotional purposes).

[15] Fainsod, *op. cit.*, 114.
[16] *The New York Times*, June 23, 1961, p. Fl; *ibid.*, Sept. 3, 1961, p. Fl.
[17] See Joint Economic Committee, *Subsidy and Subsidylike Programs of the U.S. Government* (Washington, D.C.: Government Printing Office, 1960). Especially note the listing on pp. 10–17.

CREDIT AND LOAN GUARANTEE PROGRAMS. Although government credit and loan programs are not new, most of the existing programs have been established since 1930. Perhaps the best known example of government lending to business was the program handled by the Reconstruction Finance Corporation. Set up by the Hoover administration in 1932, the RFC made loans to businesses totaling nearly $50 billion by 1954, when it was liquidated by the Eisenhower administration in partial redemption of its pledge to reduce government business operations. To partially fill the gap left by the RFC, and at the insistence of small business interests, the Small Business Administration was established in 1953. The SBA makes loans to small businesses (for which there is no precise definition) for plant expansion, modernization, and other purposes. It also assists small businesses in obtaining government contracts and helps finance Small Business Investment Companies. The Area Redevelopment Administration (1961–1965) in the Department of Commerce made loans (and grants) to aid businesses in depressed areas.

Also in this category are government loan guarantee operations of various sorts. Such agencies as the Federal Housing Administration, the Veterans Administration, and the Federal National Mortgage Association underwrite private loans and mortgages for residential housing. By assuming a large share of the risk in housing credit the government has aided large numbers of homeowners and, more to the point here, has contributed to the prosperity of home builders, real estate operators, and mortgage lenders. In another area the Transportation Act of 1958 guarantees the repayment of private loans made to railroads to enable them to maintain their existing facilities and to purchase new equipment.

SUBSIDIES. Subsidies may take the form of outright grants of cash or other things of value, such as public lands, to private businesses. Railroad construction was subsidized in the nineteenth century by grants of public land and by cash contributions. According to one estimate, federal and state grants of land to railroads amounted to 183,000,000 acres.[18] Subsidies have been given by the national government to the airlines since 1926. During the 1950's operating subsidies amounting to $477,000,000 were paid to international, domestic trunk, and local feeder airlines. Today only local airlines receive operating subsidies. Both the construction and operation of American merchant ships are currently subsidized by the government. These are designed to make up the difference between foreign and American construction and

[18] Federal Coordinator of Transportation, *Public Aids to Transportation* (Washington, D.C.: Government Printing Office, 1940), I, 13.

operating costs. The liner United States was built in the early 1950's at a cost of $76,800,000, of which $43,900,000 was provided by the government.[19]

Subsidies may also be indirect or hidden, as when the government sells services or products to private business at below cost, or when it buys products at higher than market prices. Thus newspaper and periodical publishers are subsidized by below-cost postal rates for the mailing of their publications. The newspaper which may be highly critical of subsidies for farmers is apt to view its own postal subsidy as a vital bastion of freedom of the press. Bulk mailers of advertising material benefit from low rates for second, third, and fourth class mail. Government disposal of surplus property to private business involves a subsidy when the sale price is short of the actual market value of the surplus, and it often is. The silver mining industry has been subsidized by government purchases of silver at higher than market prices. The government's program of stockpiling scarce and strategic materials for national security purposes has sometimes been used to subsidize, by means of high prices, the domestic producers of lead, zinc, nickel, and other metals.

CONSTRUCTION AND MAINTENANCE OF FACILITIES. Various types of physical facilities built and maintained by government are of much value to private business. To the extent that the users or beneficiaries of such facilities do not pay their cost they can be said to be subsidized by the government. The transportation industries have especially been served by this form of assistance. Shipping on inland waters has benefited from the billions of dollars the national, state, and local governments have spent on the construction of canals, the improvement of harbors, the dredging of rivers, and the construction of shipping terminals, locks, and lighthouses. Commercial aviation has benefited from the construction of airports by national, state, and local governments. Though the airlines are assessed for operating costs, the capital costs of airports are met by the taxpayers. The national government also spends several hundred million dollars a year on the establishment and maintenance of airways—traffic control equipment, instrument landing systems, radio beams, weather reporting services—which are for the most part free of cost to the airlines. Public construction of roads and highways has greatly contributed to the growth of the motor carrier industry. Only in recent years have motor carriers come to pay much of their share of highway costs.

TECHNICAL AND INFORMATIONAL SERVICES. The Department of Commerce has as its primary purpose the promotion and encouragement

[19] *The New York Times,* April 2, 1953, p. 55.

156

of American business at home and abroad. One of the three major "clientele" departments (the other two are Labor and Agriculture), the Commerce Department is a service agency for business and does little in the way of business regulation. Within the Department, the Office of Business Economics and the Bureau of Foreign Trade provide information on business activities and opportunities at home and abroad. The Bureau of the Census, through its decennial census and special agricultural and business censuses, provides businessmen with data on business and agricultural activity, income, employment, housing, business trends, and other matters. The Weather Bureau issues weather forecasts which are of importance to shipping, aviation, and other businesses as well as to agriculture. The Bureau of Standards engages in physical research, conducts tests of materials and products, and develops commercial and industrial product standards. The list could be extended.

Outside the Department of Commerce numerous other government agencies provide informational and technical services for business. Economic trends and forecasts are reported in the *Federal Reserve Bulletin* and the *Monthy Labor Review,* put out by the Federal Reserve Board and the Department of Labor respectively. The Bureau of Mines, the Forest Service, and the Fish and Wildlife Service engage in research and informational activities of benefit to the mining, lumbering, and fishing industries, including development of new products and resource uses.

In general, these and other technical and information services assist businessmen in making informed and intelligent decisions and in planning their operations in a more rational manner. Most of them would have to be provided privately if they were not provided by the government.

Concluding Comments

Few business groups of any importance do not receive some form of government promotional aid. Some industries, such as silver mining and merchant shipping, appear to draw heavily upon governmental aid; others do so to lesser degrees. But, whether the benefits of promotion are great or small, few groups willingly permit the termination of programs beneficial to them, even with the disappearance of the conditions which originally gave rise to the programs. Industries which benefit from protective tariffs continue to desire them long after they have passed the stage of "infancy." They now base their claims for protection on the need to offset low labor costs of foreign manufacturers and maintain employment or on their relationship to the nation's present or possible defense needs. As prevailing conceptions of the proper objectives of public policy change, the justification of promotional programs will be altered to fit them.

Promotional programs clearly tend to persist once established. As time passes and new programs are added in response to new or expanded demands, promotional programs proliferate. Not a session of Congress goes by but that several business groups can be found seeking some kind of governmental assistance or benefits. Nor, apparently, are they much discouraged from this quest by the fact that regulatory programs sometimes follow in the wake of promotional programs, a pattern particularly evident in the areas of transportation and public utilities.

It should also be noted that the success of business groups in obtaining government succor contributed to the demands of agricultural, labor, and other economic groups for promotional benefits. "If government is to dispense privileges, the argument ran, it cannot limit the beneficiaries. The logic of protection for one group led to the call for 'protection all around.' "[20] The success of non-business groups in securing government aid and assistance will be taken up in later chapters.

REGULATION AND THE MAINTENANCE OF COMPETITION

On Competition and Policy

The maintenance of competition by preventing private restrictions on competition and the development of monopoly is a cardinal feature of public policy in the United States. But public policy is concerned with more than maintaining competition as such. A closely related policy goal is the maintenance of a standard of competition by preventing unfair or unethical competitive practices. What is desired is "fair competition, competition that fights fair."[21] These policies can be collectively designated as antitrust policy.

In dealing with the matter of monopoly a number of alternative courses of action might be followed by the government in addition to that set forth in the preceding paragraph. First, the government could take no action on the assumption that monopoly would be prevented,

[20] Fainsod, op. cit., 97.
[21] Woodrow Wilson, The New Freedom (New York: Doubleday, 1914), 17.

158

or eliminated where it did exist, by the "natural" operation of competitive forces. Or, as an alternative rationale for inaction, the government could assume the public interest would be served by the monopolist, perhaps because his "conscience" would cause him to act in a socially responsible manner.[22] Second, the government could accept the existence of monopoly as desirable or inevitable and act to protect the public by direct regulation of the monopolist's prices and standards of service. Third, "industrial self-regulation" could be attempted through governmentally approved "codes of fair competition." This was tried during the period of the National Industrial Recovery Act (1933–1935) but did not prove very satisfactory. Fourth, the government could operate on the premise that "private monopolies are indefensible and intolerable" and take them into public ownership when they developed.

It presently seems unlikely that the *general* policy toward business enterprise competition of maintaining competition and preventing monopoly will be replaced by one of the other alternatives listed above. It must be said, however, that there are two major exceptions to the general procompetitive policy. Industries designated as "public utilities," regarded as a special case, have been subject to a policy of direct regulation since the turn of the century. Second, in industries that consist of a great many small businesses, such as retail distribution, a major purpose of legislation has been to restrict competition in order to protect competitors against, especially, the "hazard" of low incomes.

Why now, it may be asked, is the maintenance of competition a major goal of public policy? What advantages or benefits does it confer? One answer to such questions is statable in terms of the "ideology of competition." (The word "ideology" is here used to indicate that some of the following statements lack much empirical verification.) Competition is said to lead to the efficient allocation of resources. In a competitive economy production of goods will be more responsive to consumer desires than under monopoly conditions. Further, competition will keep prices reasonable and quality high as producers compete for the consumers' favor. Consumers have greater choice among types and qualities of goods and services. For producers, competition means freedom of entry into lines of production that offer greater profits or other advantages. Those who sell their labor or services benefit from competition by having greater freedom of choice in selecting occupations, lines of work, and employers. Competition stimulates economic growth by providing businessmen with an in-

[22] Adolf A. Berle, *The 20th Century Capitalist Revolution* (New York: Harcourt, Brace & World, 1954), esp. chs. 2, 3.

centive to adopt more efficient modes of production and to develop new or improved products in order to gain business. Politically, competition is identified with the diffusion of economic power, and consequently political power, widely throughout the society. A major line of thought holds that the best social setting for democracy is one in which the electorate consists of people relatively similar in economic position, wealth, and power. Finally, competition is alleged to foster such "desirable" personal traits as independence, initiative, and self-reliance.

Taken at face value, the ideology of competition depicted here is highly congruent with many of the basic values and beliefs of American political culture. Clearly, for example, it appears to be instrumental for the attainment of such values as equality of opportunity, freedom, democracy, individualism, and efficiency. It accords with beliefs in the desirability of private property, private enterprise, and economic growth. Acceptance of the ideology of competition, and policy action in conformity with it, are facilitated by its congruence with general cultural values and beliefs. Of course, competition as a policy is also supported because of the advantages it seems to confer, at one time or another, upon particular economic groups—producers, sellers of raw materials, workers, consumers. Competition is thus regarded as the norm, as one of the basic "rules of the game" of American society. The burden of proof tends to rest with those who would deviate from it and not with its supporters.

At this point it is necessary to muddy the clear waters of certitude. Our contention that the American people generally support competition and oppose monopoly raises a problem of definition. What, precisely, constitutes competition and monopoly? Under what conditions can a situation be characterized, i.e., defined, as competitive or monopolistic. On this matter there is lack of agreement and sometimes acrimonious conflict. The predicament here is similar to a hypothetical instance in which there is agreement on the desirability of preventing poverty but lack of agreement as to what conditions constitute poverty and are therefore to be eliminated. Here we will note some ways of defining competition and monopoly and some possible ramifications of the lack of agreed definitions.

Competition may be defined as a situation in which many buyers and sellers are engaged in rivalry in the sale and purchase of goods and services and in which prices are determined by the interaction of supply and demand. But what number of buyers or sellers comprise "many." And what kind of "rivalry" constitutes competition: rivalry in prices, product, design, advertising, supplementary services, or what? Economists have developed a concept of "workable competition" as a goal for public policy. Thus, "Workable competition is considered to require, principally, a fairly large number of buyers and sellers, no one of whom occupies a large share of the market, the absence of collusion among either group, and the possibility of market entry by new firms."[23] A lawyer, however, might define as competitive those situations in which the actions of competitors are not restrained in ways defined as illegal. What might be considered competitive in this sense would not necessarily be so regarded using "workable competition" as a standard.

Nor is there agreement as to the meaning of monopoly. In one sense, monopoly means the control of an industry by a single firm. Such situations are rare; more common are those designated "oligopoly"— domination of a market by a few firms with control over prices or production. A policy definition of monopoly more in accord with the way the word is often used holds that monopoly is "the power to raise prices or exclude competitors if it is desired to do so." This would seem applicable to many oligopolistic situations. Sometimes monopoly is equated with "bigness" in business. Having raised that notion, however, we shall simply say it produces much confusion and quietly withdraw from discussion of it.

Of what significance is this problem in definition? Is it simply a semantic controversy which can well be ignored? The answer is no. The lack of agreed-upon definitions opens the way for conflicting interest groups to employ definitions of competition and monopoly favorable to their interests when urging or opposing the need of government action to maintain competition. In this way conflict over material interests may be obscured by its transformation into symbolic conflict over the choice and meaning of definitions. The manner in which competition is defined, for example, will affect one's judgment concerning the amount of competition in a particular situation. A situation which some might view as competitive because no competitors are illegally restrained (the lawyer's definition) may be perceived as noncompetitive by others because the market is dominated by a few firms which have control over prices. Whichever definition and viewpoint is accepted by the decision maker, his decision will favor some interests over others. The lack of clear standards to guide decision may cause slowness, indecisiveness, or inaction by decision makers.

[23] Edward S. Mason, *Economic Concentration and the Monopoly Problem* (Cambridge: Harvard University Press, 1957), 354.

161

The contention that antitrust policy has not lived up to its promise is partly a result of the continuing lack of agreement as to what conditions are to be maintained as competitive and prevented as monopolistic. But this lack of agreement is produced in turn by the conflict of group interests—small business and big business, suppliers and buyers—in our society.

In the ensuing discussion, *we* will use the word "competition" to mean something akin to "workable competition" and "monopoly" to indicate power to raise prices or exclude competitors and, generally, any device to eliminate competition. The problem of definitions is not thereby resolved, but it does have the virtue of allowing the discussion to proceed.

The Sherman Antitrust Act

With the expansion of industrialism in the latter part of the nineteenth century, control of many sectors of the economy came to be concentrated in a limited number of large concerns. Competition among these large firms, as well as between them and their smaller rivals, was often cutthroat or predatory. Moreover, competitive pressures were intensified by the development of nationwide markets which threw more businesses into direct competition with one another. Concerns with large investments were often impelled to slash prices, sometimes below costs, in their quest for sales and at least a partial return on their investment. Under these and similar conditions competition seemed to threaten mutual destruction. Businessmen began to seek ways to lessen competitive pressures, and they found many. Monopolistic agreements to fix prices, to limit production, to allocate markets, and to share profits were entered into. By purchase, merger, and other means, previously independent and competing companies were welded together to form huge combinations. Such combinations or trusts,[24] as they were popularly called, dominated many industries: sugar, meat packing, steel, tobacco, petroleum refining, whisky, matches, fruit preserving, lead, coal, gunpowder, and linseed oil, to name some prominent examples.

[24] The trust form of organization, which gave its name to antimonopoly policy, was a device for combining independent firms under common control. A trust was formed by persuading the majority stockholders of a number of independent firms to give control of their shares, and voting rights, to a single group of "trustees." The trustees could then run the previously independent companies as a single enterprise. The stockholders in turn received for their shares "trust certificates," which entitled them to receive dividends from the trust's profits.

The use of monopolistic agreements and combinations enabled business groups to become somewhat immune from control by competitive forces and the "unseen hand" envisaged by the classical economist Adam Smith. Some business groups benefited from lessened competitive risks and larger profits, but many other groups in the society felt disadvantaged by the effects of such economic changes. Farmers complained of having to pay high railway rates, interest rates, and prices for the products they purchased while receiving low prices for the commodities they sold. Independent and small businessmen were hard put to survive, or were driven out of business by what many considered to be "vicious" or "anti-social" practices on the part of large firms and combinations. The sellers of raw materials were at a disadvantage when dealing with combinations able to dominate the market and manipulate the prices. Workers had to contend with large companies which controlled (or nearly controlled) particular labor markets. Many people feared that "big business" was destroying economic opportunity, competition, and the independence of the common man. The political power emanating from the trusts' control of economic resources was seen as a threat to "traditional American democracy."

The development of big business and the resort to monopolistic agreements and combinations thus altered or disrupted existing relationships among various economic groups and challenged existing political and economic beliefs and aspirations. The new economic order brought with it new group relationships and new "rules of the game" which many groups viewed as inadequate, undesirable, or unacceptable. Since "a major function of politics is the mediation of relations among groups of people,"[25] it seems only natural that farmers, small businessmen, workers, reformist elements, and others who felt in some way aggrieved or threatened by the new economic conditions should call for governmental control of big business and the trusts. They demanded laws and policies which, from the perspective of their economic and ideological interests, would be more satisfactorily geared to the changed economic order. In response to their demands and pressures, many of the states enacted anti-monopoly laws in the late 1880's. But these state laws, and also the common law applied by the state courts, proved inadequate to prevent the abuses complained of, in part because the interstate character of the operations of many large businesses and combinations put them beyond the legal power of the states.

[25] Key, *op. cit.,* 83.

163

National action on the matter of monopoly and competition came in 1890 in the form of the Sherman Antitrust Act. Although there is much conjecture as to the motives of Congress in passing the Sherman Act, there appeared to be much support for national action to control monopolistic "abuses" and to "bust the trusts" among aggrieved economic groups and the public generally. One crude indicator is the fact that by 1890 all the political parties considered it expedient (at the least) to have antitrust planks in their platforms.

The Sherman Act, which was passed by Congress without intensive deliberation or committee consideration, has as its broad policy goal the maintenance of competition. The statute is a short, simple, and general piece of legislation. The substance of its policy is embodied in the first two sections:

> Sec. 1. Every contract, combination in the form of trust or otherwise, or conspiracy, in restraint of trade or commerce among the several States, or with foreign nations, is hereby declared to be illegal. Every person who shall make any such contract or engage in any such combination or conspiracy, shall be deemed guilty of a misdemeanor. . . .
>
> Sec. 2. Every person who shall monopolize, or attempt to monopolize, or combine or conspire with any other person or persons, to monopolize any part of the trade or commerce among the several States, or with foreign nations, shall be deemed guilty of a misdemeanor. . . .

Taken at its word, Section 1 prohibits every formal arrangement between two or more persons or firms designed to limit independent economic action. This section is concerned with market conduct, with the activity of persons in the market. Section 2 is directed against market structures involving situations of monopoly, regardless of how many persons are involved and whether or not trade is restrained. Or so it would seem. However, because of its briefness and generality, the meaning of the Sherman Act is vague. No definitions are provided for such terms as "restraint of trade," "combination . . . or otherwise," "monopolize," and "monopoly."

The actual meaning and effectiveness of the Sherman Act in maintaining competition have depended and still depend upon a number of factors. These include: (1) the interpretations given to the words of the statute by the federal courts in cases brought before them; (2) the attitudes of the current administration and the Justice Department toward the purposes of the Act and the actions of the latter in bringing cases against violators; (3) the adequacy of the injunctions and decrees

164

issued and criminal penalties imposed by the courts, after successful suits, for restoring competitive conditions or preventing restraints of trade; (4) the action of Congress in providing funds for enforcement and supplemental legislation when required. These factors will be examined as the discussion proceeds.[26]

Primary responsibility for the enforcement of the Sherman Act now rests with the Antitrust Division of the Department of Justice. Techniques available to the Antitrust Division include civil and criminal proceedings in the federal courts, and the consent decree, which is an informal procedure. Criminal proceedings are punitive and if successful can result in the imposition of fines and jail sentences on violators, up to a maximum of $50,000 ($5,000 before 1955) and a year's imprisonment. Criminal suits are often used in price-fixing, predatory practices, and other "flagrant" violations. Whatever their value as deterrents, criminal penalties do little to correct noncompetitive situations. More effective for this purpose are civil proceedings, which are remedial in character. A successful civil suit results in the granting of a court injunction or decree. An injunction is negative in effect and takes the form of an order to the defendant not to take some illegal action he had planned or to discontinue illegal activities engaged in during the past. Future violation of an injunction could involve punishment for contempt of court, but, when issued, it is simply an order to go forth and sin no more. A decree issued after a civil suit is positive in form, requiring that some action be taken. It may require abolition of a trade association, sale of illegally acquired stock, separation of the units of a combination, or breakup of a business unit into several parts. Decrees of this nature were used to split the Standard Oil and American Tobacco combinations into several parts each early in this century. The courts, however, are reluctant to issue orders breaking up corporations or combinations, apparently because of "judicial reluctance to disturb private rights [such as those of stockholders, other investors, and workers] in the interest of promoting nebulous public goals."[27] Old-fashioned "trust busting" has been rare in recent decades.

Many civil antitrust proceedings are settled by the use of consent decrees.[28] Over 50 per cent of the civil proceedings brought by the government since 1906, when the consent decree was first used, have

[26] Fainsod, *op. cit.,* 450.

[27] Donald Dewey, "Romance and Realism in Antitrust Policy," *Journal of Political Economy,* LXIII (April, 1955), 102.

[28] See Mark S. Massel, *Competition and Monopoly: Legal and Economic Issues* (Washington, D.C.: The Brookings Institution, 1962), ch. 5.

been closed in this way. During the 1954–1958 period, 88 per cent of the successful civil proceedings started by the Antitrust Division ended in consent decrees. Negotiated by the Antitrust Division and the offending party before the completion of formal proceedings, the consent decree is an agreement concerning the particular actions the offending party will take or cease doing. For example, in 1958 the United Fruit Company and the Antitrust Division negotiated a consent decree whereby the company agreed to create, out of its assets and before 1970, a competitor capable of handling 35 per cent of the business of importing bananas into the United States. When accepted by a federal district court, as it usually is without question, a consent decree has the same legal standing as any other court decree.

Consent decrees have become an important and often used means for settling antitrust cases because of the advantages each side—government and defendant—may gain from their use. Consent decrees are the outcome of bilateral bargaining and compromise between the Antitrust Division and the defendants. Differences between the two parties are narrowed as proposals are advanced, counter-proposals are made, and so on until a mutually acceptable agreement is reached. Advantages which defendants may gain from consent decrees include avoidance of the high cost of legal defense (especially important to small businesses) and of adverse publicity which may flow from litigation. Also, consent decrees cannot be used as evidence against them in private antitrust suits (discussed below). The consent decree procedure is of advantage to the Antitrust Division because it is less time-consuming and expensive than litigation, and thus permits the Division to make wider use of its limited personnel and financial resources. In turn, the Division may be able to bring and settle more cases and thereby build a more impressive record for itself. The consent procedure is also more flexible and permits decrees to be shaped to the peculiarities of particular industries; and it may enable the Division to secure broader reforms than would be required by a court. But, in its eagerness to settle cases, the Division might accept less than a court would (it was frequently criticized for doing just this during the Eisenhower administration), which is another advantage of the procedure for defendants.

The fact that consent decrees are perceived by defendants to have advantages for them over formal proceedings may give leverage in bargaining to the Antitrust Division, since it initiated the antitrust action in the first place and ultimately determines what procedure will be used in settling it. But, if the Division is to gain the ostensible benefits of consent procedure, it must bargain rather than command. The final outcome, in part, will depend upon how intensely the two contending parties desire the advantages (or values) realizable through the consent procedure and their estimates of the possible advantages, and costs, of formal court proceedings.

The Sherman Act also authorized private suits for triple damages by persons injured by violators of the law. The possible award of triple damages was intended to encourage private suits (thereby augmenting public enforcement activities) and to punish violators. Less than two hundred private suits were started during the first fifty years of the act. Though the number of private suits has greatly increased in recent years, the private plaintiffs win redress in less than a third of the cases filed.[29] Private plaintiffs often lack the resources to secure evidence and establish proof of violations. Successful government proceedings usually end in a consent decree or plea of *nolo contendere,* which involve no admission or finding of guilt, and therefore cannot be used in support of the private suit. Moreover, lower federal court judges are often unsympathetic toward private suits. "The extraordinary remedy of triple damages," stated the judge in one case, "requires the closest scrutiny of the transaction . . . and . . . should be allowed only in the rarest of cases."[30]

An interesting chain of events was triggered by the conviction of twenty-nine electrical equipment companies in 1960 for engaging in price-fixing and market-rigging during the preceding eight years. More than 2,000 private triple damage suits were filed against the companies by private utility companies and municipal agencies. By the summer of 1965 most of these private suits had been settled, most of them by out-of-court negotiations. An Associated Press poll revealed that the final settlement costs might total $400,000,000, most of which would be paid by four companies (General Electric, Westinghouse, Allis-Chalmers, and McGraw-Edison). However, the financial and punitive impact of the settlements was greatly reduced by an Internal Revenue Service ruling that the settlement costs were tax deductible as "ordinary and necessary" business expenses. One government official said the ruling may have resulted from concern about the ability of the less prosperous electrical companies to survive the settlement payments. "General Electric can survive a blow like this but what about the

---

[29] Senate Select Committee on Small Business, *The Role of Private Antitrust Enforcement in Protecting Small Business—1958,* Senate Report 1855, 85th Cong., 2nd Sess., 1958, p. v.
[30] *Ibid.,* 9–10.

smaller companies?" he stated. "Do you want to clobber an antitrust violator or do you want to clobber him and then stomp on him?"[31] The official's remarks illustrate a continuing problem in antitrust activity: How severe should the sanctions be that are imposed on violators? Are factors other than punishment to be considered in shaping penalties and remedies?

The Sherman Act in Court

In this section we will outline some of the major aspects and developments in judicial interpretation of the Sherman Act. Because of its generality, the act permits different interpretations. The meaning given to the act has shifted from one time to another, Supreme Court professions of consistency in interpretation notwithstanding, as changes have occurred in judicial attitudes, executive enforcement activity, economic circumstances, and interest group configurations and conflicts.

Let us first look at the scope of the Sherman Act—the range of economic enterprises to which it has been held to apply. The first Sherman Act case to reach the Supreme Court was that of *U.S. v. E. C. Knight Co.* (1895). Involved was the American Sugar Refining Company (the "sugar trust"), which controlled 98 per cent of the sugar refining industry. In its suit the government sought to compel the refining company to dispose of some of its recently acquired firms. The Court agreed that the company had a monopoly of sugar refining but went on to state that the Sherman Act, as an exercise of Congress' power to regulate commerce, applied only to commerce and not to manufacturing. The refining company had a monopoly in manufacturing and therefore was a matter for the states to regulate because control of manufacturing was left to the states by the Constitution. Under this restrictive interpretation of the scope of the Sherman Act, which was based on a narrow view of the commerce power, about all the Sherman Act applied to were monopolies in transportation.

The above ruling of the Court has sometimes been attributed to the failure of the government to sufficiently stress the effect of a manufacturing monopoly on the interstate movement of goods. The failure to do so undoubtedly resulted in part from the hostility of Richard R. Olney, then Attorney General, toward the Sherman Act. Olney was more concerned with getting the Act repealed than with enforcing it. He later wrote: "the government has been defeated in the Supreme Court on the trust question. I always supposed it would be and have

[31] *Winston-Salem Sentinel,* May 6, 1965, p. 30.

168

taken the responsibility of not prosecuting under a law I believed to be no good . . ."[32]

A few years after the Knight case, however, the Sherman Act was held to apply to manufacturing activities which had a "direct effect" on interstate commerce.[33] Since then the scope of the commerce power has been greatly broadened and, consequently, so has that of the Sherman Act. The act has been applied to such diverse groups as railroads, manufacturing companies, trade associations, the American Medical Association, the Associated Press, newspaper publishers, the insurance business, the real estate business, the legitimate theatre, motion picture companies, and professional boxing, wrestling, and football (but not to professional baseball). Even groups which have been exempted from the Act by Congress, such as labor unions, agricultural cooperatives, and export trade associations, have been prosecuted under the Act when they join with other groups to restrain trade. As it now stands, any group or organization whose activities can be shown to have an "actual or threatened substantial effect" on interstate commerce can be prosecuted under the act.

Although the words of the Sherman Act prohibit *every* contract, combination, or conspiracy in restraint of trade, conflict soon developed over the meaning of this phrase. Did it prohibit all restraints of trade or only all *unreasonable* restraints of trade? Those who favored strong government action to maintain competition and prevent monopoly took the first position whereas business groups and others favoring broader scope for private action took the latter view. In the Trans-Missouri Freight Association case,[34] which involved a railroad rate-fixing agreement, the Court held that the act prohibited every restraint of trade whether reasonable or unreasonable.

In 1911, however, the Court reversed its position in the Standard Oil case.[35] The Standard Oil Company, which controlled about 91 per cent of the oil refining industry, was convicted of violating both Sections 1 and 2 of the Sherman Act. In his opinion for the Court, Chief Justice White held that the act prohibited only *unreasonable* restraints of trade. Standard was guilty of violating the act not merely because it restrained trade but because it had done so unreasonably. The opinion emphasized the vicious and predatory practices used by Standard to

---

[32] Quoted in Homer S. Cummings and Carl McFarland, *Federal Justice* (New York: Macmillan, 1937), 322–323.

[33] *U.S. v. Addyston Pipe and Steel Co.,* 175 U.S. 211 (1899).

[34] *U.S. v. Trans-Missouri Freight Assn.,* 166 U.S. 290 (1897).

[35] *U.S. v. Standard Oil Co.,* 251 U.S. 417 (1911).

eliminate competitors. Thus the Sherman Act was judicially amended to include the "rule of reason," an action which Congress had earlier refused to take.

The inclusion of the rule of reason in the act led to the Court's adoption of differential positions in applying the law to close and loose combinations during the next three decades. The rule of reason was used in deciding the legality of close combinations (a number of previously independent business units integrated by common ownership and control). If a company, however large, had not achieved its size and market position by undesirable, i.e., unreasonable, methods, it was held not to violate the law. This application of the act can be illustrated by the famous U.S. Steel case in 1920.[36] When created in 1901, U.S. Steel had controlled 60 per cent of the steel capacity in the United States, and in 1920 still controlled 50 per cent. Although U.S. Steel seemed to represent the type of large combination against which the Sherman Act was directed, the Court held that the company had not broken the law. It had not coerced its competitors nor, since 1911, had it conspired to fix prices. The contention that the company was so large as to constitute an illegal monopoly was rejected on the ground that "The law does not make mere size an offense. It . . . requires overt acts and trusts to its prohibition of them and its power to repress or punish them. It does not compel competition nor require all that is possible." Thus, the steel company, though big, had not acted unreasonably, and therefore, it was not bad. To use Theodore Roosevelt's terminology, the Court had drawn the line against "misconduct, not wealth" and had found the company to be a "good" trust. According to the rule of reason only monopolizing and not "monopoly" was an offense. As a consequence of this interpretation, Section 2 of the Sherman Act was a dead letter until the 1940's.

Although the law was applied with leniency in close combination cases, there was much more severity in its application to loose combinations (agreements or arrangements among independent companies for the purpose of eliminating competition). Thus, agreements among competitors to fix prices, divide markets, or limit production were held to be *per se* violations of Section 1 of the Act. The rule of reason was not used and no effort was made to determine whether the objectives or results of such agreements were reasonable or not. The mere existence of an agreement constituted a violation of the law. As the Court stated in a price-fixing case: "it does not follow that agreements to fix or restrain prices are reasonable restraints and therefore permitted by

[36] *U.S. v. U.S. Steel Corp.*, 251 U.S. 417 (1920).

the statute, merely because the prices themselves are reasonable. . . . The aim and result of every price-fixing agreement, if effective, is the elimination of one form of competition."[37]

Only when a loose combination took the form of a trade association did the Court use the rule of reason in applying the Sherman Act to such combinations. Trade associations perform a variety of useful functions—research, industry promotion, cost studies, commercial arbitration —which may improve industry performance. Some, however, may engage in activities such as price filing and reporting schemes which restrict competition. In passing on the legality of trade association activities, the Court has attempted to balance the interests opposing restrictions on competition against the interests in favor of improved industry performance. Only those activities which unreasonably restrained competition, such as efforts to eliminate price competition, were banned.

A double standard thus existed in the application of the Sherman Act because of the courts' use of the rule of reason. The differential application of the law to close and loose combinations can be accounted for as a "law—economic conflict." As Edward S. Mason states:

> The antithesis of the legal conception of monopoly is *free* competition, understood to be a situation in which the freedom of any individual or firm to engage in legitimate economic activity is not restrained by the state, by agreements between competitors or by the predatory practices of a rival. But free competition thus understood is quite compatible with the presence of monopoly elements in the *economic* sense of the word monopoly. For the antithesis of the economic conception of monopoly is not *free* but *pure* competition, understood to be a situation in which no seller or buyer has any control over the price of his product. Restriction of competition is the legal content of monopoly; control of the market is its economic substance. And these realities are by no means equivalent.[38]

The judges, because of their prior legal training and familiarity with the legal conceptions of competition and monopoly, accepted the legal attitude. They tended to regard the intent of the Sherman Act as prohibitive of restrictions on competitors and, through use of the rule of reason, so interpreted and applied it. The legal attitude was undoubtedly reinforced by the nature of judicial antitrust proceedings. It was much easier for judges to examine and weigh evidence concerning collusive

[37] *U.S. v. Trenton Potteries Co.,* 273 U.S. 392 (1927).
[38] Mason, *op. cit.,* 334.

or predatory practices than it was to devise standards for measuring corporate (or monopoly) power over output or prices. Further, "competitors aggrieved by predatory practices" could bring cases into court but abstractions such as competition could not. Consequently, the courts were inclined to concern themselves with the protection of private interests against predatory practices rather than limitation of monopoly power in the "public interest."[39] Also, the conservative orientation of most judges, including a majority of the Supreme Court, caused them to be reluctant to interfere with private property interests. Judicial use of the rule of reason was in harmony with this reluctance.

Another explanation, cynical but insightful, for the absence of effective action against large combinations, has been provided by Thurman Arnold. Writing in the late 1930's, he commented:

> Bigness was regarded as a curse because it led to monopoly and interfered with the operation of laws of supply and demand. At the same time specialized techniques made bigness essential to producing goods in large enough quantities and at a price low enough so they could be made part of the American standard of living. In order to reconcile the ideal with practical necessity, it became necessary to develop a procedure which constantly attacked bigness . . . and at the same time never really interfered with combinations. Such pressures gave rise to the antitrust laws. . . . The same pressures made the enforcement of the antitrust laws a pure ritual. . . . The actual result of the antitrust laws was to promote the growth of great industrial combinations by deflecting the attack on them into purely moral and ceremonial channels . . . the courts soon discovered that it was only "unreasonable" combinations which were bad, just as any court would decide that a big, strong neighbor should not be incarcerated so long as he acted reasonably.[40]

In the late 1930's, however, and following two decades of relative inactivity, antitrust enforcement activities were revitalized. Strong administration support for antitrust enforcement resulted in larger Congressional appropriations for antitrust. The courts, in turn, were persuaded to provide broader and more effective interpretations of the Sherman Act. Since the late 1930's the Act's prohibitions against collusive and predatory practices have been strengthened. Moreover, the courts' position concerning the rule of reason and close combinations has shifted.

[39] Fainsod, *op. cit.,* 458–459.
[40] Thurman Arnold, *The Folklore of Capitalism* (New Haven: Yale University Press, 1937), 207–208, 212.

A major interpretative change began with the decision of a federal circuit court, acting as the highest appellate court, in 1945 in the Alcoa case.[41] The government charged Alcoa with having monopolized the production of virgin aluminum in violation of Section 2 of the Sherman Act, and the court agreed. Circuit Judge Hand held that monopolization was illegal *per se,* with the Sherman Act making no distinction between "good trusts" and "bad trusts." Alcoa controlled 90 per cent of the production of virgin aluminum and this, said Judge Hand, "is enough to constitute monopoly; it is doubtful whether sixty or sixty-four per cent are enough; and certainly thirty per cent is not." But what about the fact that the Act prohibits monopolization and not monopoly as such? Alcoa, stated Hand, had not had monopoly "thrust" upon it. It had worked effectively to exclude would-be competitors by acting "progressively to embrace each new opportunity as it opened, and to face each newcomer with new capacity already geared into a great organization, having the advantage of experience, trade connections, and the elite of personnel." A monopoly position could thus be gained and held by means other than predatory practices and the destruction of competitors. In short, Alcoa had violated the law because of its excessive size, as measured by its share of the market. No use was made of the rule of reason in determining the violation, seemingly eliminating the distinction between close and loose combinations under the Act.

The Supreme Court endorsed the Alcoa decision in 1946 in the second American Tobacco Company case.[42] The three leading cigarette manufacturing companies (American, Reynolds, and Liggett and Myers) were found guilty of monopolization in a criminal proceeding. The evidence presented by the government did not show any open collusion but rather demonstrated through economic and statistical evidence that the three companies had apparently pursued common pricing and purchasing policies in an effort to "squeeze out" some of their smaller competitors. They had not succeeded and their share of the market had declined from over 90 per cent to 68 per cent from 1931 to 1938. Affirming the condemnation of monopoly power *per se* in the Alcoa case, the Court held that actual exclusion was not necessary to sustain the charge of monopolization. "The material considera-

[41] *U.S. v. Aluminum Co. of America,* 148 F.2d 416 (1945). Several Supreme Court justices had disqualified themselves from hearing the Alcoa case because of previous involvement in its prosecution. Because a quorum of six was thus not available to hear the case, the judicial code was amended to permit a circuit court to make final decisions in such instances.

[42] *American Tobacco Co. v. U.S.,* 328 U.S. 781 (1946).

tion in determining whether a monopoly exists is not that prices are raised and competitors excluded, but that power exists to raise prices or exclude competitors when it is desired to do so." The decisions in the Alcoa and American Tobacco cases produced a new interpretation by condemning "the power to abuse rather than the abuse of power."[43] They eliminated for the most part the rule of reason as a standard for determining the legality of monopoly and monopoly power.

But problems still remain. It still must be determined in particular cases how much market power a company must possess before its possession becomes illegal as monopoly power. Is it control of 90 per cent of the market, or 68 per cent, or what? No precise answer has been provided. A second problem relates to defining the market allegedly being monopolized. Depending upon whether the relevant market is narrowly or broadly defined, a company may or may not be guilty of monopolization. For example, in the 1956 cellophane case,[44] DuPont was accused of monopolizing the cellophane market because it produced over 80 per cent of the supply and its licensee the remainder. The Court defined the relevant market to include all flexible wrapping materials —glassine, waxed papers, aluminum foil, etc., as well as cellophane. DuPont produced only 18 per cent of all flexible wrapping materials and on this basis was exonerated on the monopolization charge. Had the market been defined to include only cellophane, the decision could well have gone against DuPont. Whether a company has monopoly power thus depends upon the standards of measurement used, and the selection of these standards is a matter for judicial determination.

Judicial application of the Sherman Act in recent years, especially as it relates to monopolization, has been well characterized here:

> What the courts appear to be reaching for, above and beyond the range of traditional Sherman Act violations, is a doctrine of permissible power. Some power there has to be, both because of inescapable limitations to the process of atomization and because power is needed to do the job the American public expects of its industrial machine.[45]

In summary, judicial interpretation has made the meaning of the Sherman Act more specific and, in recent decades, has made it a more effective tool for maintaining a competitive economy. The double

[43] Harold Koontz and Richard W. Gable, *Public Control of Economic Enterprise* (New York: McGraw-Hill, 1956), 340.

[44] *U.S. v. E. I. duPont de Nemours & Co.,* 351 U.S. 377 (1956).

[45] Mason, *op. cit.,* 387.

standard employed in the interpretation of the law has almost disappeared, and the rule of reason no longer provides large combinations with a shield against prosecution. But, as we have said, the "operational" meaning of the Sherman Act depends on more than judicial interpretation. Executive enforcement activity, and congressional support of it, also play important roles in shaping antitrust policy. We now turn to these matters.

The Politics of Enforcement

Historically, antitrust enforcement has been strongly affected by the policy positions of the various presidential administrations since 1890. The Harrison, Cleveland, and McKinley administrations were conservative and manifested little enthusiasm for the Sherman Act. Only eighteen antitrust cases were started during their administrations. During the Progressive era there was comparatively vigorous antitrust enforcement by the Roosevelt, Taft, and Wilson administrations in response to strong pressures for the control of monopoly and private economic power. But after 1917 a period of tax enforcement lasting two decades set in. The Wilson administration and the country became preoccupied with winning the Great War and making the world safe for democracy. Then, during the 1920's the business-minded Republican administrations were not inclined to disturb business interests, the dominant source of their political support, by active antitrust enforcement. Nor, in an era in which business values were predominant, was there much public support for antitrust activity. The early New Deal, in the form of the National Industrial Recovery Act and as an attempt to combat the depression, was more concerned with limiting competition than with promoting it. Following the revival of antitrust enforcement in the late 1930's by the New Deal, and with the exception of the World War II years, there has been active antitrust enforcement by both Democratic and Republican administrations. Vigorous antitrust activity is now both bipartisan and politically popular. But administration support is only one factor affecting enforcement.

The amount of funds made available by Congress to antitrust agencies, especially the Antitrust Division, also has a significant effect on enforcement activity. Until 1935 the annual appropriation for the Antitrust Division was less than $300,000, an amount sufficient to finance the prosecution of only a few cases a year. This state of affairs led one observer to remark that, until the late 1930's, antitrust enforcement was "merely symbolic in nature. In any one year, from half a dozen to a dozen cases were selected for investigation and trial. . . . With all available resources committed . . . the prosecution of a few lawbreakers became in effect a guarantee of immunity to the rest."[46]

Since the late 1930's the appropriation for the Antitrust Division has gradually increased, rising to more than $6 million annually since 1963. Although the costs of handling cases have also risen, an increasing number of cases have been started annually. New cases averaged 63 per year for the 1956–1964 period.[47] More than twice as many cases have been brought since 1940 as during the preceding fifty years. Other things being equal, whether antitrust enforcement is lax or vigorous depends upon the funds available.

Even with the larger recent appropriations, the Antitrust Division is still limited in the number of cases it can start. A really intensive antitrust enforcement program would require still more funds to hire personnel and finance investigations and litigation. "An increase of the over all budget of the Antitrust Division by at least severalfold is clearly called for if violations are to be deterred because of the prospect of apprehension and legal action, and if the bulk of undesirable situations and practices are to be remedied as they occur."[48] The lack of sufficient Congressional financial support to permit the intensive enforcement program thought desirable by some antitrust proponents, would seem to be the result of such things as (1) the belief that antitrust violations are not as serious, or "morally wrong," as other law violations; (2) ideological opposition to "excessive" government interference with private economic activity; (3) uncertainty among both officials and citizens on such matters as the difference between monopoly and bigness and the amount of competition presently existent, or desirable for the future, in the economy; and (4) the lack of strong, consistent, organized group support for a strong enforcement program.

Setting aside now the matter of financial support, it appears that the Antitrust Division has been and is still somewhat haphazard in its selection of cases for legal action. "There is a persistent tendency toward the selection of cases largely in response to the receipt of specific complaints, usually either from competitors of, or buyers from, allegedly offending firms, or from Congressmen who represent or reflect the opinions of such interests."[49] Cases also originate from suggestions made

[46] Corwin D. Edwards, *Maintaining Competition* (New York: McGraw-Hill, 1949), 293.

[47] Derived from Department of Justice, Antitrust Division, *Comparative Summary of Workload Statistics by Fiscal Years* (Washington, D.C.: mimeo., 1964).

[48] Joe S. Bain, *Industrial Organization* (New York: John Wiley and Sons, 1959), 612.

[49] *Ibid.*, 613.

by other government agencies and from the research activity of the Division itself. This "haphazard" selection procedure may mean that important violations are overlooked or not prosecuted in the absence of specific complaints. To the extent that private complaints are relied on, private interests help shape the Division's enforcement program; and their actions may be motivated more by the desire to gain advantage over their rivals than by an interest in maintaining a broadly competitive economy.

Roughly two-thirds of the antitrust cases filed since 1890 have dealt with collusive practices in violation of Section 1 of the Sherman Act, and price-fixing agreements have been the activity most often singled out for legal action. From 1956–1964 an average of only nine monopolization (Section 2) cases was started annually. If the double standard has disappeared from the *interpretation* of the Sherman Act it certainly has not entirely disappeared in the *enforcement* process. Moreover, antitrust enforcement has focused not only on Section 1 but also on its application to three broadly defined sectors of the economy: food processing and distribution, production and distribution of building materials, and the service trades. About half of the antitrust cases since 1890 have involved these industrial groups although they are characterized by far lower economic concentration than such groups as metals production, chemicals, and electrical goods and machinery, which have been more lightly dealt with.

Why have these trends or biases appeared in the enforcement of the Act? A number of factors help explain them and also cast some light on the enforcement process.[50] First, under procedures, as indicated above, many antitrust cases originate out of private complaints. A large proportion of the complaints received by the Antitrust Division concern industrial groupings which deal with many small customers. Second, these industrial groupings deal with the "necessities" of life (like food) or come into contact with large numbers of buyers (e.g., building materials). The focus of the Antitrust Division on such industries may be politically expedient insofar as it is seeking Congressional and public support. And the Antitrust Division, like any government agency, needs such support if it is to survive and prosper. Third, companies in industries with many firms and low concentration may be more inclined to engage in formal agreements or collusion than companies in more concentrated industries, who can gain "monopoly" profits or shield themselves against economic risks without formal restraint of competition. Fourth, Section 2 monopolization cases are more costly in time, money, and personnel to prosecute and more

[50] The following discussion draws partly on *ibid.*, 491–492.

difficult to win than are cases involving collusion. The more obvious and easily provable violations tend to occur in low concentration industries. It is reasonable to assume that in allocating its scarce resources of money and personnel the Antitrust Division will be motivated at least partly by the desire to produce the best record possible—a winning one in both total numbers and percentage of cases won. This will gratify the egos of agency personnel and perhaps help gain political support for the Division, to indicate both psychological and political bases for such a desire.

The enforcement of antitrust policy is complicated and further opened to political struggle by the fact that jurisdiction under the antitrust laws is shared by twenty agencies. Because the various agencies have different institutional and policy viewpoints, and because they respond to different interests and values, they may differ in their interpretation and application of the law. Whether lawyers for potential antitrust defendants seek to have their problems handled by the Antitrust Division or the Federal Trade Commission (the two major antitrust agencies) depends on their beliefs concerning which agency will give their clients easier treatment. Bank mergers approved by the Comptroller of the Currency and the Federal Reserve Board, who have authority over such mergers under the banking laws, have later been successfully attacked in antitrust proceedings as have some of the mergers approved by the Interstate Commerce Commission.[51]

The problems which may emerge when two agencies with different policy orientations have competing jurisdiction over the same business activity are illustrated by a situation involving the El Paso Natural Gas Company.[52] In 1956 El Paso proposed a merger with another natural gas company, the Pacific Northwest Pipeline Corporation. The Antitrust Division in 1957 filed suit in a federal district court to prevent the merger, alleging that it would substantially lessen competition in violation of the Clayton Act. Soon afterward, El Paso applied to the Federal Power Commission for approval of the merger as is required by Section 7 of the Natural Gas Act of 1938. El Paso then obtained a federal court order suspending the antitrust proceeding until the FPC reached a decision. This action by El Paso probably rested on the assumption that the FPC, because of its tendency to promote the economic health of the natural gas industry, would approve the merger.

[51] Massel, op. cit., 106, 81.
[52] This matter is treated more fully in Peter Woll, American Bureaucracy (New York: W. W. Norton, 1963), 78–80; and The New York Times, May 2, 1965, p. F1.

Once given, such a decision would militate against resumption of the antitrust action, or at least would serve as strong evidence against the Antitrust Division's position.

The FPC approved El Paso's proposed merger. The commission apparently believed the merger was thus made immune from antitrust action because, it said, it had taken the Clayton Act into consideration in making its decision that the merger was in the public interest. The State of California, acting on behalf of its citizens as natural gas consumers, appealed the FPC decision to a federal court of appeals, which upheld the FPC. The state then took the case to the Supreme Court which, in 1962, held that the FPC should have waited for the antitrust case to be completed before acting. The antitrust proceeding was then resumed and in 1964 it again reached the Supreme Court. The Court unanimously held that El Paso's merger violated the Clayton Act and ordered El Paso to divest itself of the merged company, thereby nullifying the FPC action.

The effectiveness of antitrust policy for maintaining competition has been lessened by Congressional legislation exempting various groups from antitrust prosecution. Exemptions have been extended to such groups as export trade associations, agricultural cooperatives, insurance companies, and retail distributors. It is not exaggerating too much to say that everyone favors competition for everybody except himself. Congress has occasionally responded to the demands of particular interest groups (which are often motivated by a concern for economic security in the form of sustained incomes) for protection against some of the hazards of competition. Although there is strong, if primarily latent, support for the Sherman Act and the maintenance of competition which would be activated by a direct assault on them, it has not always proved sufficient to forestall piecemeal limitations on competition. Consumers, who are generally regarded as the prime beneficiaries of competition, are notoriously unorganized and often are unable to exert sufficient pressure to prevent such limitations or other actions which may be inconsistent with the general procompetitive policy.

Additional Antitrust Legislation

Dissatisfaction with the enforcement of the Sherman Act during its first two decades produced a variety of pressures and demands for additional legislation. Critics of the Supreme Court's interpretation of the Sherman Act to include the rule of reason wanted legislation to reduce the discretion which this ruling gave to the courts. Small business interests wanted more protection from their larger competitors. Many businessmen wanted the law to be more specific so they could know with more certainty whether their actions were legal or not. In general, groups supporting the policy of maintaining competition wanted legislation against various predatory competitive practices to prevent the development of monopolies. They contended that unfair competition was a major cause of monopoly. Organized labor and some retail and wholesale groups wanted exemptions from the Sherman Act.

By 1914 two general patterns of thought concerning strengthening of the antitrust laws had crystallized out of this welter of interests and demands. There was a divergence, not on the need for additional legislation, but on the form it should take. Some contended that specific legislation was needed which would enumerate and prohibit a list of unfair practices so as to make the law more definite and eliminate the uncertainty generated by the rule of reason. Others contended that such legislation would not be effective because new unfair practices would be developed which were not prohibited. What was needed, rather, was a general prohibition of unfair competition enforced by an administrative commission with power to determine what was fair or unfair in particular cases. The first pattern of thought is reflected in the Clayton Act and the second in the Federal Trade Commission Act, both of which were passed in 1914.

The Clayton Act

Four specific sets of practices are prohibited by the Clayton Act: price discrimination, exclusive dealing and tying contracts, intercorporate stockholding, and interlocking corporate directorates. The first three, however, are banned only if their effect "may be to substantially lessen competition or tend to create a monopoly." Enforcement of the act is entrusted jointly to the Antitrust Division and the Federal Trade Commission. To avoid becoming bogged down in a morass of detail, we shall discuss the Clayton Act in simplified fashion giving especial attention to the problem of intercorporate stockholding (mergers).

Section 2 of the act prohibited sellers from discriminating in prices among buyers unless such discrimination was based on "differences in grade, quality, or quantity," made only "due allowance for differences in the cost of selling or transportation," or was done "in good faith to meet competition." This section was directed primarily at large companies which used local price cutting to eliminate small competitors while maintaining their price levels elsewhere. The Standard Oil Company and other trusts had often engaged in such predatory activity. Section 2 was rarely applied to local price cutting and was not very effective, because of both the exceptions in the law and unfavorable judicial interpretations. It was amended by the Robinson-Patman Act of 1936.

Section 3 prohibited exclusive dealing and tying contracts, which are devices for excluding competitors from market. Under an exclusive dealing arrangement a seller agrees to give a buyer access to his goods only if the buyer will not handle goods from any of the seller's competitors. Under a tying contract a seller gives a buyer access to some of his goods only if he takes others as well. An example of a tying contract declared illegal under this section was the International Salt Company's requirement that lessees of its salt dispensing machines must also purchase the salt so dispensed from International, foreclosing this market to other sellers of salt.[53] In general, exclusive dealing and tying contracts, when challenged, have been held illegal if the company using them has "dominant" or "substantial" control of the market.

Section 8 declared illegal interlocking directorates among banks with over $5 million capital or competing corporations with over $1 million capital "where the elimination of competition . . . would constitute a violation of any of the provisions of the Antitrust laws." This section has never been enforced with any vigor as the antitrust agencies have concentrated their limited resources on other matters. However, in 1963 the Congress denied a request by the Federal Trade Commission for funds to study interlocking directorates and other intercorporate relationships. Congress apparently has no desire for Section 8 to be of practical rather than symbolic significance.

Section 7 forbade any corporation engaged in commerce to acquire stock in a competing company, or in two or more companies who were competitors, where the effect "may be to substantially lessen competition or tend to create a monopoly in any line of commerce." This section, intended to combat corporate mergers, had little real significance until the 1950's. In 1926 the Supreme Court held that it prohibited mergers only through stock acquisitions and not mergers effected by one corporation's acquisition of the physical assets of a competitor, even if the merger of physical assets was done through the use of illegally acquired voting stock.[54] This decision created a large loophole in the

[53] *International Salt Co. v. U.S.,* 332 U.S. 392 (1947).
[54] *FTC v. Western Meat Co.,* 272 U.S. 554 (1926).

181

law, since competitors who desired to merge could easily and legally do so by transferring their physical assets.

Although the Federal Trade Commission and other antitrust supporters continually urged Congress to close this loophole, no action was taken until the passage of the Celler Anti-merger Act in 1950. This statute, which amends Section 7 of the Clayton Act, prohibits mergers by acquisition of either stock or physical assets where the effect may substantially lessen competition or tend to create a monopoly "in any line of commerce in any section of the country."

The antitrust agencies now give close attention to the enforcement of the antimerger provision. Their efforts have been complemented by favorable judicial action. Between July, 1956, and July, 1962, the Antitrust Division and the FTC started a combined total of 106 antimerger cases, nearly twice as many as were begun between 1914 and 1950. Important proposed mergers prevented in recent years include those involving the Youngstown and Bethlehem steel companies in 1958 and Chrysler and Mack Truck in 1964.

The Supreme Court has acted to broaden the scope of the new Section 7 in cases coming before it. In the DuPont-General Motors case in 1957,[55] the Court held that the Clayton Act prohibited combinations by vertical stock acquisitions (as when a supplier gains control of a purchaser) as well as horizontal mergers (those involving companies in the same stage of production). DuPont was convicted of using its 23 per cent stock ownership of General Motors, which it had acquired by 1919, to gain an illegal preference over its competitors in the sale of automotive fabrics and finishes to General Motors. DuPont was subsequently ordered to divest itself of its General Motors stock.

In 1963 the Supreme Court ruled that bank mergers could be proceeded against under the Clayton Act, even though the Bank Merger Act of 1961 gave the various federal banking agencies (Comptroller of the Currency, Federal Reserve Board, Federal Deposit Insurance Corporation) authority to control bank mergers, and even though they might have approved bank mergers subsequently moved against by the Antitrust Division. Experience has revealed that the banking agencies are more sympathetic toward bank mergers than is the Antitrust Division with its procompetitive bent. Consequently the banking industry is seeking legislation from Congress which would at least partially restrict the freedom of the Division to move against bank mergers.

The antitrust agencies now regard Section 7 as an effective instrument for preventing or slowing down economic concentration which

[55] *U.S. v. DuPont,* 353 U.S. 586 (1957).

182

may lessen competition. In applying the antimerger law the antitrust agencies and the courts have been inclined to reject any merger which would give the combined companies control of 15 per cent or more of their market.[56] The general viewpoint manifested by the "new" antimerger policy is that huge companies cannot be allowed to increase their size by mergers. In their actions, however, the antitrust agencies may be motivated not only by the desire to maintain competition but also by the wish to protect smaller competitors against competition. Thus, in its annual report for 1963 the Federal Trade Commission discusses its antimerger activity as part of "The Fight to Protect Small Business." But, whatever the motives behind it, present judicial and agency attitudes have produced a strengthened antimerger policy with which the business community must reckon.

The Federal Trade Commission

The Federal Trade Commission Act created an administrative commission, headed by a five-man board, with executive, rule-making, and adjudicatory functions. The commissioners are appointed by the President for seven-year terms and no more than three of them can come from the same political party. They are subject to presidential removal from office only for "inefficiency, neglect of duties or malfeasance in office." Section 5 of the act empowered the Commission to prevent "unfair methods of competition in commerce" by issuing, after formal complaint, notice, and hearing, "cease and desist" orders to those found engaging in such practices. The Commission was given jurisdiction jointly with the Department of Justice to enforce the Clayton Act. The FTC was also authorized to conduct studies or investigations and issue reports on business organizations and practices; to investigate alleged violations of the antitrust laws at the request of the President or Congress; to investigate the effectiveness of antitrust decrees when requested by the Attorney General; and to assist the courts in formulating antitrust decrees when called upon to do so. The Commission's investigational or information-gathering authority was partly a product of the belief, general at the time, that "pitiless publicity" would prevent many antitrust violations.

Legislation enacted since 1914 has greatly enlarged the jurisdiction of the FTC. It shares responsibility with the Department of Justice for enforcing the various amendments to the Clayton Act, especially the

[56] M. A. Adelman, "The Antimerger Act 1950–60," *American Economic Review,* LI (May 1961), 238–239. Cf. *The New York Times,* Jan. 11, 1965, p. 57.

Robinson-Patman and Celler Anti-Merger Acts. The Wheeler-Lea Act of 1938 amended Section 5 of the original FTC Act to prohibit "unfair or deceptive acts or practices in commerce" as well as unfair methods of competition. Deceptive acts or practices include activities (false or misleading advertising, for example) which may deceive or injure consumers without necessarily harming competitors of those engaged in deception. The Wheeler-Lea Act was passed by Congress to overcome a judicial ruling that under the original Section 5 competitive practices could be prohibited as unfair only if they hurt competitors, regardless of the harmful or deceptive effects they might have on consumers. The act thus gives the Commission clear power to protect consumers.

The FTC also enforces a number of statutes which require honest and accurate labeling of fur, wool, and textile products. Although these statutes provide consumer protection they were enacted primarily at the behest of producer groups. The Wool Products Act of 1940, for example, was passed mainly at the insistence of sheep-raisers and woolen weavers wanting to protect wool products from "unfair" competition by other fibers which, in the absence of honest labels, might be passed off as wool. Another law enforced by the Commission is the Flammable Fabrics Act of 1953, which prohibits the production or distribution of clothing made of "highly flammable" fabrics.

In enforcing the statutes under its jurisdiction, the FTC now employs a number of methods, formal and informal. The Commission presently emphasizes securing voluntary compliance with policy. Procedures used for this purpose include advisory opinions and trade regulation rules, both of which were adopted in 1963, and trade practices conferences. The Commission gives advisory opinions to business men seeking advice as to whether a proposed action is illegal, e.g., whether a particular quantity discount would violate the Robinson-Patman Act. These opinions are considered binding on the Commission unless under changed circumstances their reconsideration would be "in the public interest." Trade regulation rules, issued after all interested parties have had opportunity to be heard, express the judgment of the Commission, based on its knowledge and experience, on the substantive requirements of the laws it administers. A rule may cover all possible applications of a statutory provision, and its effects may be nationwide, or it may be limited to a particular area, industry, or product. Under the trade practices conference procedure, first used in 1919, the Commission meets with the members of an industry to draw up codes of fair trade practices. These codes include Group I rules, which condemn practices found illegal by the FTC and the courts, and Group II rules, which are directed against practices which are not illegal but are considered unfair by industry members. These procedures are designed to guide businessmen away from illegal practices and to encourage voluntary compliance by informing them of the meaning and requirements of the law.

The Commission also uses several techniques in proceeding against those accused of violating the law. A complaint against an offender may be dropped upon receipt of a letter of assurance in which he states that he has discontinued the practice complained against. When a complaint issued by the Commission is contested, the case may be formally tried (adjudicated) and, if the practice complained of is found to violate the law, the FTC issues an order directing the offender to "cease and desist." Such orders, which become effective after sixty days unless judicially challenged, are enforceable through the federal courts. At any time during a formal proceeding, or before it begins, a case may be settled by a consent order negotiated by the Commission and the offender. Under the consent order the offender agrees to stop the practices considered objectionable without necessarily admitting their illegality. The Commission makes extensive use of consent orders in settling cases. During fiscal 1963, 381 consent orders were issued compared to 65 contested cease and desist orders. This is in line with the Commission's stress on voluntary compliance with formal action only as a last resort.

The substantive work of the Federal Trade Commission involves two general categories of action: antimonopoly cases and deceptive practices cases. Antimonopoly cases involve restraints of trade under the FTC and Clayton acts. Illustrative here are cases involving price fixing, discriminatory pricing, and mergers. Deceptive practices cases involve actions which mislead or deceive consumers, and which may also have the effect of diverting trade from honest businessmen. Among the deceptive practices stopped by the Commission in 1962 were the following: The Vick Chemical Company agreed to stop advertising that "Vicks Double-Buffered Cold Tablets" would cure a common cold or shorten its duration. The Murray Space Shoe Corporation was prohibited from claiming that its shoes would correct, prevent, or relieve arthritis, high blood pressure, indigestion, or stomach ulcers. Soberin Aids Company was ordered not to claim that a drug preparation it sold would cure alcoholism.

The Federal Trade Commission in the past was the object of much criticism. It was charged with devoting too much time to anti-deception work to the neglect of antimonopoly work, which would be more valuable for maintaining a competitive economy. The Commission was criticized for using antiquated and cumbersome procedures in handling cases which resulted in long-delayed decisions and large backlogs of unfinished work. The Commission was also accused of adopting a passive, judicial attitude, waiting for cases to be brought to it rather than actively enforcing the law. Further, it was contended that: "With notable exceptions, appointments to the Federal Trade Commission have been made with too little interest in the skills and experience pertinent to the problems of competition and monopoly, and too much attention to service to political party."[57] These criticisms, and the circumstances which gave rise to them, led James M. Landis to declare that the only way to correct the "utter bankruptcy" of the FTC was to "wipe out the FTC completely and start afresh."[58] Change has come but not in the drastic manner thus suggested.

During the later years of the Eisenhower administration, and continuing during the Kennedy and Johnson administrations, efforts were made to reform the Commission. Its procedures have been improved and the backlog of pending cases has been reduced. The organization of the Commission has been revamped and more responsibility for its operations has been given to its chairman. Better, more qualified personnel have been appointed as commissioners. Further, increased Congressional appropriations, resulting in part from stronger presidential support, have enabled the Commission to expand its staff and to both broaden and intensify its enforcement activities. Better commission performance has increased judicial confidence in the Commission and today it receives far more favorable treatment at the hands of the courts than it did in the past.

The Commission presently is much more vigorous and effective as an antitrust agency than it was during most of its history. It is an active proponent and protector, especially, of the interests of small businesses and consumers. It now devotes the major portion of its efforts to antimonopoly work. Nearly two-thirds of its enforcement budget went for this purpose in fiscal 1963 and the Commission issued an all-time high of 454 cease and desist orders, including 261 in the antimonopoly area.[59] The Commission has adopted a policy of attacking

[57] Commission on Organization of the Executive Branch of the Government, *Task Force Report on Regulatory Commissions* (Washington, D.C.: Government Printing Office, 1949), 125.

[58] George W. Stocking and Myron W. Watkins, *Monopoly and Free Enterprise* (New York: Twentieth Century Fund, 1951), 548. Landis was a former member of two regulatory commissions.

[59] See Federal Trade Commission, *Annual Report,* 1963, pp. 31, 32.

law violations on an industry-wide basis when investigation reveals that a large number of industry members are engaged in violation rather than concentrating solely on individual cases. In addition, it has expanded its efforts to secure voluntary compliance with the law and to check on compliance with orders once they are issued.

Two actions started by the Commission in 1964 exemplify the range and diversity of its activity. One involved an alleged monopoly of the baseball "trading cards" found in bubble gum packages. This case, later dismissed for lack of evidence, indicates that the Commission still is sometimes concerned with what some consider "trivia."

The second action involved a proposed Commission order to require cigarette packages and advertising to include warnings that cigarette smoking could be injurious to health. In the wake of the Surgeon General's 1964 report stating that a link exists between cigarette smoking and lung cancer, the proposed order aroused much opposition among tobacco producing and manufacturing interests and their supporters in Congress and elsewhere. Led by tobacco-state Congressmen, a movement to overcome the proposed FTC action was launched in Congress. Legislation was enacted in 1965 requiring cigarette packages to carry a health warning but prohibiting the FTC from requiring warnings in advertising for a four-year period. The tobacco companies had been especially opposed to warnings in advertising and had wanted a permanent prohibition on them. A bill providing this had been passed by the House but the Senate, which is traditionally less responsive to "special interests," refused to go along.[60] The Commission will be free to take action on cigarette advertising after four years, so the issue is only temporarily resolved. This case study illustrates the new strength and vigor of the FTC. It also shows that Congressional action is a possible source of redress for economic interests lacking access and influence with a regulatory commission.

Small Business and the Moderation of Competition

Small business groups engaged in wholesale and retail distribution have been quite active, and frequently successful, in seeking national and state legislation intended to lessen the impact of competition on themselves, especially competition coming from chain stores and other mass distributors. The number of small businessmen engaged in wholesale and retail distribution is large and, when organized, they are politically potent. Every member of Congress has hundreds or thousands of them in his district or state. Their political potency is en-

[60] *Congressional Quarterly Weekly Report*, XXIII (March 26, 1965), 535.

hanced by the fact that the small businessman is something of a culture hero. He is often viewed and eulogized as epitomizing independence, thrift, self-reliance, freedom, and other values identified with the American Way of Life. John H. Bunzel has remarked: "With the possible exception of the American farmer, it is doubtful if the virtues and values of any individual have been so consistently and unanimously proclaimed as those of the small business man."[61]

For these and other reasons, legislators have shown a marked willingness to come to the aid of small businessmen, even if it meant restricting competition to do so. Indeed, the primary intended effect of the various legislative actions discussed here has been more to preserve competitors than competition. Altogether, they provide an instructive example of the use of government to promote particular group interests.

A major development in the distributive trades in the early decades of this century was the rapid expansion of chain stores and other mass distributors.[62] Between 1900 and 1929 the chain stores' share of retail trade grew from almost nothing to around 20 per cent. The essential appeal of chain stores to the consumer lay in the lower prices they were able to offer. Because of economies resulting from the scale of their operations, greater operating efficiency, better management, and because of their ability to buy at lower prices from their suppliers, the chains were able to undersell their smaller competitors and expand their share of the market while earning good profits. Although predatory practices played some part in the chains' growth, their greater efficiency was the main factor. The competitive pressures exerted by the chains on small retailers were intensified by the Great Depression, which caused both lower incomes and greater consumer price consciousness. By 1933 the chains' share of the market had increased to 25 per cent. To the small retailer the chains threatened extinction or at least greatly impaired income. Their success, moreover, was disturbing to his self-image and self-esteem.

But not only retailers felt threatened by the growth of chain stores. Wholesalers were also affected as the chains often bypassed them and dealt directly with the manufacturers. The wholesalers' bankruptcy rate was lower than that of retailers, but they undoubtedly derived little comfort from that fact. Consequently, wholesalers joined and some-

[61] Quoted in Harmon Zeigler, *The Politics of Small Business* (Washington, D.C.: Public Affairs Press, 1961), 1.

[62] An excellent discussion of the economics and politics of small business is Joseph C. Palamountain, Jr., *The Politics of Distribution* (Cambridge: Harvard University Press, 1955), on which this section draws.

times led the small business campaign against the chains in the political arena. Efforts to use legislation to combat the chains reached a peak in the 1930's.

The first attack on the chains came at the state level and took the form of legislation placing punitive taxes on them. These taxes were intended to handicap the chains, if not to drive them out of existence, by raising their costs of doing business. Beginning in 1927, twenty-seven states enacted such taxes, at rates ranging from a maximum of $100 per store in Wisconsin to $750 per store in Texas. The chain tax movement was supported by wholesalers and retailers although at this time they were not well organized for political action. Initiative in the enactment of these taxes was often taken by state legislators aware of the need and support for new sources of state revenue and of the opportunity to gain political support and favor as the champions of small business. Another causal force is indicated by the fact that chain taxes were first adopted and were most frequent and severe in the southern and western states. In these regions popular attitudes toward chains were conditioned by the "latent fear of, and animosity toward, 'foreign' corporations dominated by Northern and Eastern financial interests—'Wall Street.'"[63]

By the late 1930's the chain tax movement had ebbed. Many of the taxes were repealed or declared unconstitutional by state courts; only about half of them remain. In the long run the chain taxes were probably ineffective from the small business standpoint. Though the taxes neither drove the chains out of existence nor crippled them, they did cause the chains to close some of their marginal stores, to increase the size of individual stores, and consequently to become more efficient and more competitive than ever.

The next attack on the chains occurred at the national level. The Robinson-Patman Act of 1936 was generally intended to reduce the buying power of the chains. Small business groups contended that the chains were able to sell at lower prices because the bargaining power provided by their large size enabled them to obtain goods from suppliers at lower costs than were economically justifiable. It was much easier for the independent wholesalers and retailers to thus explain the chains' success than to admit their own relative inefficiency, which would have been far more accurate but both politically unappealing and personally ungratifying. The chains served as a convenient scapegoat for the small businessman's economic difficulties.

[63] *Ibid.*, 163.

The campaign for the Robinson-Patman Act was led by the U.S. Wholesale Grocers' Association, which drafted the original House bill. Additional support came from such groups as the retail druggists, the retail grocers, and some manufacturers who wanted protection against the buying power of large distributors. Despite its varied sources of support, the bill was depicted as necessary to protect the small retailer. Opposition came from chain stores, department stores, and other mass distributors; and they succeeded in weakening the original bill.

In brief, the Robinson-Patman Act prohibited price discrimination by a seller among his buyers when it would substantially lessen competition or "tend to create a monopoly in any line of commerce," or prevent or injure competition between or among his buyers, unless it could be justified on the basis of different costs in supplying different buyers. A price discrimination also could be defended "as made in good faith to meet an equally low price of a competitor." Other provisions prohibited allowances for brokerage services unless a broker were actually used and allowances for advertising or other services unless they were made available to all buyers on proportionately equal terms. These provisions were intended to reinforce the price discrimination prohibitions. Finally, it was made illegal for anyone to knowingly induce or receive a price discrimination. In general, the act was designed to reduce price competition between chains and their smaller competitors by restricting the alleged unfair buying advantages of the chains.

As the Robinson-Patman Act has been applied since 1936, it has probably reduced the vigor of price competition, although it would be difficult to specify how much. It has also given wholesalers and producers some protection against the chains' buying power. However, the small retailer, in whose name and defense the act was ostensibly passed, has not been much benefited. For one thing, it was not the chains' buying power but their greater efficiency and economies of scale that enabled them to outsell their smaller rivals. Second, and despite its supporters' desire to restrict competition, the inclusion of the "good faith to meet competition" clause in the act permitted the courts to interpret the act as a means of protecting competition. As the Supreme Court stated:

> The heart of our national economic policy has long been faith in the value of competition. In the Sherman and the Clayton Acts, as well as in the Robinson-Patman Act, "Congress was dealing with competition, which it sought to protect, and monopoly, which it sought to prevent."[64]

[64] *Standard Oil Company v. FTC,* 340 U.S. 231 (1951).

A third attack on chain stores was designed to restrict the freedom of mass distributors to lower their selling prices. Two types of legislation resulted: unfair practices or minimum markup laws and resale price maintenance ("fair trade") legislation. The first category of laws, enacted by thirty-one states, customarily prohibited sales below cost. The second, resale price maintenance laws, went further and permitted retailers and manufacturers or wholesalers to enter into agreements concerning the minimum prices below which trademarked or brand-name goods could not be sold. With the inclusion of "non-signer clauses" in such laws, the agreed-upon minimum price was binding on all who sold an article and not merely those directly involved in the agreement. Forty-five states enacted resale price maintenance laws during the 1930's. The prime force behind the enactment of these laws was the National Association of Retail Druggists, a well-organized, well-financed, skillfully led, militant trade association. Support also came from other retailers and from some manufacturers and wholesalers.

Resale price maintenance agreements were liable to prosecution as restraints of trade under the Sherman Act when the parties to them were located in different states, which reduced their effectiveness. Consequently, the NARD and its allies embarked on a campaign to obtain federal legislation exempting such agreements from antitrust action. Success came with the enactment of the Miller-Tydings Act in 1937. What Congress gave, however, the Supreme Court partially took away in 1951 when it held that the 1937 legislation did not exempt the non-signer clause part of the resale price maintenance laws from federal antitrust prosecution. The organized drug interests and their cohorts immediately set out to secure Congressional action to overcome the Court's decision. Notwithstanding opposition from labor and farm organizations, the American Bar Association, the Department of Justice, and others, Congress passed the McGuire Fair Trade Enabling Act by large majorities in 1952. The act exempted use of the non-signer clause from the antitrust laws, another demonstration of the political influence of organized drug interests and the responsiveness of Congress to small business interests.

Resale price maintenance laws have declined in recent years because of their opponents' success in combating them in the state courts. Many state courts have either declared them unconstitutional or have nullified their non-signer clauses. One successful ground for judicial attack is that resale price maintenance laws unconstitutionally delegate power to fix prices to private groups. Resale price agreements are now really enforceable and effective in only twenty-three states.[65]

[65] The New York Times, June 6, 1964, pp. 49, 59.

This erosion of state resale price maintenance legislation has prompted a new tack by the NARD and its "fair trade" allies, who now include many brand-name manufacturers. They want Congress to enact "Quality Stabilization" legislation which would permit manufacturers to establish minimum resale prices for their brand-name or trademark goods on a nationwide basis. Its supporters, in a now familiar refrain, argue that it is necessary to preserve the existence of the small retailer, lest he be destroyed by price cutting by chain stores and other mass distributors. Its opponents, which include the AFL-CIO, the American Farm Bureau Federation, the FTC, and the Departments of Commerce and Agriculture, contend that such legislation would lead to price fixing, the lessening of competition, and higher consumer living costs. The strategy of the opponents of the "Quality Stabilization" bill is to keep it bottled up in committee. They believe enough Congressmen, whether out of conviction or expediency, would vote for the bill to pass it, should it ever reach the floor of Congress.

Although small business groups have generally been strong supporters of antitrust policy, they have not hesitated to seek legislation restricting competition when they thought that competition, especially chain store price competition, was a threat to their economic interests. Legislative bodies have usually responded favorably to their demands. The courts, however, as guardians of the basic "rules of the game" of American society, have helped to maintain competition. Consequently, they have interpreted restrictive legislation with competitive goals in mind, thereby at least partially frustrating the efforts of small business groups.

The Effectiveness of Antitrust Policy: A Brief Comment

How effective have the antitrust laws been in maintaining a competitive economy? No simple or definitive answers are possible. Those who contend that antitrust policy has been ineffectual and of little or no significance in maintaining competition point to the general absence of "trust busting" to support their position. But antitrust policy involves more than trust busting. Although large concerns have rarely been broken up, those entrusted with antitrust enforcement have tried to prevent their use of predatory and restrictive practices. Collusive agreements among independent firms have been moved against consistently, if not always vigorously and successfully. And undoubtedly many who would have tried to restrain competition, alone or severally, have been deterred by the prospect of discovery and legal action. It seems quite safe to say that the economy is more competitive today than it would have been in the absence of antitrust policy.

On the other hand, antitrust policy has not been as effective as its more avid supporters would desire. Its impact has been reduced by exemptions granted to various groups, by the adoption of laws or policies inconsistent with antitrust (such as state laws permitting holding companies), and by the suspension of antitrust enforcement during wartime and the early New Deal years. Inadequate Congressional support for antitrust enforcement, public indifference, and unfavorable judicial action have all, at one time or another, also operated to diminish the effectiveness of antitrust policy. Collectively, these conditions have prevented the development of a really systematic and comprehensive program for the maintenance of competition.

REGULATION OF THE PUBLIC UTILITY TYPE

Some industries, such as those concerned with electricity, gas, water, transportation, and communications, are regulated by the government as public utilities. In these industries government has accepted or created monopolies (or oligopolies) and then has relied on direct regulation of them to protect the public.

Because of their economic characteristics, direct regulation is considered a particularly appropriate policy for public utility industries. They deal in the "necessities" of life—water and electricity are good examples—for which there are no available close substitutes. The buyer must either meet the seller's price or do without and the latter is often not a feasible alternative. By itself, however, necessity is not sufficient for an industry to be considered a public utility. It must be coupled with at least one of the following factors. Public utilities are often described as "natural monopolies" in the sense that good service can best be provided by single companies serving particular areas. To have several telephone companies serve the same city would result in a costly duplication of facilities and also in poorer service. A person would have to subscribe to all of the telephone services to be able to call anyone in the city. Again, public utility companies have large investments and high fixed costs. Their operations must be conducted on a large scale to achieve low unit costs (and consumer prices, or rates) because their costs decrease as their business increases. Competition among such companies is often destructive, and rate warfare

193

leads to bankruptcy for some companies and monopolistic positions for others. It is not possible, however, to draw any hard and fast lines between public utilities and other businesses.

For years legislative bodies were constitutionally limited in their power to extend what we shall call regulation of the public utility type to business enterprises. The Supreme Court recognized the need for direct regulation (especially of rates and services) of some businesses to protect the public but was unwilling to permit the possibility of such regulation being applied to business generally. It solved this dilemma by developing a concept of "business affected with a public interest," which was first set forth in *Munn v. Illinois* (1887).

Swept along by the tide of the Granger movement, the Illinois legislature had enacted a law regulating the rates and services of grain warehouses. The operators of a grain warehouse in Chicago challenged the constitutionality of the law on the ground that theirs was a private business and therefore such regulation constituted a deprivation of property (or the right to income from property) without due process of law. The Supreme Court, accepting the legislature's judgment that regulation was necessary to protect the public, upheld the Illinois statute as a reasonable exercise of the state's police power. The Chicago warehouses were described as gateways of commerce who "take toll from all who pass." When the use of private property such as this affects the community at large, the Court stated, the owner has in effect granted the community an interest in that use and "must submit to be controlled by the public for the common good."

After the Munn case, and until 1934, the general rule followed by the courts was that a given business could be constitutionally subjected to direct rate and service regulation only if it was "affected with a public interest." If the business in question was held not to be so affected, if it was a "private business" rather than a public utility, then regulation of the public utility type would be a violation of due process of law. The public utility concept was thus a legal concept. A business became a public utility if the legislature and the courts declared that it was one.

The basic problem involved here was determination of whether a business were classifiable as a public utility, a task which was complicated by the imprecise meaning of the phrase "affected with a public interest." The final decision rested with the courts. They held that the public utility category included such businesses as railroads, water companies, gas and electric companies, telephone companies, stockyards, and insurance companies. On the other hand, the conservative Supreme Court of the 1920's restricted the scope of the public utility concept.

Such businesses as those concerned with the manufacture, preparation, or transport of food, theater ticket brokers, private employment agencies, ice companies, and gasoline service stations were held to be private businesses and therefore beyond the reach of regulation of the public utility type. Only a small number of businesses could be constitutionally regulated as public utilities.

In the case of *Nebbia v. New York* (1934), however, the public utility concept as a limitation on the power of government to regulate rates and service was laid to rest by the Court. In sustaining a New York law regulating the retail price of milk, which was clearly outside of the traditionally public utility category, the Court said there was nothing "sacrosanct" about prices as a subject of regulation. The prices a business charged, as well as the other aspects of its operations, could be controlled without violating the due process clause if the legislature found their regulation essential to protection of the public. The concept of "affected with a public interest" was held to mean "no more than that an industry, for adequate reason, is subject to control for the public good."

The Nebbia case thus broke down the distinction between public utilities and private businesses. The question of constitutional power is no longer an important factor in the public utility type of regulation and the manner in which a particular business is regulated is now a matter for legislative determination. But if the public utility concept is no longer a legal limitation on governmental power, it still is with us. The concept still has significance as "a form of expression denoting that the American people think of some industries as being of such a nature that certain types of control are appropriate for them".[66] For example, most people accept the regulation of railroad and electric power rates at least partly because such companies are considered public utilities. They would probably oppose regulation of steel prices, except perhaps under emergency circumstances, because the steel companies are regarded as private businesses. Moreover, because the public utility concept remains deeply rooted in our social and legal traditions, it still may be employed by business organizations as a political (not constitutional) argument against the application of the public utility type of regulation to them as private businesses. In sum, though the public utility concept has withered, it has not departed from the regulatory scene.

Today some industries that traditionally have not been thought of as public utilities are under some degree of regulation of the public utility

[66] Emmette S. Redford, "The Significance of Belief Patterns in Economic Regulation," *Western Political Quarterly,* XIV (September, 1961), 20.

type. Stockyards and the producers of natural gas, both subjected to rate or price regulation, are examples. However, even now when we speak of public utilities we customarily refer to such businesses as railroad, electric, and telephone companies, which have the economic characteristics discussed at the beginning of this section.

The total scope of the public utility type of regulation includes the following categories of activities.

First, entry into the utility business is controlled by a regulating agency. Our norms of freedom of entry into business, at least insofar as this means the absence of legal limitations, is not followed. A company must secure a permit, or "certificate of public convenience and necessity," before it can enter the utility field. Before issuing the permit the regulating agency is supposed to consider such questions as whether the proposed service is needed, whether an existing company could supply the service, whether the applying company can adequately provide the service it wants to offer, and whether issuance of the permit would serve the public interest.

Second, the regulating agency approves and regulates standards of service, including safety standards. A general rule here is that utility companies must serve all equally (without unreasonable discrimination) in the territory they set out to serve. The regulating agency may establish minimum quality standards of service, investigate and settle consumer complaints, and determine whether existing services can be abandoned or extended. A railroad, for example, cannot abandon service to a community without the approval of the Interstate Commerce Commission or a state railroad agency.

Third, the financial structure and transactions of utilities are controlled by the regulating agency. Its approval is required before a utility company can issue new stocks or bonds and perhaps before one company can acquire or merge with another. Regulation of utility financial activities is undertaken to protect consumers and investors against financial manipulation, to protect the credit of utility companies so that funds will be forthcoming from investors when needed, and to make rate making more effective because of the relationship between a company's financial condition and its rate structure. Over-capitalization, for example, usually results in higher rates.

Fourth, the regulatory agency sets uniform rules of accounting to be followed by utility companies. Accurate and intelligible information on financial conditions and operations is required if the agency is to be effective in assuring reasonable rates, satisfactory services, and financial soundness.

Fifth, the regulatory body controls the rates charged by utility companies, which may include the setting of minimum as well as maximum rates. Rate regulation, together with control over service, constitutes the core of the public utility type of regulation. The other facets of regulation set forth here are undertaken primarily to increase the effectiveness of rate and service regulation. Moreover, rates and standards of service are closely related and regulation of one would probably be ineffective without regulation of the other. The prescription of lower rates, for example, might lead to a reduction in quality of service unless the utility company's service standards are also controlled.

Public utility rate making is a very complicated and involved matter in which there is much room for conjecture and conflicts of opinion and interest.[67] The general rule applied in utility rate making can be stated thus: The rates set must enable the company to earn a fair return on the fair value of the property devoted to serving the public, otherwise the company will be deprived of its property (or income therefrom) without due process of law. It is generally agreed that a return of from 5 to 8 per cent on a company's investment is a "fair return." The big problem arises in determining the "fair value" of the company's property (the rate base). Should it be what it originally cost to provide the facilities less depreciation, or what it would cost to construct them today (reproduction cost new), or what a "prudent man" would have spent in constructing the facilities? Each of these theories may lead to a different valuation of the property, and the higher the value of the property the higher the rates will have to be to yield a fair return, and the higher in absolute numbers of dollars the fair return will be. Utility companies tend to favor whichever theory will yield the highest return whereas the regulating agencies usually take the opposite view. Thus the scene is set for conflict. There are no clear standards to guide regulatory agencies in their actions when conflict arises and, as a consequence, rate making is more a matter of bargaining and search for the acceptable than of "scientific" determination.

The five categories of control discussed here comprise the spectrum of the public utility type of regulation. (Other forms of regulation, such as wage and hour laws and antitrust legislation, may also be applied to public utilities.) All these activities, or any part of them, may be employed in regulating a particular industry. The degree of control applied is a matter for legislative decision and is shaped by

[67] Space permits only brief treatment of rate making here. Fuller discussions can be found in Clair Wilcox, *Public Policies Toward Business,* rev. ed. (Homewood, Ill.: Richard D. Irwin, 1960), chs. 20, 21; and Martin Glaeser, *Public Utilities in American Capitalism* (New York: Macmillan, 1957), chs. 17, 18, 23.

such factors as the nature of the industry, special circumstances surrounding it, the parties-in-interest involved, their relative political and economic strength, and public attitudes. In practice, no single uniform pattern of regulation is followed in the public utility area. The entire spectrum of control set forth above is applied to the railroads by the Interstate Commerce Commission, but regulation of the radio and television broadcasting industries is mostly limited to control of entry and standards of service. Regulation of natural gas producers by the Federal Power Commission is confined to control of their prices.

The independent regulatory commission is the traditional and accepted organization used for the administration of public utility regulation. The use of commissions for this purpose is reflective of the common beliefs that utility regulation should be nonpolitical, that it should be fair to the regulated private interests (and fairness is widely equated with the use of judicial processes), and that reliance on commissions should permit the realization of these regulatory values.[68] At the national level, regulation of the interstate aspects of various public utility industries is handled by the Interstate Commerce Commission, the Federal Power Commission, the Federal Communications Commission, and the Civil Aeronautics Board. All the states have commissions (some have more than one) which regulate intrastate public utility businesses. These state commissions are variously called public utility commissions, public service commissions, and occasionally, commerce commissions, corporation commissions, and railroad commissions. In 1964, commissions regulated electric, natural gas, and water companies in forty-six states, motor trucks in forty-seven, and telephone and motor bus companies in forty-nine, with smaller numbers authorized to regulate oil and gas pipelines and interurban railways.[69]

There seems rather widespread agreement that this system of control has not worked very well. It is said, for example, that regulatory commissions have not been effective in regulating rates to keep them low, that discrimination in rates among users has been neglected, that commissions have helped create monopolies where they need not exist, and that, in general, commissions have been lethargic and haphazard in performing their tasks.[70]

[68] See Redford, op. cit., 21–24.
[69] Book of the States, 1964–1965 (Chicago: Council of State Governments, 1964), 571–572.
[70] Viewpoints on this subject can be found in Wilcox, op. cit., ch. 28; Walter Adams and Horace M. Gray, Monopoly in America (New York: Macmillan, 1955), ch. III; and Richard Caves, American Industry: Structure, Conduct, Performance (Englewood Cliffs, N.J.: Prentice-Hall, 1964), 68–73.

198

A number of factors have contributed to the lack of effectiveness in public utility regulation.[71] One is insufficient public and governmental support for regulation. Once laws regulating utilities have been enacted and commissions have been established to enforce them, public interest in regulation has often waned, apparently on the assumption that the problem of control has been permanently settled. In the absence of strong public or group support a commission may attempt to protect itself against political pressures emanating from regulated interests by acting in a routine and passive manner. Further, because of its day-to-day relationships with regulated industries, its constant association with their representatives and exposure to their problems, the commission often takes on the viewpoint of the regulated industries and becomes a promoter (or "captive," as is sometimes alleged) rather than a regulator of them.

To be most effective in regulating utilities, commissions require qualified personnel, financial support sufficient to permit hiring adequate numbers of competent staff members, and clear legislative mandates. Commissions have often lacked all these requisites for effective action. The persons appointed (or elected, in some cases) as commissioners have frequently been undistinguished, possessing little experience or knowledge of the industries they are to regulate. Legislative bodies have been rather parsimonious in providing appropriations for commissions and they have been handicapped by staffs that are inadequate in both quantity and quality. Although the federal commissions have been better financed, many state commissions have had annual budgets averaging only a few hundred thousand dollars. A large utility company may spend as much money in contesting a single rate case as a commission has for an entire year. Legislative directives are often vague or ambiguous. To tell a commission to fix "just and reasonable" rates is not very helpful. Such a directive provides little specific guidance for the commission's actions, nor does it serve as a clear mandate to which the commission can point in countering the demands of particularistic interests.

A second factor affecting the performance of the commissions is the vast amount of work they have to perform. In a year's time a commission may be called upon to handle thousands of complaints and requests relating to rates, services, and other matters. In addition to

[71] For a much different assessment of the effectiveness of public utility regulation, see Austin L. Roberts, Jr., "Developments in Public Utility Regulation," *The Book of the States 1964–65* (Chicago: Council of State Governments, 1964), 563–570.

its regulation of interstate electric companies and natural gas pipelines, the Federal Power Commission now has the task of regulating some fifteen or twenty thousand producers of natural gas. Some 200,000 tariff applications and 9,000 requests for motor carrier certificates are part of the business confronting the ICC annually. Commission regulation is greatly complicated by the sheer volume of administrative work involved, let alone its technicality and complexity.

In the past the courts handicapped the efforts of commissions to regulate utility rates by issuing vague and confusing decisions concerning the procedures commissions had to follow in fixing rates and the level of rates that had to be set if the requirements of due process were to be met. The courts also displayed much willingness to engage in detailed review of the commissions' work when it was challenged. The Supreme Court moved away from this position in 1946 when it held that "it is the result reached and not the methods employed which is controlling. . . . If the total effect of the rate order cannot be said to be unjust and unreasonable, judicial inquiry . . . is at an end."[72] The Court's ruling gave commissions a freer hand in fixing rates but no definite standards for determining whether the rates set were reasonable in their impact. "The Court has relaxed its grip on regulation. But it has left the regulators in the dark."[73]

Fourth, the commissions operate primarily in a negative fashion. They can veto or modify proposals from utility companies but, from the nature of things, they cannot effectively compel positive action. They can prevent a proposed rate increase but they really cannot require that a utility company lower its rates to achieve a larger volume of sales. Initiative, then, rests with the private parties involved. Here, as in most life situations, an advantage in shaping action rests with those who can take the initiative and determine the agenda for decision making.

Much of the support for commission regulation of utility industries today comes from the regulated interests themselves. Even though it may conflict somewhat with their short-run interests regulation has not, partly because of the factors cited above, proved overly restrictive. Acceptance of such regulation may be a means of preventing the emergence of effective demands for more severe regulation of even worse, from the viewpoint of private utility companies, public ownership. Further, the opposition of public utilities to rate regulation "has been considerably tempered by the realization that in any event consumers

[72] *FPC v. Hope Natural Gas Co.,* 320 U.S. 591, 602 (1944).
[73] Wilcox, *op. cit.,* 575 .

200

would probably sooner or later organize to restrict the power of monopolies to fix their own prices."[74] When the Iowa State Commerce Commission was given jurisdiction in 1963 over all of the state's major utilities providing transportation, water, electricity, gas, and communications services, "the legislation did not stem from an aroused public demanding protection from monopolies, but was actively sponsored by the utilities themselves."[75] It is doubtful that the utilities were motivated by masochistic tendencies in this situation.

PUBLIC ENTERPRISE

Public enterprise—government ownership and operation of economic enterprise—may be viewed as an alternative to the control of economic activity by regulation to maintain competition or by regulation of the public utility type. As a form of regulatory control, public enterprise could be substituted entirely for private enterprise in a particular sector of the economy (e.g., the railroad industry). Or a sector could be occupied jointly by public and private enterprise, with competition between them ("yardstick regulation"). The government, however has seldom gone into business to deliberately control economic activity or to compete with private business. Public enterprises, rather, have usually originated to provide needed or desired services which private businesses were unable or unsuited to provide, or which they sometimes started but proved incapable of providing on a permanent basis.

What are public enterprises? Some would include under public enterprise only government economic activities producing goods and services for which direct payments are required of the users. This interpretation would make a government toll road a public enterprise, whereas a road financed by taxation would not be one. This is a rather fine distinction. Further, in enterprises like the Post Office the prices charged pay only part of the cost of operation; the remainder comes from tax revenues. Here we will simply define as public enterprise any government activity of a business-like or commercial nature which might be carried on (at least conceivably) by private enterprise.

National, state, and local governments maintain a wide variety of public enterprises. A fairly complete listing includes the following: educational institutions, libraries, and museums; hospitals and other

[74] Herbert A. Simon, Donald W. Smithburg, and Victor A. Thompson, *Public Administration* (New York: Alfred A. Knopf, 1950), 462–463.
[75] Roberts, *op. cit.*, 563.

medical facilities; public lands, forests, and parks; swimming pools, golf courses, and other recreational facilities; river development projects, such as the Tennessee Valley Authority; the Post Office; credit and insurance programs; atomic energy installations, shipyards, and arsenals; public housing programs; electricity, water, sewerage and other "household" utilities; transportation facilities—airports, port facilities, subways; liquor stores; and the Government Printing Office. Very few manufacturing enterprises, at least outside of the Defense Department, are under government operation.

So listed, the variety of public enterprise is extensive. In its contribution to national income, however, public enterprise plays only a minor role in the economy. In 1961, national income in the United States, the total earnings of labor and property from current production of goods and services, was $427.8 billion. Of this total, $5.6 billion originated from government activities defined as public enterprises by the Department of Commerce. Of this amount, $3.8 billion was accounted for by federal enterprises and $1.8 billion by state and local enterprises. In all, according to this measure, public enterprises accounted for less than 1½ per cent of the nation's income.

Public enterprise plays a more significant role in the economies of the Western European democracies than it does in the United States. In these countries, the governments typically control banking, transportation, communication, and other public utility industries. Most of them own and operate some mining and manufacturing enterprises: iron and steel in Italy, coal mining in France and Great Britain, automobile manufacturing in France and West Germany, gold and copper mining and lumbering in Sweden, and so on. The United States is unique among the Western democracies in being the only country with privately owned and operated railroad and electric companies.

One explanation for the failure of public enterprise to develop in the United States to the same extent and magnitude as it has in Western Europe is our political culture. The ideology or philosophy of socialism has never had much appeal here; socialist parties have always been quite small and have practically ceased to function as electoral groups. Nor has the tradition of the strong positive state had the same acceptance here that it has had in Europe. These two phenomena have run counter to American beliefs and values relating to the desirability of private property, private enterprise, individualism, and limited government. Government regulation of private economic activity and provision of services without charge have been the preferred American approaches to the solution of economic problems. Indeed, regulation has often been viewed as a barrier to socialism, a way of avoiding the "extremes" of both government ownership and uncontrolled private activity, as the "moderate" approach to economic control.

Public enterprises have been established in this country for practical and pragmatic reasons and not, it must be emphasized, because of adherence to socialist doctrine. In various situations public enterprise has appeared to be the best, or at least the most satisfactory, way to solve particular problems and meet particular needs. The actual causes of public enterprise are many and varied. In Nebraska, which has never been known for socialist proclivities, public electric power agencies have completely replaced private power companies. According to Firth, public power became a monopoly in Nebraska, not because of ideological reasons but "as an outgrowth of many factors such as drought, depression, the experience of municipal ownership, the advent of PWA [Public Works Administration, a New Deal agency] to provide a means of financing public hydroelectric projects, federal antitrust legislation—for example, the Holding Company Act of 1935 which forced the breakup of private utility empires—electrification of rural areas, and temporary and local expediencies."[76]

A somewhat standard and unadorned inventory of the causes of public enterprise follows. They are not mutually exclusive and several may have contributed to the development of any particular enterprise. First, some public enterprises have been started because they were considered essential to the needs of warfare and national defense, e.g., atomic energy installations, shipyards and arsenals, and the World War II synthetic rubber plants. And certainly national defense considerations contributed to the decision to build the Panama Canal.

A second group of enterprises were created as a means of alleviating economic distress and bringing the country out of the Great Depression, leading to the Reconstruction Finance Corporation, the Home Owners' Loan Corporation, and other public housing agencies. Firth states that the desire to combat depressed economic conditions contributed to the development of public power projects in Nebraska as they provided employment and helped stimulate the economy.[77]

A third group of government enterprises has been established as incidental to other government undertakings. Prison industries have followed from the operation of prisons; public power production has sometimes resulted from the construction of dams primarily for irriga-

[76] Robert E. Firth, *Public Power in Nebraska* (Lincoln: University of Nebraska Press, 1962), 3.
[77] *Ibid.*, 2.

tion purposes. The operation of the Panama Canal, plus financial difficulties, led to government control of the Panama Railway.

Another group of government enterprises has originated because the resources required were too large, the risks too great, or the prospects of profits too small to make their conduct attractive to private enterprise. In this category we can put the Panama Canal, river development projects, including the Tennessee Valley Authority, farm credit programs, crop insurance, rural electrification, and the Alaskan Railroad.

Some enterprises have been taken over by the government because of the failure of private enterprises. The federal government acquired the barge lines on the Mississippi River for this reason during the 1920's. Many municipal governments have taken over the operation of street railways, subways, and bus systems because of the financial difficulties of private companies.

Sixth, some forms of economic enterprise traditionally have been regarded as proper governmental functions, e.g., the Post Office, the Government Printing Office, and municipal water, sewerage, garbage collection, and recreational facilities fall into this category. Thus, when a city proposes to construct swimming pools and other recreational facilities debate over them normally centers on such matters as need and cost rather than the ideological issue of public versus private enterprise.

Seventh, some enterprises have been established deliberately to control particular forms of economic activity. Some states have chosen to control liquor traffic by the use of state-owned liquor stores rather than by regulation of privately owned liquor stores. Occasionally a cause of government production and distribution of electricity has been "yardstick regulation" of private companies, to cause them, by competition and example, to improve their services and lower their costs.

Finally, it must be recognized that, whatever the economic justifications for public enterprises, political factors contribute significantly to their establishment. Pressures for them are exerted by groups, and their spokesmen, who will benefit from the services they provide. Political support for government enterprises may also stem from the fact that they create jobs and involve the expenditure of government funds in particular regions or localities.

What, now, of the future of public enterprise? In the developing nations in Asia, Africa, and Latin America socialist ideologies and the desire to speed industrialization and economic development, together with shortages of private capital and entrepreneurs, have produced much reliance on public enterprise. In contrast, in the United States, and perhaps to a lesser extent in Western Europe, the trend appears to be moving from public enterprise back to private enterprise. Numerous public enterprises have been liquidated or sold to private enterprise since the end of World War II, and especially during the Eisenhower administration. Among the public enterprises that have been eliminated are the wartime synthetic rubber plants and various other defense plants, the Mississippi barge lines, the Reconstruction Finance Corporation, and various small enterprises within the Defense Department. Although there has been expansion of public enterprise in some fields in which it existed before the war, such as public housing and power production, one is hard pressed to find new areas of public enterprise.

A good illustration of movement from public to private enterprise appears in the area of atomic energy. The McMahon Act of 1946 created the Atomic Energy Commission and gave it complete control of the production and use of atomic energy, thereby creating what one writer called "an island of socialism in the midst of a free enterprise economy."[78] As the peacetime uses of atomic energy became more apparent, private business and power interests began to press for greater scope for private enterprise in the atomic area. These and other pressures led to the Atomic Energy Act of 1954, which authorized the AEC to license private industry to build and operate atomic plants, primarily to generate electric power, although the Act still required government ownership of all fissionable materials. Then, in 1964, Congress enacted additional legislation requiring the AEC to sell nuclear fuels to private companies. In the future (after June, 1973) atomic power companies will be able to buy uranium ores directly from the producers on the commercial market. This legislation is apparently intended to prevent the government from becoming deeply involved in the expanding atomic power industry. What was once a government monopoly will now come increasingly under private enterprise, at least so far as peacetime uses of atomic energy are concerned.

If the expansion of public enterprise into new fields presently appears unlikely so also does the probability of significant reduction of its present scope in the foreseeable future. Public enterprise, in limited amount, and along the periphery of the private enterprise economy, has become an accepted part of the American economic system. But it is regarded as a supplement to, and not a substitute for, private enterprise, which remains the preferred alternative.

[78] J. R. Newman, "America's Most Radical Law," *Harper's Magazine* (May, 1947), 436.

Chapter Six

GOVERNMENT AND LABOR

The transformation of the United States from an agrarian to an urban, industrial society has produced an economic system characterized by Big Labor as well as Big Business. The masses of workers in an industrial society are confronted with many problems: the necessity of bargaining for jobs and wages with large corporate employers, insecurity in employment because of fluctuations in the business cycle and their loss of self-sufficiency, industrial accidents and sickness, and the loss of creative job satisfactions because of the routinization of work tasks. In dealing with these problems workers may act individually, through private collective organizations (unions), or through government. In the twentieth century American workers have come to rely rather heavily on the latter two methods in protecting and promoting their interests in relation to employers and other groups in the economy. They have formed unions for economic bargaining with employers and they have sought legislation, both to protect their right to organize and bargain collectively and to promote directly their interests (e.g., minimum wage laws). Indeed, most labor legislation in this country is a twentieth-century phenomenon, as is the development of labor as a significant political force along with agriculture and business.

We shall begin our discussion of government and labor by examining the labor force, the role of labor unions, and the general nature of labor legislation. Then we shall focus on three particular areas of labor policy: minimum labor standards, unionization and collective bargaining, and the settlement of labor disputes. National policy will be emphasized.

WORKERS, UNIONS, AND THE
AMERICAN ENVIRONMENT

In March, 1963, the total civilian labor force of the United States, including all persons over the age of fourteen working or seeking work, numbered 71.6 million. Of this figure 4.3 million were engaged in agricultural work and 4.5 million were unemployed. Approximately 55 million persons were employed as wage and salary earners in non-agricultural establishments. The remainder of the labor force, 16.6 million, comprised the self-employed, proprietors, farm workers, domestic workers, and unpaid family workers. As these figures would indicate, most people now earn their livelihood by working for someone else, or they depend on those who do.

Since 1900 there have been some significant changes in the composition of the labor force. Although its total size has grown greatly since 1900—it numbered about 28 million in that year—the percentage employed in agriculture has declined from 37.5 per cent in 1900 to less than 7 per cent in 1960. Changes in the occupational composition of the labor force are indicated in Table Six-1.[1]

The data in Table Six-1 illustrate the often remarked fact that white-collar employment is increasing and blue-collar employment is decreasing. Craftsmen, operatives, and laborers can be considered blue-collar, whereas professional, managerial, sales, and clerical workers fit into the white-collar category. Blue-collar workers constituted 37 per cent of the nonfarm labor force in 1940 and 36 per cent in 1962. White-collar workers made up 32 per cent of that labor force in 1930 and 44 per cent in 1962. Thus, in recent decades there has been some decline in the proportion of blue-collar workers but a sharp rise in the proportion of white-collar workers and they now outnumber blue-collar workers. Also, there has been a sharp drop in the proportion of "laborers," that is, unskilled and manual workers. These trends are consequences of the growing complexity, mechanization, and automation of production, which requires fewer "production" workers and more people to distribute goods, keep records, and handle technical planning, design, and research activities.

[1] Lloyd G. Reynolds, *Labor Economics and Labor Relations,* 4th ed. (Englewood Cliffs, N.J.: Prentice-Hall, 1964), 335. The data on the labor force and union membership in this section are taken from Reynolds, especially chs. 2 and 13; and H. James Neary, "American Trade Union Membership in 1962," *Monthly Labor Review,* LXXXVII (May, 1964), 501–507.

TABLE SIX-1

OCCUPATIONAL DISTRIBUTION OF THE LABOR FORCE, 1910–1975*

Occupational group	1910	1940	1962	Projected 1975
Total employed	100.0%	100.0%	100.0%	100.0%
Professional, technical, and kindred workers	4.6	7.9	11.8	14.2
Farmers and farm managers	17.3	11.4	3.9	*
Managers, officials, and proprietors, except farm	7.2	8.1	10.9	10.7
Clerical and kindred workers	5.5	9.7	14.9	16.2
Sales workers	5.0	6.8	6.4	6.7
Craftsmen, foremen, and kindred workers	11.7	11.5	12.8	12.8
Operatives and kindred workers	14.1	18.9	17.8	16.3
Service workers	9.6	11.8	12.9	14.3
Farm laborers and foremen	13.4	6.9	3.4	*
Laborers, except farm and mine	11.6	7.0	5.3	4.5

* The two farm occupational groups are combined for the 1975 projection. It is estimated that together they will comprise 4.5 per cent of the total labor force.

The proportion of women over 14 at work has increased from 20 per cent in 1900 to nearly 40 per cent today, and women now account for over 30 per cent of the labor force. However, the percentages of teen-age boys and men over 65 who are gainfully employed is falling. Only one in four men over 65 was employed in 1962 as compared to three in four in 1900. This drop is the function of such factors as improved economic conditions, social security and pension programs, and the reluctance of employers to hire older workers. The drop in proportion of teen-age male employment results principally from compulsory school attendance laws and the growing emphasis on completing high school and going to college. These changes in employment ratios have roughly balanced each other and the percentage of people over 14 in the labor force today (57.4) is about the same as it was in 1890.

Labor unions, organizations formed by wage earners to maintain or improve their conditions and terms of work by bargaining with employers, have existed in the United States, at least at the local level, since the 1790's. The numbers of workers belonging to unions has increased greatly in the last three decades. In 1933 there were 2.3 million union members; in 1962 there were 17.6 million members in 181 national and international labor unions (international unions are those having some members outside of the U.S., usually in Canada). This figure, however, represents a decline from the peak union membership of 18.5 million in 1956.

Today roughly one in four gainfully employed persons, or one in three persons in nonagricultural employment (a better measure) is a labor union member. Only one in six female workers, however, belongs to a union and, as we have seen, more and more women are going to work. Figures of this sort are somewhat deceptive, however, because there is much diversity in union strength among both different industries and geographical areas. Four sectors of the economy—manufacturing, mining, transportation, and construction—account for more than 80 per cent of the total union membership. Large numbers of the wage earners in each of these industry groups are unionized. Only small percentages of the workers in service industries, wholesale and retail trade, and finance and insurance are organized. These sectors include large numbers of white-collar workers, who traditionally have been difficult to organize. Agricultural workers are almost completely unorganized. As one might guess from these data, outside of agricultural employment union membership is much more frequent among blue-collar workers than white-collar workers.

Geographically, union membership as a percentage of nonagricultural employment is highest in the Middle Atlantic, East North Central (Ohio, Illinois, etc.), and Pacific Coast regions whereas, by comparison, workers in the Mountain, South, Southwest, and West North Central (Kansas, North Dakota, etc.) regions are poorly organized. On a state basis, the ratio of union membership to nonagricultural employment is highest in Washington (43 per cent). The ratio ranges between 30 and 40 per cent in Pennsylvania, New York, Massachusetts, Illinois, Michigan, Missouri, Montana, and Alaska. States with low ratios of union membership to nonagricultural employment include South Carolina (6 per cent), North Carolina and New Mexico (7 per cent), Oklahoma and Georgia (9 per cent), and Florida, Georgia, and Mississippi (11 per cent). This disparity in unionization exists partly because industries with high rates of union membership are concentrated in some states and regions (those with the higher ratios above) and are not uniformly spread throughout the country. But other factors are also operative. In the South, for example, strong resistance by business interests and an unfavorable political climate also contribute to the low rate of unionization.[2]

Great disparity also exists in the size of the various national (or international) unions. The Teamsters, Automobile Workers, and Steelworkers each count more than a million members. The next seven largest unions, with memberships ranging from 900,000 to 400,000, include the Machinists, Carpenters, Electrical Workers (IBEW), United Mine Workers, Ladies Garment Workers, Hotel and Restaurant workers, and the Hod Carriers. In all, these ten unions have about eight million members, or nearly half of the total union membership. In contrast, there are approximately a hundred unions with less than 25,000 members each. This group includes more than half of the national unions in the country but only around 5 per cent of total union membership. Included in this small union category are the International Broom and Whisk Makers Union, the International Die Sinkers' Conference, the Amalgamated Lace Operatives of America, and the International Association of Siderographers. Our point here is simply this: to consider the Steelworkers, or Teamsters, or Machinists as "typical" of all unions, as many people apparently do, is to distort reality. Many unions are small, often poorly organized or financed, struggling to survive, and possess very little economic or political power.

For two decades prior to 1955, the labor movement was divided between two rival and often sharply antagonistic national labor federations. The American Federation of Labor, created in 1886 and long the dominant force in American unionism, was composed principally of unions of skilled craftsmen: machinists, carpenters, electricians, plumbers, musicians. The Congress of Industrial Organizations, which began as a faction within the AFL in 1935 and became a separate federation in 1938, was essentially comprised of industrial unions formed to include all workers in particular industries: steelworkers, automobile workers, rubber workers. The CIO represented a response to the development of mass production and other industries employing large numbers of unskilled and semiskilled workers. Such industries could be only partially and ineffectively organized along skilled craft lines. In the late 1940's and early 1950's, the pressures created by declining union membership, political reverses (e.g., enactment of the Taft-Hartley Act), and a Republican administration in Washington, caused many leaders in both federations to adopt the position that unity in the labor movement was necessary if organized labor were to preserve its eco-

[2] Marian D. Irish, "Political Thought and Behavior in the South," *Western Political Quarterly*, XIII (June, 1960), 406–420.

nomic gains and be able to fend off political attacks. In December, 1955, and after the failure of various previous attempts, the two federations were merged to form the American Federation of Labor and Congress of Industrial Organizations (AFL-CIO).

The AFL-CIO in 1962 comprised 130 national unions having a total membership of 14.8 million. About 50 national unions having approximately 2.8 million members were not affiliated with the AFL-CIO. Prominent among these independent unions are the Teamsters (expelled from the AFL-CIO in 1957), the United Mine Workers, the Locomotive Engineers, and the Railway Conductors and Brakemen. The AFL-CIO can be described as a loose federation of national unions, largely autonomous in the conduct of their internal affairs and in bargaining with employers.

> Each sets its own economic course. Each conducts its own organizing efforts. Each maintains its own staff, both field and professional. The largest unions have resources that dwarf those of the national center, the AFL-CIO. In theory, the activities of these member unions are correlated to some degree through the AFL-CIO, its trade and industrial departments, and its state and local central bodies. In practice, the correlation has been limited, with very few exceptions, to political and legislative action, and has been less than perfect even there.[3]

In sum, the national unions are the real power centers of the labor movement. Their relationships to the AFL-CIO are more like those of the states to the central government under the Articles of Confederation than those of the states to the national government under our present federal system.

A well-known student of labor affairs, Jack Barbash, has remarked that "No political democracy has offered a more hostile environment to unionism than has the United States."[4] A number of aspects of American society, which have both handicapped the development and expansion of labor unions and helped determine the nature and form of the American labor movement, can be noted here in summary form.

First, private property and its attendant rights constitute a valued and widely supported institution in American society, today as well as in the past. Although labor unions by and large have accepted the capitalist system and have worked within its framework to improve the

[3] Solomon Barkin, *The Decline of the Labor Movement* (Santa Barbara: Center for the Study of Democratic Institutions, 1961), 12.
[4] Jack Barbash, *The Practice of Unionism* (New York: Harper & Row, 1956), 2.

211

position and well-being of the working man, they have sought to limit the employer's ability to control and use his property. As a consequence, the labor movement has been interpreted historically as an attack on private property and "the right of a man to run his business as he sees fit." This interpretation, in turn, has lowered the status of labor unions in our society, reduced support or tolerance for them among middle-class and other elements, and strengthened business interests in their efforts to resist unionism by enabling them to pose as defenders of private property against "radical" attack. "Unlike the organization movement among businessmen," Harmon Zeigler has written, "labor activity . . . has faced the impediment of transmitting an image which deviates from social norms."[5]

Individualism as an American trait has also worked to the disadvantage of unions. A product of such phenomena as our self-reliant frontier psychology, militant Protestant heritage, and the concept of America as a land of opportunity, individualism emphasized individual initiative, self-reliance, and responsibility in preference to collective or cooperative action. Even today as one commentator has observed, "While individual action and competition are given the most exalted value, few Americans share a profound belief in the constructive contributions of group or collective action [to the solution of economic and social problems]."[6] This tradition of individualism has militated against the acceptance of unions, even by workers in many instances, as a necessary and proper part of the American socio-economic system, even when the individual alone is unable to care for his own interests (as when dealing with large corporate employers).

The absence of strong class consciousness among workers is another factor which still lessens the appeal of unions. Many workers have preferred to regard themselves as temporary workers on the way to becoming employers or entrepreneurs rather than as permanent members of a "working class." Although the prevalence of such beliefs among workers is probably lower now than in the past, large numbers of workers, especially white-collar workers but also many blue-collar workers, see themselves as having middle-class rather than working-class status.[7] Workers with such perceptions, and particularly white-

[5] Harmon Zeigler, *Interest Groups in American Society* (Englewood Cliffs, N.J.: Prentice-Hall, 1964), 127.

[6] Barkin, *op. cit.,* 71.

[7] See Richard Centers, *The Psychology of Social Classes* (Princeton: Princeton University Press, 1949), 86; and Neal Gross, "Social Class Identification in the Urban Community," *American Sociological Review,* XVIII (August, 1953), 398–404.

collar workers, are likely to feel that unionism is beneath them and resist joining unions. The weakness of class consciousness among American workers has undoubtedly slowed the growth of unionization. It has also affected the political power of unions.

One characteristic of the American experience, because of the emphasis on individualism and other factors, is distrust of government. Workers have shared this distrust with farmers and businessmen, although it must be said that none of these groups has carried this distrust to its logical conclusion of rejecting government aid and protection of its interests. However, workers were long skeptical of the use of government as an instrument of economic reform. Union leaders, such as Samuel Gompers, long-time president of the American Federation of Labor, preferred to rely primarily on unions and collective bargaining to advance worker interests and, until the 1930's, only occasionally sought positive assistance from government. In recent decades, however, organized labor has become actively and deeply involved in political action.

ORGANIZED LABOR AND POLITICAL ACTION

Labor unions employ two general methods in promoting and protecting their interests: collective bargaining, including strikes, picketing, and boycotts; and political activity. Political action by unions has been necessary because of their existence in a socio-economic environment, which has generally been critical if not always hostile toward them and which has often produced unfavorable governmental attitudes and actions. Thus, at the least, organized labor has determined to defend itself in the political arena against labor injunctions, right-to-work laws, and other legislative restrictions, and executive intervention in strikes on behalf of management. Labor political activity, then, has appeared as a necessary condition for its survival and for the opportunity to bargain collectively. But, especially in recent decades, the political objectives of labor have been more than merely defensive, or negative. Unions now rely on political action, in addition to collective bargaining, to promote the economic interests of their members (and often those of other workers as well). They have had to do so, according to Gus Tyler, because:

The American economy of the second half of the twentieth century is much too much of a legislated economy for the unions to believe they can defend the economic status of their workers solely through contract [collective bargaining]. . . . To give the worker more than make-believe protection, a modern union must be concerned with influencing the legislation that goes to make up our legislated economy.[8]

The present-day objectives of labor's political activity, beyond its desire to protect its right to organize and bargain collectively, can be categorized thus:

1. There are general goals which labor seeks and which cannot be obtained by collective bargaining. These include unemployment compensation, other social security programs, policies to maintain full or maximum employment, job retraining programs, and employment services.

2. There are general objectives which could possibly be attained by collective bargaining but which may be more readily secured by government legislation: minimum wages, maximum hours, prevention of child labor, and improved standards of industrial health and safety.

3. Particular objectives are sought by individual unions relating to their respective industries and their positions therein. The railroad brotherhoods have advocated legislation to protect or improve the competitive position of the railroads with relation to other forms of transportation. The Bricklayers and other unions in the building trades usually strongly support public housing programs. The United Mine Workers favor restriction (in the name of conservation) of domestic oil production and limiting of the importation of foreign oil. In taking policy positions of this sort unions are motivated by a desire to protect (or increase) the job opportunities of their members. A drop in rail traffic, for example, may lead to a decline in railroad employment.

4. Organized labor expresses its views and takes policy positions on a wide range of matters of general social concern but not directly related to their economic interests. In its proposals to the Republican and Democratic national platform committees in 1964 the AFL-CIO made recommendations on foreign aid, civil rights legislation, federal aid to education, agricultural price support policy, Congressional reform, the Peace Corps, and civil defense.[9] That labor takes positions on such matters does not mean it supports and works for them with the

[8] Gus Tyler, *A New Philosophy for Labor* (New York: Fund for the Republic, 1959), 11.

[9] *Platform Proposals of the AFL-CIO to the Republican and Democratic National Conventions, 1964* (Washington, D.C.: AFL-CIO, 1964). This publication illustrates well the wide range of matters on which the AFL-CIO expresses views.

same vigor as it does on matters of more immediate concern to workers. However, it does indicate that labor, probably because of its increasing social and political consciousness, no longer confines its legislative attention to the traditional area of "job-centered" matters, as it customarily did before the New Deal.

In seeking its legislative goals, organized labor has chosen the course of pressure politics, striving first to influence the election or appointment of public officials favorably inclined toward its interests and, second, to persuade them to adopt policies supported by labor once they are in office. Labor has rejected the alternative, favored by some intellectuals and minor labor leaders, of establishing an independent labor political party. Attempts to establish labor parties were unsuccessful in the nineteenth century and there is little prospect for their success today. In many states the election laws make it difficult for new parties to get on the ballot; in other states a labor party probably would be weak because of the paucity of union members. "Fears of electoral failure, of antagonizing employers, of rupturing labor unity, 'of taking a risk in a hostile environment' impel pragmatic union leaders to resist efforts to form a new party."[10]

In its political activities organized labor still holds, at least formally, to the traditional policy, first enunciated by Samuel Gompers, of promoting its interests by rewarding its friends and punishing its enemies without regard to their party affiliation. Especially since the New Deal years, however, labor has become increasingly committed to the Democratic party. Most of the candidates for office endorsed by labor are Democrats. In 1956 labor groups reported spending $1,024,258 in support of candidates for federal office. Of this sum, all except $3,925 went to Democratic candidates.[11]

Labor, at the national, state, and local levels, engages in a wide range of electoral activities, operating through three types of labor union organizations; the trade unions themselves, the AFL-CIO, and "independent" political action committees (e.g., the Committee on Political Education of the AFL-CIO). Labor endorses candidates, distributes copies of candidates' voting records and other literatures, engages in campaigns to register voters and to get them to go to the polls on election day, and contributes to the campaign funds of favored candidates. Since the Taft-Hartley Act of 1947, labor unions have been pro-

---

[10] William J. Keefe and Morris S. Ogul, *The American Legislative Process* (Englewood Cliffs, N.J.: Prentice-Hall, 1964), 317.

[11] Alexander Heard, *The Costs of Democracy* (Chapel Hill: University of North Carolina Press, 1960), 186–187.

hibited from expending funds in connection with the nomination or election of federal candidates. This ban has been rather handily circumvented by the use of "independent" union political action committees to solicit voluntary contributions entirely separate from union dues for campaign purposes.

Organized labor also maintains many lobbyists, or legislative representatives, in Washington on a permanent basis to look after labor's legislative interests. In addition to lobbyists on the staff of the AFL-CIO, many of the larger national unions have their own legislative representatives. In contrast, at the state legislative level, lobbying is frequently a part-time activity of officials of individual unions and state labor federations. The lobbying techniques employed by labor groups include testifying before committees, help in bill drafting, personal contacts with congressmen, logrolling and alliance building, and the stimulation of "grass roots pressures" on legislators. In all, organized labor is a very active participant in legislative politics.

The question now arises: How successful has labor been in securing its political objectives? Although labor has gained some impressive legislative victories, as during the early New Deal years, it has often failed to win acceptance of its legislative proposals. In comparison with business and agricultural interests labor appears to be the weakest political force. "He who would understand politics in the large may ponder well the status of labor: a numerically great force in a society adhering to the doctrine of the rule of numbers, yet without proportionate durable political power as a class."[12]

Although it might be assumed that because labor groups are large, well-organized, and politically active they must almost automatically gain acceptance of their policy proposals, a brief look at the historical record will show that this is not at all the case. In the early 1930's labor unions were numerically weak and not especially adept in the political arena. Yet, Congress enacted the Norris-La Guardia Act (1932), section 7(a) of the National Industrial Recovery Act (1933), and the Wagner Act (1935), all of which were favorable to organized labor. In contrast, in 1947 and 1959 Congress passed the Taft-Hartley Act and the Landrum-Griffin Act. Both of these statutes, widely labeled "anti-labor" by unions, came during a time when organized labor was numerically strong and politically wise and active.

What factors, then, affect the political success of labor? How can we account for the relative weakness of labor in comparison to busi-

[12] V. O. Key, Jr., *Politics, Parties, and Pressure Groups,* 4th ed. (New York: Thomas Y. Crowell, 1958), 52.

ness and agricultural interests? (We are concerned here with the political power of organized labor and not its economic power, which is another matter.) We can suggest a number of hypotheses and some evidence in support of them.

1. Although there appears to be general public hostility toward unions and some of their goals, the "climate of opinion" is more favorable toward labor at some times than at others. During the early 1930's, when labor made some of its greatest legislative gains, business prestige was low because of the Great Depression. Further, because labor was weak, legislation to strengthen unions in dealing with management appeared equitable to many people. By 1947, however, business had regained its former status and labor, in turn, was widely regarded as too powerful and in need of restraint. A number of serious strikes in the immediate post-World War II years further diminished public support for labor. This shift in the climate of opinion was to the advantage of groups supporting restrictive labor legislation.

2. There is no controlled "labor vote" subject to the dictates of labor leaders. Note the following statement: "Union members and their families comprise one-third of all eligible voters in the United States. If they were to go to the polls and vote overwhelmingly in one direction, they could carry almost any national election."[13] This, however, has never happened. Union members think of themselves not only as union members, but as Democrats, Republicans, homeowners, veterans, southerners, Irish-Americans, taxpayers, and so on; and they will be influenced by such group memberships as well as union membership in their voting behavior. Labor unions may endorse candidates and urge their members to vote for them but many will not. Thus, large numbers of union members voted for Eisenhower in 1956 rather than Stevenson, who was endorsed by the AFL-CIO and many national unions. Using a variety of voting behavior data, Scoble has estimated that the influence of unions on worker voting patterns may mean a net gain of perhaps as much as 2,800,000 votes for the Democratic party in presidential elections.[14] (Union members are more likely to vote, and to vote Democratic, than are nonunion members.) This is about one-eleventh of the popular vote necessary to win the election. The President, and most other candidates for public office, must appeal to more than organized labor to be elected.

[13] Arthur Kornhauser, Harold L. Sheppard, and Albert J. Mayer, *When Labor Votes* (New York: University Books, 1956), 261.
[14] Harry J. Scoble, "Organized Labor in Politics: Some Questions for the Discipline," *Western Political Quarterly,* XVI (September, 1963), 673–674.

3. The uneven geographical distribution of union members may also lessen the political strength of labor. Organized labor has more influence in Northern urban-industrial states having large numbers of union members, e.g., Michigan, than in the mountain states or the South, where union membership is low. This predominance undoubtedly affects the attitudes of Congressmen from these areas. Democratic Representatives from Northern industrial states are much more likely to support labor's policy proposals than are those from the South. Geographical distribution of union membership is related to the legislative under-representation of urban areas, in which union membership is concentrated. This imbalance may lessen the access of labor groups to legislative bodies, and it is often so assumed. It will be interesting to see whether labor gains in legislative support as legislatures are reapportioned in conformity with recent Supreme Court decisions to give more representation to urban areas.

4. The structure and customs of Congress are another set of factors that may work to the disadvantage of labor. Under the seniority system many committee chairmen tend to come from one-party dominated districts in the South and in rural and small-town areas in the Middle West where there is often strong opposition to labor unions (and where unions are usually weak). During the 1950's the House Committee on Education and Labor was presided over by a conservative Southern Democrat, Graham Barden of North Carolina (except from 1953–1954, when a conservative Republican was chairman), who ran the committee with a strong hand. Barden's attitude toward labor legislation was indicated by his statement that "everybody knows that minimum-wage legislation is basically counter to our democratic form of government and our competitive economy."[15] Another Southern Democrat, Representative Howard Smith, often used his power as chairman of the House Rules Committee to support conservative interests in labor legislation.

5. As a consequence of its origin as a protest movement against the existing economic order and unfavorable public attitudes (discussed above), organized labor occupies a low status in the American social system. "The labor leader's social status is equivalent to that of a street car conductor."[16] Professor Truman has suggested that "the position of a group or its spokesmen in the social structure" is the most important factor affecting its access to the government.

[15] Gus Tyler, *A Legislative Campaign for a Federal Minimum Wage* (1955) (New York: Holt, Rinehart and Winston, 1959), 3.
[16] A. A. Imberman, "Labor Leaders and Society," *Harvard Business Review,* XXVII (January, 1950), 53. Quoted in Zeigler, *op. cit.,* 130.

The deference accorded a high-status group not only facilitates the acceptance of its propaganda but also eases its approach to the government. . . . Even an official who shares the attitudes of a competing group may be flattered into aiding one of these high-status organizations [e.g., a major corporation or the Chamber of Commerce]. Even where flattery is not an influence, the high-status group is aided by the large proportion of key officials . . . whose class backgrounds are such that they have similar values, manners, and preconceptions.[17]

After observing that most political decision makers come from the middle and upper classes, and that most labor leaders come from working-class families, Zeigler concludes: "The great disparity between the class affiliations of labor and those of public officials is surely a disadvantage to labor in its political competition with other groups."[18]

6. Organized labor may be handicapped, at least sometimes, by a lack of unity in its political efforts resulting from the divergent interests and attitudes of various unions and labor groups. "Today the lobbying of the AFL-CIO is hampered by the contradictory political pressures exerted by the jurisdictional groups within it. The bitterest complaints about labor lobbying often come from labor-supported legislators faced with the conflicting demands made upon them by different unions or groups of unions."[19] McAdam reports that disunity within the labor movement concerning the form labor reform legislation should take was an important factor in labor's inability to prevent the passage of the Landrum Griffith Act.[20] McAdam also states that the Teamsters Union's rather crude lobbying techniques, which included "threats of certain election defeat for voting 'wrong,'" antagonized many Congressmen and probably lost votes for labor, thereby contributing to passage of the act.[21]

7. Finally, the political activity of labor evokes strong opposition from conservative business groups and, at times, similarly minded farm and professional groups. The National Association of Manufacturers is usually at the head of the opposition to labor. Depending upon the particular issue in question, it may draw allies from such groups as the Chamber of Commerce, the American Farm Bureau

[17] David B. Truman, *The Governmental Process* (New York: Alfred A. Knopf, 1951), 265.

[18] Zeigler, *op. cit.,* 133.

[19] Paul Jacobs, *Old Before Its Time: Collective Bargaining at 28* (Santa Barbara: Center for the Study of Democratic Institutions, 1963), 35.

[20] Alan K. McAdam, *Power and Politics in Labor Legislation* (New York: Columbia University Press, 1964), 270–271.

[21] *Ibid.,* 199, 210–211.

Federation, the American Medical Association, or the American Bar Association. In competing with such groups labor is at a disadvantage because of its lower social status and because it has fewer political resources (e.g., money and propaganda skills).

AN OVERVIEW OF LABOR LEGISLATION

Jurisdiction in the area of labor legislation is divided constitutionally between the national government and the states. Although federal legislation is limited to businesses engaged in or affecting interstate commerce, the concept of interstate commerce has been greatly broadened, especially since 1937. No longer, for example, do the courts hold that labor matters are an aspect of production and thus primarily for the states to regulate. If a labor matter has some substantial affect on interstate commerce, it can be dealt with by the national government.

Since the early decades of the nineteenth century, legislative bodies, national, state, and occasionally local, have enacted much labor legislation. Most nineteenth-century legislation was at the state level and concerned such matters as child labor, hours of work for women and sometimes men, industrial safety, methods of wage payment, and mediation of labor disputes. State legislation on minimum wages, workmen's compensation, and unemployment compensation were twentieth-century developments, as were laws relating to hours of work for men (for the most part), labor relations, and fair employment practices.

A few statutes affecting labor were enacted in the nineteenth century by the national government, as on the hours of work of government employees and the mediation of railway labor disputes (the Erdman Act). Between 1900 and 1930 federal activity increased but was confined mostly to efforts to prevent child labor (which were declared unconstitutional) and to regulate the hours, working conditions, and labor relations of railroad workers. The dominant view during this period was that labor (except when the employees of interstate railroads were involved) was essentially under the jurisdiction of the states. Since 1930, as a consequence of changing economic, political, and constitutional conditions, the national government has legislated on wages and hours, child labor, unemployment compensation, labor relations, employment services, worker retraining, and fair employment practices. Labor, as we have suggested elsewhere, has

220

come to look primarily to the national government for protection and promotion of its interests.

The existing body of labor legislation can be classified by the subjects with which it deals: wage and hour legislation, child labor laws, labor relations legislation, and so on. Another way of categorizing labor legislation is according to its purposes, centering attention on the purposive nature of legislation and the problems at which it is directed. Using purpose as our organizing criterion, we can group labor legislation in the categories listed here, which are not mutually exclusive.

Numerous laws have been enacted by the state and national governments for the express purpose of preventing the exploitation of workers by employers. Because of the generally weaker bargaining power of workers, and particularly of such groups as women and children, the terms and conditions of work in most instances would be unilaterally determined by employers in the absence of governmental controls (and, we should add, labor unions). Consequently, the government has often acted to protect the interests of workers in their relationships with employers. Such action, supported by the middle-class ideal of protecting the weak against the strong, has taken the form of legislation on minimum wages and maximum hours, health and safety, child labor, and the methods of wage payment (e.g., outlawing payment in scrip redeemable only at company stores).

Closely related to the above is legislation intended to guarantee minimum standards of existence for workers. Minimum wage laws obviously serve this purpose, as do unemployment compensation and workmen's compensation legislation. These contribute to the economic well-being of workers and reflect humanitarian motives and the welfare state ideal that every one is entitled to a minimum standard of living simply because he is a human being.

Another purpose of labor legislation is to promote greater equality of opportunity for workers. A number of types of legislation fit into this category. Child labor laws, together with compulsory school attendance laws, contribute to the future employment opportunities and earning capacities of workers. It is statistically demonstrable that a person's income will increase with his level of education, that the average high school graduate, for example, will earn more money during his working career than the average person having an eighth-grade education or less. More job opportunities will also be available to the better-educated person. Some states have adopted fair employment practices acts intended to prohibit discrimination against workers on the basis of race, religion, or national origin. The Civil Rights Act of 1964 set up an Equal Employment Opportunity Commission at the national level to prevent such discrimination. Legislation providing for employment services, aid to depressed areas, and manpower retraining is designed to improve employment opportunities for unemployed or underemployed workers.

Legislation has been enacted to protect the right of workers to organize and bargain collectively through unions of their own choosing. Fifth, there is both national and state legislation designed to regulate unions in order to lessen or prevent the abuse of their economic power, to prohibit union activities considered unfair or undesirable, and to ensure the ability of union members to participate meaningfully in union government and to control their leaders. Finally, agencies and procedures for the resolution of labor-management disputes have been established by legislation.

Legislation falling into each of the above categories, and in support of the included objectives, has been enacted at both the national and state levels. But the national government and the various state governments have not been equally vigorous in enacting legislation in pursuit of the listed purposes. There is much diversity among them in the nature, scope, effectiveness, and enforcement of the legislation they have enacted. For example, the states differ in the emphasis their labor policies give to the possible objectives. Northern industrial states have given more attention to providing greater equality of opportunity for workers, including the prevention of job discrimination, than have Southern states. The latter, in turn, along with some of the North Central states, have been more active in regulating and restricting unions. Even if there is general agreement on the desirability of a particular objective, such as the resolution of labor-management disputes, there is often much disagreement as to the form government action should take, a fact which manifests itself in policy diversity.

Broadly, the function of labor legislation is the establishment of socially approved norms of behavior to be followed by labor and management in their relationships. Another function of labor legislation is the distribution of advantages and disadvantages among labor and management groups. Because it performs these functions, the substance of labor legislation will be affected at any given time and place by economic circumstances, public attitudes and beliefs, and the balance of power among contending interest groups. Whether the resulting policy is "good" or "bad" will depend upon the interests and values of those passing judgment on it.

MINIMUM LABOR STANDARDS

Legislation establishing minimum labor standards is intended to protect the interests of economically weak workers in such matters as hours and wages, working conditions, equal job opportunities, and insurance against industrial accidents and unemployment. This legislation rests on the general premise that, because of their unequal bargaining power, unregulated bargaining between employers and workers often results in undesirable or unjust terms and conditions of work. This eventuality was attested to by the Supreme Court in an 1898 case upholding the constitutionality of a Utah statute providing an eight-hour day for miners;

> The legislature has also recognized the fact . . . that the proprietors of these establishments and their employees do not stand upon any equality, and that their interests are, to a certain extent, conflicting. The former naturally desire to obtain as much labor as possible from their employees, while the latter are often induced by the fear of discharge to conform to regulations which their judgment, fairly exercised, would pronounce detrimental to their health or strength. In other words, the proprietors lay down the rules and the laborers are practically constrained to obey them. In such cases, self-interest is often an unsafe guide, and the legislature may properly impose its authority.[22]

Until the late 1930's the opponents of protective labor legislation were buttressed by constitutional barriers erected by a conservative Supreme Court. With the exception of laws dealing with child labor (children were recognized as "wards" of the state and were without legal power to contract) protective labor legislation modified the person's "freedom of contract," a "freedom" that the Court read into the Constitution in the 1890's as part of the liberty protected by the due process of law clauses. The idea of freedom of contract, derived from the concept of the free individual in laissez faire economics, assumed that workers and employers bargained as equals over terms of work and that, guided by their self-interest, they would not enter into contracts detrimental to their interests. Legislation held by the courts to be an arbitrary or unreasonable limitation of the right of the individual to enter into labor contracts, and thus to infringe on his liberty,

[22] *Holden v. Hardy,* 169 U.S. 366 (1898).

was declared unconstitutional. In 1905, for example, the Supreme Court struck down a New York law limiting the hours of bakery workers to ten per day as a "mere meddlesome interference with the rights of the individual. . . ."[23] What was arbitrary or unreasonable seemed to depend more on the social and economic philosophies of the judges than on any clear legal principles. Various state and national laws fell by the constitutional wayside as a consequence of adverse judicial action.

The division of powers under the American federal system also worked to the disadvantage of those seeking legislation on minimum labor standards. Under the commerce power as interpreted before 1937, Congress could regulate working conditions only for federal employees, persons engaged in interstate transportation, and (indirectly) employees of government contractors. Workers engaged in the production and exchange of goods and services were held to come under the jurisdiction of the states. The states, however, were unable to provide the uniform action required for effective governmental action. Further, they were often more responsive to conservative and business interests than was the national government, a condition that still exists in many of the more rural and agrarian states and the South, as a comparative examination of labor legislation will indicate.

A caution: in explaining the slow growth of minimum labor standards legislation in the United States too much emphasis should not be given to constitutional limitations by themselves. The erosion of these barriers after 1937 was not automatically followed by a large volume of labor legislation. Most states still do not have general wage and hour laws for men and many do not have minimum wage laws (or effective ones) for women. The interpretation of the Constitution has changed but in many cases the actual distribution of political power among interest groups in the community (what some would call the "real constitution" as opposed to the "nominal" or written constitution)[24] is still balanced in favor of groups with interests and values opposed to various types of protective labor legislation.

Child Labor Legislation

In the early decades of our national history, child labor was generally regarded as a righteous institution, being both economically necessary and morally desirable. From colonial times onward, traditions em-

---

[23] *Lockner v. New York*, 198 U.S. 45 (1905).
[24] See the discussion of these concepts in J. Lloyd Mecham, "Latin American Constitutions: Nominal and Real," *Journal of Politics*, XXI (May, 1959), 258–275.

phasizing the virtue of work and the vice of idleness contributed to favorable attitudes toward child labor. So did such factors as the need to foster domestic industry, the scarcity and high cost of adult male labor, and the desire to prevent poor children from becoming public charges. Large numbers of children were members of the labor force. All the workers in the first textile mill in the United States, established in 1790, were children between the ages of seven and twelve years.[25] Throughout the nineteenth century and into the twentieth, many factories continued to employ children. During the past century, however, an almost complete reversal has occurred in public attitudes toward child labor. Rising standards of living, pressures from organized labor, concern for the education of children, growing awareness of the harmful moral and social effects of child labor, and humanitarian motives produced the attitude that child labor is socially and economically undesirable and resultant pressures for legislative action to control child labor.

Massachusetts was the first state to regulate child labor; in 1842 it limited the hours of work for children under twelve in manufacturing establishments to ten per day. In 1848 Pennsylvania prohibited the employment of children under twelve in textile factories and, by 1860, seven states had enacted child labor legislation. These early laws were not very effective because they were poorly enforced and contained a variety of loopholes. In the second half of the nineteenth century most states enacted some sort of child labor legislation but, except for the very young, child labor was generally not prohibited outright until the twentieth century.

All the states now have laws regulating the conditions under which children may be employed. These laws usually include the following: a minimum age of from fourteen to sixteen for general employment; prohibition of employment in dangerous occupations, often for minors up to eighteen years of age; limitation of the workday to eight hours; prohibition of night work; and the requirement of employment certificates for children under sixteen. Most states permit the employment of children outside of school hours in domestic work, the street trades (selling newspapers, etc.), entertainment businesses, and agriculture. The regulatory standards governing child labor in agriculture are generally lax, perhaps reflecting the favored position of agriculture in our society. These generalizations should not be permitted to obscure the

---

[25] U.S. Department of Labor, *Growth of Labor Law in the United States* (Washington, D.C.: Government Printing Office, 1962), 1. Much of the factual material in this discussion of minimum labor standards comes from this excellent source.

differences among the states, both in the standards set in their child labor laws and in the vigor with which they are enforced.

Early in this century, after some of the states had enacted fairly strong child labor laws, limitations on effective state action became apparent. States often hesitated to enact legislation with adequate standards. Such action placed their industries at a disadvantage in competing with those in other states who profited from the lower wages that traditionally accompanied child labor. Despairing of effective action by the states alone, the proponents of child labor legislation turned to the national government for supplementary action. After a decade of struggle Congress passed the Owen-Keating Act of 1916, prohibiting the shipment of child labor-made goods in interstate commerce. Although other national laws prohibiting the movement of objects in interstate commerce had been upheld earlier, the Supreme Court ruled the Owen-Keating Act unconstitutional because its effect was to regulate conditions of production. This, said the Court, was a matter reserved for the states to regulate.[26] Congress responded by enacting a tax of 10 per cent on the net profits of mines or factories using child labor. This effort was also declared unconstitutional by the Court as an attempt to regulate production and not, therefore, a legitimate use of the taxing power.[27]

In 1924, to overcome these court rulings, Congress submitted an amendment to the states authorizing the national government to regulate child labor. The proposed amendment was vigorously opposed by the National Association of Manufacturers, the American Farm Bureau Federation, Southern textile manufacturers, and various industrial groups though it received support from many civic, labor, and religious organizations. Only six states ratified the amendment during the 1920's. Twenty-two more states did so during the early New Deal years, in part as a response to the deterioration of employment conditions and child labor standards caused by the depression. This was still short of the two-thirds required for adoption of the amendment. The need for the amendment, however, was eliminated by the broadening of the commerce power after 1937.

The Fair Labor Standards Act was passed by Congress in 1938. Among other things, the Act prohibited the employment of children under sixteen in most manufacturing establishments, and under eighteen in occupations found to be hazardous by the Department of Labor, when the goods produced were to be shipped in interstate commerce.

[26] *Hammer v. Dagenhart*, 247 U.S. 251 (1918).
[27] *Bailey v. Drexel Furniture Co.*, 259 U.S. 20 (1922).

Child labor in retailing, personal services, street trades, entertainment places, and agriculture was exempted. The coverage of the act was extended in 1949 to include industries such as transportation and communications. Also, it was made illegal for children under sixteen to be employed in agriculture during school hours.

There is now a network of federal and state laws regulating child labor. This legislation is supplemented by state compulsory school attendance laws, growing popular interest in the education of children, the changes in attitudes mentioned above, and labor union opposition to child labor. Child labor has not been entirely eliminated, but children now constitute only a peripheral part of the labor force.

Hours and Wages Laws

For most of the nineteenth century a working day extending from "sun-up to sun-down" was regarded as normal for men, women, and often children. Attempts to shorten the working day by governmental action began in the second quarter of the century, directed first at hours of work for children and next for women. Hours of work for men, except for employees of the federal government, went generally unregulated until the end of the century.

A number of factors have contributed to the group interest supporting limitation of the hours of work. These include the belief that workers need adequate leisure to develop "good citizenship"; evidence that excessive hours are detrimental to physical and mental health; the desire to eliminate fatigue as a cause of accidents in transportation and hazardous occupations; the increased productivity of workers; and, especially during periods of unemployment, a desire to "share the work." In addition, organized labor has strongly supported legislation on both hours and wages since the 1930's.

New Hampshire was the first state to legislate on women's hours, limiting them to ten per day in 1847. Several other states followed before 1860. These early state laws were customarily declaratory and the stated maximums were applicable only in the absence of contracts calling for a longer workday. Effective legislation did not exist until the late 1870's. Much action has occurred in this area in the twentieth century and today forty-three states and the District of Columbia have laws limiting the daily and weekly hours that women may work in one or more industries. In about half the states the maximums are eight hours a day and forty-eight hours or less a week. In the others, the standards are nine or ten hours a day and fifty to sixty hours weekly. The coverage of the laws is diverse. Manufacturing establishments are usually covered; agricultural, domestic, managerial, and professional employees are almost always exempted.

State regulation of the hours of work for men is still primarily restricted to government employees and to those engaged in transportation and hazardous occupations. Most states, along with the national government, now prescribe an eight-hour day for government employees. In addition to transportation, hours are limited by many states for workers in such places as mines and smelters, cement plants, coke ovens and blast furnaces, stamping and rolling mills, and firms using cyanide and chlorinating processes. In these cases restriction of hours is considered necessary to protect the health and safety of workers and, in public transportation, the public safety as well. Only three states have general laws regulating the hours of work for men, despite the absence now of constitutional barriers.

Minimum wage legislation first appeared during the Progressive Era but was of little importance until the 1930's because of adverse judicial action. Massachusetts enacted the first minimum wage law in 1912, but it was a weak measure and provided only for the publication of the names of employers who paid less than the recommended minima. A number of other states followed with legislation and, in 1917, an evenly divided Supreme Court upheld the constitutionality of an Oregon law against the charge that it violated the freedom of contract.[28] A few years later the Court changed its position and, in a 5–3 decision in 1923, struck down a District of Columbia law setting minimum wages for women.[29] Several state laws also were soon declared unconstitutional and the minimum wage movement entered a dormant period. In the early 1930's, the poor wage and employment conditions resulting from the Great Depression caused a revival of interest in minimum wage legislation. The Court again intervened and held the New York minimum wage law unconstitutional in 1936.[30] This decision, however, marks the end of judicial rejection of such legislation. In 1937 the question of the constitutionality of minimum wage legislation again came before the Court. A shift in the voting position of one judge (Justice Roberts) converted the former minority into a five-man majority, which upheld the Oregon minimum wage law for women as within the scope of the state's police power. The constitutionality of minimum wage legislation was established

[28] *Bunting v. Oregon*, 243 U.S. 426 (1917).
[29] *Adkins v. Children's Hospital*, 261 U.S. 525 (1923).
[30] *West Coast Hotel Co. v. Parrish*, 300 U.S. 379 (1937).

228

beyond doubt when the Court in 1941 unanimously sustained the federal wage and hour law.[31]

Thirty-five states, plus the District of Columbia and Puerto Rico, currently have some sort of minimum wage legislation on their statute books. All of these laws apply to women and almost all to children. In recent years there has been a tendency to include men under the wage laws and fifteen states now do so. It is difficult to generalize on this legislation because of its diversity. Some states set statutory minimum wages; others authorize wage boards to fix minimums on an industry to industry basis; still others employ a combination of these two methods. In a few states the wage laws are not currently operative. In other states, because the prescribed minima are so low in relation to present wage levels, the wage laws are mostly symbolic. The Arkansas law sets a minimum of $1.25 *a day* for women. In South Dakota the rate is $12 *a week* except in towns of more than 2,500 population, where the rate is raised to $15 per week!

Action by the national government in the wage and hour field began in the nineteenth century with legislation on the hours of federal employees. Early in the present century Congress began to regulate the hours of transportation. A 1907 law limited railroad workers to no more than sixteen consecutive hours on the job, to be followed by at least ten hours of rest. This was intended to protect both workers and the public against fatigue-induced accidents. The Adamson Act of 1916, stimulated partly by the threat of a national railway strike, provided a basic eight-hour day for railroad employees. By 1938 the hours of employees in water, motor, and air transportation were also the subjects of national legislation. The Walsh-Healey Public Contracts Act of 1936 provided that contractors with the federal government must pay not less than the prevailing minimum wage in their industry, observe the eight-hour day and forty-hour week, pay time and a half for overtime work, and not employ child labor. This act, which utilizes government purchasing as a lever to improve working conditions, has grown in significance as government expenditures, especially for national defense, have expanded.

In 1938 Congress enacted a general wage and hour law, the Fair Labor Standards Act, which applied to both men and women. The original FLSA provided for a minimum wage of 25 cents an hour, which was to rise to forty cents an hour in 1945. The standard set for working hours was forty-four per week, decreasing to forty in 1940. Compensation of employees at time and a half of the regular rate was

[31] *U.S. v. Darby Lumber Co.,* 312 U.S. 100 (1941).

required for work in excess of the standard. Subsequent amendments to the FLSA in 1949 raised the minimum wage to 75 cents, to $1.00 in 1955, and to $1.25 in 1961 (fully effective in 1965). The FLSA covers workers engaged in interstate commerce or in the production of goods for interstate commerce, with the exception of those specifically exempted. The coverage of the act was broadened in 1961 to include an additional 3.6 million workers, mainly in the service, retail trade, and construction industries. As a result, about 27.5 million employees are covered out of a possible 44.3 million (this figure is derived by subtracting government employees, military personnel, the self-employed, professional workers, etc., from the total labor force).[32]

Of the 16.8 million workers not protected by the federal law, 11.4 million were not engaged in interstate commerce or in the production of goods for interstate commerce. The other 5.4 million were eligible under these criteria but were specifically excluded from coverage. Among the exempted groups are farm workers, outdoor salesmen, laundry workers, employees in cotton gins and a number of other establishments engaged in primary processing of agricultural commodities, fishermen, lumbermen, employees of small newspapers, and taxicab drivers. Most of these groups are unorganized, politically inarticulate, and unable to effectively protect their interests in the political arena.

Although the coverage of the FLSA was expanded in 1961 (along with an increase in the minimum wage), the expansion was not as great as the Kennedy administration had originally proposed (3.6 million compared to 4.3 million). Proposals to extend the act to laundry workers, employees in small chainstore units, and persons employed by automobile and farm equipment dealers were dropped. Moreover, workers in cotton gins and some other agricultural processing establishments, who had previously been covered, were now exempted. These concessions were made to conservative business and agricultural interests and were considered necessary by the administration to secure the enactment of legislation fairly close in substance to that originally proposed. A strong Northern Republican-Southern Democrat coalition opposed the administration's proposals in the House and, in the absence of concessions, might have prevented the 1961 legislation from being passed. Political pressures and "realities" thus took their toll on the proposed expansion.

Federal action is now far more important than state action in the wage and hour field. With respect to minimum wages, much more

[32] See Robert D. Leiter, "Coverage Confusion Under the Fair Labor Standards Act," *Labor Law Journal*, XXIII (February, 1962), 139–150.

than half the workers of the sort usually protected by minimum wage legislation (27.5 million out of 44.3 million in 1961) are covered by the federal law. Of course, most of these workers plus many not covered receive wages above the $1.25 minimum because of the workings of market forces and labor unions. But of the 16.8 million workers not covered by the federal law only 4.8 million are protected by state laws, which often set low standards, as we have seen. In the group of workers protected by neither federal nor state legislation, nor by the action of labor unions, are large numbers of poorly paid and depressed workers, in laundries, agricultural work, domestic service, and so on. For them, the rule of laissez faire prevails and low wages are a fact of life. A survey by the Bureau of Labor Statistics in 1960 revealed that in the South 31.6 per cent of the workers in industries not covered by the federal wage law earned less than 75 cents an hour.[33] To the extent that low wage rates can be remedied by legislative action, much has been done. But much room remains for additional action, especially by the states, if the desired goal is minimum wage standards for all workers.

Workmen's Compensation

With the industrialization of the American economy after the Civil War came greatly expanded use of powerful, complex, and often dangerous machinery. Working conditions in mines, factories, and transportation presented many hazards and risks, and the number of industrial accidents, injuries, and illnesses multiplied. Safety legislation enacted to prevent job hazards was only partially successful. Consequently, society was confronted with the problem of providing support or compensation to workers or their dependents for injuries, temporary or permanent disability, and death.

Throughout the nineteenth century an injured employee whose employer refused to provide voluntary compensation had only two alternatives: to bring a law suit for damages against the employer or to fend for himself as best he could. The common law rules developed by the courts for handling compensation cases were weighted to the employer's advantage. Three specific defenses open to the employer greatly reduced the worker's chances of winning his case for compensation. Under the assumption of risk doctrine, the burdens

[33] Bureau of Labor Statistics, "Wages in Nonmetropolitan Areas, Southern and North Central Regions," *Monthly Labor Review,* LXXXVI (September, 1963), 1033–1039.

of inherent occupational risks were held to be assumed by the employee and to be reflected in his wages. The fellow-servant rule stated that the employer was not legally responsible for injuries to one of his employees caused by the negligence of another of his employees, i.e., a fellow servant. Finally, under the contributory negligence rule the employer was not liable if the employee was in any way responsible for an accident, regardless of how great the employer's negligence may have been.

Workers were highly dissatisfied with these common-law procedures as it was very difficult for the worker to win his case. Agitation for change led to the enactment of laws in some states modifying or even partially abrogating the common law procedures. The employee's legal position was strengthened but criticism of the lawsuit as a means of recovering damages continued. The employee still had to use costly and time-consuming court actions, for which he often lacked adequate resources. He also ran the risk of losing his job if he sued his employer and, for this reason also, his fellow employees were often reluctant to testify in his behalf.

Beginning in the 1880's, Western European countries increasingly adopted compulsory workmen's compensation insurance legislation. This legislation made the employer responsible for providing compensation to workers injured on the job, regardless of who was at fault. The underlying theory was that compensation for injuries should be treated as part of the cost of doing business and should ultimately be borne by the consumer of the product. The European experience stimulated interest in similar legislation in the United States on the part of private and official groups. Opposition to workmen's compensation came from employers and also from some of the railroad brotherhoods. The latter long preferred the occasional recovery of large sums in damages to systematic compensation. Three states passed workmen's compensation laws in the first decade of this century but they were challenged immediately by employers in the state courts and declared unconstitutional. The states continued to pass such laws—nine did so in 1911—and in a series of decisions between 1915 and 1917 their constitutionality was firmly established by the Supreme Court. The principle of workmen's compensation is now generally accepted by all concerned.

Since 1948 all the states have had workmen's compensation laws. (Two federal laws apply to federal employees and to longshoremen and harbor workers.) In place of court suits for damages these laws substitute compensation for industrial injuries and illnesses on a fixed scale. Payments are made from insurance funds built up by employers' premiums in private companies or, sometimes, in state-operated funds. As an alternative many states permit self-insurance by the employer if he can demonstrate ability to pay benefits. The compensation systems are usually administered by the state labor department or a separate independent agency, although there is court administration in five states. The use of administrative agencies is favored as a means of simplifying procedures, hastening award of benefits, and providing the flexibility and continuous supervision considered necessary for effective compensation administration.

In no state are all workers protected by workmen's compensation. Many states exempt employers having fewer than a specified number of employees, ranging from two to fifteen depending upon the particular state. Groups of persons not usually covered include farm workers, domestic workers, employees of religious or charitable institutions, and those engaged in casual employment. For protected workers, most job-related accidents are covered and all but two states provide full or partial coverage for industrial diseases. Compensation benefits are paid for medical care, temporary or permanent disability, death, and burial expenses. The benefits paid vary widely in amount and duration among the various states. About half the states include vocational rehabilitation programs in their workmen's compensation system. These are intended to restore (at least partially) the earning capacity of injured workers.

Because employers must meet the costs of many accidents and illnesses, and because insurance premiums are generally reduced for employers with good safety records, workmen's compensation has stimulated efforts by employers to prevent industrial accidents and illnesses. But only a few states have strong and active programs of accident prevention to supplement employers' efforts. Many accidents still occur. In 1960 there were 1,960,000 serious work injuries, including 13,800 deaths. Most states now provide full or substantial medical care benefits for covered workers, but death and disability benefits are frequently not sufficient to meet family needs. And many workers are not protected at all. Many gaps thus remain in the protection of workers and their families against the hazards of industrial accident and death. However, many labor unions are able to obtain similar benefits for their members by collective bargaining. This has lessened the pressure for expansion of state compensation programs, which is to the disadvantage of workers currently protected by neither union nor governmental action.

PUBLIC POLICY, UNIONIZATION, AND
COLLECTIVE BARGAINING

Collective bargaining is the process by which a labor contract or agreement governing terms of work, fringe benefits, and working conditions is negotiated by an employer and a union representing his employees. An agreement at least minimally acceptable to each party is reached by give and take, proposal and counterproposal, bargaining and compromise. Most such agreements are arrived at without actual use of the economic weapons available to each side: strikes, boycotts, slowdowns, lockouts, and the like.

Collective bargaining is conducted within a framework of public law—both statutory and common (judge-made) law; the former is most important now—which sets forth rules concerning the rights and duties of, and the limitations on labor and management. This framework of legal rules has been developed and modified in response to changing social, economic, and political circumstance. First one party in the bargaining relationship and then the other has been favored. Since 1789 public policy has moved from a period in which labor unions were of doubtful legality, to one in which unions were legal but often treated hostilely, to positive support and encouragement, to detailed regulation of labor-management relationships.

Doubtful Legality: Until 1842

In the nineteenth century, and indeed until the 1930's, little legislation relating to labor unions was enacted, but labor unions have been subjected to judicial controls since their appearance in this country. Employers confronted with unions in the early nineteenth century turned to the courts for assistance. Beginning in 1806 the courts held in a number of cases that any sort of union activity constituted an illegal conspiracy in restraint of trade under the common law. Such activity was consequently subject to punishment by fine or imprisonment. In other cases the courts were less harsh toward unions but, in any event, there was substantial doubt as to the legality of unions until 1842. In that year, in the famous case of *Commonwealth v. Hunt*, the highest court of Massachusetts ruled that union activities were not illegal *per se*, but rather that their legality depended on the objectives

234

they were seeking to attain. Other state courts followed this ruling and the doctrine that unions were illegal criminal conspiracies fell from grace. The legality of unions was thus established.

Judicial acceptance of the legality of unions was not accompanied by judicial approval of them as economic organizations. Throughout the nineteenth century, and to a lesser extent in the present century, most judges were rather hostile toward unions. This judicial hostility stemmed partly from the judges' legal training and partly from their personal beliefs and group affiliations. The common law, in which the judges were trained, was conservative and strongly directed to the protection of property rights. Unions were historically viewed as an attack on property rights and, consequently, they appeared to be in conflict with the spirit of the common law. The judicial dislike of unions was strengthened by the judges' political predilections. As Reynolds notes:

> [The judges] were drawn mainly from the property class, mingled more frequently with employers than with workers, and tended naturally to sympathize with the propertied interests. Their political thinking was influenced also by the classical economics, which could find no useful place for joint action by wage earners.[34]

More will be said regarding judicial hostility to unions as our discussion continues.

Legality, Hostility, Neutrality: 1842–1932

During this span of ninety years, unions existed as lawful organization but there was very little governmental protection of their rights to organize and bargain collectively. Employers were required neither to recognize nor to bargain with unions representing their workers. Rather, they were legally free to interfere with, obstruct, or combat the development and activities of unions as they saw fit within the broad confines of criminal law. Among the methods used by individual employers or associations of employers in combating unions were: discharging or discriminating against union members; blacklisting to prevent them from obtaining other jobs; the use of labor spies and strikebreakers; lockouts; and the requirement that as a condition of employment workers sign "yellowdog" contracts forbidding union membership. Violence on the part of both sides often accompanied labor disputes.

[34] Reynolds, *op. cit.*, 112.

Government not only left management unrestricted but often intervened in its behalf in labor matters. This was especially true of executive and judicial officials at the state and local levels. Local law enforcement officials, the state militia, and occasionally federal troops were employed against strikers. Local authorities prohibited union meetings, helped drive organizers out of town, clothed company police or guards with legal authority, and in other ways helped employers harass unions. Moreover, employers usually enjoyed the sympathy and support of middle-class elements and the owners of newspapers and other opinion-shaping communications media.

In the 1880's the labor injunction was developed by the courts as a means of limiting unions. Employers who believed that a strike or some other type of concerted worker activity threatened their property interests could go to court and seek an injunction enjoining such activities on the ground that they would cause irreparable harm or injury to their property. The judges had wide discretion in issuing injunctions and, because of the factors mentioned above, were usually sympathetic to the pleas of employers. Injunctions against union activity were often issued without any notice or hearing to the union. They were frequently both sweeping and vague, prohibiting "all persons whomsoever" from aiding a strike. Violators of an injunction could be tried without a jury as being in contempt of court and, if guilty, punished by fine or imprisonment. If the injunction was broadly drawn and strongly enforced by the police it was an almost infallible method of breaking strikes. Even if it was not well-enforced, the injunction stigmatized the union before the public, interfered with union activities, and generally helped demoralize the union and its supporters.[35] Unions were bitterly opposed to the use of labor injunctions and long sought legislation restricting their use. They were not really successful in this endeavor until the Norris-La Guardia Act of 1932.

Although it was generally thought that the Sherman Antitrust Act applied only to restraints of trade and monopolistic activities by business organizations, the Supreme Court in 1908 held that the act was applicable to labor unions if their activities had the effect of restraining trade. The Sherman Act was thus transformed into a legislative obstacle for labor unions. Amendment of the act to exempt labor unions joined elimination of "government by injunction" on labor's list of legislative objectives.

At the urging of labor groups, and under the leadership of the Wilson administration, Congress included some labor provisions in

[35] *Ibid.*, 115–116.

the Clayton Act. Section 6 of the act stated that the laws should not be construed to prohibit the existence of labor unions or to forbid "members of such organizations from lawfully carrying out the legitimate objects thereof." Section 20 was designed to prevent the issuance of labor injunctions against such union activities as strikes, boycotts, and picketing except to prevent irreparable damage to property or a property right. These provisions were hailed by Samuel Gompers and other labor leaders as "labor's Magna Carta." Labor's victory was of short duration, however, because hostile judicial interpretations soon deprived the Clayton Act provisions of most of their intended meaning. The courts continued to apply the antitrust laws to unions and to issue injunctions against union activities held to be neither "lawful" nor "peaceable." By the early 1920's the courts had largely frustrated this effort by Congress to protect unions against unfavorable judicial action.

Early attempts by both Congress and state legislatures to aid labor by prohibiting the use of yellow-dog contracts were declared unconstitutional by the Supreme Court as violations of the freedom of contract.[36] Moreover, in 1917 the Court held that an employer could secure an injunction to prevent unions from attempting to organize employees who had signed yellow-dog contracts on the ground that they were "inducing a breach of contract." Here we have another example of judicial rejection of legislative policy favorable to unions.

In 1932 labor won its greatest legislative victory up to that time when Congress passed the Norris-La Guardia Act. The act prohibited the enforcement of yellow-dog contracts in the federal courts. It deprived the federal courts of jurisdiction to issue labor injunctions against strikes, union membership, payment of strike benefits, peaceful picketing, or publicizing a labor dispute by any persons, singly or in concert, participating or interested in a labor dispute. The act also set down procedural rules governing the issuance of injunctions and making them more difficult to obtain. The Norris-La Guardia Act, in short, "neutralized" the courts in labor disputes and gave labor as much freedom from injunctions as management had long enjoyed. The philosophy reflected in the Act has been stated as follows:

> The law should intervene [in labor disputes] only to prevent damage to tangible property and to preserve public order; otherwise, the disputants should be left to their own resources to work out their own problems. Both labor and business would now be free to promote

[36] *Adair v. U.S.*, 208 U.S. 161 (1908), and *Coppage v. Kansas*, 236 U.S. 1 (1915). The 1917 case is *Hitchman Coal and Coke Co. v. Mitchell*, 245 U.S. 229 (1917).

their own interests in the field of labor policy through self-help without interference of the courts.[37]

A "liberalized" Supreme Court later interpreted the statute to provide labor unions with almost complete freedom from judicial action in labor disputes. Most of labor's grievances against "government by injunction" were finally remedied, to the dismay of business interests.

Throughout this period labor unions were handicapped by hostile executive and judicial action. With the exception of the Norris-La Guardia Act, which came at the end of the period, legislation favorable to unions usually was rendered ineffective by the courts. Although such factors as unfavorable community attitudes and periodically depressed economic conditions also worked to the disadvantage of organized labor, a hostile judicially-created legal environment was certainly an important obstacle to the growth of unionization and collective bargaining. Between 1900 and 1933 union membership was usually below 10 per cent of non-agricultural employment. Outside of the railroad industry and the skilled crafts, unions were almost nonexistent.

Protection and Promotion: 1933–1947

From 1933 until 1947 the policy of the national government toward unions can be described as one of protection and positive support for unionization and collective bargaining. During this period the New Deal-Fair Deal administration provided a favorable politico-legal environment for organized labor.

The first New Deal measure that directly aided unionism was the National Industrial Recovery Act of 1933. This act attempted to alleviate the problems of unemployment, economic insecurity, and declining production by encouraging business self-regulation through industry codes of fair competition. Section 7(a) of the NIRA provided that each such code should contain a guarantee of labor's right to organize and bargain collectively through unions of its own choosing. This effort to help unions proved ineffective because of employer resistance and because the administrative boards later created to enforce Section 7(a) had no meaningful sanctions to use against employers who refused to bargain collectively. Indeed, the only sanction available to the boards was withdrawal of the Blue Eagle emblem,

---

[37] Herbert R. Northrup and Gordon F. Bloom, *Government and Labor* (Homewood, Ill.: Richard D. Irwin, 1963), 22.

which was used to symbolize compliance with the law, from non-compliers.

When the NIRA was declared unconstitutional in 1935, Congress quickly replaced Section 7(a) with the National Labor Relations Act, better known as the Wagner Act after its leading sponsor, Senator Wagner of New York. The general purpose of the Wagner Act was to guarantee labor's rights to organize and bargain collectively through unions of their own choosing, free from employer interference. To make this guarantee effective, the act prohibited a number of unfair employer practices. (1) It forbade employers to "interfere with, restrain, or coerce" employees in exercising their rights to organize and bargain collectively. (2) It prohibited employers from dominating or interfering with labor organizations or giving them financial or other support. This provision was directed against "company unions," unions set up and really controlled by management. (3) Employers were forbidden to discriminate against workers in hiring, firing, or conditions of employment because of union membership. (4) Discharge or discrimination against workers filing charges under the act was banned. This rule was intended to prevent employer retaliation. (5) It was declared unfair for an employer to refuse to bargain collectively with a union representing his employees. Employers were thus obligated to bargain with unions but not necessarily to agree with them.

To enforce these prohibitions, the act established the National Labor Relations Board, an independent regulatory commission headed by a three-man board (later increased to five by the Taft-Hartley Act). The Board was authorized to investigate and hold hearings on complaints of unfair employer practices and to issue cease and desist orders to employers found guilty of specified unfair practices. The Board's orders were enforceable through the federal courts of appeals. In addition, the Board was given the duty of determining the appropriate unit for collective bargaining: craft unit, plant unit, company unit, or others. If there were controversy concerning which union should represent the employees in a particular bargaining unit, the NLRB was to determine by secret election or other suitable methods which union (if any) the majority of employees wanted to represent them. This union was then certified as bargaining agent for the unit.

In general, then, the Wagner Act provided a procedure for selecting the employees' bargaining representative, required the employer to bargain, and placed some restraints on employers in dealing with unions. So far as the results of the bargaining process were concerned, unions and management were left free to agree or disagree on terms of work, working conditions, fringe benefits, and union security arrangements. The NLRB was given no authority to directly intervene in the bargaining process. The act did, however, place the weight of government on the side of the unions and provided them with support and protection which they previously had not enjoyed. Under the Norris-La Guardia Act, in contrast, the government had taken an essentially laissez-faire position on labor relations.

The Wagner Act and the twelve years of experience with it were effective in establishing collective bargaining as an accepted method of conducting labor-management relations.[38] The act did not require union membership, but unions prospered during this period and their membership rose from four million in 1935 to about fifteen and a half million in 1947. Although such other causes for this growth as a favorable economic environment (especially after 1940), the vigor of unions during the 1930's, and the strong organizing efforts of the newly established CIO in mass-production industries cannot be disregarded, certainly the favorable politico-legal environment created by the Wagner Act was an important factor. The act clearly achieved its purpose of promoting unionization and collective bargaining. On the other hand, the act did not generally reduce the causes or numbers of labor disputes. It was intended only to reduce strikes by unions to gain recognition and the opportunity to bargain and here it was apparently successful. The proportion of strikes over recognition declined sharply between 1939 and 1947. Disputes over wages, hours, and other conditions of work were outside the scope of the act.

A variety of criticisms were directed at the Wagner Act, involving both the law itself and the way in which it was administered by the NLRB. Because it embodied a rather sharp shift in national policy to the advantage of unions, most of these criticisms came from business and conservative sources. The National Association of Manufacturers, the Liberty League (a conservative lawyers' organization), and other conservative groups initially contended that the law was unconstitutional because it exceeded the scope of the commerce clause. This contention was rejected by the Supreme Court in 1937. The Court upheld the act as a legitimate means of preventing obstructions to interstate commerce in the form of work stoppages.[39]

[38] R. W. Fleming, "The Significance of the Wagner Act," in Milton Derber and Edwin Young, eds., *Labor and the New Deal* (Madison: University of Wisconsin Press, 1957), 121–156, esp. 149.

[39] *NLRB v. Jones & Laughlin Steel Corp.,* 301 U.S. 1 (1937).

The Wagner Act was often criticized by business interests as one-sided because it restricted the activities of employers but not those of unions. For example, the employer, but not the union, was required to bargain in good faith. The act did favor unions because its essential purpose was to promote collective bargaining by unions. Most legislation is partial (or one-sided) in the sense that it favors some groups over others. But partiality is not necessarily the equivalent of unreasonableness here. Whether a law is reasonable or unreasonable depends upon the criteria of judgment used. Consequently, those opposed to unions were likely to view the act as one-sided, i.e., unreasonable.

Another criticism of the Wagner Act was that it violated minority and individual rights because some employees in a bargaining unit might not want the union selected by the majority to bargain for them. Furthermore, if a closed shop or union shop were established, those not favoring the union would have to join it or give up their jobs. In reply it was frequently said that the principle of majority rule was not alien to a democracy. Senator Wagner and other proponents of the law believed that democracy in industrial relations, which they saw as an objective of the Wagner Act, also supported political democracy. The remarks of Professor Lane merit quotation at some length because they offer insight into the controversy over the act.

> The proponents of regulation clearly select symbolic references which have the weight of cultural approval. . . . [T]he National Labor Relations Act was commonly supported on the ground that it would extend the accepted right of freedom of association to the employee and substitute democratic electoral processes for violence. In this society businessmen writing for a closed circle of other businessmen did not challenge these objectives, but, accepting their validity, said that the law was confused because it would "foment strikes," "cause trouble," "shackle labor," and put labor under John L. Lewis who sought "to become the virtual dictator of labor policies." That is, at the deeper level of basic objectives, symbols, and myths, there is a remarkable consensus. Ideologically we are a high consensus society. Hence, manufacturers will say that measure will not achieve these objectives, or better will destroy them, which is the way businessmen most frequently express "contrary to the public interest."[40]

[40] Robert E. Lane, *The Regulation of Businessmen* (New Haven: Yale University Press, 1954), 42–43. See also Murray Edleman, *The Symbolic Uses of Politics* (Urbana: University of Illinois Press, 1964), 137.

Questions of democracy aside, it was also contended that collective bargaining would not be very effective if small groups or individuals in the bargaining unit were permitted to bargain on their own. Protection of dissenting groups might thus weaken the union in the bargaining process. Opposition to strong unions, more than a concern for rights of minorities, was probably the motivation behind many employer complaints that the Wagner Act was "undemocratic."

Finally, it was often charged that the NLRB was biased in favor of unions in its administration of the law. Many of these criticisms applied directly to the law itself because the Board, in administering the law as written, could not avoid helping or protecting unions. Concerning NLRB decisions applying the act in unfair employer practices cases, Edleman has noted: "By their inherent nature . . . [these] decisions either favored union growth or permitted the status quo to continue. Under the Wagner Act they could not place the company in a stronger bargaining position than it already enjoyed for there were no union unfair labor practices."[41] In some instances NLRB officials did directly involve themselves in union organizing activities and otherwise acted beyond the agency's proper concern, but such action was not representative of the Board, on the whole.

Charges of bias against the NLRB also came from unions, especially those in the AFL, as an outgrowth of the Board's responsibility for determining bargaining units. The AFL often alleged that the Board favored the CIO by selecting plant and company rather than craft units for bargaining purposes. The CIO sometimes responded that the Board went out of its way to be fair to the AFL. The Board was never able to fully satisfy either of the two. In 1940 the AFL was sufficiently dissatisfied to join forces with a conservative coalition in the House of Representatives seeking amendments to the Wagner Act to weaken the Board's position and restrict unions. Included in the package were amendments protecting AFL craft unions. The efforts of this rather strange alliance failed because the bill was not acted upon in the Senate, where support for the Wagner Act was stronger, although it passed the House by a two-to-one majority.

The dissatisfaction of business and conservative groups with the Wagner Act policy and with the growth and activities of unions caused them to devote much time and energy to seeking amendments to the law which would curb unions and strengthen the position of

[41] Murray Edleman, "New Deal Sensitivity to Labor Interests," in Derber and Young, *op. cit.,* 171.

employers. The attitude of business groups can be illustrated by brief reference to the National Association of Manufacturers. The NAM had opposed the enactment of the Wagner Act as both unconstitutional and undesirable. But, after 1939, following the Court's upholding of the act and the development of general acceptance of the principle of government intervention in labor relations, the NAM changed its position. The NAM ceased its efforts to disprove the validity of labor's rights to organize and bargain collectively and instead gave limited approval to them. "Attention was then directed to injustices that resulted from a law which guaranteed these rights. The injustices were characterized as violative of the rights of employees and employers and destructive of the welfare of employers." Government legislation favorable to employers' interests rather than a policy of laissez faire now became the goal of the NAM. It set out to use lobbying, public relations, and electoral activities to secure this new, positive objective.[42]

In the late 1930's a reaction against labor unions set in and the states began to enact restrictive labor legislation. By 1947 three-fourths of the states had passed legislation restricting unions on such matters as strikes, picketing, secondary boycotts, jurisdictional and sympathetic strikes, use of coercion and violence, and prohibition of union and closed shops. At the national level the movement to place restraints on labor unions moved more slowly. Many bills amending the Wagner Act in ways unfavorable to labor were introduced in Congress but opposition by the administration and Democratic congressional leaders was strong enough to prevent their adoption (one such attempt was mentioned above). The efforts of those seeking restrictive legislation intensified after the end of World War II, and in 1947 they bore fruit when the Taft-Hartley Act was passed by large majorities in both Houses of Congress. Composed primarily of Republicans and conservative Southern Democrats, they were sufficient to override President Truman's veto, which was strongly urged by labor groups and their allies.

A number of factors contributed to the enactment of the Taft-Hartley Act, some of which are summarized here. By 1947 labor had lost much public support because of jurisdictional disputes between AFL and CIO unions and misuses of power by unions, such as failure to bargain in good faith and coercion of employers to recognize unions despite the wishes of employees. Internal conflict also lessened labor's

[42] This paragraph rests substantially on Richard W. Gable, "NAM: Influential Lobby or Kiss of Death?" *Journal of Politics,* XV (May, 1953), 254–273.

political power and effectiveness. Serious strikes in the steel, automobile, meat-packing, railroad, and other industries after World War II cost labor public favor, as did the resentment created by John L. Lewis and the United Mine Workers when they defied a government order against a coal strike in the fall of 1946. For many people an "arrogant and malevolent" John L. Lewis became the stereotype of the union leader. While labor was losing prestige that of business groups was rising because of their contributions to "winning the war," the return of prosperity, and their many "image-building" activities. The Republican party, which had little support among unions, gained control of Congress in the 1946 elections; its leadership believed it had a mandate to enact legislation curbing unions. Conservative Southern Democrats supported them in this endeavor, apparently on the assumption that restrictive legislation would retard unionization in the South and help the region attract new industries. Neither organized labor nor the Truman administration was able to agree on proposals for moderate labor reform legislation which might have prevented or softened the sweeping changes embodied in the Taft-Hartley Act.[43]

Detailed Regulation: 1947 to the Present

THE TAFT-HARTLEY ACT. The Taft-Hartley Act, formally entitled the Labor-Management Relations Act, marks a major change in national labor relations policy. It replaces union promotionalism with a policy of detailed regulation intended to restrict unions and "equalize" the power of labor and management. Although the Taft-Hartley Act is not as harsh as was desired by some of the more extreme anti-labor spokesmen in and outside of Congress, in no way does the law enhance the status or power of unions. But neither has it appeared to be a "slave-labor law," as labor contended. The Taft-Hartley Act is a complex and detailed piece of legislation and only a few of its salient aspects are covered here.

First, the act attempts to strengthen the prerogatives of management and to reduce those of unions in their relationships. The series of unfair employer practices in the Wagner Act were retained but their impact on employers was partially reduced. Employers were accorded greater freedom of speech in opposing unions and more freedom to

---

[43] See Seymour Z. Mann, "Policy Formulation in the Executive Branch: The Taft-Hartley Experience," *Western Political Quarterly,* XIII (September, 1960), 597–608.

discharge employers, as when they engaged in the unfair union practices listed below. Employers were given more opportunity to secure NLRB elections on union demands for recognition and on petitions for decertification of unions. To supplement the Wagner Act's unfair employer practices, the following union activities were declared unfair:[44]

1. Restraining or coercing employees in their right to join or refrain from joining a union.

2. Causing an employer to discriminate against or discharge an employee for nonmembership in a union in the absence of a legal union shop arrangement.

3. Engaging in or encouraging any strike or concerted refusal by employees to use, manufacture, transport, work, or handle goods where the purpose is to force or require:

(a) an employee or self-employed person to join a union or an employer organization.

(b) an employer or other person to cease dealing in the products of another employer or to stop doing business with any other person. (This was directed against secondary boycott.)

(c) any employer to recognize or bargain with one union if another union is already the certified bargaining agent or to force another employer (not the strikers' employer) to recognize an uncertified union.

(d) an employer to assign particular work to employees in one union or craft rather than employees in another union or craft. (This was designed to prohibit "jurisdictional strikes" over controversies as to what union should perform a particular job.)

4. Charging, under a union shop agreement, initiation fees found by the NLRB to be "excessive or discriminatory under all the circumstances."

5. Causing or attempting to cause an employer to pay for services not performed or not to be performed. (The practice aimed at here is popularly designated as "featherbedding".)

6. Refusing to bargain collectively in good faith with the employer.

The act also regulates some internal and political practices of unions. They were required to file annual reports with the Secretary of Labor on their finances, compensation of principal officers, internal rules and procedures, and initiation fees and dues. Union officers were required to file affidavits stating that they were not members of the Communist party or other organizations advocating overthrow of

[44] The list of unfair union practices below is derived from Northrup and Bloom, *op. cit.*, 87–94.

the government by violence or unconstitutional methods. Failure to comply with these requirements deprived the union involved of protection under the act and of the use of NLRB machinery for certification and handling of unfair employer practices complaints. The unions were vigorously opposed to the noncommunist affidavit requirement, arguing that it was unnecessary and unfair since it was not required of employers. It was repealed by Congress in 1959. As stated earlier, the act also prohibited union expenditures in connection with any federal election.

Various aspects of collective bargaining procedure were dealt with by the act. Refusal to bargain in good faith, as mentioned, was made an unfair union practice, as were jurisdictional strikes. In the latter instance, the NLRB is directed to "hear and determine" jurisdictional disputes unless the parties arrive at a voluntary settlement within ten days after a case is filed. This has encouraged unions to establish procedures for settling jurisdictional disputes by themselves. Existing labor contracts can be legally modified or terminated only if the party desiring change gives sixty days' written notice to the other party and, after thirty days, to the Federal Mediation and Conciliation Service and any state agency with jurisdiction. During the sixty-day period the parties are bound by the existing contract. Any workers who strike during this period lose their status as an employee unless the employer decides to retain them. Unions have come to give strike notices as a matter of routine so this provision has not proved overly restrictive.

The courts were brought into the bargaining process by a provision authorizing suits for damages, by either unions or employers, resulting from violations of existing contracts. Furthermore, the General Counsel of the NLRB was authorized to obtain court injunctions against secondary boycotts, strikes by uncertified unions, and other unfair union practices. Taft-Hartley's limited revival of the use of injunctions provoked opposition from unions because of their old fear and distaste for "government by injunction." However, little actual use has been made of the authorization.

A special procedure for dealing with "emergency disputes" involving the "national health or safety" was also established.

Employees of the federal government are absolutely prohibited from striking although they may join unions and bargain with the government. The penalty for striking is immediate discharge, loss of civil service status, and ineligibility for re-employment for three years.

Strikes against the government are viewed in the United States as something akin to "insurrection" against public authority.

The Conciliation Service in the Department of Labor was abolished and its mediation and conciliation activities were given to a new independent agency, the Federal Mediation and Conciliation Service. The old Conciliation Service had helped to successfully settle a large majority of the cases referred to it. Employer groups, however, believed that its location within the labor-oriented Department of Labor prevented it from being fully impartial. Supposedly a new independent agency would not have this shortcoming.

Finally, in contrast to the Wagner Act, the 1947 legislation regulates what can be included in agreements reached by collective bargaining. Limitations were placed on union security arrangements negotiated by labor and management. The closed shop, which requires that employers hire only union members, is prohibited. Union-shop agreements, under which workers must join the union within a certain amount of time after being hired in order to keep their jobs, are permitted. Also accepted are maintenance of membership agreements, in which the worker is free to join or not to join the union but must retain his membership for the length of the agreement if he does join the union. Originally, the Taft-Hartley Act permitted those two union security agreements only if approved by a majority of the workers affected in an NLRB election. This requirement was removed in 1951, because up to that time workers had approved union security agreements in 97 per cent of the elections held.

The Taft-Hartley Act went on to provide that when a state had legislation more restrictive of union security arrangements, the state law should take precedence over the federal law. In other words, in this area of policy national supremacy is replaced by state supremacy. The way was left open for the states to enact "right to work" laws which, by stating that union membership or nonmembership shall not be a condition of employment, outlaw all the union security arrangements listed in the preceding paragraph. What remains permissible is the "open shop" where the worker is legally free to join or not join a union as he sees fit. Nineteen states now have right to work laws.[45] The proponents of right to work legislation have been suc-

[45] Alabama, Arizona, Arkansas, Florida, Georgia, Iowa, Kansas, Mississippi, Nebraska, Nevada, North Carolina, North Dakota, South Carolina, South Dakota, Tennessee, Texas, Utah, Virginia, and Wyoming. Louisiana once had a general right to work law but repealed it except as it applies to agricultural employment.

cessful primarily in the more rural states, and particularly in the South, where unions are weakest. Among the major industrial states, only Indiana enacted such a law. However, in the 1964 elections the Democrats gained control of both houses of the Indiana legislature and early in 1965, in accordance with the desires of labor groups, the state's right to work law was repealed.

Strong support for right to work legislation has come from employer groups seeking to increase (or retain) their power in relation to unions by eliminating the union shop and compulsory unions. Their arguments, however, are usually phrased in terms of voluntarism and the worker's right to freedom from coercion by unions or "labor bosses." The appelation "right to work" is itself a misnomer since these laws guarantee no one the right to work—that is, a job. But, like such phrases as "fair trade" and "states' rights," it has strong emotional and ideological appeal. Unions have outspokenly opposed right to work legislation as a form of "union busting" and because it permits "free riders" to gain the benefits of collective bargaining without sharing the costs (dues) or risks (strikes) involved. (The union is required to serve all workers in the bargaining unit which it represents.) Repeal or prevention of this sort of legislation is a major objective of organized labor.

The effect of right to work laws is difficult to determine. Studies of the right to work laws in Texas and Virginia reveal that in those states closed shops sometimes still exist, being acceptable to both employers and unions, especially in the building trades.[46] Professor Meyers concludes that the " 'right to work' proposals are of much less importance than either side to the controversy has been willing to admit. The issue is symbolic. What is at stake is the political power and public support of management and unionism."[47] The enactment of a right to work law probably both reflects and helps to create an unfavorable political environment for unions. There is some evidence, however, that right to work laws may adversely affect union membership and union strength. Workers who would have to join the union under a union shop arrangement may not do so when membership is made non-mandatory by a right to work law.[48] Although the social pressures generated by fellow workers may "compel" some to join

[46] Frederic Meyers, *"Right to Work" in Practice* (New York: Fund for the Republic, 1959); and J. M. Kuhlman, "Right to Work Laws: The Virginia Experience," *Labor Law Journal,* VI (July, 1955), 453–461.

[47] Meyers, *op. cit.,* 45.

[48] See the discussion in Northrup and Bloom, *op. cit.,* 232–238.

the union, these will not always be effective. But, whatever the actual impact of right to work laws on unions, the controversy over them continues.

Having had little success in obtaining the repeal of right to work laws in the states, the AFL-CIO decided to seek Congressional action repealing Section 14(B) of the Taft-Hartley Act, the provision permitting right to work laws. With the sweeping Democratic Presidential and Congressional victories in the 1964 elections, the AFL-CIO believed it had sufficient support to obtain favorable action during the 89th Congress. Repeal of Section 14(B) was given top priority on the AFL-CIO's legislative agenda and, in the spring of 1965, President Johnson sent a message to Congress supporting repeal. Although the repeal measure passed the House, a conservative filibuster prevented its passage by the Senate in 1965, thereby at least temporarily frustrating organized labor and a majority of the Senate.

The Taft-Hartley Act further affected union security by providing that the "check-off" could be used only if authorized annually by each union member. The check-off is an arrangement whereby the employer agrees to deduct union dues from the employee's wages and pay them directly to the union, which greatly facilitates dues collection by the union. (In Wisconsin, state law requires that the check-off be authorized by both the worker and his wife. One can only speculate on the legislature's motivation here.) In addition, it was made an unfair practice for a union to attempt to cause an employer to discharge a union member except for failure to pay dues or fees (where the union shop was permitted). This was intended to lessen the union's disciplinary controls over its members. Content of the agreement was also regulated by a provision permitting welfare funds financed by employer contributions only when they were jointly administered by union and management representatives.

TAFT-HARTLEY: IMPACT AND ADMINISTRATION. An unintended consequence of the Taft-Hartley Act, especially since it attempted to restrict labor in this regard, was an expansion and intensification of labor's political activities. The passage of the act sharply indicated to labor that, in promoting and protecting its interests, it could not neglect the political process. Since 1947 labor as a whole has been quite active politically.

Moreover, the Taft-Hartley Act has been a focal point of labor politics since its enactment. Denouncing the act as a "slave labor law," its repeal or substantial modification became a major legislative objective for organized labor. President Truman promised to work for its repeal during the 1948 Presidential campaign and made various efforts to redeem his pledge. In 1954 President Eisenhower proposed a series of amendments to the act, some of which were favorable to labor. There have been no significant legislative modifications of the statute, however. (Several changes were made by the Landrum-Griffin Act of 1959, discussed below.) The absence of major changes has resulted in part because of lack of agreement among those favoring change concerning the specific form it should take. Moreover, the act has become a symbolic issue on which both supporters and opponents have often taken extreme and intransigent positions, which has made it difficult to get proposed amendments considered on their merits and has reduced the possibility of compromise solutions.[49] With the passage of time labor has learned to "live" with the act but, at the same time, it has not stopped seeking favorable changes in the law.

It should be clear, then, that the Taft-Hartley Act restrained unions in a variety of ways to the advantage of management and in some cases, individual workers. This was the intent of the limitation placed on the bargaining process, the content of agreements, and union organizing and bargaining practices. However, it seems agreed that the law has probably affected new or weaker unions more seriously than it has such strong, well-established unions as the Teamsters, Steelworkers, or Auto Workers. Its impact on existing unions has been softened by generally prosperous economic conditions since 1947. Consequently, "employers [generally] have found it more profitable to get along with unions than to provoke them."[50]

The rate of growth in union membership slowed down after 1947 and, in fact, since 1956 total union membership has declined from 18.5 million to 17.6 million in 1962. Union officials often attribute this situation to the Taft-Hartley Act and the state right to work laws which, they say, have given an unfair advantage to employers in combating unions. A number of other factors, however, have probably been at least equally important in their effect on union organizing activities. These include the growth in white-collar employment, the shift of many industries to the South and Midwest, more mature and less dynamic leadership in many unions, and the increasing number of women in the labor force. All have made it more difficult for unions to secure new members.

[49] Melvin W. Reder, *Labor in a Growing Economy* (New York: John Wiley and Sons, 1957), 256.
[50] *Ibid.*, 227.

250

The "operational" meaning and the effect of the Taft-Hartley Act on labor-management relations is conditioned by the way in which it is administered by the National Labor Relations Board. Although the Board does not have a free hand in applying the law, its provisions permit varying interpretations, affording considerable discretion to the Board in its implementation. As stated in Chapter Three, the supporters of the Taft-Hartley Act included provisions in the law revamping the NLRB—its membership was increased to five and a separate office of General Counsel was created to handle case prosecution—in an effort to ensure that the statute would be administered as they intended. The unexpected re-election of President Truman in 1948, however, resulted in the appointment of Board members during 1947–1953 who were favorably inclined toward unions. Consequently the impact of Taft-Hartley on labor during its first five years was frequently eased by Board decisions favorable to unions. Management groups often complained that the Board was biased in favor of unions and that it was perverting the meaning of the act. In early 1953 a Chamber of Commerce spokesman contended that: "A dispassionate review of the decisions of the Board seems to disclose a studied attempt to evade the clear-cut intent of Congress, as expressed in the Taft-Hartley Act, and to revert to the principles established under the Wagner Act."[51]

When the Eisenhower administration took office in 1953 it was urged by business groups to "do something" about the NLRB. The course of action decided on was the appointment of persons to the Board favorable to business interests, which the administration proceeded to do as vacancies appeared. The "Eisenhower Board," as it was dubbed by labor, reversed many of the pre-1954 decisions which had been favorable to labor. This created unhappiness among labor groups and satisfaction in the business community. As the National Association of Manufacturers commented in late 1954:

> Though the language of Taft-Hartley has remained unchanged, its interpretation by the Labor Board has not. On numerous and important issues, a new Board, a majority of whose members have been appointed by President Eisenhower, has overturned long established rulings, and given the Act a new, and almost always anti-labor meaning. Indeed, the Eisenhower appointees seem to have taken office

[51] Quoted in Seymour Scher, "Regulatory Agency Control Through Appointment: The Case of the Eisenhower Administration and the NLRB," *Journal of Politics,* XXIII (November, 1961), 669.

with that end consciously in mind. . . . They have proceeded to imbue the Board with the employer-oriented interests of the new Administration.[52]

After 1961, however, the pendulum swung back in the direction of labor. Responsive to labor interests, the Kennedy administration appointed to the NLRB members who were sympathetic toward unions and collective bargaining. As a consequence, the Board now reversed or modified many of the decisions favorable to management made by the "Eisenhower Board." These labor-oriented decisions have blunted restrictions on union tactical weapons, such as picketing, restricted employer counterweapons, such as speeches opposing unions, and defined the bargaining unit so as to facilitate union organizing.[53] For example, the Board held that a single store in a retail chain was an appropriate bargaining unit whereas the "Eisenhower Board" had held that the appropriate unit for bargaining should embrace all the employees in all the stores located in an employer's administrative division or geographic area.[54] The new decision will undoubtedly make it easier for unions to organize stores in a chain one at a time. Once more employer groups have begun to criticize the NLRB for being biased toward labor.

THE LANDRUM-GRIFFIN ACT. In the last half of the 1950's there were continuing and increasing complaints about corruption, abuses of power, and undemocratic procedures in unions.[55] From 1957 to 1959 the McClellan Committee, officially designated the Senate Select Committee on Improper Activities in Labor-Management Affairs, conducted investigations and held hearings on alleged corruption and racketeering by unions. The attention of the McClellan Committee was especially focused on the Teamsters Union, James Hoffa, and his predecessor as Teamsters president, David Beck; and a few other unions, such as the Carpenters. The Committee's findings and charges were widely reported by the mass communications media and many people came to believe that the unsavory and corrupt practices of some unions were typical of all unions. Specific actions such as the indictment (and later conviction) of Dave Beck for misuse of Teamsters' funds and the expulsion of the Teamsters and a few other unions from the AFL-CIO for unethical practices, seemed to confirm the Committee's allegations of extensive union wrongdoing.

[52] Quoted in *ibid.*, 687.
[53] Northrup and Bloom, *op. cit.*, 136.
[54] *Sav-On Drugs, Inc.*, 138 NLRB 1032 (1962).
[55] The discussion in this section draws extensively from McAdam, *op. cit.*

By 1959 there was widespread agreement that union reform legislation was needed. Anti-union and management groups and their congressional supporters wanted "tough" legislation to restrict unions. The Democratic party and its congressional leadership, and the AFL-CIO, believed that some kind of reform legislation was a political necessity. The Democratic leadership saw the mood of the public as favorable toward union reform and consequently believed legislative action was necessary to demonstrate the responsibility of the Democratic party. While the AFL-CIO had attempted to clean its own house, it came to regard reform legislation as "necessary to rebuild the waning prestige of labor as a law-abiding group worthy of public respect." The AFL-CIO was questing for what the sociologist would call a new "identity."

A reform bill fairly acceptable to labor was passed by the Senate but in the House, where anti-union sentiment was much stronger, a conservative coalition of Northern Republicans and Southern Democrats succeeded in passing a stringent bill strongly opposed by labor. The Landrum-Griffin Bill, as it was called, included amendments to the Taft-Hartley Act as well as provisions on internal union affairs. It was strongly supported by President Eisenhower and many executive officials. Before the Landrum-Griffin Bill became law, however, a number of the provisions most objected to by labor were eliminated or modified at the insistence of the Senate participants in the conference committee which met to resolve differences between the two Houses. Nonetheless, its enactment was considered a defeat for labor.

The Landrum-Griffin Act, officially titled the Labor-Management Reporting and Disclosure Act of 1959, injects the government far more deeply into internal union affairs than did the Taft-Hartley Act. It is also much more specific and detailed than the earlier act. Section 1 of the Landrum-Griffin Act contains a "bill of rights" intended to guarantee union members equal rights to participate in union meetings and vote in union elections, to protect their rights to sue the union, and to free them from unfair disciplinary action. Procedures for increasing union dues and initiation fees are regulated. A later section provides that officers of national or international unions must be selected at least every five years by secret ballot of the members, or by a convention of delegates chosen by secret ballot. Local labor organizations must choose their officers at least every three years by secret ballot. Detailed procedures governing union elections are also set forth. These provisions are obviously intended to increase member control of union affairs (or at least make it possible) and are based on the assumption that the interests of union leaders and members sometimes are divergent.

Other sections of the act require that unions file with the Secretary of Labor detailed reports on their financial practices and condition, operating procedures, and loans to officers, members, or employers; regulate the administration of trusteeships (local unions taken over and directly managed by the national union); require the bonding of union officials; and prohibit persons convicted of felonies or persons belonging to the Communist Party from serving as union officials until five years after their release from prison or the termination of their party membership. Criminal penalities are provided for most violations of the act and the Secretary of Labor is given broad investigatory power to uncover violations.

The last section of Landrum-Griffin (Title VII) contains a number of amendments to the Taft-Hartley Act. This part of the act caused most of the controversy during its enactment because it directly affects the balance of union-management power. Restrictions on secondary boycotts and organizational picketing were strengthened and the use of "hot cargo" contracts, whose legality under Taft-Hartley had been unclear, was outlawed.[56] The "no-man's" land created by the NLRB under Taft-Hartley was eliminated. The Board had declined to take jurisdiction over some disputes because of the small size or the character of the industry involved. The Supreme Court had then held that since the Board could take jurisdiction the states were excluded from doing so even in the absence of Board action. Landrum-Griffin dealt with this situation by authorizing the states to act in this area. The relevant state laws usually provide less protection for labor than does Taft-Hartley. Title VII also contained a number of "sweeteners" for labor. Something approaching the closed shop was in effect legalized in the building industry, lessening the opposition of the building trades unions to the new legislation and helping to create disunity in the ranks of labor. Unions in the building and clothing industries were also exempted from the restrictions on secondary boycotts when attempting to control subcontracting in their respective industries.

The main target of the Landrum-Griffin Act was the Teamsters Union but its power appears to be little affected by the statute. In 1961 the election procedures prescribed by it were scrupulously fol-

[56] A "hot cargo" contract is an agreement between a union and an employer whereby the employer agrees that he will not require his workers to handle materials coming from another employer with whom the union has a dispute. It is a form of secondary boycott and was much used by the Teamsters.

lowed and Hoffa was unanimously re-elected president by the Teamsters Convention. Hoffa has since run into legal difficulties but for matters mostly unrelated to Landrum-Griffin. On the whole, existing unions do not appear to be seriously disadvantaged by Landrum-Griffin although new and weaker unions may now find it more difficult to organize and win elections.[57] The extensive reporting requirements of the law have not revealed widespread misuses of union funds or violations of the rights of members. In fiscal 1962 over 52,000 unions submitted reports to the Bureau of Labor-Management Reports in the Department of Labor. The Bureau conducted 5,408 investigations of unions on the basis of "spot checks" and complaints. Of the 3,174 cases closed during the year, 1,263 revealed no violations. In 96 per cent of the remaining cases (1,911), violations were technical or without criminal intent and were settled voluntarily. In only 76 instances was legal prosecution started, mostly for misuse of union funds.[58] Thus, only a small percentage of unions were involved in even technical violations of the Act. This has led Taft to conclude: "One of the great contributions of the Landrum-Griffin law is . . . to show that for probity and integrity the labor movement compares favorably with other American institutions."[59] However, it must be said that if labor's house is reasonably clean, it is less than spotless. Abuses do occur and therein lies the need and justification for the 1959 legislation. Most of the controversy over the act since its passage has involved the provisions which amended the Taft-Hartley law.

SETTLEMENT OF LABOR DISPUTES

One of the basic issues raised for public policy by collective bargaining is "the problem of work stoppages which interrupt production considered essential to acceptable levels of welfare."[60] The strike, or the threat thereof, is an effective means by which a union can influence employer behavior in the bargaining process, primarily because it

[57] Edward B. Shils, "The Impact of Landrum-Griffin on the Small Employer," *Annals of the American Academy of Political and Social Science*, CCCXXXIII (January, 1961), 142, 152.

[58] United States Department of Labor, *Annual Report, 1962* (Washington, D.C.: Government Printing Office, 1962), 135.

[59] Philip Taft, *Organized Labor in American History* (New York: Harper & Row, 1964), 706.

[60] Robert A. Dahl and Charles E. Lindblom, *Politics, Economics, and Welfare* (New York: Harper & Row, 1953), 485.

interferes with production. But, because it does so, a strike will also affect the goals or desires of others in the community—persons who are neither strikers nor struck employers—by depriving them of desired services, products, or commodities, by interfering with national defense activities, or by indirectly putting others out of work. Consequently, there are demands for government action to prevent or aid in the resolution of strikes and disputes. Such demands have been especially strong when work stoppages disrupt national defense industries or when they involve activities considered highly essential to community well-being, such as hospitals, police protection, government agencies, and, often, public utilities. Governments have sometimes acted to prohibit strikes in these areas. Recall Taft-Hartley's prohibition of strikes by federal employees. Generally, however, government action has not taken the form of prohibition of strikes. Rather, government policy makers have focused their efforts on developing means for settling labor-management disputes which keep government intervention as minimal as possible and which preserve freedom of action for the private bargainers. Before discussing some of the methods used by government in dispute settlement, it would be well to look briefly at the problem they are designed to meet: labor disputes and strikes.

Most work stoppages are the result of strikes—collective refusal by employees to work—rather than employer lockouts. In the case of a strike the union has to take the first overt action; the employer can cause a strike simply by rejecting the union's proposals. The union is thus typically regarded as the "aggressor" by the public when strikes occur; and this attitude probably costs the union public acceptance and support. But the mere existence of a strike tells us nothing about who caused it. Whether it was caused mainly by the union, or the employer, or both, can be determined only by an examination of the parties and circumstances.

Although strikes do not occur as frequently as is often thought, they are a normal part of the collective bargaining process. In 1963 there were 3,362 strikes, averaging twenty-three days in duration, and involving an aggregate of 941,000 workers.[61] The major issues in disputes leading to strikes were wages, fringe benefits, union organization and security, worker job security, plant administration and work rules, and intra- and inter-union matters. For a number of reasons the bar-

[61] *Statistical Abstract of the United States, 1964* (Washington, D.C.: Government Printing Office, 1964), 249. This is about 2 per cent of the nonagricultural labor force. About one in every sixteen union members was involved.

gaining parties are unwilling or unable to reach agreement on a particular issue or set of issues. Brief consideration of these factors will tell us more about the actual causes of strikes, and the problems involved in their settlement, than will a listing of disputed issues.[62] First, one of the parties may want a strike. The employer may see a strike as an opportunity to eliminate the union. Union leaders may believe a strike necessary to demonstrate that the union has not "gone soft." Second, the parties may be unable to reach an acceptable compromise. The employer may insist on a change in work rules which the union regards as threatening to its security and survival. Or, the union may insist on a wage increase which the employer cannot or will not pay. Third, external factors may prevent agreement even when the negotiators themselves are willing to compromise. Union leaders may believe that to retreat from their demands will weaken their position within the union because of the members support for the initial demands. A plant manager may be directed by an absentee board of directors to take a position that leads to a strike. Fourth, one party may underestimate the strength and willingness to resist of the other party because of past behavior. An employer who made concessions to the union frequently in the past may decide that he can no longer afford to do so. Those seeking to settle disputes must take matters of this sort into account as well as specific contested issues.

Governments have relied primarily upon mediation and conciliation in trying to settle labor management disputes. Mediation agencies at the national level include the Federal Mediation and Conciliation Service and the National Mediation Board (the NMB has jurisdiction over railroad and airline disputes). Many of the states have mediation services, as do some larger cities. Mediation is a voluntary approach under which the government does not compel a settlement or the acceptance of its services. Nor is the right to strike denied. In general, mediation involves working with the parties to a dispute to get them to discuss their differences, to help define the essence of the dispute, and to suggest possible solutions. Much depends upon the skill and experience of the mediator and he must fashion his role to fit a particular dispute situation. He may be able to devise and persuade the parties to accept a solution not previously thought of. Or he may be able to employ the threat of adverse public opinion in promoting a settlement. There is no way of determining how many disputes have been settled by government mediation, but most observers believe it

[62] Reynolds, *op. cit.*, 267–268.

has been of much benefit in dispute settlement.[63] It is probably more effective in the earlier stages of a dispute than after a strike has started and the positions of the parties have become hardened.

Because there are mediation agencies at the national, state, and local levels, and because there are no clear jurisdictional lines between them, two or more agencies often intervene in the same dispute. The result is frequently conflict and competition among the mediators, who try to get their services accepted by the parties to a particular dispute. In one situation it is reported that a mediator "urged one party to withdraw the dispute from a rival agency on the promise that a shift would assure a better settlement."[64] Because alternative mediators are available, disputants may pick and choose among them, each favoring the mediator he believes to be most agreeable to his own interests. And thus choice of a mediator can become a new issue for labor and management to struggle over. Conflict and competition among different mediators for "business" may actually hinder the resolution of disputes.

Why do such conflicts occur when the use of mediators is voluntary and when a government mediator receives the same salary regardless of the number of cases he handles? Mediators are human and they undoubtedly desire opportunities to display their talents, both to enhance their self-esteem and to gain the respect or approval of others. Moreover, a larger case load serves to justify the mediation agency's existence and its budgetary requests. In a move to eliminate jurisdictional friction and conflict and to improve the effectiveness of mediation, federal and state mediators in 1964 adopted a "code of professional conduct" to govern their relationships and to promote cooperation among themselves.[65] Thus did the mediators attempt to mediate their own "jurisdictional dispute."

Thus far we have spoken of mediation of labor disputes by permanent, legislatively established government agencies. Mediation of disputes, and particularly of serious ones, may also be undertaken on an *ad hoc* extralegal basis by top level executive officials or others at the direction of the President. During the Eisenhower administration Secretary of the Treasury Humphrey and Secretary of Labor Mitchell in 1956 and Vice-President Nixon in 1959 were instrumen-

[63] See, for example, David L. Cole, "Government in the Bargaining Process: The Role of Mediation," *Annals of the American Academy of Political and Social Science,* CCCXXXIII (January, 1961), 42–58.

[64] Edward J. Silberfarb, "Who Will Mediate the Mediators?" *The Reporter,* XXVIII (March 14, 1963), 25.

[65] *The New York Times,* Sept. 13, 1964, p. 53.

tal in settling disputes in the steel industry. In such instances there is usually an intertwining of political pressure and mediation. Of Mr. Nixon's role in 1959 it has been written: "In conferring with Mr. Nixon, the company and union representatives were not unaware that they were dealing with the man who could be the next occupant of the White House, the man who, in this situation, was obviously functioning as the President's alter ego."[66] In 1964 President Johnson, his Secretary of Labor, and other executive officials, together with some nationally known mediators appointed by the President, brought about a settlement of the five-year-old dispute over work rules in the railroad industry.[67] Because of their high status and the political pressure they can exert, the parties to a dispute find it difficult to reject efforts by the President or top level executive officials to gain a settlement.

Presidential action in dispute settlement has also involved the establishment of extralegal and seemingly permanent boards to mediate disputes in the atomic energy industry and at missile sites and bases. These boards—the Atomic Labor-Management Relations Panel and the Missile Sites Labor Commission—were established by executive order and not specific legislation. The latter Commission was established by President Kennedy in 1961 to counter strong demands by Senator McClellan for legislation prohibiting strikes in the missile industry.

A special procedure for dealing with "emergency disputes" that "imperil the national health or safety" was provided by the framers of the Taft-Hartley Act. If the President believes that a dispute fits into this category, he first appoints a "board of inquiry" to investigate and report on the facts of a dispute. After this board reports the President may direct the Attorney General to seek a federal district court injunction postponing the strike or lockout for an eighty-day period. The courts have always issued such injunctions when requested. The Federal Mediation and Conciliation Service is then brought in to help the disputants reach agreement. If the dispute is unsettled after sixty of the eighty days have elapsed, the NLRB enters onto the scene and polls the employees to determine whether they would accept "the employer's last offer of settlement." The employees

---

[66] John Perry Horlacher, "A Political Science View of National Emergency Disputes," *Annals of the American Academy of Political and Social Science,* CCCXXXIII (January 1961), 90.

[67] See the excellent account of this situation by John D. Pomfret in *The New York Times,* April 27, 1964, pp. 1, 16.

have always upheld the union by overwhelmingly rejecting the employer's last offer when these polls have been held. When the eighty-day period is over the injunction is dissolved and a strike or lockout becomes legal. The President then submits a report on the dispute to Congress, together with recommendations for legislative action he may care to make.

This procedure was employed twenty-three times between 1947 and April, 1963, primarily in longshore, atomic energy, and coal industry disputes. Most observers are agreed that it has not been very effective in controlling emergency disputes. The Presidents in office since 1947 have often preferred to use extralegal forms of action, as discussed above, rather than the Taft-Hartley procedure.

Another alternative open to government in resolving labor disputes is arbitration. Under arbitration the terms of a settlement are determined by a third party after a formal or informal judicial type of hearing. Arbitration may be either voluntary, agreed to by the contending parties; or compulsory, made mandatory by law. Voluntary arbitration is frequently used by labor and management as the final step in settling grievances arising under labor contracts. Under the Railway Labor Act of 1926, as amended, public boards are provided for voluntary arbitration of disputes in the railroad and airline industries. This procedure has been little used, however, in recent years in these industries. Other means of settlement, such as mediation, have been preferred.

Compulsory arbitration has not been used extensively in the United States. Both labor and management have generally opposed it, because its effect is to substitute government action for collective bargaining in determination of terms of work. Some use of compulsory arbitration to settle disputes has been made by the national government during wartime (when "national emergency" serves as a justification) and by a few states in labor disputes affecting public utilities. Experience with these state laws indicates that they encourage weak bargainers to avoid private bargaining in the hope of better promoting their interests through government arbitration.

The first peacetime use of compulsory arbitration by the national government in a major dispute came in 1963. In order to prevent a nationwide rail strike, Congress passed a law providing for compulsory arbitration of the conflict between the major railroads and five railway unions on two issues: the employment of firemen in diesel locomotives and the make-up of train crews. The AFL-CIO and the railway unions strongly opposed this legislation and, though they were not successful in preventing it, they did succeed in having the arbitration handled by a special board rather than the Interstate Commerce Commission as proposed by the Kennedy administration. The unions contended that the ICC was biased in favor of the railroads. Whether use of compulsory arbitration in this case will lead to its use in other instances is problematical. Because of their vital relationship to the operation of the economy, railroads have come to represent a special case. Since World War II, Congress and the President have not permitted a railroad strike to last more than a few days.

A variety of means thus exist by which government can deal with labor-management disputes and work stoppages. Other possibilities are the use of fact-finding boards, compulsory delay of strikes to permit settlement efforts, and government seizure and operation of struck plants (frequently used during World War II). The trend in recent decades has been toward greater government intervention in disputes. Although government action can lessen the possibility of work stoppages which affect important public or group goals, it cannot do so entirely without eliminating collective bargaining by prohibiting strikes and providing for government determination of the terms and conditions of work. In short, strikes and the resulting inconvenience are part of the costs of collective bargaining and economic freedom. Those who value the latter must be prepared to accept some of the former.

Chapter Seven

GOVERNMENT AND AGRICULTURE

In their efforts to improve their economic situation and to strengthen their position vis-a-vis other groups in the economy, farm groups have long and often successfully sought to invoke the power of government in their behalf. The farmers' success in this pursuit is attested to by the large volume of legislation dealing directly with farm needs and problems and by the favorable treatment accorded agricultural interests in much nonfarm legislation. In the first instance we can cite a multitude of programs involving such matters as agricultural price supports, agricultural education, research, and extension, the marketing of farm commodities, soil conservation, land reclamation, and irrigation, farm credit, crop insurance, and animal and plant pest control. During the early 1960's the total cost of the programs administered by the Department of Agriculture was between five and seven billion dollars annually.

Additionally, it seems to be a rule of American politics that farm interests shall be given actual or symbolic preferential treatment when they are affected by nonfarm legislation. For example, agricultural co-operatives are exempted from the antitrust laws and most vehicles transporting agricultural commodities are exempted from national motor carrier legislation. In the interests of farm operators, farm workers are not covered by minimum wage, unemployment compensation, and workmen's compensation laws. The federal tax code contains a variety of provisions of advantage to farmers. Even in immigration legislation the farmer receives preference, as in the law which long permitted the importation of bracero (cheap) labor from Mexico to work on farms in the West and Southwest. All of this simply indicates that the farmer has frequently mixed agriculture and politics to his advantage.

Our primary focus here is on agricultural price support policy because that has been of most concern to farm policy makers in the past three decades. It has cost the most money and generated the most conflict, both within and outside of the farm community, and, in short, it epitomizes the politics of agriculture. Some consideration will be given to a number of other farm programs to indicate the variety and scope of government aid to agriculture.

AGRICULTURE AND THE ECONOMY

American agriculture was largely of a subsistence type in the early decades of the nineteenth century. Farmers produced most of their own food, clothing, and tools, depending very little on the market either for selling their products or for purchasing goods (except such items as salt, metal products, or cotton cloth, which they could not produce themselves). After the Civil War, however, profound changes occurred in agriculture. Mechanization of farming methods and growing specialization of production in the latter decades of the century led to the commercialization of agriculture. Farmers increasingly concentrated on the production of one or a few crops for sale in the market. The farmer became *interdependent* along with other groups in the economy—meatpackers, grain merchants, elevator operators, railroads, manufacturers of farm equipment—and *dependent* upon the market conditions of supply and demand and prices for his income. Farming became a business as well as a way of life.

In the twentieth century, and especially since the 1930's, a vast and far-reaching technological revolution has been in process in American agriculture. This technological revolution has manifested itself in mechanical, chemical, biological, and managerial forms.[1] Mechanically, tractors and trucks have almost entirely replaced horses and mules as the sources of farm power. Along with them have come such machines as grain combines, mechanical corn and cotton pickers, gang plows, and a host of other machines. Rural electrification has permitted the use of a wide range of equipment such as milking machines, feed mills, and grain dryers. Chemically, commercial fertilizers have led to great improvements in soil productivity. Insecticides, pesticides, fungicides, and herbicides have been developed to combat insects, pests, and plant and animal diseases which adversely affect agri-

[1] Don Paarlberg, *American Farm Policy: A Case Study of Centralized Decision-Making* (New York: John Wiley and Sons, 1964), ch. 4.

cultural production. Biologically, new and improved plant varieties and livestock breeds have been developed. Hybrid seed corn (e.g., "Steckley's Genetic Giant") has greatly increased the production of corn per acre, while in the poultry world hybrid hens lay more eggs more often and hybrid broilers grow drumsticks more rapidly than their non-hybrid compatriots or ancestors. Other biological advances have come in animal nutritions, disease control, and sanitation. Managerially, farm operators (at least the more successful ones) give more attention to cost and output data in planning their operations, to the proper organization of production and marketing, to the abandonment of uneconomic activities, and to specialization in the production of the crops they can grow most efficiently and profitably.

The broad consequences of this technological revolution have been a sharp increase in agricultural productivity (per acre, farm worker, etc.), a decline in the number of farms and the farm population, and a trend toward concentration of farming operations in fewer and larger units capable of using the new technological developments to best advantage.

That agricultural production has increased significantly since the early 1930's can be demonstrated by a few statistics. The farm output index, a measure of the annual volume of farm production (1957–1959 = 100), was 61 in 1930, 86 in 1950, 103 in 1959, and 112 in 1963.[2] In other words, in a little more than three decades, agricultural output nearly doubled. To cite two major crops, average yields per acre of wheat increased from 17.2 to 25.1 bushels and of corn from 36.7 to 64.1 bushels. Many other crops showed increases of similar magnitude. Because agricultural productivity has increased so greatly, only a small proportion of the population is needed to produce food for the nation (about 6 per cent of the labor force in 1963). Whereas one farmer fed five people in 1850 and ten people in 1940, today he feeds more than thirty people.

Expanding farm output made possible by increased productivity will not bring greater farm income, however, unless the demand for farm products expands at a similar rate. This has not happened: the population of the United States has increased, but not as rapidly as farm output. Moreover, though standards of living have risen, only up to a point do people buy more food as their income increases. As incomes rise people customarily spend a smaller proportion of their income for food and a larger proportion for housing, clothing, entertainment, and other purposes. Because of these factors, and others to be noted,

[2] *Statistical Abstract of the United States, 1964* (Washington, D.C.: Government Printing Office, 1964), 643.

the supply of farm commodities has often exceeded demand in recent years and, consequently, farm prices have fallen.

At the same time, because of rises in the general price level and because of the expense involved in making use of the new technological developments, the costs of farm production have swollen. This situation, often designated the "cost-price squeeze," has reduced the proportion of gross farm income remaining as net income after farm expenses have been met. (See Table Seven-1.)

TABLE SEVEN-1
THE FARM INCOME SITUATION, 1940–1963*

Year	Total net income (millions)	Percentage of gross income	Average net income per farm[a]	Parity ratio
1940	$ 4,289	38.9	$1,607	81
1946	15,223	51.2	3,618	113
1950	13,185	40.6	2,714	101
1955	11,470	34.4	2,622	84
1959	11,279	30.1	2,726	81
1960	11,692	30.8	2,932	80
1961	12,803	32.1	3,294	79
1962	12,900	31.7	3,396	80
1963	12,500	30.0	NA	78

* Data are from Congressional Quarterly, *U.S. Agricultural Policy in the Postwar Years* (Washington, D.C.: Congressional Quarterly Service, 1963), 5, except for 1963, which is derived from *Statistical Abstract of the U.S. 1964,* pp. 630, 632.

[a] In 1957–1959 dollars, not millions.

The cost-price squeeze is reflected by the declining percentage of gross income which farmers receive as net income and by the parity ratio. For example, the parity ratio of 80 in 1962 indicates that the purchasing power of farm commodities, in relation to the goods and services the farmer buys, was 80 per cent of farm purchasing power in the base period (1910–1914). During this period farm prices are said to have been in "fair" relationship to nonfarm prices.

The cost-price squeeze in agriculture together with the possibility of higher incomes in industrial and other nonagricultural employment has caused a farm-to-city population movement. Both the number of farms and the farm population have declined markedly in recent decades. In 1935 there were 6,814,000 farms in the United States—an all-time high. By 1945, in spite of wartime farm prosperity, the number had declined to 5,967,000. The figure for 1954 was 4,782,000 and for

1959, 3,704,000.[3] As a percentage of the total population, the farm population stood at 30 per cent in 1920, 24.9 per cent in 1930, 23.1 per cent in 1940, 16.6 per cent in 1950, and 12 per cent in 1959. In 1962, on the basis of a census method which excluded rural residents not actually involved in commercial farming, the farm population was estimated at 14,313,000 (or 7.7 per cent of the total population).

As the farm population and the number of farms have declined, the average size of farms has increased from 148 acres in 1920, to 215 acres in 1950, to 302 acres in 1959. The total amount of land under cultivation has not changed significantly in the last twenty-five years. As the poorer and smaller farmers (they are often synonomous) have left agriculture, their land has often been taken over by other and better farmers. Consequently, farm production has become concentrated in the hands of the larger, more efficient, and more well-to-do farmers, though many low income farm units still remain.

As Table Seven-2 indicates, roughly 95 per cent of farm production, as measured by value, is accounted for by the 55 per cent of farm units selling at least $2,500 of farm commodities. More significantly, the top 21 per cent of farm units produced 71 per cent of farm output. On the other hand, more than a million of the units counted as farms (those in the noncommercial category) are less than full-time farming operations and account for a very small percentage of total farm production. Many of the farm operators in this group are not engaged meaningfully in agriculture. In another category are the 349,000 farmers who sell less than $2,500 of agricultural commodities, and who are neither part-time nor semi-retired. These represent the hard core of farm poverty and contrast sharply with the well-to-do, or relatively well-off, farmers who comprise the top 21 per cent of farm units. The latter may believe that farm prices are too low, or perhaps that farm incomes are unsatisfactory, but, by and large, farming yields them a comfortable if not elegant way of life. There is in short, much disparity among the income situations of various farm groups, a fact often glossed over by spokesmen for farm interests.

Agriculture is often referred to as the principal sector of the economy in which (in the absence of government price support action) conditions approaching pure competition prevail. In any area of farming there is usually a large number of producers, no one of whom can affect prices by controlling the quantities he offers for sale. And, for

[3] When data from the 1964 Agricultural census become available they will undoubtedly reveal a further decrease in the number of farms by several hundred thousand.

ECONOMIC CLASSES OF FARMS, 1959*

Class[a]	Number	Percentage of all farms	Percentage of total farm sales
I. Commercial	2,416,017	65.2	96.2
$40,000 or more sales	102,099	2.8	31.5
20,000 to 39,999	210,402	5.7	18.4
10,000 to 19,999	483,004	13.0	21.9
5,000 to 9,999	653,881	17.6	15.4
2,500 to 4,999	617,677	16.7	7.4
50 to 2,499	348,954	9.4	1.5
II. Noncommercial	1,292,046	34.9	3.8
Part-time	884,875	23.9	2.3
Part-retirement	404,110	10.9	1.1
Other	3,061	0.1	0.4
Total, all farms	3,708,063	100.0	100.0

* Congressional Quarterly, *U.S. Agricultural Policy,* 4.

[a] Commercial farms are the main source of their operators' income. Noncommercial farms are those where the operator depends largely on nonfarm income or employment. "Other farms" include prison farms and Indian reservations.

whatever reasons (geographical dispersion, independence, etc.), farmers have been unable to voluntarily cooperate to reduce supply so as to increase prices. Nor can the individual farmer afford to withhold his products from the market until he considers that prices are satisfactory. Consequently, the farmer sells his products for whatever the price, as set by supply and demand in a highly competitive market, happens to be.

Farm prices frequently fluctuate widely from season to season. It is characteristic of agriculture that a small increase in the supply of a commodity often produces a relatively great decrease in price. As a result, a larger quantity of a commodity may result in a smaller total return for the farmer. A decrease in production, in turn, may lead to a proportionately greater increase in price and gross receipts. An illustration may help here. During the period 1951–1955 there was steady, high-level consumer demand for pork. Prices for pork, however, fluctuated between $10 and $25 per hundredweight during this period as high prices brought increased production, which drove prices down, which led to cutbacks in production, which led to a price increase, and so on.[4] Such price instability obviously is detrimental to farm interests. It causes farm income to be unstable, especially as farmers become more specialized and concentrate on the production of one or two commodities.

Out of this farm economic situation, has emerged the "farm problem." The "farm problem" may be defined in a number of ways, and the proposed solution is substantially shaped by the definition used. Some would describe the farm problem as a price problem: farm prices are unstable and too low. Those who take this position may point to the parity ratio to support their beliefs, pointing out that farm prices are quite a bit lower than nonfarm prices. The solution, then, is to raise farm prices, make them more stable, or both. The emphasis is usually on raising prices.

Others would say that the farm problem is an income rather than a price problem and cite low average farm incomes in recent years to substantiate their position. Thus, the Department of Agriculture reported that in 1963 per capita farm income was $1,480 (with $510 coming from nonfarm sources), compared to $2,515 for the nonfarm population.[5] Disagreement may arise, however, concerning whether the problem is low average income for all farmers or only for those at the lower end of the farm income scale. In any case farm income may be raised by raising farm prices, making direct payments to supplement farm incomes, or increasing the efficiency of farming operations, to cite three possibilities.

A third view is that low farm prices and low farm income (per capita) are only symptoms of the basic farm problem: continued overproduction of farm products relative to the demand for them, with a resultant low gross national farm incomes and an excess supply of farmers. Together the two factors keep per capita farm incomes low in comparison to nonfarm income. More concisely, there are just too many farmers. Those who take this third position often cite the need for programs to facilitate migration off the farm. "The real farm problem, then, is a farmer-adjustment problem resulting from a continual excess of potential farmers being born on farms, and a continued reduction in the number of farmers being needed."[6] This definition of the problem is often unpopular with farm groups, as one might suspect.

[4] See Lauren Soth, *Farm Trouble* (Princeton: Princeton University Press, 1957), 149–150.

[5] *The New York Times,* March 11, 1964, p. 53.

[6] Geoffrey Shepherd, *Farm Policy: New Directions* (Ames: Iowa State University Press, 1965), 94. The preceding discussion relies extensively on Shepherd, chs. 1–6.

268

Most commonly, however, the farm problem is diagnosed, for policy purposes, as a combination price and income problem: low farm prices produce low farm incomes. The solution is to raise prices in order to raise farm incomes. To this end, the government has adopted a wide variety of "price support programs" during the past three decades at the urging of farm interests.

THE POLITICS OF AGRICULTURE

Historical Aspects

Though often characterized as a rugged individualist wanting nothing more than to be left alone by the government to "hoe his own row," the American farmer has not hesitated during the past century to turn to the government for political redress of his economic grievances. Whatever the specific cause of his dissatisfaction—low market prices, high railroad rates, insects and pests—economic insecurity in the form of low, unstable, or otherwise unsatisfactory income has been back of most agrarian political demands. And, as Key has shown, agrarian political discontent and agitation has waxed and waned with decline and improvement in the economic fortune of the farmer.[7]

In the last four decades of the nineteenth century agrarian discontent was frequently manifested in third-party movements which sought control of the centers of political decision making. The Granger movement of the late 1860's and early 1870's, the Farmers' Alliances of the late 1880's, and the Populist party in the early 1890's are important examples. These movements, generated by agricultural distress, were directed against the "traditional enemies" of the farmer: railroads, monopolists, bankers, and "middlemen" generally. Their political programs called for antimonopoly laws, regulation of railroads and grain storage facilities, and currency reform, which often involved proposals to increase the currency supply to enable farmers to pay their debts more easily. These third-party movements initially enjoyed some electoral success but were short-lived since, in each case, they dwindled into insignificance with the return of agricultural prosperity. They were not totally unsuccessful or without influence, however. The Granger movement gave rise to laws regulating railroads and grain warehouses in several Midwestern states. Agrarian

[7] V. O. Key, Jr., *Parties, Politics, and Pressure Groups* 4th ed. (New York: Thomas Y. Crowell, 1958), 27–36.

discontent and action was also an important factor in the adoption of the Interstate Commerce Act and the Sherman Antitrust Act.

In the twentieth century no real effort has been made to organize a national third party appealing primarily to farmers. The relative numerical decline of the farm population has undoubtedly helped account for this, as has the lack of success of third parties in general. Some efforts to establish agrarian third parties did occur at the state level, most notable of which was the Nonpartisan League. Organized in 1915, it became strongest in North Dakota, where it gained control of the Republican party and the state government. Legislation provided for state-owned grain warehouses, elevators, and flour mills, a state-owned bank, a graduated income tax, regulation of railroad rates, and a state hail insurance company. After a few years, however, the League declined in significance.

In the early 1920's the agricultural depression touched off by the decline of wartime demand for farm products led to the development of a new strategy by farm groups for exerting political influence: electing members of Congress who were sympathetic to agricultural interests, regardless of their party affiliation, and then organizing them into a disciplined and unified "farm bloc" to secure desired farm legislation. The American Farm Bureau Federation had much to do with the creation of the "farm bloc" and was joined by most other farm groups. The farm bloc in Congress, composed primarily of Midwestern Republicans and Southern Democrats, operated with vigor and effectiveness. By 1926 it had secured legislation on such matters as agricultural tariffs, farm credit, supervision of packers and stockyards, regulation of the sale of grain futures, and cooperative marketing.

Conflicts among farm groups and interests led to the decline of the farm bloc. Benedict suggests that it had disintegrated by the late 1920's and certainly by the late 1930's,[8] whereas Zeigler implies that it ceased to function, at least as a formal group, after the mid-1920's.[9] Whichever may be the case, most observers agree that during the 1930's and 1940's there existed in Congress a bipartisan group of legislators sufficiently strong and unified to pass price support and other legislation desired by farm interests and to prevent the enactment of undesired legislation.

[8] Murray R. Benedict, *Farm Policies of the United States 1790–1950* (New York: Twentieth Century Fund, 1953), 199.

[9] Harmon Zeigler, *Interest Groups in American Society* (Englewood Cliffs, N.J.: Prentice-Hall, 1964), 179, 182.

Farm organizations came into their own during the New Deal years and since then agricultural politics have been characterized by continuous pressure-group activity intended to influence the formation and administration of agricultural policies. As the technological revolution in agriculture has increased the economic pressures on farmers, and as farm production has become more specialized, sharp conflicts and divergencies have either developed, or become manifest, among farm groups and interests. To understand farm politics and policy issues today, we must examine the nature of farm groups and the conflicts among them.

Agricultural Group Politics Today

It is elementary but nevertheless highly important to recognize that there is no single farm interest. Though we sometimes speak of "farmers" as if they all came out of the same mold, or hay field, they differ greatly in such matters as size of farm, amount of investment, efficiency of operation, income, education and background, political loyalty and involvement, and commodities grown.

Dairy farmers, tobacco growers, sheep and cattle raisers, feed grain producers, vegetable farmers, and wheat growers—all have more or less separate and distinct problems and interests "which induce commodity consciousness rather than broad agrarian consciousness."[10] Dairy farmers and fruit growers are likely to have little or no interest in a price support program which is considered vital by tobacco growers and which stirs them to political action to secure and maintain it. Tobacco growers, in turn, are not much concerned with the problems of rice farmers. But, what is more pertinent here, the interests of different commodity groups may directly conflict rather than merely diverge. A price support program which will raise the price of feed grains may draw the opposition of poultrymen and dairymen because it will raise the cost of the feed they buy. Dairymen producing butter and growers of soybeans and cottonseed, which yield oil used in making oleomargarine, have long struggled over the issue of oleomargarine taxation. Conflict may also occur among the growers of a particular commodity. Cotton growers in the Southeast compete with the producers of cotton on large, modern, irrigated farms in Califor-

[10] Merle Fainsod, Lincoln Gordon, and Joseph C. Palamountain, Jr., *Government and the American Economy* (New York: W. W. Norton, 1959), 40. Also see Jack Heinz, "Those Annoying Farmers: Impossible But Not Really Serious," *Harper's Magazine,* CCXXVII (July, 1963), 62–64.

nia and the Southwest, and each of the two groups seeks cotton support policies favorable to itself. Here, it will be noted, the conflict is regionally based, as is the recently developed conflict between Southern livestock raisers and Midwestern feed-grain producers over the level of price supports for corn and feed grains.

The differences in the interests of farmers are reflected in the variety of farm organizations which serve as their spokesmen. Many of these organizations have been formed around commodity interests, including the National Milk Producers' Federation, the National Wool Growers' Association, the American National Cattlemens' Association, the National Wheat Growers' Association, the National Turkey Federation, and the Vegetable Growers' Association of America. There are also a number of associations comprised of both processors and producers, including the National Cotton Council, the American Sugar Cane League, and the Western Growers' Association (vegetables). Key remarks: "it is not uncommon for leaders of food processing industries to adorn their ears with wisps of straw and attempt, with some success, to camouflage themselves as farmers to gain legislative advantage."[11] Among other things, such action attests to the status which farmers enjoy in our society.

Notwithstanding the melange of organizations claiming to speak for farmers, most attention has been directed toward the large general farm organizations which claim, at least, to represent general farm interests. These are the American Farm Bureau Federation, the National Grange, and the National Farmers Union. These organizations are of major political importance and, in their programs and actions, they reflect some of the broad ideological and economic differences within the agricultural population.

The American Farm Bureau Federation is the youngest, the largest, and the most conservative of the general farm organizations. Organized in 1919, the Farm Bureau now claims a membership of 1,600,792 families,[12] although this figure includes many nonfarmers. "Every county has local businessmen in the Farm Bureau. They join for social and strategic reasons."[13] Although the Farm Bureau has members in

[11] Key, *op. cit.,* 37.

[12] The data on farm organization membership in this section are taken from Robert L. Toontz, "Membership of General Farmers Organizations, United States, 1874–1960," *Agricultural History,* XXXVIII (July, 1964), 143–156. The Grange and Farm Bureau figures are for 1960 and the Farmers' Union figure is for 1956.

[13] Wesley McCune, *Who's Behind Our Farm Policy* (New York: Praeger, 1956), 2.

every state, the bulk of its membership is located in the Midwest (especially the cornbelt) and the South and it has frequently been described as a coalition of corn and hog raisers and cotton farmers. It speaks primarily for the larger, more prosperous commercial farmers and has been a rather constant opponent of programs designed to benefit tenant farmers, farm laborers, migratory workers, and other marginal farm groups. Regarded by many observers as the most powerful of the farm organizations, the Farm Bureau's leaders do nothing to refute this notion. For many years the Farm Bureau was described as a "veto group" which could prevent the enactment of any legislation it opposed. If such were the case in the past, it would no longer seem true as most of the farm legislation enacted during the Kennedy administration was opposed by the Farm Bureau.

The Farm Bureau was a vigorous supporter of agricultural price support programs during the New Deal years but, since the end of World War II, its policy position has shifted. The Bureau now favors movement toward a "free market" for agriculture, apparently on the premise that "the iron laws of supply and demand will, if unfettered by government controls, govern farm yield so that it is produced as efficiently as possible and only in such amounts as the market can sustain."[14] To this end, the Farm Bureau advocates the elimination of controls on production and lower, more flexible, price supports designed primarily to lessen price instability. It gave strong support to the agricultural policy proposals of the Eisenhower administration and Secretary of Agriculture Ezra Taft Benson and consistently opposed those of the Kennedy administration, which stressed higher price supports along with rigorous controls on production. Some of the state Farm Bureau organizations, especially in the South, have occasionally opposed the national Farm Bureau leadership and have pushed for higher price supports. The national leadership, in turn, has been somewhat pragmatic, accepting or acquiescing in high fixed supports for tobacco, for example, rather than risk alienating some of its Southern members.

Outside of agriculture, the Farm Bureau usually takes a conservative position on economic and other issues and is often found allied with the National Association of Manufacturers and the Chamber of Commerce. It has favored state control of the offshore oil lands, the Taft-Hartley and Landrum-Griffin acts, and right to work laws and

[14] Ross B. Talbot, "Farm Organization and the National Interest," *Annals of the American Academy of Political and Social Science,* CCCXXXI (September, 1960), 112.

has opposed the expansion of minimum wage legislation, federal medicare, and federal aid to education.[15] Comments favoring states' rights and "free enterprise" and opposing "the trend toward centralization" and "socialism" in government often appear in its official policy statements and in speeches by its leaders. "Federation leaders at times come perilously close to converting their organization into a tool of business without much regard to the concern of farmers with the issues at stake." But, as Key continues, "On the other hand, the Federation looks to business for support on farm issues and may feel obliged to reciprocate."[16]

A second farm organization is the Farmers' Educational and Cooperative Union of America, more commonly known as the National Farmers Union. Started in 1902, the National Farmers Union now has a membership of 278,216 families, located primarily in the wheat states of the Great Plains region and with strong affiliates in Wisconsin, Minnesota, and Montana. The most liberal of the farm groups, the NFU advocates an active and expanded role for government in agriculture and stresses that "farm prices are made in Washington." Especially concerned with promoting the interests of the family farm and low income farm groups, the NFU favors high price supports, strict production controls, limitation of the government benefits available to any one farmer, rural relief programs, more agricultural credit facilities, and expanded federal crop insurance programs. The liberal economic position of the NFU may be partly explained by the fact that its main strength is in an area where the weather is especially hazardous for farming. This factor increases the economic insecurity of farming, a condition which the NFU wants to remedy by extensive government action.[17]

The National Farmers Union has become rather closely identified with the Democratic party in recent decades and has enjoyed much influence in the Department of Agriculture during Democratic administrations. Alone of the major farm organizations, the NFU supported the Brannan Plan (discussed below) proposed by President Truman's Secretary of Agriculture. It generally opposed the price support proposals of the Eisenhower administration and favored those

[15] A more extensive and detailed discussion of current policy positions of the Farm Bureau and the other major farm organizations can be found in R. Joseph Momsen and Mark W. Cannon, *The Makers of Public Policy* (New York: McGraw-Hill, 1965), ch. 4.

[16] Key, *op. cit.,* 43.

[17] See Seymour Martin Lipset, *Political Man* (New York: Doubleday, 1959), 232–233.

of the Kennedy administration. The NFU usually takes a liberal position on nonagricultural matters and, in contrast to the Farm Bureau, often is effectively allied with organized labor. The Farmers Union was part of the "liberal labor lobby" behind the Employment Act of 1946 and frequently joins the AFL-CIO in supporting labor and welfare legislation. In general, the National Farmers Union and the Farm Bureau have taken sharply opposing positions on most issues of public policy since World War II.

The National Grange is the oldest of the general farm organizations, dating back to 1867. Its present membership totals 394,069 families, concentrated principally in New England, New York, Pennsylvania, Ohio, and the Pacific Coast states. Fruit and vegetable growers, poultrymen, and dairymen are predominant among its members. The Grange is deeply committed to maintaining the family farm and it stresses the virtues and benefits of farming as a way of life. (It is, incidentally, an historic foe of drinking, smoking, and gambling.) Once the prime symbol of agrarian discontent and radicalism, the Grange has been the least politically aggressive of the general farm organizations since the 1920's. During the New Deal years it was the most conservative.

For a long time the Grange supported the "two-price plan" for agriculture, under which price supports or production limitations would be used to keep prices high in the United States for a portion of farm production while the rest was sold on the free market at world prices. Since the late 1940's the Grange's farm policy position has shifted and it now usually favors high price supports and production controls, but not as enthusiastically as the National Farmers Union. The Grange generally supported the Kennedy and Johnson administrations on agricultural policy and, in 1963, joined with the NFU in supporting a favorable vote in the referendum among wheat farmers on whether there should be high supports and stringent production controls for wheat. This was in opposition to the Farm Bureau's stand against controls—a stand taken by a majority of the wheat farmers voting in the referendum.

While the Grange occupies a position between the Farm Bureau and the Farmers Union on farm policy, it usually assumes a conservative stance on nonfarm matters. Thus the Grange likes balanced budgets and right to work laws and dislikes deficit spending, federal aid to education, and public power projects. There is, as one might guess, little cooperation between the Grange and organized labor.

A fourth farm organization, the National Farmers Organization, merits mention. It contrasts sharply with the "big three" in style and mode of action. Originating in Iowa in 1955, the National Farmers' Organization now has around 100,000 members, located primarily in the Midwest and drawn mostly from small and medium-sized farms. These are the farmers who feel squeezed the hardest by the agricultural revolution. Expressing dissatisfaction with both government efforts to support farm prices and the Farm Bureau's position, the NFO advocates direct action and "farm bargaining power" to improve the farmer's economic situation. By concerted action to withhold farm products from the market, the NFO hopes both to raise prices and to induce food processors to sign contracts for the purchase of farm commodities at high prices. Withholding actions, as these concerted efforts are known, were tried by the NFO in 1962 and 1964, but neither had much success. Too few farmers participated and when market prices did go up a little, many farmers (including some NFO members) hastened to sell their products.

In its way, the NFO symbolizes the discontent of less prosperous farmers, both with farm prices and income and with present-day governmental efforts to improve them. The appeal of the NFO is reduced by its evangelistic fervor because: "Conservative by tradition, many farmers recoil from what they regard as a fanatical organization."[18]

When the various farm organizations are relatively united, as they were during the early 1920's and the New Deal era, they have been a strong political force. More often, however, the farm organizations have urged conflicting or differing programs and viewpoints on Congress because each of them represents different interests within the agricultural community. This lack of unity has probably reduced the political effectiveness of farm groups as a whole. Diversity and conflict among agricultural groups also has undoubtedly contributed to the tendency of Congress to follow a commodity-by-commodity rather than a general farm approach in enacting price support legislation. Additionally, it has probably helped stimulate the increase in party voting in Congress on agricultural policy. Given the complexity of the farm problem, the divided and conflicting interests involved, and the apparent inadequacy or unacceptability of every proposed solution, the Congressmen may well believe that voting with

[18] Richard T. Cooper, "Why the Drive to Raise Cattle Prices Failed," *New Republic*, CLI (October 3, 1964), 7. Also see Julius Duscha, "Farmers on Strike," *The Reporter*, XXVII (November 22, 1962), 32–35.

their party is both the easiest and the most defensible course of action.

When all is said, however, it is clear that well-organized, well-led, active organizations have served to increase the influence of some farm groups on public policy. The farm groups most neglected in the policy process are the small marginal farmers, farm workers, and migratory workers, who are mostly unorganized and whose interests are for the most part unarticulated.

In addition to pressure groups, ideological factors and political over-representation have also augmented farm influence. These factors have helped to maintain the political strength of agriculture and shape the course of policy by offsetting such factors as conflict among farm organizations and the lessening importance of the farm population in the total population.

Ideology and Over-representation

There appears to be a broad if somewhat ill-defined belief in the United States that government is obligated to aid people in difficulty. As Boulding has remarked: "agricultural policy is frequently sold politically, even in countries with predominantly urban populations, by an appeal to social justice; farmers are poor, the argument goes, and should, therefore, be aided."[19] Are not farm incomes, on the average, lower than nonfarm incomes? Are there not many low income farmers? The proponents of price support programs often urge, or defend, them as necessary to protect small and low income farmers. And does not the concept of parity, which measures "fairness" in the relationship between farm and nonfarm prices indicate that the former are too low and need raising? Parity is often equated with social justice, a highly valued goal and symbol in American politics.

Beyond this matter there is the "myth of agricultural fundamentalism" which is manifested in a number of ways. It is expressed in the belief that agriculture is the basic industry of a people, that it provides the food which all need for survival. Farming is thus indispensable to the welfare of all and so the material benefits accruing to farmers should at least be on a par ("parity") with those of other economic groups. Again, the myth is given form in the slogan, "Depressions are farm led and farm fed." An argument often used to justify farm price support legislation is that general prosperity is

[19] Kenneth Boulding, *Conflict and Defense* (New York: Harper & Row, 1962), 205.

dependent upon agricultural prosperity. This statement of the House Committee on Appropriations will serve as an illustration:

> A review of the economic history of the United States will show that every economic recession in this country has started on the farm. Every recession has been preceded by a period of reduced income to the agricultural segment of our population. Since agriculture is the principal segment of our economy which generates new wealth, it is inevitable that a prolonged depression in agriculture will eventually reflect itself in more aggravated economic distress throughout the rest of the economy.[20]

Without involving ourselves with the highly questionable validity of this viewpoint,[21] it does appear to be popular and, therefore, can at the least serve as an appealing rationale for aid to agriculture.

The myth of agricultural fundamentalism also appears in the notion that farm or rural people are better, more virtuous, better suited to govern than are urban dwellers. Moreover, out in the country the air is fresh, the water is pure, beauty abounds, and life is pleasant and tranquil, a sharp contrast with the hustle and bustle, the noise and dirt, the vices and sins of urban life. So many appear to believe. A Cornell University study based on a broad sample of the population found that nearly every group surveyed believed a rural environment to be the best place in which to raise children, presumably because of the values of rural living.[22] Beliefs of this sort contribute to the status of agriculture and to favorable attitudes toward it. They have also served to justify over-representation of rural areas in American legislative bodies.[23]

The relative and absolute numerical decline of the agricultural population has not been accompanied by a proportionate decline in the representation of rural areas in Congress. The constitutional prescription of equal representation of the states in the Senate means that rural states like Mississippi and South Dakota will have the same voting strength as urban states like New York and California, regardless of population. Rural inhabitants have also been over-

[20] House Committee on Appropriations, *Department of Agriculture and Farm Credit Appropriation Bill,* H. Report 1584, 85th Cong., 2nd Sess., 1958, 5.

[21] Today few economists would argue, for example, that the depressed condition of agriculture during the 1920's was a major, let alone the main or only, cause of the Great Depression.

[22] W. A. Anderson, *A Study of the Values of Rural Living, Part VIII, Summary of Findings,* Rural Sociology Publication No. 34 (Ithaca: Cornell University Agricultural Experiment Station, 1952).

[23] See Noel Perrin, "In Defense of Country Votes," *The Yale Review,* LII (Autumn, 1962), 16–24, for an example.

represented in the House because Congressional districts, drawn by rural-minded state legislatures, have often favored rural areas. A study made by the *Congressional Quarterly* in 1962 concluded that rural areas in the nation had twenty-seven more representatives than they were entitled to on the basis of population (and the "one man-one vote" criterion).[24] Although the benefits of over-representation to the farmer cannot be specified precisely, it has, at a minimum, enlarged his access to political decision makers.

Probably more important than over-representation is the fact that Congressional structure and customs function to increase farm political power in Congress.[25] Congressional committees are major centers of legislative decision and their operation and output is much influenced by their chairmen. Committee chairmen are selected on the basis of seniority, which means that the "safer" a congressional district is, the more apt its incumbent is to be continually re-elected, to acquire seniority, to become a committee chairman, and to remain one (assuming, of course, majority party membership). Among the safest Congressional districts are rural districts in the South and Midwest. When the Democratic party controls the House, from half to two-thirds of the chairmen come from rural districts in the South. When the Republican party has been in the majority in recent decades a similar share of committee chairmen have come from rural and small-town districts in the Midwest. A somewhat similar situation appears in the Senate in that many committee chairmen come from states in which agriculture is an important economic interest. Farm and rural people have more than their "fair share" of influential friends in Congress. We now turn to a more detailed look at Congress and the making of agricultural policy.

Congress and Agricultural Policy

In agricultural policy, as in most other areas of public policy, the initiative in proposing new legislation or modification of existing legislation rests mainly with the executive branch. Congress has maintained and exercised a great deal of control over farm policy, however, and has not hesitated to modify, reject, or sometimes substitute its own policy proposals in place of those emanating from the President

[24] *Congressional Quarterly Weekly Report,* XX (February 2, 1962).
[25] Our discussion draws on Chares M. Hardin, "Farm Political Power and the U.S. Governmental Crisis," *Journal of Farm Economics,* XL (December, 1958). Reprinted in Joseph R. Fiszman, ed., *The American Political Arena* (Boston: Little, Brown, 1962), 477–487.

and the Secretary of Agriculture. The Farm Bureau is an especially strong supporter of Congressional power in agricultural policy, believing that it can work more effectively with Congress than with the President, particularly if the latter is a Democrat. Because of the wide geographical dispersion of its members the Farm Bureau has access to most Senators and Representatives coming from rural-farm states and districts.

Within Congress the major centers of decision on agricultural policy are the House and Senate agriculture committees,[26] which are constituted almost entirely of Senators and Representatives from farm states and districts in the South, Midwest, and Great Plains regions. In making assignments to the House Agriculture Committee, for example, "Both parties take it for granted that wheat, cotton, and tobacco interests should have the majority of representation on the committee."[27] In the Democratic-controlled Eighty-ninth Congress (1965–67) the leadership of the agriculture committees, including both chairmen (Cooley, N.C., in the House and Ellender, La., in the Senate) and most of the subcommittee chairmen, came from the South. This situation, which is a function of the committee selection process, plus the safe district-seniority syndrome noted above, gives Southern farm interests a large voice in agricultural policy formation.

The agriculture committees are organized along commodity lines for the handling of price support legislation. The House committee has a number of permanent subcommittees (on cotton, tobacco, wheat, livestock and feed grains, etc.), each of which is controlled by representatives from districts producing the commodity in question.[28] In the Senate committee the chairman, under an informal arrangement, relies for decisions on particular commodities on member Senators whose states have substantial farm interests.[29] Consequently, committee structure and action have contributed to the decline of general farm legislation and to the substitution for it of a series of commodity programs acceptable to congressmen from areas in which each commodity is important.

[26] Also important are the subcommittees on agricultural appropriations of the House and Senate appropriations committees. See David C. Knapp, "Congressional Control of Agricultural Conservation Policy: A Case Study of the Appropriations Process," *Political Science Quarterly*, LXXI (June, 1956), 257–281.

[27] Nicholas A. Masters, "Committee Assignments in the House of Representatives," *American Political Science Review*, LV (June, 1961), 354.

[28] See Charles O. Jones, "Representation in Congress: The Case of the House Agriculture Committee," *American Political Science Review*, LV (June, 1961), 358–367.

[29] Dale E. Hathaway, *Government and Agriculture* (New York: Macmillan, 1963), 188–193.

The domination of the agriculture committees by farm oriented congressmen, makes it nearly impossible to obtain farm legislation unacceptable to the major interests represented on the committees since they must approve such legislation. On the other hand, the decline in rural representation means that farm area congressmen are no longer sufficiently numerous to secure the enactment of farm legislation without the help (votes) of many nonfarm congressmen. Most farm legislation reported to the floor by the committees in recent years has been passed, probably because of the skill of the committee leadership in judging what kind of legislation will be accepted by a majority of the House or Senate (and later the President, especially if he is from the opposition party).

Since World War II, voting in Congress on price supports has been rather strongly partisan, most Democrats usually backing high price supports and production controls and most Republicans favoring lower or no price supports and minimal controls on production. Those voting patterns are in general accord with the ideological positions of the parties concerning government intervention in the economy. The pattern of party voting is shown by the Agricultural Act of 1961, which was in line with the Kennedy administration's proposals for higher price supports and production controls. The bill was passed in the House by a vote of 224–170 (Dem. 175–58; Rep. 49–112). In the Senate the crucial vote came on a Republican amendment to eliminate the feed grain program from the bill; it was rejected 36–59 (Dem. 10–51; Rep. 26–8). Here, as usual, most Democrats opposed most Republicans but with some crossing of party lines. The *Congressional Quarterly* has characterized postwar congressional voting patterns in terms of high support and low supports blocs:

> The high-supports bloc consisted of a majority of Southern and Western Democrats, a small number of Republicans from heavy farm districts of the Lake States (Minnesota, Wisconsin, Michigan), corn belt and plains (Iowa, downstate Illinois, Indiana, Kansas, Nebraska, Dakotas), and a fluctuating number of Northern urban Democrats. In a typical House vote on high supports, Southern and Western Democrats usually produced some 100 or more votes in favor of high supports, the small group of Midwestern farm Republicans any where from half a dozen to 40 or 50 votes in favor, and the urban Democrats from 30–70, the fluctuations depending on the exact nature of the issue and the party pressures involved.
>
> The low supports bloc consisted of Northern urban and suburban Republicans, Republicans from feed-deficit farming districts, particularly in the Northeast, some of the urban Democrats, and a few

Southern and Western Democrats, generally from feed-deficit areas. The Republican groups usually produced about 150 votes against high supports, urban Democrats from 20–50, and Southern and Western Democrats a handful, usually no more than a dozen.[30]

To a large extent, voting by congressmen in opposition to the position taken by a majority of their party can be satisfactorily explained by "constituency interests." Some urban Democrats have opposed higher price supports as meaning higher food prices for consumers. Southern Democrats from areas in which there is much livestock, dairy, and poultry production, and a resultant demand for cheap feed, have sometimes voted against high price supports for feed grains. Some plains-state Republicans have supported high price supports and production controls as the best way of maintaining the income of wheat farmers (lower wheat prices usually do not result in expanded consumption of bread and other wheat products and thus greater demand for wheat). In sum, Congressional voting on price support legislation reflects mixture of party pressures and constituency interests.

A major proposal to change the decision-making structure for farm policy was presented to Congress by President Kennedy early in 1961. Essentially, it was proposed that Congress should grant the Secretary of Agriculture authority to select an advisory committee of producers for each basic commodity. These committees would help draft income-support programs for their respective commodities. If a commodity program were approved by two-thirds of the producers in a referendum, it would be submitted to Congress and unless vetoed by either house within sixty days, it would go into effect. Congress was to have power only to approve or disapprove of programs, not to amend them.

This proposal, which acknowledged the fragmentation of farm interests, would have much reduced the control of Congress and the agriculture committees over farm policy in favor of the Secretary of Agriculture and the various commodity group committees; and the latter could have been stacked to represent the policy viewpoints of the administration (as some Congressmen pointed out). Further, the proposal was designed to take advantage of the well-known fact that it is easier to block congressional action than to obtain it.

The administration proposal drew the support of the Grange, the National Farmers Union, and a dozen other farm groups. The Farm Bureau was the main source of farm group opposition, being joined

[30] Congressional Quarterly, *U.S. Agricultural Policy*, 9.

282

by a few lesser farm groups and also by the Chamber of Commerce. Both the House and Senate agriculture committees rejected the proposal. Many congressmen, especially Southerners, were strongly opposed to yielding to the executive branch any of their power to write farm legislation. Chairman Cooley of the House Agriculture Committee stated that: "[The proposal would] put Congress on the spot of [sic] the so-called farmer committee which would really be controlled by the administration, which would be out there building up the pressure and, I can just see the arguments being made, 'Would you, a member of Congress, go against a million corn-growers, and 500,000 something else?' No, we cannot see any possibility of agreeing to this."[31] Conservative Republicans and Southern Democrats also opposed the plan on ideological grounds because of the expansion of federal power in general and executive power in particular which it appeared to entail. Congress continues to have a major role in agricultural policy making.

A Case Study: Wheat Policy

A short look at policy making for wheat during the 1962–1964 period will illustrate more fully the complex nature of agricultural politics, policy making, and policy.

Early in 1962, in line with the "supply management" concept, the Kennedy administration asked Congress to provide tough production controls for wheat (along with feed grains and milk products) to reduce surpluses while raising wheat prices for the farmer. A bill to this effect was passed by the Senate after the proposed program for all dairy products was eliminated by the Senate Agriculture Committee at the insistence of dairy groups. The bill was killed in the House, however, mostly because of Republican and some Southern Democratic opposition to the stringent feed-grain controls it contained (the vote was 215–205; Dem. 48–204, Rep. 167–1). Subsequently, a compromise bill devised by the House Agriculture Committee provided mild controls for both wheat and feed-grain production. It passed the House by 229–163 (Dem. 199–37; Rep. 30–126) but, before Senate passage, it was amended to include the stiff controls on wheat originally requested by the administration. These wheat provisions were retained in the final version of the bill and it was adopted over the almost unanimous opposition of the Republicans in both Houses.

[31] *Hearings,* House Committee on Agriculture, 87th Cong., 1st Sess., 1961, part 2, p. 253.

The Food and Agriculture Act of 1962, as this legislation was designated, provided the following program for wheat: In 1963 the policy was continued whereby wheat farmers who cut back production 10 per cent from their acreage allotments were eligible for price supports of about $1.80 a bushel. Then, beginning in 1964, wheat farmers would have a choice of two alternatives. The first required approval of two-thirds of the wheat-growers to go into effect, and imposed stringent mandatory controls on wheat production, based on bushels rather than acreage. In return, under a certificate plan, the price of wheat would be supported at around $2.00 a bushel. If less than two-thirds of the growers approved this program, the second alternative would automatically go into effect. Under it, growers who complied with the existing acreage allotments would be eligible for price supports at 50 per cent of parity (probably $1.25 a bushel); non-compliers would be ineligible for any supports.

The referendum to decide which of the alternatives would be followed was scheduled for May, 1963. It touched off a hard-fought, bitter struggle among farm groups. Lined up in support of the stringent control-high support alternative, which the Kennedy administration wanted, were the National Grange, the National Farmers Union, the Missouri Farmers Association, the National Association of Wheat Producers, the National Federation of Grain Cooperatives, and the Grain Cooperative of the Great Plains. These groups formed an alliance known as the National Wheat Committee and cooperated with the Department of Agriculture in seeking a favorable vote. Leading the opposition to the stringent controls was the American Farm Bureau Federation, which believed the time had come "for wheat growers to blow the whistle on the administration's 'supply management' program."[32]

The groups supporting the production control alternative emphasized economic factors in advocating a favorable vote. Unless it was approved, they contended, wheat prices would fall to $1.25 or lower, with resultant "chaos," low incomes, and depressed conditions generally for farmers. The Department of Agriculture estimated that an unfavorable vote would cost wheat growers $700,000,000 in income in 1964. Secretary of Agriculture Freeman stated the issues involved in the referendum in this fashion: "A 'yes' vote means $2.00 a bushel for wheat, high farm income, no overproduction, a stable world wheat market. A 'no' vote means '$1.00 wheat,' a $700,000,000 drop in farm income, 300 to 400 million bushels of overproduction, and possible

[32] *The New York Times,* May 19, 1963, p. E5.

collapse of world wheat trading agreements."[33] During the referendum campaign, both Secretary Freeman and President Kennedy stressed that no new legislation would be enacted to "bail out" the wheat farmers should they reject the control plan. Moreover, to make a favorable vote more attractive, the administration pushed a new feed-grain bill through Congress a few days before the scheduled referendum. It permitted farmers to interchange wheat and feed-grain acreage, which would be advantageous to many farmers, should the wheat controls be approved.

The American Farm Bureau Federation, in opposing stringent controls, put the issue largely in moral terms. "The battle is being fought now in the wheat fields," AFBF President Shuman told his audiences, "but adoption of the wheat certificate plan would be a signal for the Federal Government to move in and impose controls on all of agriculture—dairy, livestock, poultry, fruits, and vegetables."[34] "Freeman or Free Men" and "For freedom, vote no," proclaimed AFBF literature and billboards. However, the Farm Bureau also contended that if farmers rejected the tough controls a more acceptable program would be provided by Congress. Many Republicans took the same position but neither they nor the Farm Bureau were very explicit about the form the "more acceptable" program would take.

In the referendum, the wheat farmers rejected the strict production controls by a vote of 638,572 to 584,284, which was far short of the two-thirds vote required for approval. In the twelve previous wheat referenda production controls (marketing quotas) had been approved by 70 per cent or more of the farmers voting (except in 1962, when 68.4 per cent approved). Only in six states, mostly in the South,[35] did two-thirds of the farmers approve controls. As to why controls were rejected, available data do not permit a firm answer but the all-out campaign against wheat controls waged by the Farm Bureau was probably a factor. Never before had the Farm Bureau worked so strongly and actively against controls. Many observers believe that small wheat farmers (those growing less than fifteen acres) voted

[33] *Winston-Salem Journal,* May 20, 1963, p. 4.

[34] *The New York Times,* May 19, 1963, p. E5.

[35] The six states were Tennessee, Kentucky, North Carolina, South Carolina, Georgia, and Maine. In Maine the control program was approved by 24 of the 32 farmers voting. Approval in the Southern states may have resulted from the greater experience of farmers in the South with production controls, as on tobacco and cotton, making controls not as disagreeable to them as to Northern farmers.

overwhelmingly against controls, except in the South. Previously unable to vote, these small growers were permitted to vote in 1963 provided they signed up for the control program. Part of the Farm Bureau's strategy was to persuade these small farmers to sign up and then vote "no" in order to preserve their freedom from controls.[36] Whatever the specific explanations for the outcome of the referendum, it indicated that many farmers do not want strict production controls. But it also showed that many farmers are willing to accept such controls in the absence of other forms of economic security.

Following the referendum, the initial reaction of the Kennedy administration was that the farmers had made their choice and would have to live with it. Low price supports and voluntary production controls were to go into effect in 1964. In the fall of 1963, however, the administration's position began to shift because 1964 would be an election year and many Democrats (especially in Congress) were concerned about the possible political repercussions of low wheat prices. In December, 1963, Secretary of Agriculture Freeman told the press that Congress was "more receptive to a wheat program than it would have been last spring" and that President Johnson had "strong feelings" that new wheat legislation was needed.[37] In his message to Congress in January, 1964, the President called for enactment of a voluntary wheat certificate plan which would raise farmers' income but would not raise food prices. Most farm groups favored a program of the sort recommended. The major exception was the Farm Bureau, which wanted a program featuring low price supports and payments for retiring land from production.

The President's recommendation set off a movement in Congress to pass legislation which would apply to the 1964 wheat crop. In the Senate a wheat program was attached to a cotton bill previously passed by the House. The amended bill was then returned to the House and, under tight leadership control, agreed to by a 211–203 vote (North. Dem. 113–25, South. Dem. 88–11; Rep. 10–167). (Some needed support from northern urban Democrats in the House was gained by leadership's promise of quick action on a food stamp plan which urban interests desired.) President Johnson signed the bill into law and the wheat growers were indeed "bailed out" of a low-price situation.

As enacted, the new wheat program provided for a voluntary "certificate plan" which, through a complicated subsidy arrangement,

[36] *Congressional Quarterly Weekly Report,* XXI (May 24, 1963), 823–824.
[37] *Congressional Quarterly Weekly Report,* XXII (January 24, 1964), 158.

provided for price supports of around $1.80 a bushel for wheat farmers who kept within their acreage allotments. Those failing to do so were not eligible for supports. Out of the wheat controversy thus came a system of moderate controls and moderate price supports with which farmers are comfortable if not completely happy. President Johnson recommended a continuation of this sort of program for wheat farmers in 1965, which was done by Congress.

PRICE SUPPORT PROGRAMS

Many proposals for direct governmental support of farm commodity prices have been advanced since the early 1920's and, beginning with the Agricultural Adjustment Act of 1933, a large volume of price support legislation has been enacted. It is not our intention to examine these matters in fine detail here because of their volume and complexity.

The Evolution of Price Support Programs

Demands for government action to support farm prices began as a response to the agricultural depression that followed the end of World War I and the disappearance of wartime markets and demand. Depressed agricultural conditions persisted throughout the 1920's and then went from bad to worse when the Great Depression set in. Disequilibrium in the marketplace stimulated the quest for political solutions for depressed farm prices and income.

Under the spur of the farm bloc, the first attempt to raise farm prices utilized a traditional instrument, the protective tariff. Tariffs on farm commodities were raised in 1921 and again in 1922. In most cases, though, their effect was only symbolic because domestic production exceeded domestic consumption of practically all farm products and the tariff consequently worked to keep out commodities that had never come in. Attention soon shifted to "making the tariff effective" through the use of a two-price plan for export crops. Most important of the proposals with this intent were the McNary-Haugen Bills. Essentially, they provided that the federal government should purchase sufficient quantities of farm commodities to raise their domestic prices to suitable levels. The stocks thus accumulated would be sold abroad at the presumably lower world price and the losses would be recouped by a tax on domestic sales. Strongly supported by the Grange and the Farm Bureau, the McNary-Haugen bills were defeated in Congress in 1924 and 1926 because of opposition from the South and Northeast. Then in 1927 and 1929 versions of the bills were passed, only to be vetoed each time by President Coolidge, who took the position that not much could be done to help the farmer.

President Hoover came into office in 1929 committed to "do something" about farm prices. A moderate measure, the Agricultural Marketing Act of 1929, was passed in order to forestall more far-reaching or "radical" proposals. The Agricultural Marketing Act created a Federal Farm Board with a revolving fund of $500,000,000 to be used in supporting the price stabilization activities of agricultural marketing cooperatives and stabilization corporations. Commodities were to be purchased when prices were low and sold when they were high, thereby stabilizing prices. The Federal Farm Board began financing the purchase of large quantities of wheat, cotton, and other commodities. A bumper crop harvest in 1931 and the depression combined to produce record surpluses and low prices, with which the Farm Board could not cope. It ceased operations, having lost $400,000,000 in its stabilization efforts. A major reason for the failure of the Farm Board experiment was its inability to control production. The Board exhorted farmers to curtail output but they refused to do so voluntarily, production was maintained or increased, and prices continued to fall. The lesson here was obvious for later policy makers: Efforts to raise farm prices, without increased demand, require restriction of supply by means of production controls to be effective.

In 1933, Congress passed the first Agricultural Adjustment Act. This legislation, mutually agreed to by farm group leaders and the Roosevelt administration, provided for production controls to reduce the supply of farm commodities and thereby raise farm prices. Farmers who agreed to restrict production were eligible for cash benefit payments, financed by a tax levied on the processors of agricultural commodities. Also, commodity loans were made available to farmers to encourage the withholding of commodities from the market and direct purchases were made of surplus commodities. The goal of the act was "parity," which was defined as the establishment of "prices to farmers at a level that will give agricultural commodities a purchasing power with respect to articles farmers buy equivalent to the purchasing power of agricultural commodities in the base period . . .

288

August, 1909–July, 1914."[38] Legislation enacted in 1934 made production controls mandatory for producers of cotton and tobacco when approved in a referendum by two-thirds of the growers of a commodity.

The Agricultural Adjustment Act came to an end in 1936 when it was declared unconstitutional by the Supreme Court on the grounds that agricultural production was a matter for state control and, further, that the tax on processors was for the benefit of "special interests" rather than the general welfare.[39] Congress quickly responded by passing the Soil Conservation and Domestic Allotment Act of 1936 to help maintain farm income. The act provided for payments to farmers for taking soil-depleting crops out of production and planting the land to soil-improving crops and for various other soil conservation practices. The "soil-depleting" crops happened to be those in excess supply. The real purpose of the act was, of course, to provide income assistance for farmers in the guise of payments for soil conservation.

The 1936 measure did not reduce surpluses enough to raise prices so, in 1938, Congress adopted the second Agricultural Adjustment Act, which restored the policy of direct price supports and production controls to raise farm income. Price supports were authorized at rates ranging from 52 to 75 per cent of parity. Farmers who reduced their production and stayed within their allotted acreages were eligible for commodity loans, parity payments, and/or soil conservation payments. When necessary to reduce excess production of wheat, cotton, corn, tobacco, or rice (and later, peanuts), the Secretary of Agriculture could impose mandatory marketing quotas with the approval of two-thirds of the growers in a referendum. Penalties were provided for producers who exceeded their marketing quotas. The act also included a number of surplus disposal programs, including a food-stamp plan to help families on relief, free distribution of food to needy families, provision of food for school lunch programs, and subsidization of the export of cotton and wheat. In 1939 and 1941 decisions, the Court held that the act was a legitimate exercise of the commerce power.[40]

[38] See Gilbert C. Fite, "George N. Peek: Equality for Agriculture," *Current History*, XXVIII (June, 1955), 351–355. The concept of parity was initially developed by Peek, head of a farm equipment company, as a basis for increasing farmers' income and their ability to purchase goods, including farm equipment.

[39] *United States v. Butler*, 297 U.S. 1, (1936).

[40] *Mulford v. Smith*, 307 U.S. 38 (1939); and *Wickard v. Filburn*, 317 U.S. 111 (1942).

World War II began before the effectiveness of the second AAA in controlling surpluses and raising prices could be assessed. During the war years the prices of many farm commodities were supported at 90 per cent of parity so as to encourage production adequate for wartime needs. Such supports were mandatory for the "basic" commodities—corn, wheat, cotton, tobacco, rice, and peanuts—and were eventually applied to a dozen or so other commodities (e.g., hogs, eggs, soybeans, and potatoes). Legislation enacted in 1942 provided that price supports at 90 per cent of parity should continue for these commodities for two years after the formal cessation of hostilities (which turned out to be December 31, 1948). Farm groups were also able to secure amendments to the Emergency Price Control Act of 1942 prohibiting price ceilings on farm products until they reached 110 per cent of parity. Needless to say, farmers generally prospered during the war years.

In 1948, with the wartime legislation due to expire at the end of the year, new legislation was required. Although there was general agreement among farm interests on the need for some kind of price support protection, there was disagreement as to the form it should take: high, fixed price supports or lower, flexible supports. The latter were favored by President Truman, many Democrats, and most Republicans, whereas high supports were desired by Southern Democrats, some Western Democrats, and a number of farm-area Republicans. The Agricultural Act of 1948 represented a combination of these positions. High supports (90 per cent of parity) for the basic commodities and hogs, chickens, eggs, and milk products were extended through May, 1950, after which time a system of flexible supports ranging between 60 and 90 per cent of parity would go into effect.

In the 1948 fall election President Truman won a presidential term in his own right and Democratic majorities regained control of Congress. Because of the party's apparent success in farm areas, the President and many Democratic Congressmen perceived the election as a mandate to help farmers by means of high price supports. Consequently, laws were enacted in 1949 and 1952 continuing price supports for the basic commodities at 90 per cent of parity through 1954.

A major controversy over the nature of farm policy was touched off in 1949 by Secretary of Agriculture Charles Brannan's proposals for dealing with the farm problem.[41] According to the Brannan Plan, as his proposals were soon designated, prices of farm products should

[41] Reo M. Christenson, *The Brannan Plan: A Study in Farm Politics and Policy* (Ann Arbor: University of Michigan Press, 1959).

be supported at high levels of parity with a limitation on the amount of benefits available to any one farm (only on the first $26,000 of production). Rigorous production controls would be instituted for storable commodities such as wheat, corn, and cotton. Perishable commodities (fresh milk, meat, eggs) would be sold on the market for what they would bring. Direct payments would then be made by the government to the farmer to make up the difference between what he actually received and what he *should* have received according to the price support standard. The plan was advocated as a means of supporting farm income while controlling surpluses and making an abundance of perishable commodities available at reasonable prices to consumers. Moreover, by limiting the payment of benefits to the first $26,000 of production on any one farm, it would provide the most help to the small and family sized farmers. Backing for the Brannan Plan came from the Farmers' Union, the AFL, the CIO, and many Northern Democrats. Opposition to the plan, spearheaded by the Farm Bureau, included most farm groups, various conservative business groups, most Republicans, and many Southern Democrats. Arguments against the Plan stressed that it was "radical," that it would be excessively costly, and that the level of supports was too high. Also, it is said that many farmers opposed the plan because of their distaste for direct subsidies, preferring to have their subsidies somewhat concealed, as in the form of loans. Large farmers objected to the limitation on benefits. The Brannan Plan failed to survive committee action in Congress because most members of that body preferred the traditional and more orthodox price support techniques.

When the Republicans returned to office in 1953, agricultural policy changed direction. President Eisenhower and his Secretary of Agriculture, Ezra Taft Benson, advocated lower and flexible price supports as a means of reducing both the cost of farm programs and the amount of government control of agriculture. The Agriculture Act of 1954 represented a moderate victory for the proponents of flexible supports over the advocates of high supports. With the exception of tobacco (whose supports were maintained at 90 per cent of parity), the prices of basic commodities were to be supported at between $82\frac{1}{2}$ and 90 per cent of parity in 1955 and between 75 and 90 per cent thereafter. Support for other commodities was continued on an optional basis.

There was much criticism of the Eisenhower-Benson farm policies by some groups, especially the Farmers' Union, and by Democrats and some farm-area Republicans in Congress. In 1956 and 1958 Congress passed bills designed to halt the administration's efforts to reduce price supports. The 1956 bill provided for the restoration of price supports at 90 per cent of parity while the second (1958) bill was an attempt to prevent the Secretary of Agriculture from reducing price supports on corn, wheat, rice, and dairy products below existing levels. Both bills were vetoed by President Eisenhower on the ground they would contribute to overproduction. Subsequent to the veto of the "price freeze" bill, the Eisenhower administration was able to secure the enactment of legislation permitting reduction of price supports on rice, cotton, and corn to 65 per cent of parity over a period of years. Following the 1958 Congressional elections, which returned heavy Democratic majorities, Congress in 1959 passed bills to increase or maintain support prices for wheat and tobacco. Both of these were also vetoed by President Eisenhower. In short, during the 1955–1960 period, agricultural policy making was characterized by stalemate between a Republican President and a Democrat-controlled Congress. Each was fairly able to deny what the other considered desirable in the way of price support policy—higher price supports in the case of the Democrats and further movement toward a "free market" for the Eisenhower administration.

The Kennedy administration came into office in 1961 espousing a policy of "supply management" (or adjustment) for agriculture.[42] Briefly, their idea was that by rigorous production controls and higher price supports, agricultural surpluses could be controlled and supply could be brought into better balance with demand while farm income was being increased. Congress, however, was unwilling generally to provide stringent controls on production. While price support levels were increased somewhat, controls on agricultural production and surpluses were only mildly strengthened. Congress did provide for strong production controls in the case of wheat but, as we have seen, these were rejected by the wheat growers. Following this action, neither the Kennedy administration nor the Johnson administration made further efforts to secure strong controls over production.

Out of two decades of struggle over agricultural price supports there has emerged a policy condition under which production is controlled, but not very rigorously, and prices are supported, but only moderately. Price support programs have become an accepted feature of agricultural policy, in spite of continuing controversy over their form and substance. Although it is an alternative, there seems little

[42] See Hans Landsberg, "A New Approach to the Farm Problem," *The Reporter*, XXVI (April 12, 1962), 34–37.

real desire to return agriculture to a "free market." It was, after all, dissatisfaction with the operation of the market which led to demands for government price support assistance in the first place.

The Price Support Operation

In broad outline, the pattern of agricultural price supports includes the following features: (1) prescription of price goals for farm commodities, usually as a percentage of parity; (2) a system of loans, payments, and purchases designed to maintain farm prices (or incomes) at the prescribed levels; (3) limitations on the amounts of commodities that can be produced or sold; (4) a series of programs for the disposal of surplus commodities acquired by the government. Although the details of price support programs have been changed or modified frequently, this broad pattern has remained constant.

Parity and Price Goals

Parity is a relationship (or ratio) between the prices farmers receive for the products they sell and the prices they pay for the goods and services they purchase, based on some period in the past (as being 100, or "ideal"). The period usually selected is 1909–1914, a time of favorable economic conditions for farmers generally (1919–1929 has been used as the base period for tobacco and a few other commodities because their economic condition was better at that time). If farmers were guaranteed 100 per cent of parity, the price received for their commodities should give them buying power equivalent to what they had in the base period. Thus, if the prices of goods purchased by farmers have tripled since 1909–1914 (as in fact they have) then the prices of farm commodities should also be three times as high as in the base period (which they now are not). As a farmer once put it, parity means that "If a man could take a bushel of corn to town in 1912 and sell it and buy him a shirt, he should be able to take a bushel of corn to town today and and buy a shirt."[43]

There is nothing scientific about the concept of parity. It is essentially a political device which reflects the endeavor of agricultural groups to gain income at the expense of other groups in the economy through government action. (Whether or not this is desirable depends upon one's point of view.) Parity is open to political manipulation

[43] Quoted in Clair Wilcox, *Public Politics Toward Business* (Homewood, Ill.: Richard D. Irwin, 1960), 471.

or tinkering, as in 1949 when labor costs were included in computing the farmer's "prices paid" index. This had the effect of raising the parity prices of farm products because it raised the index of farm costs. Nonetheless, parity has come to be regarded as a symbol of "fairness" or "equality" for agriculture, and farm groups and their official supporters have generally been successful in resisting efforts to change the manner of computing parity to their disadvantage or to eliminate use of the concept in computing price goals. A proposal by the Eisenhower administration to set support prices at 90 per cent of the average price of a commodity for the three preceding years (a "three-year moving average") got nowhere in Congress.

Price support goals are customarily stated as a percentage of parity and may be either "rigid" or "flexible." A rigid price support goal is set by Congress at a specific percentage of parity, say 90 per cent, and can be changed only by further legislation. Flexible price supports provide that price goals for a commodity may range between 75–90 per cent of parity, for example. The specific level of support is then determined by the Secretary of Agriculture, ostensibly according to supply and demand conditions. If the prospects were for an above normal supply of a commodity at the beginning of a growing season, the price support would be set low so as to discourage production. The opposite would be done if supply appeared likely to go below normal, again with the general purpose of balancing supply and demand at an acceptable price level. Whether or not flexible supports work in this fashion is another question.

Political considerations may also influence the choice of a support level. After vetoing a bill providing for high price supports in 1956, an election year, President Eisenhower directed Secretary of Agriculture Benson to use his discretion under the flexible price support system to raise price goals to a minimum of 82.5 per cent of parity. Many farm-area Republican congressmen considered this necessary to prevent a "farm revolt" at the polls.

When Congress legislates on price supports, it may be restrained by the belief that if support prices are set too high sufficient opposition and discontent may be engendered among nonfarm groups to discredit the entire price support program. Or, when a commodity produced by one group of farmers is used by another group, as are feed grains by livestock and poultry producers, the price levels set may reflect bargaining between spokesmen for the two groups. In other words, political expediency and bargaining among groups within the farm sector may help shape the policy result.

The farm commodities under price supports are usually divided into three groups. First are the "basic" commodities (wheat, corn, cotton, tobacco, peanuts, and rice) for which price supports are mandatory under existing law. That four of the six basic commodities are grown in the South attests to the influence of Southern Congressmen on agricultural legislation. Second are non-basic commodities for which supports are mandatory. Present examples of this category include milk products, wool, small feed grains, and honey. Third are other commodities on which price supports are optional at the discretion of the Secretary of Agriculture. Cottonseed, flaxseed, soybeans, and crude pine gum are in this category. Most of the controversy and legislation involving price supports has concerned the basic commodities.

Guarantee of Price Goals

A number of techniques are used to assure eligible farmers that they will actually receive the prices specified for their commodities. The most popular of these has been the nonrecourse loan: a government loan is made to a farmer in an amount equal to the support price times the amount of his output which he cannot sell on the market at or above the support price. His commodity is stored as collateral for his loan. If the market price goes above the support price, the farmer can sell his commodity, pay off his loan, and pocket the difference. If the market price is below the support price, he can default on his loan, retain the money loaned to him, and let the government have his commodity. In either case he gets no less than the support price and, from his standpoint, its a matter of "Heads I win, tails you lose." What appears to be a lending operation at first glance turns out to be a price support operation.

Similar to the nonrecourse loan is the purchase agreement, whereby the government agrees to purchase from a farmer, at his option, not more than a specified amount of a commodity at the support price. The government is required to buy but the farmer can sell some, all, or none of the specified quantity to the government as he sees fit. This technique provides price guarantees to farmers who cannot meet storage requirements or who do not want to bother with a loan operation.

For a few commodities—milk products and cottonseed are current examples—the government attempts to support prices by purchases in the market or directly from producers. In the case of wool, direct payments to producers are used. The wool grower sells his product

295

on the market for the going price. The government then makes a direct payment to him to make up the difference between what he received and what he *should* have received according to the price support goal. This is called an "incentive payment" and is justified as necessary to encourage wool production since the United States uses more wool than it produces. The wool program has been described as a "Brannan plan in sheep's clothing." A variant of the direct payment support technique is the "certificate plan" provided for wheat in 1963. In addition to price support loans, eligible farmers received wheat marketing certificates which were redeemable in cash. Here, in a polite fiction, a price support payment was disguised as a "marketing certificate." Only limited use has been made of direct payments in price support programs because of continued farm group opposition to open subsidies.

Production Controls

To prevent price support activities from leading to increased farm output, larger surpluses, and ever growing government expenditures, controls have often been placed on farm production. The two most common devices used for this purpose are the acreage allotment and the marketing quota. The major difference between the two is that compliance by farmers with acreage allotments is voluntary whereas, marketing quotas are mandatory and non-compliance is penalized.

When acreage allotments are used, the Secretary of Agriculture first determines a national acreage allotment, i.e., the total number of acres of production needed. This figure is then broken down by states, by counties, and finally by individual farms on the basis of their past production records. If acreage allotments are in effect, and if the farmer wants to be eligible for price support benefits, he must stay within his allotment. If the farmer does not desire price support benefits, he is free to grow as much as he wants and take the market price for it.

If the Secretary of Agriculture determines that the supply of a commodity (usually one of the "basics") is seriously above "normal," and if two-thirds of the growers approve in a referendum, marketing quotas can be instituted to control production. A farmer's marketing quota consists of whatever he can grow on his acreage allotment. When marketing quotas are in effect for a crop all farmers must stay within their allotted acreages or be penalized for excess production. Marketing quotas rarely have been rejected by growers when proposed by the Secretary of Agriculture because, in the referenda, growers are usually confronted with a choice of marketing quotas and high price supports or no quotas and low or no price supports. In 1964, the growers of flue-cured tobacco were faced with the alternative of a 20 per cent reduction in their existing marketing quotas and continued high price supports or no quotas and no supports. More than 95 per cent of those voting in the referendum chose the former alternative. In general, farmers are under strong economic pressure to accept marketing quotas and the rejection of them in the 1963 wheat referendum was exceptional.

Acreage allotments and marketing quotas have not been overly effective in restricting production, however. Many farmers have chosen not to comply with acreage allotments because of such factors as favorable market prices or disagreement with the concept of price supports. With the exception of tobacco, there has been an unwillingness to impose really strict marketing quotas or controls. Among other things, Congress has often provided minimum levels below which acreage in allotments or quotas could not be reduced. For wheat, the minimum of 55,000,000 acres set by the 1938 AAA remained in effect until 1963, even though production per acre increased greatly in the interim. Surpluses were the result. Again, a farmer who by choice or requirement stays within his allotted acreage may first take his poorer land out of production and, second, may increase his use of fertilizer and other technological inputs to increase his productivity. Consequently, he may produce as much as or more than he did previously but on less acreage. It has been suggested that production quotas be specified in bushels, pounds, and other volume measures but so far farm interests have been able to prevent their adoption except on flue-cured tobacco. In 1965 poundage quotas were substituted for acreage quotas with the approval of four-fifths of the tobacco growers voting in a referendum. Tobacco farmers have traditionally been willing to accept stringent marketing controls in return for high price supports.

Two other methods that have been tried in an effort to reduce production merit discussion here. These are the Soil Bank and the Kennedy administration's feed grains program. At the request of the Eisenhower administration, the Soil Bank program was established in 1956, as a means for retiring land from production and reducing surpluses. There were two facets to the program. Under the *acreage* reserve, a farmer could retire annually part of his allotted acreage for basic commodities in return for compensatory payments, which averaged about 50 per cent of what he would have received in income had the land been cultivated. The *conservation reserve* enabled farmers to contract to convert land from production to conservation uses for periods of three to ten years. Participants received payments for retiring land and for the costs of conservation practices. Both programs were to run for four years but, in 1958, Congress terminated the acreage reserve. In 1960, the Democrat-controlled Congress rejected President Eisenhower's recommendation that the conservation reserve program be extended.[44]

Many criticisms were directed at the Soil Bank during its existence. Farmers often retired their least productive land, thus lessening the effect of the "bank" on production. In some areas entire farms were taken out of operation, causing "substantial non-farm opposition—from merchants, machinery dealers, and the sellers of other inputs used in agricultural production" as they found extensive whole-farm retirement bad for business.[45] Congressional Democrats characterized the Soil Bank as a Republican effort to "buy votes" when it was set up. They continued to criticize it as a Republican effort to prevent the use of "proper" programs to raise farm income, e.g., high price supports. They also argued that the Soil Bank endangered the total farm program because nonfarmers widely resented the payment of farmers not to produce.[46] Few tears attended the demise of the Soil Bank. It cost more than two billion dollars and apparently did little to reduce farm surpluses.

The program for corn and feed grains established by Congress in 1961 differs from the Soil Bank in that it applies to specific commodities and, though participation is voluntary, nonparticipants are not eligible for price support benefits. Under this program, farmers who agree to shift from 20 to 50 per cent of their normal planted acreage to conservation uses receive compensatory "acreage-diversion" payments and are eligible for price supports. ("Acreage diversion" is a euphemism for "land-retirement," which has Soil Bank connotations.) Nonparticipating farmers would have to sell their crops for the market price; and the Secretary of Agriculture was authorized to sell surplus commodities to keep the market price below the support price. This provision, strongly opposed by the Republicans as coercive, was considered necessary by the Kennedy administration to obtain adequate participation in the program. In 1961, the first year of the pro-

[44] Conservation reserve contracts in effect in 1960 will continue until their expiration dates.
[45] Hathaway, *op. cit.*, 304.
[46] Congressional Quarterly, *U.S. Agricultural Policy,* 39.

gram, farmers reduced total corn and feed grain acreage by 18 per cent, though total production declined only by 7 per cent.

This program, like the Soil Bank, is based on the theory that paying a farmer to idle some of his land and thereby reduce production costs less in the long run than buying his surplus production and paying to store it.

Surplus Commodity Disposal

Since the early 1950's large quantities of surplus agricultural commodities have been acquired by the Commodity Credit Corporation, the unit within the Department of Agriculture handling the financial and storage aspects of the price support operation, because control programs have often failed to match supply with demand. Acquisition and disposal of farm surpluses has come to be a large and costly operation; in June, 1963, the CCC's investment in commodities and price support loans was nearly $7.3 billion. Storage and related costs come to almost a billion dollars annually. Surpluses do not simply accumulate, since there are now a variety of programs for their disposal. The cost of these programs was two to three billion dollars a year during the early 1960's.

Pending their disposal, surplus commodities acquired under the price support programs are stored in government-owned bins and facilities (including idle Maritime Administration ships), commercial warehouses and elevators, and on the farms where produced. Surplus storage has become a big business and commercial storage interests are much concerned with protecting their stake in it. Thus, the CCC is directed by law to make the maximum use practicable of commercial facilities and is prohibited from constructing its own cold-storage facilities. An unintended consequence of the price support programs has been the generation of interest groups whose well-being depends on the continued existence and storage of farm surpluses.

There are two basic types of surplus disposal programs. Some are designed to dispose of surplus commodities already acquired by the Commodity Credit Corporation under the price support programs. These include domestic and foreign sales for dollars, barter abroad for strategic materials, and outright donations to the needy, both in the United States and abroad. The second type of program is designed to remove surpluses from the market before they have to be acquired by the CCC. Examples include sales for foreign currencies under Public Law 480, the school lunch and milk programs, and the food stamp program. In either case, the purpose is to enlarge the market for farm commodities beyond what would move in regular commercial channels.

A look at a few of the disposal programs will convey a better picture of their variety and multiple purposes. Sale of surplus commodities under Public Law 480 and donations to needy people overseas have become an important part of the foreign aid program. Under that law, surplus commodities drawn from commercial stocks are sold to other countries for their own currencies. This money is ultimately deposited to the account of the United States in banks in the purchasing country. Much of this money is loaned or granted to the purchasing country for economic development projects. Needy people in various countries benefit from donation of U.S. farm surpluses. In the early 1960's, a large portion of the Algerian population received food from this source. Both of these programs have generally been well supported although objections and criticisms have arisen when assistance is proffered to Soviet satellites (like Poland) or countries not especially "friendly" toward the United States (e.g., the United Arab Republic).

Within the United States, surplus disposal activities have been tied in with a number of programs of the welfare type. These include the school lunch and school milk programs, donations to families on relief and to private and public charitable institutions, and distribution to victims of floods and other natural disasters. Programs of this nature have been especially popular with Democrats. In 1961 the Kennedy administration initiated a pilot food stamp program which was made permanent and expanded by Congressional action in 1964.[47] There had been strong support for such a program among Democrats, especially Northern Democrats, in Congress since the 1930's. The food stamp program enables needy families to buy food stamps at a discount and use them to purchase domestic foodstuffs in authorized retail stores. The program is as much, if not more, an attempt to improve the diets of needy people as it is a means of removing surplus agricultural commodities from the market.

During the period 1953–63, the Commodity Credit Corporation moved more than $30 billion worth of commodities through its various disposal channels. New ways are constantly being sought to move surpluses into use but, so far, the farmers' ability to produce has exceeded the government's permissible capacity to dispose. But, to add a moral, too much food seems more desirable than too little food, a problem still facing much of the world's population.

[47] *The New York Times,* August 12, 1964, p. 21.

Price Support Policy: Impact and Evaluation

What has been the actual effect of the agricultural price support programs on the economy? How effective have they been in raising farm income? How costly have they been? A few general remarks are in order.

First only selected farm commodities, about twenty out of nearly three hundred, have been subject to price support operations since World War II. Measured by dollar value, the supported commodities account for around 40 per cent of agricultural production. For the supported commodities, it is apparent that price support operations have often kept their prices above market levels (as shown by government surplus acquisition), ostensibly increasing farm income. The influence of price supports in this respect is not limited to the commodities directly supported, however. The accumulation of feed grains by the government, for example, has protected the income of livestock producers (who receive no direct price support aid) by providing an outlet for feed grains other than the feeding of them to livestock, preventing an increase in livestock production and a consequent decline in livestock prices.[48]

It is often contended that price support programs, by holding farm prices above "normal" market levels, have caused a misallocation of economic resources (which could be used more efficiently elsewhere in the economy), keeping them unnecessarily in agricultural production. So runs the argument.[49] In response it may be said that price support programs have not prevented a shift of many workers from agricultural to industrial employment, as is indicated by the declining size, both relatively and absolutely, of the farm labor force. Put differently, farm prices and incomes have not been supported at levels sufficient to render nonfarm employment opportunities unattractive to many farm people in an era of general prosperity.

Most of the direct benefits of the price support programs go to a small portion of the farm population. In 1963, it was reported that 80 per cent of price support assistance went to the 27 per cent of farmers (approximately a million) who had gross cash receipts of at least $10,000. (The average net income of farmers in this group was $9,500 in 1963.) The remaining 20 per cent of price support assistance was scattered among the other 73 per cent (two-and-a-half million)

[48] Hathaway, *op. cit.,* 260.
[49] See the discussion in John Kenneth Galbraith, "Economic Preconceptions and Farm Policy," *American Economic Review,* XLIV (March, 1954), 40–52.

of the farmers.[50] Low income farmers benefit but little from price supports because of the small quantities of commodities they sell. Price supports do very little to alleviate agricultural poverty or to help the small farmer. Rather, within the agricultural sector, price supports intensify the disparities between high and low income farm groups by providing most benefits to the larger, well-to-do, commercial farmers. If the objective one wants to achieve is the elimination of farm poverty some instrument other than price supports is needed.

The financial cost of the price support programs should also be considered. Although it is not possible to say what price support programs have cost consumers in the form of higher food prices, data are available on the "realized costs" of these programs to the government. During the 1932–61 period, the total "realized costs" of programs primarily for the stabilization of farm prices and incomes" was nearly $24 billion. In the early 1960's they ran from three to four billion dollars per year. The price support programs have increased greatly in cost since the middle 1950's because of increases in productivity and inadequate production controls. This situation has led many observers to ask how long the taxpayers will stand this burden.[51] It has also stimulated the Johnson administration to seek ways to reduce the size of the agricultural budget without seriously irritating agricultural groups.

OTHER FARM PROGRAMS

In addition to its price support programs, the Department of Agriculture carries on a wide range of other activities which have as their broad purpose the improvement of agricultural productivity and marketing performance and, as a result, increased farm income. Some of these programs (e.g., research in food processing and meat inspection) benefit nonfarm groups and the general public as well as farmers.

[50] Kermit Gordon, "How Much Should Government Do?" *Saturday Review* (January 9, 1965), 25–27, 76.

[51] Pennock estimates that British farmers receive two or three times as much in government subsidies, proportionally, as do their American counterparts. The annual costs of farm subsidies averaged 84.9 per cent of net agricultural income and 5.1 per cent of national government expenditures in Great Britain, compared to 19.2 per cent and 3.2 per cent, respectively, in the United States during 1954–60 years. J. Roland Pennock, " 'Responsible Government,' Separated Powers, and Special Interests: Agricultural Subsidies in Britain and America," *American Political Science Review*, LVI (September, 1962), 621–633.

Such assistance to farmers predates price supports and generally does not involve regulation or limitation of farm activity. It is, rather, basically promotional. Regulation of the farmer did not become a feature of agricultural policy until 1933, when it was accepted as a necessary condition for effective price support programs.

Education, Research, and Extension

The national government has been involved with agricultural research and education for more than a century, these being two of the earliest forms of aid to agriculture. Government action in these areas is intended to improve agricultural methods, techniques, and products and thereby make farming more efficient, productive, and profitable. Indeed, government-conducted or assisted educational and research programs have been a major contributor to the technological revolution in agriculture. This has led to frequent comments that the government is promoting agricultural productivity with one hand while, with the other, it is attempting to restrict production under the price support programs. The apparent inconsistency stems from the fact that the two activities were started at different times in response to different interests and, further, are administered almost independently of one another within the Department of Agriculture. This holds true for a number of other programs.

The Morrill Act of 1862 was one of the first major efforts to promote agriculture. The act provided for grants of public lands to the states (10,000 acres for each member of Congress that a state had) to aid them in establishing colleges to offer instruction in the "agricultural and mechanic arts." These colleges, the familiar land-grant institutions, are still important centers for agricultural education and research although most of them have become, or are becoming, general institutions of higher education. The Smith-Hughes Act of 1917 made grants-in-aid available to the states to help them maintain vocational agriculture education programs in the high schools.

Within the Department of Agriculture, the Agricultural Research Service carries on a vast range and variety of research activities. Government laboratories conduct research on such matters as the development of improved livestock breeds and plant varieties, the eradication and control of animal and plant diseases and parasites, and the development of better processing and handling methods and new uses for agricultural products. In the latter regard, precooked, dehydrated sweet potato flakes is one of the Department's more recent innovations. Investigation and study are also undertaken concerning water and soil conservation, agricultural engineering, and farm economic problems. A federal grant-in-aid program administered by the Research Service helps the states maintain agricultural experiment stations which engage mainly in applied or practical research to improve production, distribution, and marketing of farm products. A good portion of the federal research effort involves cooperation with the state experimental stations. Scientific agricultural research has been primarily a government undertaking.

If agricultural research and experimental activities are to have their fullest impact, their results must be made available, in understandable form, to individual farmers. This function has been performed in large part by the cooperative agricultural Extension Service. Established by the Smith-Lever Act of 1914, the Extension Service is jointly financed by the federal and state governments. Agricultural, home-demonstration, and youth agents are located in most of the nation's counties. Through educational, demonstration, and technical service activities the Extension Service and the county agents put the farmer in touch with the latest developments in agricultural research and experimentation and seek to help (and persuade) him to improve his operations. The more prosperous farmers have proven to be the most receptive to extension activities, and the extension program has centered on their needs and problems.

A close relationship has existed between the Extension Service and the American Farm Bureau Federation. In the early years of the extension program, the county agents often promoted the formation of "farm bureaus," both to gain financial support for the program and to facilitate the dissemination of information. Some of the states soon began to form federations of these county bureaus and, in 1919, the national federation (AFBF) was organized. The Farm Bureau, which got its start from the Extension Service, soon came to dominate the agency. Although formal ties between the two organizations have been severed at the insistence of other farm groups, the Extension Service remains under the sway of the Farm Bureau in most states. As a result, the Farm Bureau has favored extending the Service's responsibilities to include other farm programs. The Farm Bureau, the Extension Service, and the congressional agriculture committees constitute a subsystem nearly autonomous in the formation and administration of extension policy.[52]

[52] Theodore Lowi, "How the Farmers Get What They Want," *The Reporter*, XXX (May 21, 1964), 34–37.

Agricultural Credit Programs

The beginning of government provision of credit to farmers followed years of agrarian complaints that private sources of credit were undependable, interest rates were too high, and terms were too short. In 1916, Congress passed the Federal Farm Loan Act, establishing a system of twelve federal land banks to provide long-term credit to farmers for the purchase of land, buildings, and other property. Demands for additional credit facilities produced the Agricultural Credit Act (1923) and the Farm Credit Act (1933). The 1923 legislation created twelve intermediate credit banks to lend to livestock companies, production credit associations, and similar groups on a short-term basis. The Farm Credit Act set up a series of banks for cooperatives to make loans to farm marketing, purchasing, and service cooperatives.

These various banks collectively comprise the Farm Credit System, which operates under the supervision of the Farm Credit Administration, an independent agency headed by a thirteen-man board. One member is appointed by the Secretary of Agriculture; the other twelve are appointed by the President on the basis of nominations by various farm credit organizations. For administrative purposes, the country is divided into twelve districts, in each of which is located a land bank, an intermediate credit bank, and a bank for cooperatives. All the banks in the System initially operated on federal funds but, as provided by law, ownership of the land banks has been transferred to the farmer-borrowers who use them. The same process is under way for the intermediate and cooperative banks. Ultimately the System will be entirely owned by the borrowers.

The extent of the Farm Credit System's activity is revealed by the fact that in 1962 it made loans totaling over five billion dollars to farmers and their cooperatives. In recent years the Farm Credit Administration has become more conservative and "businesslike" in its supervision of the System. Many small and low income farmers have been unable to borrow from it.

A second agency operating in the farm credit area is the Farmers Home Administration, which primarily serves lower income farmers. The Farmers Home Administration is a lineal descendant of two New Deal agencies: the Resettlement Administration and its successor, the Farm Security Administration. The Resettlement Administration was originated by executive order in 1935 to aid the rehabilitation of low income rural families, to retire land unsuited for farming, and to resettle impoverished families on good land. Then, in 1937, the Bankhead-Jones Farm Tenant Act was passed to combat the problems of tenant farming by furnishing poor farmers with federal credit when they were unable to obtain low-interest loans elsewhere. The act authorized long-term (ownership) loans for the purchase of land and buildings and short-term (operating) loans for the acquisition of equipment, fertilizer, and related needs. The Farm Security Administration was established to handle these loan programs and to take over the various activities of the Resettlement Administration.

The Farm Security Administration thus was responsible both for purely loan programs and for a number of other activities assisting low income farm groups. These included farm purchasing cooperatives, cooperative land-leasing associations and farm communities, camps for migratory workers, and subsistence homesteads. These projects generated much political controversy and were denounced by businessmen, well-to-do commercial farmers, landlords, and others as "Communistic," or "Socialistic," or "collectivistic," and the like. The assault on the Farm Security Administration was led by the Farm Bureau (the spokesmen for well-to-do farm interests), which regarded the FSA as both radical and a threat to its own dominant position in farm politics. The conservative campaign against the FSA reached a peak in 1946, when the agency was abolished. In its stead a stripped-down Farmers Home Administration was provided.

The Farmers Home Administration was authorized to make Bankhead-Jones loans but could not carry on any of the other FSA activities. Aid to low income farmers was thus restricted to more conventional loan programs. Various legislation enacted since 1946 has authorized the FHA to make loans for a number of other purposes (not necessarily limited to low income farmers) including soil and water conservation facilities, construction and improvement of housing for rural farm and nonfarm families, emergencies such as floods and droughts, and conversion of farm land to recreational, conservation, and wildlife uses ("rural renewal"). In 1963 the Administration had over a billion and a half dollars outstanding under the programs it administers. Its losses have been small even though it lends primarily to low income farmers.

A third credit agency, and a quite interesting one, is the Rural Electrification Administration. In the early 1930's only about 10 per cent of the nation's farms had electric power service. The private power companies were quite slow and reluctant to extend service to rural areas, viewing them as poor markets and high service cost areas. To help bring electricity to the farms, the New Deal established the Rural Electrification Administration (1935) to make loans to rural electric cooperatives and others for the generation, transmission, and distribution of electric power in rural areas. (In 1949 the REA was authorized to make loans for the development of rural telephone service.) The REA proved to be quite popular among farmers, especially in the South and the Plains states. Actively promoting the formation of rural electric cooperatives, the REA provided them with technical and managerial assistance in addition to loans at low rates of interest. Its success is shown by the fact that practically all farms (about 98 per cent in 1962) have been electrified. The REA has now directed its attention to expanding and improving existing services rather than helping unserved areas as in the past. An aggressive agency, the REA has shown no desire to decline despite the accomplishment of its original task.

Criticism and opposition for the REA have come from private utility interests, who initially opposed its creation and who have developed no affection for it since then, and from conservatives who are ideologically opposed to government involvement in the electric power business. The REA's program is strongly supported by the National Rural Electric Cooperative Association, an organized interest group generated by its activities, and various farm groups. Efforts to reduce or restrict REA activities on the grounds that the agency has served its purpose or that private utility companies can now handle the job have usually been defeated. Most Democrats and many rural area Republicans in Congress customarily support the REA.

Soil Conservation

Exploitation and abuse of the soil was a common occurrence in, the nineteenth and early twentieth centuries. Soil erosion and depletion rendered tens of millions of acres of land unfit for agricultural uses or else reduced their productivity, leading often to abandonment of farms and movement away from the affected areas. Soil erosion also intensified the severity of floods and caused the silting-in of streams and water reservoirs. Despite growing concern about this wastage of a valuable national resource, really effective governmental action to counter soil erosion did not begin until the New Deal.

307

The Soil Conservation Service was organized in 1935 to combat soil erosion by demonstration projects to encourage better land use and by providing technical advice and assistance to farmers organized in soil conservation districts. These districts are established under state enabling legislation as units of local government and are controlled and administered by farmer-elected committees. They perform such tasks as obtaining equipment and machinery needed for conservation work, coordinating conservation projects involving several farms, and handling requests for technical assistance. There were nearly three thousand of these soil conservation districts in 1963, covering more than 90 per cent of the nation's farm land.

The Soil Conservation Service, located in the Department of Agriculture, provides the districts, and the farmers located within them, with technical advice and supervision and aid in securing equipment and materials required for conservation practices. Although costs are held down because only technical advice and supervision are provided without charge, the Soil Conservation Service's expenditures averaged over eighty million dollars a year in the early 1960's.

Although its program of long-term soil conservation appears to be both widely accepted and generally successful, the Soil Conservation Service has been attacked by the Extension Service and its ally, the Farm Bureau, in the postwar period. The Extension Service has sought to absorb the functions of the SCS, arguing that these are properly a part of Extension's "general approach" to farm problems and improvement. The Farm Bureau has viewed the SCS's field service and farmer committee system as a rival to its established relationships in agriculture. Thus far, the SCS, the National Association of Soil Conservation Districts, and other conservation groups (e.g., the Izaak Walton League) have been able to maintain the agency. Concerning group support for the Soil Conservation Service, it has been stated:

> One of its strengths . . . lies in the impregnable and unassailable character of the conservation concept. Being for conservation is like being for motherhood and against sin. In the public mind, a direct connection exists between the Soil Conservation Service and conservation in general . . . hence any criticism of SCS is often portrayed as an attack on the basic resources of the nation instigated by those who would exploit and despoil our heritage and leave posterity to starve.
>
> Another advantage of the Soil Conservation Service lobby is the simplicity of its position. "Save the Soil" is a better slogan than that

of building better farm units as a means of preserving the family farm.[53]

An approach to soil conservation considerably different from that of the SCS is represented by the Agricultural Conservation Program, which is currently administered by the Agricultural Stabilization and Conservation Service and its farmer-committee system. The Agricultural Conservation Program provides financial assistance, averaging about half of the costs involved, to farmers for soil conservation practices such as the construction of erosion control structures, the planting of grasses, legumes, and other cover crops, and the application of fertilizers (especially limestone) to the land. Financial assistance also is available now for wildlife conservation practices and the conversion of land to recreation uses. The cost of this program runs from $200 to $250 million annually.

The Agricultural Conservation Program has been criticized as an unneeded subsidy for farmers in that, it is argued, they are paid for doing things they ought to undertake on their own as good farming practices. The financial assistance involved, plus the identification of the program with conservation generally, has made it popular with farmers. A proposal by the Johnson administration to drastically cut ACP expenditures as one means of reducing the agriculture budget met with strong opposition from farm leaders and farm-area congressmen. Support for the program is particularly strong in the South, which with its many poor-farm, soil-depleted areas, received two-fifths of ACP funds in 1961.[54]

Marketing Aids and Services

Various activities of the Department of Agriculture, especially its Consumer and Marketing Service, are designed to aid the farmer in disposing of his products and improving his income situation. These activities, some of which date back to the nineteenth century, can generally be grouped into two categories: regulation of middlemen to prevent them from unfairly depriving the farmer of his income and promotional or regulatory programs designed to facilitate or increase the distribution and sale of farm products. That some of these programs benefit consumers will become apparent. The Department attempted to emphasize this aspect of its operations when, in late

[53] Norman Wengert, *Natural Resources and the Political Struggle* (New York: Doubleday, 1955), 54.

[54] Congressional Quarterly, *U.S. Agricultural Policy,* 25.

1964, it set up the aforementioned Consumer and Marketing Service to replace the Agricultural Marketing and Meat Inspection services.

The Department carries on marketing research, looking toward the development of better methods, facilities, and equipment for the handling, processing, transportation, storage, and retail sale of farm commodities. Information, or market news, is made available to farmers, processors, and others on the supply, demand, prices, and quality of farm products to help them conduct their buying and selling activities.

The Consumer and Marketing Service is continually engaged in the determination and revision of standards for farm products and in the inspection, grading, and classing of such products. The Service has developed grades such as U.S. No. 1, U.S. Choice, U.S. Grade A for most of the important farm commodities. Nearly three hundred U.S. grade standards are in effect for fresh and processed fruits and vegetables. The use of these standards, and the government's grading and classing services, is mostly voluntary although they are required for a few commodities, grain and cotton moving in interstate commerce, for example. Processors and distributors of food products make wide use of the government's grading services, reflecting growing consumer awareness and demands for information on food quality. For example, half of the beef, two-fifths of the broilers, and nine tenths of the frozen fruits and vegetables marketed in 1962 were under federal grade standards.[55] A closely related but distinct activity of the Service is the mandatory inspection of meat and poultry to prevent the sale of unwholesome or diseased meat.

The Packers and Stockyards Act of 1921 requires that the services and facilities of stockyards must be adequate and must be made available to livestock shippers on a nondiscriminatory basis and for a reasonable charge. Full and accurate information on sales must be provided buyers and sellers. Unfair, discriminatory, and deceptive practices in stockyards operations are banned, including manipulation or monopolizing of the market by meat-packers (buyers), giving unreasonable preferences, and conspiring to apportion purchases and thereby eliminate competition. This law was enacted in response to farmers' claims that they were often overcharged for the use of stockyards facilities and services and "victimized" by price-rigging on the part of meat-packers (of whom there were primarily four at the time) when they sold their livestock on the market. Similarly, the

[55] U.S. Department of Agriculture, *Annual Report 1962*, 33.

Perishable Commodities Act of 1930 was passed to protect farmers marketing fresh fruits and vegetables by prohibiting such practices as fraudulent charges for marketing services, refusal of dealers to take delivery of produce without just causes, and the making of false or misleading statements about quantity and quality of produce received. In the situations dealt with by these statutes, the farmer was, and is, usually unable to protect his interests without government aid.

Commodity exchanges are markets in which farm commodities are bought and sold for both present delivery and delivery sometime in the future (e.g., wheat may be bought and sold now for delivery six months after the sale contract is made). They are regulated by the Commodity Exchange Authority on the basis of the Grain Futures Act of 1922, as amended by the Commodity Exchange Act of 1936. The general task of the Authority is to ensure fair practices and honest dealing on the commodity exchanges (or boards of trade). Price manipulation, cornering (or monopolizing) the market, and false and deceptive practices are among the prohibited actions. The Authority can also limit the amount prices may change in a given period in order to prevent sharp fluctuations in the market. The objectives of regulation here are the maintenance of honest markets and prevention of market speculation in commodities which may be detrimental to farmers.

One other type of marketing assistance is illustrated by the Agricultural Marketing Act of 1937. This statute authorizes the Secretary of Agriculture to enter into marketing agreements and to issue marketing orders to ensure the "orderly" marketing of such commodities as milk, fruits, nuts, and vegetables. Both orders (which are mandatory) and agreements (which are voluntary) regulate the actions of processors and distributors of farm products for the benefit of producer (farmer) interests. Marketing orders are currently in effect for milk in seventy or so milkshed areas; they prescribe the prices that handlers are to pay producers. Agreements and orders for fruits, vegetables, and other products do not directly establish commodity prices. However, prices are often affected (raised) by rules relating to quality, rates of shipment, and control of surpluses. "Orderly" marketing, in practice, involves efforts to raise commodity prices as well as to reduce fluctuations in them. Consumers are represented in neither the formation nor the administration of marketing orders and agreements. Whatever the future may hold, the Department of Agriculture has with few exceptions promoted farm producer interests.

Price Support Policy: A Postscript

In October, 1965, after this chapter was completed, Congress passed the Food and Agriculture Act of 1965.[56] This legislation, which is to run for a four-year period, takes a major step toward a new system for subsidizing farmers and includes programs for wheat, feed grains, cotton, wool, rice, and dairy products, along with a voluntary land retirement program. The programs for wheat, feed grains, cotton, and wool, which comprise the major substance of the act, contain two general features. First, the act provides for lower support prices (21 cents a pound for cotton in 1966 compared with a high of 34 cents in 1954) so as to reduce both the incentive to increase production and the need for export subsidies to permit American commodities to compete in the world market. Second, income supplements in the form of straight cash subsidy payments or their equivalent on a fixed amount of production are provided for cooperating farmers who voluntarily reduce their crop acreage. The 1965 legislation thus focuses on maintaining farm income rather than farm prices, making substantial use of direct subsidies or their equivalent to support farm income while market prices are kept low for the benefit of domestic users and exporters.

How successful the Food and Agricultural Act will be in solving the problems of commercial agriculture remains to be seen. It does, however, appear to mark the demise of the old political maxim against direct payments to farmers. On the other hand, the rejection as a "bread tax" of the Johnson administration's attempt to shift much of the cost of the wheat program to consumers indicates that political potency still remains in the maxim that price supports should not increase food costs.

[56] See Dale E. Hathaway, "Farmers and the Great Society," *Challenge*, XIV (Nov.–Dec., 1965), 24–27; and *Congressional Quarterly Weekly Report*, XXIII (Oct. 15, 1965), 2079–2081.

GOVERNMENT AND WELFARE

Governments in the United States, especially in the twentieth century, have adopted a broad range of welfare programs directly concerned with protection and promotion of the social and economic security of individual citizens. The necessity and the propriety of governmental action to enhance and assure individual security is generally accepted. The big question today is to what extent government should protect the individual. On this point there is still much conflict between liberal and conservative, businessman and union official, the needy and the affluent, rural and urban dwellers.

Although there is not complete agreement as to which governmental programs fit into the welfare category, it seems fair to include the following: old age, survivors' and disability insurance; old age assistance; aid to the needy blind, disabled, and dependent children; workmen's compensation; unemployment compensation; vocational rehabilitation; child welfare services; distribution of surplus farm commodities to school lunch programs and the needy; veterans' pensions and education and medical services; railroad retirement; public health programs; medical care for the aged; public housing; public education; and some aspects of the programs to aid economically depressed areas.[1] The total cost of public welfare programs in 1964 was over $71 billion, divided about equally between the national government and the state and local governments (see comparative figures in Table Eight-1).

[1] See Ida C. Merriam, "Social Welfare Expenditures, 1963–1964," *Social Security Bulletin,* XVII (October, 1964), 3–7 for a complete listing of welfare programs.

TABLE EIGHT-1

SOCIAL WELFARE EXPENDITURES
BY PROGRAM CATEGORIES AND LEVEL OF GOVERNMENT
SELECTED YEARS 1934–1964
(in millions)*

	1934–35	1939–40	1944–45	1949–50	1954–55	1959–60	1963–64
Total—all expenditures	6,416.9	8,765.9	8,860.1	23,007.6	32,316.7	52,396.5	71,008.6
Social insurance	383.9	1,217.7	1,418.5	4,873.0	9,854.2	19,294.5	26,846.0
Federal	98.9	354.9	759.8	2,028.1	6,404.7	14,297.9	20,523.0
State and local	285.0	862.8	658.7	2,844.9	3,449.5	4,996.6	6,323.0
Public assistance	2,997.6	3,598.7	1,030.5	2,396.2	3,003.0	4,101.1	5,564.8
Federal	2,373.7	2,245.9	420.1	1,103.2	1,504.2	2,116.9	3,161.0
State and local	623.9	1,352.8	610.4	1,393.0	1,498.8	1,984.2	2,403.8
Health and medical programs	434.4	681.7	2,331.0	2,087.1	3,054.4	4,471.7	6,077.9
Federal	50.1	159.9	1,775.6	586.0	1,174.4	1,748.4	2,742.3
State and local	384.3	521.8	555.1	1,501.1	1,880.0	2,723.3	3,335.6
Other welfare programs	52.9	81.2	160.4	457.6	647.1	1,242.1	1,934.8
Federal	2.1	9.7	72.3	168.1	245.6	410.0	608.3
State and local	50.8	71.5	88.1	289.6	401.5	832.1	1,326.5
Veteran's programs	449.8	535.1	892.1	6,380.8	4,369.5	5,106.4	5,667.2
Federal	449.8	535.1	892.1	5,918.8	4,307.9	4,994.5	5,647.2
State and local	—	—	—	462.0	61.6	111.9	20.0
Education	2,098.3	2,647.3	3,017.3	6,698.3	11,299.2	18,003.9	24,647.0
Federal	132.9	162.3	161.0	180.8	521.6	1,014.8	2,207.0
State and local	1,965.4	2,485.0	2,856.5	6,517.5	10,777.6	16,989.1	22,440.0
Housing	—	4.2	10.4	14.5	89.3	176.8	270.9
Federal	—	4.2	10.4	14.5	74.7	143.6	207.4
State and local	—	—	—	—	14.6	33.2	63.5
Total federal	3,107.5	3,472.0	4,091.3	9,999.5	14,233.1	24,726.1	35,096.2
Total state and local	3,309.4	5,293.9	4,768.8	13,008.1	18,083.6	27,670.4	35,912.4
Total, all governments	6,416.9	8,765.9	8,860.1	23,007.6	32,316.7	52,396.5	71,008.6

* Derived from Merriam, op. cit., 5–7.

GROWTH OF THE WELFARE STATE

Aid to the poor, the needy, and the unfortunate was long considered to be mainly a local responsibility—something to be handled by local governments, private charitable organizations, or the family. This attitude was in line with the Elizabethan poor law system which was reproduced in seventeenth-century America and which continued to influence welfare organization and attitudes until the twentieth century. Public relief programs were typically mean and niggardly; assistance was given sparingly and its acceptance was made distasteful and demeaning to the individual. One often had to swear that he was a pauper in order to qualify for help.

In the nineteenth century relief for the needy and the unfortunate often took the form of almshouses, or poorhouses, in which all those needing help—orphans, the aged, the blind, the feeble-minded—were lodged together. Such care was favored as being both cheaper to provide and less conducive to idleness and pauperism than "outdoor relief" (aid to the needy in their own homes). The poor, it was thought, were in necessitous circumstances because of their own faults or weaknesses; they were improvident, lazy, shiftless, immoral, or given to vice of some sort. Therefore, their distress and misery was their proper due. If relief were given too generously, or if its receipt were made too pleasant, it would only create further (and worse) problems because some people would prefer living off the government to supporting themselves.

Contributing to such attitudes and action toward the poor and needy were a number of factors. The traditions of individual initiative and self-reliance, together with the view that America was a land of opportunity, fostered the belief that anyone who was thrifty and willing to work hard could secure a minimum of economic security for himself and his family. From the Puritan ethic and frontier individualism came the notion that the individual, not society, was responsible for his own fate. In the second half of the nineteenth century, when industrialism and the closing of the frontier reduced opportunities for self-help and self-employment, the philosophies of Social Darwinism and laissez faire economics provided rationales to support hard attitudes and inaction toward the poor.

Action by the state governments to help the needy and unfortunate began in the second and third quarters of the nineteenth century. The local approach to welfare caused public dissatisfaction with the inadequate care provided for such groups as orphaned children, the blind, the deaf and dumb, and the mentally disturbed (or the "insane," in the language of the time). Some of the states began to provide institutional care for such groups, setting up orphans' homes, insane asylums, schools for the deaf and dumb, and so on. Not until the twentieth century did the states begin to provide for assistance to persons outside of institutions. Two landmark statutes here are a 1907 Wisconsin law providing aid to the blind in their own homes and a 1923 act in Montana authorizing the payment of old age pensions. By 1930 state activities in this vein had so expanded that twenty states gave aid to the blind, twelve to the needy aged, and forty-five to mothers with dependent children (a federal grant-in-aid program was a stimulant here). Some of these programs were poorly financed, however, and others only authorized the local governments to take action. Consequently, only a portion of those in the needy groups were actually benefited.

Welfare activity by the national government was generally confined to assisting impoverished veterans, Indians, and merchant seamen until the 1930's. This situation, plus the limited character of state action, meant that the main responsibility for aiding the poor and needy continued to rest with the local governments up to the time of the New Deal. The Great Depression and the New Deal mark the "passing of the old order" in welfare, as in many other areas of government activity, and during the last three decades there has been a proliferation and expansion of public welfare programs. These programs are not limited to relief of the poor and needy but, frequently, they seek to protect people generally against economic insecurity and distress. The notion that welfare programs are beyond the constitutional or political concern of the national government has been rejected and there are now very few welfare programs without national participation. Only a modest portion of the total cost of welfare programs is currently borne by the local governments.

The welfare programs now operative have not come about according to any well thought out, systematic plan or because of the acceptance of a particular ideology. Rather, they have been established, modified, and extended, with passing time, as piecemeal and pragmatic responses to particular needs or problems—old age, unemployment, sickness, loss of family support, and the like—and the group interests centered around them. We turn now to an examination of some of the factors contributing to the growth of welfare activity.

First, the transformation of the United States from a rural agrarian society to an urban industrial society, well under way by the end of the nineteenth century, has had a tremendous influence on individual and society alike. The self-sufficiency of the individual has been eroded and he is often confronted with problems with which he, alone and unaided cannot cope. Since most individuals depend upon wages and salaries for their income and livelihood, unemployment, underemployment or "forced retirement" may become their lot when job opportunities are reduced by automation, shifts in consumer demand, or economic recession. This set of circumstances has produced demands for government action to protect people against loss of jobs and income when they could not protect themselves.

Second, the number of old people in our society is increasing both absolutely and relatively as advances in medical science and care enable more people to live longer. In 1900, there were 3.1 million people (4.1 per cent of the population) over 65 years of age in the United States; in 1963 there were 17.3 million people (9.3 per cent of the population) in that age bracket.[2] These older people generally have lower incomes, higher rates of sickness, and greater medical costs than the rest of the population; without governmental assistance they are often unable to meet the costs of living. A commonly expressed view has been that people should provide for their security in old age by saving. But, as Sumner Schlicter has remarked: "The usual method by which men have provided for their old age has never been thrift—it has been by having plenty of children and expecting the children to help the parents."[3] Low incomes while working, large families, unemployment, disability, medical expenses, social pressures to spend—all these make it difficult for people to save. They cannot be fairly classified as forms of improvidence.

But what now of family responsibility for the aged and the needy and improvident, whether aged or not? American culture traditionally held that the family had primary responsibility here. Moreover, the cohesiveness of the family, together with the rural or small-town residence of most people, actually enabled the family in a great many instances to provide minimum support (at least) for its needy or improvident members. But this has changed as urbanization, industrial-

[2] Department of Health, Education and Welfare, *Health, Education, and Welfare Trends,* 1963 Edition (Washington, D.C.: Government Printing Office, n.d.), 3.

[3] Sumner Schlicter, "The Pressing Problem of Old-Age Security," *The New York Times Magazine,* October 16, 1949, p. 9.

ization, and greater population mobility have altered the nature of the family. The modern urban family is less able, and often less willing, to take care of aged parents or relatives. The smaller size of families and of urban houses or apartments have made older people less acceptable as additional family members. And many older people would rather not be dependent upon their children for support. Government is now called upon to do what the family once did.

A fourth cause of expanding public welfare activity is changing attitudes toward the needy and unfortunate. Many people have come to believe that poverty and economic distress are often the result of poor or unfavorable social and economic conditions and other matters beyond the control of the individual, and not just laziness, immorality, or sheer improvidence as was once believed. Empirical investigation and research and actual experience and work with the poor and needy have led to greater understanding of their problems, and the actual causes of them. Knowledge is often a good antidote for myth and copybook maxims.[4] The Great Depression, which left ten to twelve million people unemployed in the winter of 1932–33, clearly revealed that people were not always masters of their destinies. The Depression also demonstrated that aid to the needy and unfortunate was beyond the capacity of local governments and charities alone to provide.

Fifth, attitudes on the use of government to provide security against economic distress and dislocation have also changed. People have always been motivated by a desire for security and, when other means have proved unavailing, they have turned to government. As local and state governments have appeared unable, or unwilling, to provide the desired level of security, recourse has been to the national government. Most people now believe that the guarantee of individual security through welfare programs is a proper function of American government, although questions about how much protection, in what form, by which level of government in a given case, still are open to debate.

Sixth, as the nation has become wealthier, or more "affluent," and as more people have shared in this affluence, the conscience of the "haves" has been more greatly disturbed by the existence of "have nots" who clearly do not share in the general prosperity. As the country's capacity to provide welfare assistance has increased, it has become morally imperative to aid the unfortunate. With respect to capacity to provide aid, a recent study indicates that a close relationship exists between the wealth of the various American states and their rates of

[4] Robert R. Bremmer, *From the Depths: The Discovery of Poverty in the United States* (New York: New York University Press, 1956), esp. chs. 8 and 9.

spending on welfare programs. "The level of public social welfare programs in the American states," it is concluded, "seems to be more a function of socio-economic factors, especially per capita income [than of such political factors as inter-party competition]."[5]

Finally, the Western European nations have usually been in advance of the United States in the adoption of social welfare legislation. The European experience seems to have provided a model, an inspiration, and an argument for American proponents of welfare programs.

THE POLITICS OF WELFARE

Although newly proposed welfare programs may be highly productive of controversy, once adopted they usually become rather quickly and widely, if not universally, accepted. This situation may result because the arguments against proposed welfare legislation are of necessity hypothetical—if this bill is passed such and such will happen. When the legislation is enacted, and the predicted evils do not come to pass, the arguments of the opposition lose their force and it becomes difficult to mobilize further opposition.[6] Political attacks on established welfare programs are apt to be both unpopular and unrewarded at the polls, as Senator Goldwater discovered in the 1964 presidential campaign. An especially illustrative anecdote concerns the 1949 New York senatorial race between Herbert Lehman and John Foster Dulles. Dulles waged a strenuous campaign against the "Welfare State," which was supported by Lehman, the decisive winner in the election. In a speech a few weeks later, Governor Thomas E. Dewey (Rep., N.Y.) remarked that "it must have been a very clumsy Republican" who tried to gain votes by attacking the welfare state. "Anyone who thinks an attack on the fundamental idea of security and welfare is appealing to the people," he added, "is living in the Middle Ages."[7]

But, despite the general acceptance and lack of controversy over established welfare programs, there is still much room for struggle and conflict in the welfare field. With regard to existing programs, conflict may occur on such matters as allocation of costs, amount and distribution of benefits, and organization and methods of administration. And,

[5] Richard E. Dawson and James A. Robinson, "Inter-Party Competition, Economic Variables, and Welfare Policies in the American States," *Journal of Politics,* XXV (May, 1963), 289.

[6] Cf. John Kenneth Galbraith, *Economics and the Art of Controversy* (New York: Vintage Books, 1959), ch. VI.

[7] Taken from *ibid.,* 73–74.

of course, sharp controversy may be stimulated by proposals for new welfare programs—medical care for the aged financed through social security and general federal aid to public education are contemporary examples. Conflicts over welfare policy may emanate from economic, ideological, and political differences among individuals and groups.

Lower income groups are usually strong supporters of welfare programs, especially when they benefit directly from such programs. Upper income groups often oppose such programs because they are better able to provide for themselves, dislike the higher taxes associated with welfare programs, and are likely to have conservative or individualistic philosophies. Although they are more numerous, the lower income groups frequently are poorly organized or inarticulate politically; thus the balance of power on welfare programs often rests with middle income groups and their spokesmen. Middle-class support is generally regarded as having been a significant force behind the enactment of the Social Security Act of 1935. Public education has also received much support from middle-class groups, who place a high value on enlarged and improved educational opportunities. On the other hand, public housing programs which primarily benefit low income groups have not received much active support from the middle class, which has helped to keep such programs at a minimum. The middle- and upper-class supporters of urban renewal are typically more concerned with the elimination of blighted areas than with finding or providing adequate housing for those displaced by renewal activities, who are often Negro as well as poor. This has caused some critics of urban renewal, including former supporters, to label it "Negro removal."

Further, it can be demonstrated that the poorest, the neediest, the most deprived groups in American society, the inhabitants of what Michael Harrington calls "the other America," often have received little or no benefit from welfare programs. Many are excluded from coverage under social security and unemployment compensation. Or they may lack the knowledge and awareness to look after their interests. And, as Harrington states, "the poor are politically invisible. . . . The people of the other America do not, by far and large, belong to unions, to fraternal organizations, or to political parties. They are without lobbies of their own; they put forward no legislative program. As a group, they are atomized. They have no face; they have no voice."[8] Many of them are not really a part of the political system.

[8] Michael Harrington, *The Other America* (Baltimore: Penguin Books, 1963), 14. And see generally chs. 1, 9.

Conflict over welfare policy may also occur between rural and urban interests. Urban dwellers in our modern, industrial society are both more susceptible to and more aware of conditions of dependency and insecurity than are the inhabitants of rural areas and small towns. Where depressed economic conditions may mean lower incomes for the latter, it often involves a total loss of income for the urban worker, who understandably seeks government protection against such a contingency. However, many farmers and small-town businessmen are hostile, or at best indifferent, toward welfare programs which appear of most benefit to urban groups and which run counter to their traditionally conservative, low tax ideology. The opposition or indifference of rural small town groups to such programs also derives from the needs and the problems of urban life, which are outside the frame of reference through which they view the world.

Rural and small-town interests have often been over-represented in the state legislatures and they have used their disproportionate political representation to oppose "costly and unnecessary" welfare programs. In turn, urban groups have gone to the national government for the social services they could not secure at the state level.[9] Many people believe that the state legislatures will become more favorably inclined toward welfare legislation as, in pursuance of *Baker v. Carr* (1962) and subsequent Supreme Court decisions,[10] they are reapportioned to give equitable (i.e., greater) representation to urban areas.

Pressure groups, whether motivated by material interests, ideology, or whatever, are much concerned with welfare policy. Organized labor is a general supporter of welfare programs whereas general opposition comes from many business groups, especially the Chamber of Commerce and the National Association of Manufacturers. They tend to oppose most strongly welfare programs involving increased business payroll taxes. Ideological groups such as Americans for Democratic Action (liberal) and the Committee for Constitutional Government (conservative) make their views known on a wide range of issues. Functional groups frequently limit their attention to a particular area of welfare policy. Schoolteachers want federal aid to education, real estate interests oppose public housing programs, medical doctors op-

[9] Charles R. Adrian and Charles Press, *The American Political Process* (New York: McGraw-Hill, 1965), 60–62. Cf. Thomas R. Dye, "Malapportionment and Public Policy in the States," *Journal of Politics,* XXVII (August, 1965), 586–601.

[10] Especially *Reynolds v. Sims, 377* U.S. 533 (1964), in which the Court held that representation in *both* houses of a state legislature must be equitably based on population to square with the Fourteenth Amendment.

pose some medical care programs. Associations of state and local welfare officials attempt to influence the substance and administration of national programs in their areas; public health, vocational rehabilitation, public education.

As the number of aged people has increased in recent decades, and as their economic problems have intensified, old age groups have been organized to seek governmental assistance in the form of old age pensions, and medical and other benefits. In the 1930's the Townsend Movement (which wanted $200 a month for everyone over sixty), the National Annuity League, the American Pension Union, Inc., and a variety of other groups strove to represent and promote the interests of the aged.[11] Their efforts were a factor in the enactment of the Social Security Act. Today, following a period of relative quiescence after World War II, there is a resurgence in organized activity in behalf of older citizens. In 1959 a Senate subcommittee estimated that two million persons belonged to "Golden Age" clubs and other organizations for older persons which strive to improve their social and economic status by political action. Concerning such developments, Cohen states:

> While it is evident that most older people retain group loyalties developed early in life, there is, indeed, some indication of the appearance of a subculture—a self-identification among older people based on recognition of common problems of preserving income security without the indignity of means tests, of retaining the social status afforded to autonomous, participating members of the community, and seeking meaningful opportunities to use the retirement years.[12]

The aged thus represent an important dimension of the politics of welfare.

In Congress, action on welfare programs is clearly affected by voting differences between the two parties. Generally speaking, the Democratic party has been significantly stronger than the Republican party in its support of welfare legislation. Although the Republicans have accepted existing programs such as social security—indeed, this program was significantly expanded during the Eisenhower administration—they are more likely than not to oppose the adoption of new welfare programs or major liberalization of existing ones. In 1964 in

[11] Abraham Holtzman, *The Townsend Movement* (New York: Bookman Associates, 1963), presents an insightful and interesting account of "pension politics," especially in the 1930's.
[12] Wilbur J. Cohen, in *ibid.*, 15–16.

322

the House, for example, a majority of Democrats voted in favor of legislation on food stamps, poverty, library services, housing, and education. They were opposed by a majority of House Republicans on all but housing. In the Senate a majority of Democrats favored legislation on poverty, medicare, housing, and Appalachia. Majorities of Republicans opposed them on the first two issues and united with them on the last two (housing and Appalachia).[13] Greater Democratic support for welfare legislation is also confirmed by the *Congressional Quarterly's* analysis of party voting on legislation which enlarges the responsibilities of the federal government. Using key roll call votes on legislation that would increase federal action (e.g., area redevelopment, aid to education, public housing, poverty, medicare, manpower retraining, Appalachia), the *Congressional Quarterly* found the Democrats generally supported, and the Republicans generally opposed, a larger federal role, as Table Eight-2 indicates.

TABLE EIGHT–2

CONGRESSIONAL PARTY VOTING,
LARGER FEDERAL ROLE*

	86th Congress (1959–1961)		87th Congress (1961–1963)		88th Congress (1963–1965)	
	Dem.	Rep.	Dem.	Rep.	Dem.	Rep.
Both houses	74%	19%	75%	24%	75%	40%
Senate	74%	27%	65%	26%	79%	47%
House	74%	17%	78%	24%	74%	40%

* Data are from *ibid.*, XIX (October 20, 1961), 1751; XX (December 28, 1962), 2290; and XXII (October 23, 1964), 2549.

The parties, then, clearly have different viewpoints on welfare legislation although the difference is obscured somewhat because some Democrats, especially Southern Democrats, often oppose welfare legislation and some Republicans, particularly "liberal Eastern" Republicans, often support welfare programs. Nonetheless, most observers agree that the enactment of welfare legislation wanted by President Johnson during the 89th Congress was greatly facilitated by the large Democratic majorities in both houses (especially because these included larger numbers of Northern, i.e., non-Southern, Democrats).

Political conflict on welfare policy today can usefully be conceptualized as centering on three general issues: What is the extent of the

[13] *Congressional Quarterly Weekly Report*, XXII (October 23, 1964), 2549

individual's responsibility for his own welfare? What level of government should handle welfare activity? What form should welfare assistance take? Here as elsewhere in political life, conflict stems from differences in the ideological and material interests of groups and individuals, some of which we have already mentioned.

The view that the individual and the family have primary responsibility for meeting economic and security needs continues to be expressed.[14] Conservatives and traditionalists still are likely to contend that welfare programs should be kept at a minimum because they reduce individual initiative and self-reliance, increase the recipient's dependency on the government, and generally weaken the moral fabric of society. (They also increase the cost of government.) In response, it is argued that welfare programs increase the freedom of the individual and enlarge his opportunities by helping to eliminate such barriers to individual action as ignorance, disease, disability, and low income. Moreover, because of the interdependency of society, welfare programs are said to promote general social and political stability and well-being by reducing privation and misery. There is also the humanitarian argument that government must, because it can, protect the poor, the weak, and the unfortunate.

Conflict also occurs over the proper roles of the national government and the state and local governments in welfare activity. Some argue that the state and local governments should be primary here, both because welfare was traditionally their responsibility and because decentralization is necessary to preserve personal freedom and maintain flexibility in government action. Such contentions, often made by conservative and business groups, sometimes amount to arguments for minimal, ineffective, or no welfare action. The states often lack adequate resources and, further, may be politically unable or unwilling to act. State executives and legislatures are often more conservative than their national counterparts. As one critic hostile to the states comments: ". . . state governments are notoriously weighted in the direction of caution, pinchpenny economics, and indifference to the plight of the urban millions."[15] The proponents of national action argue that only the national government has the needed resources, the willingness to act, and the ability to adequately cope with the problems of insecurity, which are mostly national. They believe the need for action outweighs whatever risks centralized action may entail.

[14] A splendid example is Barry Goldwater, *The Conscience of a Conservative* (New York: Hillman Books, 1960), ch. 8.

[15] Harrington, *op. cit.,* 182. And see William Anderson, Clara Penniman, and Edward W. Weidner, *Government in the Fifty States* (New York: Holt, Rinehart and Winston, 1960), 448.

324

A third cause of conflict is the administration of welfare programs. Shall they be handled on a grant basis or on the insurance principle? Shall payments be made on the basis of need as determined by a means test or shall benefits be available to all in a given category, as those over 65, regardless of need? In the case of cooperative programs, to what extent should the national government supervise state and local action? Middle-class groups usually favor the insurance principle, as in social security, because it connotes thrift and paying one's own way and because it avoids the stigma of charity or the "dole." (As in: "No self-respecting American would accept a government dole.") Means tests for determining eligibility for benefits are opposed by liberals, who view them as degrading to the individual and as discouraging the acceptance of aid. Conservatives often favor means tests, perhaps because they see them as a way of holding down the size and cost of welfare programs and of preventing "freeloading" on the government.

The way in which these conflicts are resolved varies from one area of welfare to another, and from one time to another, depending in each case upon the balance of strength among the groups and interests involved. In education broad governmental action is both accepted and expected whereas real estate and other group interests have been successful in keeping public housing programs minimal. Most welfare programs have been set up on a cooperative national-state-local basis, but general assistance and Old Age, Survivors, and Disability Insurance are important exceptions. National aid to higher education has been more readily accepted than general aid to elementary and secondary public schools. Most of the welfare programs directed against economic insecurity because of old age, disability, or other dependency provide only a minimum of protection for the individual, since traditional attitudes continue to influence action here.

THE SOCIAL SECURITY ACT PROGRAMS

Whereas previously national participation in welfare activity had been more or less peripheral, limited, or temporary, with the adoption of the Social Security Act in 1935 ". . . the constitutional dedication of federal power to the general welfare began a new phase of national history."[16] The Social Security Act represents a permanent, large-scale, and extensive commitment of national power and resources to providing people with a measure of protection against social and economic

[16] Arthur M. Schlesinger, Jr., *The Coming of the New Deal* (Boston: Houghton Mifflin, 1959), 315.

insecurity and privation. The act can also be viewed as a response by the New Deal to the underprivileged and disadvantaged groups in American society, to that third of the nation which President Roosevelt described as "ill-housed, ill-clad, and ill-nourished."

The Social Security Act of 1935, and the various amendments made to it since that time, provides for four major programs: (1) a national system of old age insurance, financed by national taxes and administered by the national government, (2) a system of federal grants-in-aid to help the states carry on public assistance programs, (3) a nationwide but state-operated system of unemployment compensation (or insurance), and (4) federal grants to the states to help them provide maternal and child welfare services. Each of these programs is directed at a different aspect of insecurity and dependency and each follows a somewhat different approach to the provision of assistance.

Because the Social Security Act constitutes a major change in the direction of national policy, we shall list some of the factors contributing to this decision. First, President Roosevelt and most of the members of his administration believed in the necessity and propriety of national action to protect people against insecurity and destitution. Roosevelt clearly rejected Herbert Hoover's belief that federal relief activity was incompatible with American individualism and that the protection of individuals against economic distress and privation was a state and local responsibility. Second, the widespread unemployment and privation caused by the Great Depression was far beyond what could be adequately coped with by voluntary agencies and the state and local governments. It is estimated that a third of American families were on relief at one time or another during the Depression.[17] Third, a variety of temporary relief programs started by the New Deal emphasized the national nature of economic insecurity and destitution and also caused people to become accustomed to national action in this field. Among the various New Deal programs were the Federal Emergency Relief Administration, the Civilian Conservation Corps, the Civil Works Administration and the Works Progress Administration (WPA).[18] Fourth, by 1935 President Roosevelt, most of his administration, most members of Congress, and a great many citizens believed that permanent national action was required to effectively combat

[17] Edwin E. Witte, "Organized Labor and Social Security," in Milton Derber and Edwin Young, eds., *Labor and the New Deal* (Madison: University of Wisconsin Press, 1957), 247.

[18] On the WPA, see Sherwin D. Smith, "Boondoggle That Helped 38 Million People," *The New York Times Magazine,* May 2, 1965, pp. 38 ff.

welfare problems. There was, of course, opposition to the Social Security Act, coming especially from organized business and conservative groups, such as the American Liberty League and the American Bar Association. In Congress there was Republican and conservative opposition. But when all was said and the chips were down, when constituency opinion was assessed, and when considerations of societal need and personal political survival were weighed, the bill was passed by a vote of 371 to 33 in the House and 76 to 6 in the Senate. The Social Security Act programs have since become an accepted part of the fabric of American society.

Old Age, Survivors, and Disability Insurance

This is the only program established by the Social Security Act which is handled solely by the national government. Old Age, Survivors, and Disability Insurance (OASDI) provides protection to workers and their families, by the payment of cash benefits, against the loss of income because of old age retirement, death, or disability. The program is commonly referred to as "social security."

More than 90 per cent of the labor force is now covered by OASDI. Coverage is compulsory for most persons but it is optional for the self-employed. Employees of religious, charitable, and private educational organizations, along with employees of state and local governments, may be covered by voluntary agreement; and many have been brought under the program. The primary groups now excluded from coverage by law are railroad workers and federal civilian employees, who are under separate retirement programs; self-employed medical doctors, who have rejected coverage; and some of the lowest income groups in the nation. In the latter category are self-employed persons who earn less than $400 a year; domestic workers who earn less than $50 a quarter from any one employer; and farm workers who earn less than $150 annually from any one employer. Thus some of those who are at the very bottom of the income ladder, and are least able to protect themselves, are excluded from income protection under OASDI.

The program is financed by a tax on payrolls which is paid in equal amounts by the employee and his employer. In 1966 each paid 4.2 per cent of the first $6,600 of wages paid the employee, with the rate being scheduled to rise to 5.65 per cent each in 1987. (These rates include the medicare tax added in 1965.) The self-employed, for whom there are obviously no employers to contribute, pay a higher tax. The tax monies paid for OASDI are placed in a separate trust fund, out of which benefits and other program costs are paid. No money from general government revenue is spent for the program. The program is administered by the Social Security Administration of the Department of Health, Education and Welfare, which keeps a record of the payments made into the program on behalf of each employee, determines eligibility for benefits, and pays the benefits. The agency operates through eleven regional offices and more than six hundred district offices scattered throughout the country.

The structure of benefits under OASDI includes payments for old age retirement, survivors of covered workers, and disability. (In 1965 OASDI was expanded to include hospital and medical care benefits for those over 65). The amount of benefits paid to a worker depends upon the amount he has paid into the program, which in turn depends upon his earnings during his working career. "This accords with a firmly ingrained belief on the part of the American people that a man should receive rewards in accordance with his individual efforts and contributions."[19] Eligibility for retirement benefits begins at age 65 (or 62, if the worker is willing to take a reduced benefit payment), the specific amount depending upon his contribution plus need as measured by family dependents. The monthly benefit (in 1966) for a worker retiring at 65 ranges from $44 to $136. If the worker has a wife over 62, or children under 18, or a dependent husband over 62, the monthly benefit increases for each dependent up to a maximum of $309. Survivors' benefits are paid to the dependents of a deceased worker who are under eighteen (twenty-two if they are enrolled in college) or above retirement age. Disability benefits are paid to workers who are unable to work for an indefinite period because of physical or mental disability.[20]

During fiscal 1963 benefits totaling $15 billion were paid to 18.6 million beneficiaries (14.4 million retirement; 3.4 million survivors, and 0.8 million disability). Retirement benefits went to around 70 per cent of persons over age 62. The average retirement benefit for a worker was $73 a month; when both the worker and his spouse received benefits, the average was $128.70 monthly.[21] Although OASDI does

[19] Charles I. Schottland, *The Social Security Program in the United States* (New York: Appleton-Century Crofts, 1963), 68.

[20] For further information on social security benefits, see the Department of Health, Education and Welfare's best seller, *Your Social Security* (Washington, D.C.: Government Printing Office).

[21] Department of Health, Education and Welfare, *Annual Report, 1963*, p. 9. Unless otherwise noted data on welfare costs and benefits in this section are from this source.

provide people with a minimum level of income protection, the level of benefits is widely regarded as too low and there is continual pressure on Congress to increase it. Those who want adequate retirement income must combine OASDI with income from savings, private pension programs, or part-time employment.

Two aspects of the OASDI benefit payment system need to be mentioned. First, benefits are paid out under the program as a matter of right; they do not depend on the discretion of administrators (benefits, however, may be reduced or denied to those between 65 and 72 because of income they receive from employment which they choose to engage in after retirement age); they are not charity. This arrangement is regarded as of much psychological importance to the individual recipient.

> Since the security he derives under the program grows out of his own work, the person who is covered views his social security benefits as an earned right. He can feel good about taking his benefits, just as he does about accepting wages for the work he does; he has earned the right to both.[22]

Thus, OASDI avoids the social stigma attached to charity or the "dole."

Second, practically every gainfully employed person makes contributions to the programs, and so becomes entitled to benefits, resulting in widespread support for OASDI. This was envisaged by President Roosevelt who insisted that there be employee contributions. As he later explained: "We put those payroll contributions there so as to give the contributors a legal, moral, and political right to collect their pensions and their unemployment benefits. With those taxes in there, no damn politician can ever scrap my social security program."[23] Labor groups, consumer groups, veterans' groups, and others have strongly supported the program and opposed hostile or unsound changes in it.

Public Assistance

Under public assistance the national government makes grants-in-aid to the states to help them aid four categories of needy people: the aged, the blind, dependent children, and (since 1950) the permanently and totally disabled. (Grants are also made for medical care for the aged.) The public assistance programs differ from OASDI in that they are financed from general tax revenues, they are based on need, and they involve federal-state-local cooperation.

[22] *Ibid.,* 6.
[23] Quoted in Schlesinger, *op. cit.,* 308–309.

The national government participates rather heavily in the financing of these programs, federal grants helping the states to meet both administrative and benefit payment costs. In 1963 the national government provided 60 per cent of the $4.2 billion paid out in benefits by the states under the public assistance programs. (The specific proportions ranged from 47 per cent in California to 82 per cent in Mississippi.) Under the programs for the needy aged, blind, and permanently and totally disabled, the national government will provide 29/35 of the first thirty-five dollars of a benefit payment, plus half of the next thirty-five dollars (or $46.50 out of a total of $70). Any amount above seventy dollars is provided solely by the state government. However, if the per capita income of a state is below the national average, the national government will put up 65 per cent of the second thirty-five dollars (or $51.75 of $70). This system of matching represents a compromise between the equal matching favored by the wealthier states and the larger federal contributions favored by the poorer states. It is designed to help the poorer states make payments that are more nearly adequate and more nearly equal to those of the higher income states.

The federal grants for public assistance are administered by the Welfare Administration, which is another part of the Department of Health, Education and Welfare. To be eligible for federal grants the state programs must conform to certain nationally prescribed standards. Here it can be observed that whether the federal requirements for a particular program are "federal controls" (bad) or "national standards" (good) depends more upon the interests or ideological position of the judgment-passer than on the intrinsic nature of the requirements. Among the requirements for public assistance grants are administration of the program by a single state agency, selection of agency personnel on a merit basis, statewide operation of the program, state financial participation (states can require local governments to put up some but not all of the state matching funds), and reasonable standards of need and eligibility. Within the framework of the national standards, the states have much discretion with respect to levels of assistance, definitions of need, and other matters. What the various states do in the way of public assistance activity is shaped by such factors as historical background, local attitudes and customs, group pressures, and economic conditions. In general, northern and industrial states have been more generous in coverage and in benefits paid than southern and agrarian states. In the former, labor and other groups supporting welfare programs are stronger, the ability of the state to pay is greater, and rural attitudes are less prevalent.

Old age assistance (OAA) was for a long time after 1935 the largest of the public assistance programs. Along with OASDI, it represented a two-pronged attack on the problem of old age economic dependency. Old age assistance provides benefits for the needy aged who are either ineligible for OASDI payments or who receive payments which are excessively low. In 1963 several hundred thousand aged people received both OASDI and old age assistance payments. Since the coverage of OASDI has been expanded since 1955, the number of recipients of old age assistance has declined. In 1963 old age assistance payments averaged $77 a month on a national basis with state averages ranging from $35 in Mississippi to $109 in Minnesota.

Aid to families with dependent children (AFDC) has become the largest of the public assistance programs in the number of people aided (3.9 million in 1963). This program provides financial aid for the maintenance of dependent children in the home of a relative (usually the mother) because of need created by the death, continued absence, or incapacity of a parent (usually the father). The rationale of the program has been stated in this manner:

> The purpose . . . is to enable needy children who are deprived of parental support and services they need for health and development, to assure to them an opportunity to grow up in their own family setting, to receive an education that will help them to realize their capacities, and to share in neighborhood and community living. In these ways the program supports and strengthens family life.[24]

In 1962 payments were also authorized when the need of the child was caused by parental unemployment. Unemployed fathers had been "deserting" their families so they would become eligible for aid. Average AFDC payments per family in 1963 ranged from $36 monthly in Mississippi to $199 monthly in Illinois.

The assistance programs for the needy blind and permanently and totally disabled have caused little controversy since their establishment. Most people would agree there is a clear need to help people in these categories, although this should not be taken to mean that levels of assistance are especially high. They are not. In 1963 monthly payments averaged $81 for the blind and $75 for the disabled. Many of the disabled now provided for by this program will be covered by OASDI in the future.

Although it is not part of the system of public assistance programs,

[24] Department of Health, Education, and Welfare, *Public Assistance under the Social Security Act* (Washington, D.C.: Government Printing Office, 1961), 4.

a few comments are in order concerning "general assistance" or "relief": programs of assistance for needy persons financed by the state and local governments, paying benefits in cash or kind. General assistance covers those needy persons not included under public assistance (or sometimes those for whom such assistance is inadequate). There is no federal participation. Eligibility requirements and the amounts and kinds of aid vary widely from state to state and, especially in those states in which primary responsibility rests with the local governments, from locality to locality. What is done depends upon the resources and prevailing attitudes in the particular state or locality. Demands on limited local funds for police and fire protection, education, roads, and other needs may leave little money for general assistance purposes. In general, standards are more stringent and benefits are lower than under the public assistance programs.

Unemployment Compensation

This program is designed to protect workers against loss of income during limited periods of unemployment resulting from fluctuations in the business cycle, technological changes, seasonal variations in employment, and other factors beyond the control of the individual worker. In addition to providing workers with a measure of economic security, unemployment compensation helps counteract fluctuations in the business cycle by adding to aggregate purchasing power in times of falling employment and restraining demand (through the taxes levied to finance it) during prosperous times. Our concern here is with unemployment compensation as an economic security program.

Although most of the Western European nations had set up unemployment compensation programs by the 1920's, strong interest in unemployment compensation did not develop in the United States until the Great Depression. Under pressures generated by that catastrophe some of the states began to consider proposals for unemployment compensation and, in 1932, the first program was enacted by the state of Wisconsin. (Its operation was suspended.) In the same year the American Federation of Labor abandoned its traditional opposition to public unemployment compensation and began to support government action. The states were reluctant to act, however, because of a desire not to burden their employers with a program which other states did not have and so put their businessmen at a competitive disadvantage. The lack of state action contributed to the inclusion of unemployment compensation provisions in the Social Security Act.

As adopted, the law provided for a federal-state cooperative program, with the major role therein being made available to the states. The law utilized a "tax-offset" device to "encourage" (opponents said "coerce") the states to establish unemployment compensation programs. A national payroll tax of 3.0 per cent (now 3.1 per cent) was levied on employers on the first $3,000 of wages paid each employee. However, if a state set up an unemployment compensation program which met federal standards and levied a payroll tax to finance it, employers in the state would be relieved of up to 90 per cent of the federal tax (2.7 per cent out of the 3.0 per cent). In short, the states and the employers within them had a choice of either a solely federal program or a program controlled principally by the state. With the benefits of inaction eliminated, the states began to act and by the end of 1937, all of them had adopted programs which received the approval of the U.S. Department of Labor.

The federal aspects of the unemployment compensation program are now handled by the Bureau of Employment Security in the Department of Labor. This agency sees that the state programs meet the federal standards, which are not very restrictive and permit the states much discretion, and determines the size of the grant-in-aid each state receives for the administration of its program. (This money is raised by the part of the federal tax—0.3 per cent—not offset by the state tax.) Each state has an "employment security agency" which administers the unemployment compensation program, usually with the aid of a number of local field offices which also customarily serve as employment offices.

Unemployment compensation is financed almost entirely by the payroll taxes on employers. The funds so raised by each state are deposited to its separate account in the U.S. Treasury, from which it may withdraw funds to pay benefits. Although the state tax was originally set at 2.7 per cent, most employers in most states pay less than that and in 1963 the state tax averaged around 2.4 per cent. During the 1950's the average was about 1.5 per cent.[25] These lower tax rates have been made possible by the use of experience (or merit) rating systems in most of the states. Under experience rating the payroll tax levied on each employer depends upon his employment experience —how many workers he has had unemployed in a given period. The logic here is that the individual employer "causes" unemployment in

[25] These and other numerical data on unemployment compensation come from U.S. Department of Labor, *Annual Report, 1963* (Washington, D.C.: Government Printing Office, 1963), 53–105.

his plant and will therefore be stimulated to prevent unemployment by the prospect of a lower tax in recognition of his efforts. Organized labor and many economists have opposed experience rating, contending that unemployment is often beyond the control of the employer and is most fairly treated as a social risk. In practice it appears that experience rating has often encouraged employer groups to work to keep benefits low and difficult to obtain in order to keep program costs, and their taxes, low.

Around 80 per cent of the wage and salary earners in the nation are now protected by unemployment compensation. All employees in firms of four or more who worked at least twenty weeks are covered. Usually excluded from coverage by law are farm workers, domestic workers, state and local government employees, employees of educational, charitable, and nonprofit organizations, and the self-employed. Employees in firms with less than four workers are excluded in half of the states. In comparison to OASDI, coverage under unemployment compensation is clearly narrower.

Benefits under the program are paid to workers as a matter of right; there is no test of need because of the insurance principle on which the program is based. To be eligible for benefits a person must have been engaged in covered employment for a specified period, be out of work through "no fault of his own," be registered with the state employment agency, and be willing to take a "suitable" job if it is available. The amount of benefits paid and the length of payment vary widely from one state to another. In 1963 the maximum weekly benefit ranged from $30 in Mississippi to $57.50 in New Mexico; minimum weekly benefits fell between $3 in Missouri and $25 in California. The specific amount paid to a worker depends upon his earnings while working: the larger the earnings the larger the benefits. The maximum benefit payment period runs from twenty-six to thirty-nine weeks in most states, with about two-thirds of them having twenty-six as the maximum. The large industrial states, in which organized labor is strongest, usually are the most generous in amount and length of benefit payment.

In its present form unemployment compensation is not adequate to deal with unemployment on a widespread and long-term basis. During the recessions of 1958 and 1961, both of which were regarded as "moderate," many workers exhausted their unemployment compensation benefits before there were able to return to their old jobs or find new jobs. This produced demands for national remedial action and in 1958 Congress authorized loans to the states to enable them to extend their benefit payment periods. Only seventeen states did so because the loans were repayable, a fact which diminished state interest considerably (as it usually does). In 1961 a different approach was followed so as to avoid state nonparticipation. This time the states were authorized to extend benefit periods for thirteen weeks (up to a maximum of thirty-nine) during the next two years, with the money to be recovered by an increase in the federal payroll tax. Under this arrangement all of the states decided to participate because they would all share in the cost whether they participated or not. The use of both the carrot and the stick produced better results.

Some persons and groups have urged either nationalization or greater national supervision of unemployment compensation. The AFL-CIO has advocated national legislation to expand its coverage, require the states to pay benefits equal to at least 50 per cent of wages, pay benefits for no less than thirty-nine weeks, and make eligibility requirements more uniform among the states. Legislation of this sort was supported by the Kennedy administration, but Congress took no action. The business community has opposed such legislation, arguing that each state knows its own needs best and should be permitted to develop a program in accord with local conditions, that the cost of proposals like those of the AFL-CIO would endanger the financial soundness of the program, and that the states are increasing benefits on their own. The states and their employment security agencies have an interest in the program as it now exists and have shown little enthusiasm for further federal controls; nor, indeed, has Congress. The struggle over the nature and scope of the unemployment compensation program continues in the state political arenas, where the advantage rests with business groups who, by and large, neither want to do away with the program nor expand it significantly.

Maternal and Child Welfare Programs

Title V of the Social Security Act authorizes the national government to make grants-in-aid to the states to help them establish or strengthen their maternal and child health services, services for crippled children, and child welfare services. (The original act also provided grants for vocational rehabilitation and public health services but these provisions have now been incorporated into other legislation.) No cash benefits are paid under these programs; rather, the national funds assist state health and welfare agencies in providing services. A large part of the funds expended pays the salaries of doctors, dentists, nurses, medical social workers, child welfare workers, and other trained professional people "who help give children a better start in life."[26]

About $75 million in grants-in-aid was distributed to the states in 1963 for these programs. The grants are administered by the Childrens' Bureau, a part of the Department of Health, Education and Welfare's Welfare Administration. The Bureau's staff also conducts studies of childrens' problems and helps the states to develop and improve their programs. To illustrate what is done under these programs, maternal and child welfare services include medical care for expectant mothers, school health programs, immunization programs, and clinics for the mentally retarded. Crippled childrens' services include diagnostic services, clinical treatment, hospital care, and therapy for children with speech and hearing defects, congenital heart disease, physical malformation, or other ailments and defects. In the category of child welfare services there are such activities as day care services for children of working mothers, efforts to prevent parental abuse of children, and arranging foster home or institutional care for children when necessary. Several million children received help under these programs in 1962, especially through school health programs. In many cases the services provided are not limited to needy or low income groups.

Recent Trends in Welfare

A number of trends in welfare activity in the last three decades have been mentioned already: the expanded scope of welfare activity, increasing participation by the national government, and concern with the problem of insecurity of people generally, not just the poor. Two other trends in welfare merit attention and will be briefly treated here.

First, there has been definite and continued movement toward the "professionalization" of welfare administration, the operation and direction of welfare agencies and programs more and more coming under the control of trained, skilled, professional welfare personnel. Schools of social work have been established in many universities to provide such personnel and welfare workers have their own professional associations and conferences. Agents of political machines and party "hacks" are disappearing from the welfare scene.

Second, and partly as a consequence of the above trend, greater attention is being devoted to the prevention of economic dependency

[26] Department of Health, Education and Welfare, *Social Security in the United States* (Washington, D.C.: Government Printing Office, 1959), 32.

336

and to the rehabilitation of needy persons to enable them, if at all possible, to become self-supporting (or, to convert them from tax-eaters to taxpayers, to use President Johnson's somewhat inelegant phraseology). Increased time and money is being given to research into the causes, problems, and possible solutions for economic dependency. The Public Welfare Amendments of 1962, enacted by Congress at the urging of the Kennedy administration, reflect this trend. The legislation increased federal funds for such purposes as rehabilitative services, child welfare services, the training of welfare personnel, and permitted the use of federal money in community work projects or on-the-job training for persons on welfare. The general thrust of the 1962 legislation is to reduce the long-term human and economic costs of dependency by increased effort and spending on rehabilitative activities. It is a "pay more now and save later" program.[27]

PUBLIC POLICY, POVERTY, AND DEPRESSED AREAS

It is well known to anyone who reads the newspapers and who is somewhat in touch with his environment that many people have not shared in the "affluence" which has been characteristic of the United States since World War II. If one-third of the nation is no longer "ill-housed, ill-clad, and ill-nourished," it is nonetheless true that millions of people are still afflicted with poverty. Much debate has occurred in recent years over what constitutes poverty and how many poverty-stricken people there are. Is poverty definable as a family income of less than $3,000 annually, or $4,000, or $2,000, or what? Do the poor number 35 million, or 40 to 50 million, or how many? Or is poverty only a state of mind?[28] There is a lot of room for statistical manipulation in this debate. Conclusions may often be influenced by ideological considerations, the conservative defining poverty more narrowly and consequently finding both less poverty and less need for government action than does the liberal. But, as one writer has concluded:

> . . . it would be a mistake to conclude from this [lack of agreement] that there is no evidence to demonstrate that tens of millions of people have incomes that are insufficient to provide minimum levels of living for this society. Most Americans would agree that a family

[27] *The New York Times,* July 27, 1962, p. 6.
[28] Herman P. Miller, "Statistics and Reality," *The New Leader,* XLVII, (March 30, 1964), 15–18.

is poor if its income is below the amount needed to qualify for public assistance. Many would also count as poor some families with incomes well above this level. . . . The 1960 Census data show that *at least 23.5 million people—one person out of eight in the United States—lives in a family with an annual income that is less than the amount needed to qualify for aid under the public assistance laws of each state.*[29]

Galbraith distinguishes between two kinds of poverty—case poverty and insular poverty.[30] Case poverty relates to the personal qualities or characteristics of the individuals involved. Some persons and families have been unable to participate fully in the general prosperity because of such things as old age, inadequate education, lack of needed job skills, poor health, racial discrimination, and the like, regardless of where they live—rural areas, small towns, large cities. Insular poverty manifests itself in "pockets of poverty" or "depressed areas," as in West Virginia, most of Appalachia, and many parts of rural America. Such areas are characterized by high rates of unemployment and under-employment because of the lack of adequate job opportunities for the population. (Some of these may, of course, lack job skills, etc., because the two poverty categories are not mutually exclusive.) This situation in turn may be the consequence of factors like technological change (as in the West Virginia coal mines), depletion of natural resources (the timber of upper Michigan), or the movement of industry to other regions (textile companies moving to the South from New England).[31]

Neither case poverty nor insular poverty can be adequately remedied by general use of fiscal and monetary policy to maintain prosperity and continuing economic growth (although anti-poverty action does presume the existence of general prosperity). The individual inadequacies characteristic of case poverty prevent such persons from sharing in continuing growth and prosperity. Nor will general growth and prosperity necessarily eliminate or correct the environmental factors causing insular poverty, as we noted in an earlier chapter. Consequently, if poverty is to be effectively prevented or remedied, other efforts will be needed. Since 1960 a variety of antipoverty programs have been started by the national government, the general effort now being referred to

[29] *Ibid.,* 17–18. (His italics.)

[30] John Kenneth Galbraith, *The Affluent Society* (Boston: Houghton Mifflin, 1958), ch. XXIII.

[31] Cf. Sidney C. Sufrin and Marion A. Buck, *What Price Progress?: A Study in Chronic Unemployment* (Chicago: Rand McNally, 1963), esp. chs. 1, 2.

as a "war on poverty." Some of these programs, and the various approaches to the "poverty problem" they follow, are described here. Their general purpose is to increase the economic opportunities for individuals to provide for themselves, either by increasing the employability of the individual or the number of jobs available to him, or both.

The Area Redevelopment Program

Efforts to provide national aid to localities affected by chronic and heavy unemployment began in 1955, with Senator Paul Douglas (Dem., Ill.) leading the way. Bills which would have established programs to aid such areas were passed by Democratically controlled Congresses in 1958 and 1960. Both times they were vetoed by President Eisenhower, in part because he believed they involved too much national participation in local affairs. Aid to depressed areas became a major issue in the 1960 Presidential campaign and President Kennedy took office pledged to aid such areas. His observations and contact with poverty in West Virginia during the Presidential primary had been instructive and had convinced him of the need for government action.

As enacted, the Area Redevelopment Act of 1961 established a four-year program of assistance for depressed areas which was to be administered by an Area Redevelopment Administration located in the Department of Commerce. The broad objective of the act was to reduce unemployment by encouraging the formation of new businesses, or the relocation or expansion of existing businesses, in areas designated as depressed so as to provide more jobs. To this end, the act authorized the Area Redevelopment Administration to make loans and grants for commercial and industrial development purposes in urban and rural depressed areas. (Rural areas were included in the bill in an effort to win Southern Democratic votes for its passage.) The funds provided could be used for such projects as the construction of new factory buildings or the renovation of existing ones and the improvement of community facilities: water systems, sewage disposal plants, and the like. Funds were also made available to finance the retraining of workers in the depressed areas. Some 1,035 counties, constituting roughly one-third of the nation's total and containing a sixth of the population, were eventually designated as depressed areas by the Area Redevelopment Administration and thus made eligible to share in the $394,000,000 authorized by Congress for the four-year program. The large number of counties designated as "depressed" was the function of loose ARA criteria for designation plus pressures from farm and labor interests and "congressmen who had voted for the legislation and who had promised constituents that their areas would benefit from the law...."[32]

During the first three years of its operation, the ARA approved 512 area development projects involving $244.5 million in federal loans and grants. The agency claimed that these projects would directly generate 72,000 new jobs and indirectly provide employment for an additional 44,000 workers. Several hundred worker retraining projects were also authorized, covering more than twenty-five thousand workers.

The ARA early came in for criticism and it led a hectic and harried life. Contributing to its difficulties were administrative problems (e.g., many of its activities required cooperation of other government agencies), Congressional impatience for results, dissatisfaction with some ARA projects (one was a $1.8 million loan to help build a motor hotel in Detroit), Republican charges that the program was used in 1962 as a "pork barrel" to help elect Democrats, and continued opposition from business groups.[33] Congress refused to act favorably on Presidential recommendations for continuation of the ARA in 1963 and again in 1964. It subsequently expired in June, 1965.

To replace the Area Redevelopment Administration, early in 1965 President Johnson requested the Congress to establish an Economic Development Administration which would emphasize a broader area approach to economic development than the policy of aid to particular communities and counties followed by the ARA. According to the President, a broader approach was necessary because "Individual counties and communities are often not capable of economic growth."[34]

In August, 1965, Congress passed the Economic Development Act, providing for a five-year, $3.25 billion program of grants and loans for public works, development facilities, technical assistance, and other activities to help economically depressed areas. The bulk of the money will go for public works projects, such as water works, waste treatment plants, industrial streets and roads, airports, tourist facilities, and other facilities which will directly or indirectly improve employment activities in depressed areas or, in the words of the act, "primarily benefit the long-term unemployed and members of low-income families or otherwise substantially further the objectives of the Economic Opportunity

[32] Sar A. Levitan, *Federal Aid to Depressed Areas* (Baltimore: Johns Hopkins Press, 1964), 61–64. The quotation is on 63.

[33] Jules Duscha, "The Depressed Areas," *The Progressive,* XXVII (September, 1963), 29–32; and Levitan, *op. cit., passim.*

[34] *The New York Times,* March 26, 1965, p. 16.

Act of 1964. . . ." The new legislation also provides for the establishment of multi-county and multi-state development areas and districts to broaden the scope of development planning and for the establishment of additional multi-state regional planning commissions similar to the Appalachian Regional Commission. (See below.) The establishment of the Appalachia Commission had stimulated demands by Congressmen from other regions for such commissions.

In short, the Economic Development Administration differs from the ARA in three primary respects: It has a broader orientation, considerably greater funds, and a new name. Whether the new EDA program will be more effective in stimulating employment and economic development and in combating poverty is a question for the future. In any event, its stress on public works will probably increase its popularity with Congressmen and local officials, both of whom are much concerned with such matters.

Manpower Development and Retraining

A second approach to the poverty problem is stressed by the Manpower Development and Training Act of 1962. This act is intended to attack the problem of unemployment wherever it may exist, in depressed areas or elsewhere, by helping workers who are unemployed or underemployed to acquire new job skills or to improve their existing ones. The 1962 legislation created a three-year program of loans and grants for vocational training programs to be operated by existing state agencies or private institutions. Funds were also made available for on-the-job training programs conducted by employers, the states, labor unions, or other groups. Subsistence payments were authorized for many workers while they were enrolled in retraining programs. Basic literacy training may be given those who need it in order to benefit from vocational training. The vocational training programs are supervised by the Department of Health, Education and Welfare; the Department of Labor oversees on-the-job training activities and is in charge of selecting worker trainees for both programs. The MDTA is credited with having made possible the training of 320,000 unemployed workers during the first two-and-a-half years of its existence. Three-fourths of those trained subsequently found jobs.

Although the MDTA program originally was to expire in 1965, it has proved to be quite popular with members of both parties in Congress. The program was extended for a year in 1963 and then, in 1965, it was enlarged and continued until June, 1969. (The 1965 House vote on extension was 392–0.) Under the terms of the original act, most of the training programs were to be jointly financed by the national and state governments after the first two years of operation. However, most of the states manifested inability or unwillingness to participate financially and full federal financing was extended through June, 1966.[35] After that time the 1965 legislation requires that *local governments* involved in training programs pay 10 per cent of the in-school training costs. (Under the initial act, the states were to have provided 50 per cent of the training costs.) The new matching requirement seemingly should not be a serious impediment to state-local participation.

Vocational Education Act of 1963

The Vocational Education Act of 1963 represents another effort by the national government to improve job training facilities and opportunities. A major goal of the act is to bring high school vocational education activities into line with the needs of the modern American economy. Although the national government has given financial support for vocational education since 1917, these programs have given disproportionate emphasis to agriculture and home economics. The Vocational Education Act both increases the amount of federal aid to the states and broadens the purposes for which it can be used. Vocational agriculture training can now include training for such related occupations as food processing and farm equipment repair work. Further, the act gives greater emphasis to training for distributive occupations, as in retail and wholesale marketing, and for jobs in trade and industry. Funds are also allocated to the states to help them maintain work-study programs to give financial assistance to full-time students in vocational education programs. Priority here is given to communities with substantial numbers of high-school "dropouts" and unemployed youth. Administration of the federal assistance is handled by the Office of Education in the Department of Health, Education and Welfare.

[35] During the first year of the MDTA forty-nine states undertook training programs but only four authorized matching of the federal funds. A U.S. Office of Education survey of state directors of vocational education revealed that, of those surveyed, eighteen believed their states would not match the federal funds and thirteen more expressed serious doubts about this. Only eight were "reasonably certain" their states would participate and match the federal funds. *Congressional Quarterly Almanac, 1963* (Washington, D.C.: Congressional Quarterly, Inc., 1964), XIX, 525.

The Economic Opportunity Act of 1964

This act, frequently called the Anti-Poverty Act, was enacted by Congress in response to President Johnson's call for a "War on Poverty." Its primary focus is on youth and breaking the "cycle of poverty," whereby poverty in one generation of a family begets poverty in the next generation and so on. Administered by the Office of Economic Opportunity in the Executive Office of the President, the Economic Opportunity Act authorizes a series of programs using education, vocational training, loans, and other techniques to alleviate poverty and improve people's employment skills and opportunities. The various programs include: a Job Corps to provide education, vocational training, and work experience in camps and residential schools for youth 16 to 21 years of age; federal assistance for state and community work training programs (the "Neighborhood Youth Corps") to provide vocational training and work experience for youths aged sixteen to twenty-one while living at home; a work-study program to provide financial assistance to students from low income families so they can remain in college; federally assisted community action programs to help low income families in such matters as job training, vocational rehabilitation, housing, health, and home management; grants and loans to low income rural families to help them increase their income earning capacity; loans to small businesses, especially as these may increase training and job opportunities for low income persons; and a domestic service corps (VISTA: Volunteers in Service to America) under which volunteers would work in state and local projects combating poverty in somewhat the same fashion as the Peace Corps abroad.

Under the direction of Sargent Shriver, who was put in charge of the Office of Economic Opportunity while continuing as head of the Peace Corps, the "War on Poverty" got off to a good start. In the first six months of the "anti-poverty program" some five hundred anti-poverty projects were approved. These included several urban job-training centers and several dozen rural conservation camps under the Job Corps program; one-hundred fifty community action programs; and more than sixty communities with Neighborhood Youth Corps projects. More than 40,000 college students were receiving financial aid under the work-study program. Several hundred VISTA volunteers had been recruited and were in training and thousands more had

343

applied for service.[36] Approximately $750 million was appropriated for the overall program in fiscal 1965. Twice that amount was requested by the Johnson administration for fiscal 1966 in order to expand activities. The Congress went beyond this and actually provided $1.78 billion.

As one would suspect, a variety of conflicts, controversies, and complaints were soon generated by the operation of the antipoverty program. Some communities objected to the location of Job Corps camps near them on the ground that the trainees would be "undesirables." Business groups, conservative politicians, and others objected to a decision that Neighborhood Youth Corps members should be paid no less than $1.25 an hour for working. This was often more than their parents or other low paid workers in the community earned. Political struggles developed over who should control the community action programs in New York, Chicago, Cleveland, and other cities. Some local politicians evidently viewed them as a form of political patronage. And there were complaints that the poor were being excluded from a role in policy making and administration under the antipoverty program in some areas by "the powers that be" in order to keep the poor from becoming a new political force. Finally, we might mention that conflicts have developed among the various federal agencies concerned with the antipoverty program. Although the Office of Economic Opportunity is charged with coordinating the entire program, various parts of it are actually implemented by the departments of Health, Education and Welfare, Labor, and Agriculture, the Small Business Administration, and other agencies. Each has its own vested interests to protect, its own "ideology," and notions as to what should be done.

The Regional Approach: Appalachia

In March, 1965, Congress passed the Appalachian Regional Development Act, which embodies still another approach to the poverty problem—the use of federal funds to promote the social and economic uplift of an entire geographic region. The name Appalachia denotes an eleven-state region centered around the Appalachian Mountains. Extending from northern Pennsylvania to mid-Alabama, the region embraces all of West Virginia and parts of Pennsylvania, Ohio, Maryland, Kentucky, Virginia, Tennessee, North Carolina, South Carolina, Georgia, and Alabama. "The victim of both geography and automation, Appalachia lags behind the nation as a whole in employment, educa-

[36] "As the Poverty Program Gets Into Gear," *U.S. News and World Report,* LVIII (March 8, 1965), 56–58. Also, *The New York Times,* April 28, 1965, p. 22.

tion, health facilities, housing, road-construction, and virtually every other yardstick used to measure a healthy economy."[37] It is generally conceded to be the largest economically depressed area in the nation. (There are, of course, "pockets of prosperity" within the region, such as Charleston, West Virginia.)

The Appalachian Regional Development Act permits the expenditure of $1.1 billion in federal funds to encourage the economic development of the region. About four-fifths of this money will be used over a five-year period to help pay the cost of building development (or major) highways and local access roads. The national government will pay up to 70 per cent of the cost with the remainder coming from the state or states involved. Roadbuilding is stressed primarily because the governors, senators, and representatives of the Appalachia states wanted roads to be given priority and because adequate highways were lacking in many parts of the region. The remainder of the funds authorized by the act, for a two-year period, are for health facilities, vocational schools, land improvement, reclamation of mining areas, and the development of timber and water resources. (A program for pastureland improvement was dropped because of the opposition of Western cattle interests.)

The various programs under the Appalachia Act will be carried out by the appropriate federal and state agencies, e.g., the Bureau of Public Roads and the State Highway departments. However, the entire program will be supervised and coordinated by an Appalachian Regional Commission, to be comprised of the governor of each state (or a representative selected by him) in the region and a federal representative chosen by the President. Subject to a veto by the federal representative, a majority of the state members on the Commission have the power to determine what specific projects will be undertaken. The states are thus given a major share in the decision making involved in the program. This, it is hoped, will result in greater local participation and in better adaptation of the program to local conditions.[38]

The Appalachia program is geared to the economic needs of the region and is intended to increase economic growth and employment opportunities in the region as a whole. The funds expended will not go directly to needy people nor, necessarily, to the most depressed towns and counties. There is no "means test" to determine eligibility for aid as there was in the Area Redevelopment Act. The idea here, rather, is to

[37] *The New York Times,* Feb. 7, 1965, p. E5.
[38] Jerald Ter Horst, "No More Pork Barrel: The Appalachia Approach," *The Reporter,* XXXII (March 11, 1965), 27–29.

focus aid on those areas with the best potential for economic growth. The program is thus an attempt to substitute regional action for the "scattershot" approach often followed in the past, as under the ARA. Further, "Most programs of economic help in the past have been based on the theory that a man has a right to a job where he lives and that government should help bring him that job. The Appalachia approach is that a man has a right to a job, but it is reasonable to expect him to be willing to commute to it or move to it if necessary."[39] This approach is made manifest by the emphasis on roadbuilding and aid to areas of high growth potential.

Observations on Antipoverty Policy

Whether or not the various antipoverty programs thus far established will eliminate poverty is problematical. So indeed is the possibility that poverty can ever be entirely eliminated by any means. However, taken together the various antipoverty programs constitute a clear rejection of laissez faire and indifference on this matter and a strong commitment to positive action. They also represent a pragmatic attempt to find new and effective ways to counteract poverty.

In contrast to the welfare programs established by the Social Security Act, which seek to provide the individual with a floor of security in the form of minimal maintenance, the various antipoverty programs are designed to increase the economic opportunities open to the poor. To this end efforts are being made both to increase the number of available jobs in the economy and to equip the poor, by education, job training, and work experience, to secure jobs or better paying jobs. But if the antipoverty programs represent a departure in *technique* from the New Deal approach to welfare, they are nonetheless based on the "traditional" view of poverty—that is, poverty is individual and peripheral and is not the consequence of major structural weaknesses or malfunctions in the American socio-economic system. But there are those who believe poverty is the product of the latter conditions and they are likely to criticize the present antipoverty programs as too mild, as substitutes for really far-reaching reform. In response the supporters of the present programs contend that they represent a good start and that they can be expanded in future years as political conditions become more favorable.

The antipoverty programs, in contrast to most economic legislation of similar magnitude, did not evolve with strong, organized interest

[39] *Ibid.*, 28–29.

group support. They are the product, rather, of a *general* concern for poverty manifested by the President, members of Congress (especially Democrats), civic groups, and others. Unless the antipoverty programs can develop stronger and better focused political support in the future, they may be restricted or weakened by political attack and indifference. The war on poverty has only begun and its outcome will be much affected by future political battles.

TWO CURRENT ISSUES IN HEALTH AND EDUCATION

Two subjects which have been highly productive of political struggle since World War II are general federal aid to public education and compulsory national health insurance schemes. Although these issues are on the frontier of welfare policy today both are relatively old. Efforts to provide general federal aid to education date back to the 1870's; public health insurance proposals were first advanced around 1915. Political issues do not stop being controversial simply because of advanced age and familiarity. Nor has the enactment of a wide variety of other federal educational and medical programs significantly reduced the fervor of the contending sides. An examination of these two issues will cast light on the formation of welfare policy and some of the broad implications of particular welfare programs.

Federal Aid to Education

Education at the elementary and secondary levels has been traditionally regarded as the primary responsibility of the state and local governments. Historically, the local school district has been the principal unit for administration of local school systems and today there are still more than 40,000 school districts in the several states. (This figure represents a major decline from the 127,000 plus school districts existent in 1932 and is mainly the product of the school consolidation movement.) In the twentieth century the states, on whom the local school districts have always depended for legal authority, have come to exert increasing control over the public schools on such matters as curricula, textbooks, quality of teaching personnel, attendance, and periods of operation. State financial support for the schools has also grown, now accounting for around 40 per cent of their revenues, and is often the lever by which state controls are made effective. Each state has a department of education, (or, perhaps, public instruction), headed by a chief state school office, which supervises the state's public school system. Public higher education has been the customary preserve of the state governments. Education remains as the major area of governmental activity assigned primarily to the state and local governments in our federal system. In fiscal 1964 twenty-two of the twenty-four billion dollars expended by governments on education in the United States came from the state and local governments.

Although public schools have been the source of education for most children at the elementary and secondary levels, private and parochial schools have annually enrolled several million pupils in recent years. Most of these are in schools operated by the Catholic Church. It has been part of the American tradition that parents should have the right to send their children to private rather than public schools if they so choose, and many have done so. The existence of parochial schools has complicated the issue of federal aid to education because such aid, if it should go to parochial schools as well as public schools, raises questions concerning the separation of church and state. More will be said about this in a moment.

The tradition of state and local control of education and attitudes in support thereof have been reinforced by the belief that control of education is reserved to the states (and their local subdivisions) by the Tenth Amendment. State control of education consequently has become an aspect of states' rights and of decentralization and local self-government. The proponents of state control and support of education, or, to put it negatively, the opponents of federal aid or control, are frequently heard to proclaim that the Founding Fathers "clearly" intended to leave education to the states. This contention is probably a better argument than a description of historical reality because, when the Constitution and the Tenth Amendment were adopted, there was no real state government responsibility for public education.[40] Most elementary and secondary education was privately provided; the little public education that did exist was handled by towns and communities. Nonetheless, the states' rights contention has political appeal and usefulness for those who oppose federal aid.

However, in spite of the tradition of state and local control of education, the history of federal aid to education in the United States dates back to at least 1785 and the Northwest Ordinance. That statute provided that one section of land in each township in the Northwest

[40] On this point, see Homer D. Bobbidge, Jr. and Robert M. Rosenzweig, *The Federal Interest in Higher Education* (New York: McGraw-Hill, 1962), ch. 1.

Territory should be set aside for the support of education. Since that time a great many programs of aid for education have been started by the national government.[41] A few examples follow.

The Morrill acts of 1862 and 1890 provided for first land and then cash grants to help the states maintain colleges offering instruction in the agricultural and mechanical arts. The Office of Education, established in 1867, handles a wide range of research, advisory, and grant-in-aid programs for all levels of education. The Smith-Hughes Act of 1917 and later legislation have given financial support to high school vocational education. Since the late 1930's food and money have been made available for school lunch programs and with the Lanham Act of 1940, Congress began to provide financial aid for the construction, maintenance, and operation of public schools in "federally impacted areas." This program, which has been especially popular in Congress (there is a bit of the pork barrel about it), aids schools in areas where school enrollments have been increased by the presence of large numbers of federal personnel or where school revenues are reduced by large amounts of tax-exempt federal property. The National Defense Education Act of 1958, which was stimulated by public and congressional concern over Soviet space exploits, authorizes expenditures for the improvement of teaching in science, mathematics, and foreign languages at all educational levels. Funds were also made available for scholarships and loans for various categories of college students. Other federal postwar legislation has provided for veterans' education, including the famous "G.I. Bill," loans and grants for the construction of college dormitories and academic buildings, and grants and contractual arrangements for college research activities, e.g., grants from the National Science Foundation. More than half of the research conducted in American colleges and universities is federally financed.

It is fair to say, however, that until 1965 federal aid to education was essentially peripheral or indirect. It clearly did not satisfy the demands of the proponents of general federal aid for elementary and secondary education in the form of funds for school construction, or teachers' salaries, or both. Their general contention has been that both existing school facilities and current levels of state and local support for education are inadequate and that a major federal effort was needed to im-

---

[41] Charles A. Quattlebaum, "Federal Policies and Practices in Higher Education," in Douglas M. Knight, ed., *The Federal Government and Higher Education* (Englewood Cliffs, N.J.: Prentice-Hall, 1960), 29–75, gives a picture of the wide variety of federal programs for both higher and secondary and elementary education.

prove the quality of the schools, to broaden educational opportunities, and to provide classrooms and teachers for an ever growing school population. Since 1945 some sort of federal aid legislation has been before Congress almost continuously.

In their efforts to secure federal aid, its proponents have had recourse to a variety of arguments over the years.[42] Following World War I, federal aid was viewed as necessary to combat and to help Americanize immigrants, many of whom could not speak English. There were also some who, interestingly enough, saw federal aid to education as a bulwark against Communism, which would be unappealing to the educated. During the 1930's federal aid was advocated as necessary to help solve the fiscal emergency in the schools created by the depression as well as a means to stimulate increases in employment and economic activity. After World War II, federal aid proponents stressed the need to close the "classroom gap" and alleviate the shortage of teachers which stemmed in part from insufficient school construction during the war years and rising enrollments. With the Soviet space exploits in the late 1950's the federal aid argument focused on the needs of national security and "keeping up with the Russians." Finally, in the middle 1960's attention was directed toward improved educational facilities and opportunities as a means of combating poverty. Thus, while the belief in the need for and desirability of federal aid has remained constant, the substance of the argument for it has been geared to changes in the current conception of the needs and problems of the educational system. Whether this has had the effect of securing new supporters, however convincing it may be to the already committed, is problematical.

Various opinion surveys during the 1950's and early 1960's revealed widespread popular support for federal aid to education.[43] But it also appears that interest in federal aid has not been very intense. Consequently, very few Congressmen have apparently believed that their chances for re-election would be adversely affected by Congress' failure to enact a general federal aid law. Moreover, a number of divisive issues long prevented the development of a consensus on federal legislation sufficient to obtain positive action.

Coalitions of interests supporting and opposing federal aid to education have developed. The supporters of federal action have generally

---

[42] See Frank J. Munger and Richard F. Fenno, Jr., *National Politics and Federal Aid to Education* (Syracuse: Syracuse University Press, 1962), 176.

[43] V. O. Key, Jr., *Public Opinion and American Democracy* (New York: Alfred A. Knopf, 1961), 88, *passim*.

included the National Education Association, the American Federation of Teachers, the Council of Chief State School Officers, the AFL-CIO, and various Negro, liberal, and womens' service organizations. In opposition have been the Chamber of Commerce, the National Association of Manufacturers, the American Farm Bureau Federation, "patriotic" organizations like the Daughters of the American Revolution, and various other business and conservative organizations. Resistance to federal aid has stemmed from opposition to increased federal spending and taxes and the belief that federal aid will inevitably lead to federal control of education, which is considered both intrinsically bad and a contradiction of states' rights. Opposition to federal aid as leading to federal control often rests on the Victorian premise that one kiss must necessarily lead to the total surrender of virtue. Fears of federal control have probably been stronger when funds are to be made available for teachers' salaries rather than just for school construction since the "threat" is perceived to be more immediate in the former instance. To mollify such fears, school aid bills have usually contained provisions prohibiting "federal controls."

The coalition supporting federal aid has been split by a number of controversial issues in the past, including times when success has seemed imminent. Questions always arise concerning the way in which federal funds, once available, should be allocated among the states. Spokesmen for the poorer states have favored formulas which would channel larger shares of the funds to them in order to help equalize educational opportunities among the states. The wealthier states have objected to paying federal taxes which go for education benefits in other states and favor flat per pupil grants rather than equalization formulas. This issue has not been nearly so troublesome as have two others: aid to segregated schools and to parochial schools. Here differences of "principle" are involved and it is much more difficult to secure compromise on such "moral issues," because of the emotional attachments involved, than on differences over money. Liberal and Negro groups have often secured provisions in federal aid bills prohibiting the granting of funds to segregated school systems, which in turn has made such bills objectionable to Southern Democrats. In the past, conservative interests have manipulated this issue to divide the supporters of federal aid. For example, in 1956, in the House, a combination of Republicans and Northern Democrats attached an anti-discrimination clause (the "Powell amendment") to a federal aid bill. Then, on final passage, most of the Republicans joined with the Southern Democrats to defeat the entire bill.

351

Protestants and other groups have opposed aid to parochial schools as a violation of the constitutional principle of separation of church and state. Catholic groups, however, have often opposed federal aid to education programs which would not assist parochial as well as public schools. The Kennedy administration's 1961 school aid bill, which provided funds for school construction and teachers' salaries for public schools only, was killed in the House for this reason. Two members of the House Rules Committee, both Catholics, who normally supported the administration joined with the conservatives on the committee to prevent floor consideration of the bill.[44]

In April, 1965, the dike against general federal aid to education finally gave way and Congress passed the Elementary and Secondary Education Act of 1965. Although the act was put forward as an antipoverty measure, it will provide funds to about 95 per cent of the nation's school districts.[45] Some $1.3 billion in federal spending is authorized for fiscal 1966, with the amounts for later years to be set by subsequent legislation. Most of the money will go to the states for allocation to school districts with substantial numbers of children from low income families (i.e., families with incomes below $2,000 a year or on relief) to be used for activities of benefit to such children. Each state receives funds equal to the sum of half of its annual education expenditure per child times the number of children from low income families. The larger a state's education expenditure, the more federal money it receives per child, a formula to the advantage of the wealthier states. Federal funds will go for a variety of special services such as remedial education, educational television, mobile education units, guidance and counseling, and speech therapy. These programs are administered by public schools or other public agencies but are available to low income children who are attending either public or parochial schools. Money is also made available for purchase of nonsectarian textbooks and library materials by both public and parochial schools.

Why was federal aid to education legislation finally enacted in 1965? A number of contributory factors can be mentioned. First, President Johnson was a much stronger supporter of such legislation than either of his immediate predecessors, Presidents Eisenhower and Kennedy. Second, the large Democratic majorities in the Eighty-ninth Congress, especially Northern Democrats, provided votes in Congress

[44] The political struggle over federal aid to education during the Kennedy years is well discussed in Hugh Douglas Price, "Schools, Scholarships, and Congressmen," in Alan F. Westin, ed., *The Centers of Power* (New York: Harcourt, Brace & World, 1964), 53–105.
[45] *The New York Times,* April 10, 1965, pp. 1, 14.

that were not available in earlier years. Third, by emphasizing assistance to schools with children from low income families and antipoverty action, the supporters of the act were able to avoid much of the controversy over aid to parochial schools that had been a stumbling block in the past. Aid was provided for children in parochial schools, which satisfied Catholic groups, while the fiction that the aid was going to the children and not parochial schools as such made it less unacceptable to opponents of aid to parochial schools. Fourth, by getting the Senate to pass the House bill without amendment, the Johnson administration and its congressional allies were able to avoid some of the roadblocks on which federal aid had perished in past years. Normally, on their way to becoming law, major bills must receive favorable action at seven points: House committee, House Rules Committee, House floor action, Senate committee, Senate floor action, House Rules Committee action to permit the House to go to conference, and conference committee. The strategy employed by the administration eliminated the last two steps, much to the displeasure of many Congressional Republicans who opposed the legislation. Finally, the Civil Rights Act of 1964, which generally prohibited federal funds from being used for programs which discriminated against Negroes, made the dispute over aid to segregated schools a nullity.

Now that the proponents of general federal aid to education have succeeded in passing legislation, will they be satisfied? In all likelihood they will not because success in achieving a political objective, such as federal aid to education, often leads not to satiation but to demands for greater amounts of the same benefits.[46] This principle is well illustrated by the many successful efforts to secure increased benefits and broader coverage under the Social Security Act and federal minimum wage legislation.

Health, Medical Care, and Politics

As with education there is a long history of national government activity in the area of health and medicine. We shall begin with a discussion of some of the various forms of federal and state involvement in health and medicine generally and shall then focus on the issue of national health insurance.

Government activity to protect and promote the public health dates back to colonial times. By the early nineteenth century many cities had established health departments for this purpose and, at the end of the

[46] See Murray Edleman, *The Symbolic Uses of Politics* (Urbana: University of Illinois Press, 1964), ch. 8, esp. 153–157.

century, public health departments had been created by most of the states. State and local health departments are now concerned with such matters as the control and prevention of communicable diseases, inspection and control of public water and sanitation facilities, inspection and licensing of restaurants and other food-service establishments, air pollution control, public health education, collection of vital and medical statistics, and research into the causes of cancer, heart disease, diabetes, and other diseases. The states, usually through their health departments, also operate hospitals for the treatment and care of persons having tuberculosis and mental illnesses. The expenses involved in the treatment of these illnesses are often too great for families to meet. About 85 per cent of all patients with mental illnesses are in state or local hospitals, making this a government-dominated area of medical care.[47]

In general, though, the state and local health departments have confined their efforts to the prevention of diseases and health hazards—mental illness is a major exception here. The actual treatment of persons with illnesses and ailments has been left mostly to private doctors. Although most public health programs now create little controversy, an exception worth noting is the fluoridation of community water supplies. This program is widely supported by dentists and public health groups as an effective means of reducing dental cavities in children. Some have opposed fluoridation of water for religious reasons; others have opposed it as dangerous to health, since fluorine is a poison. Ultra right-wing groups have viewed it as sinister, communist-inspired, and the like. Regarding their viewpoint, it has been written:

> Of fluoride, we are told that the Russians depended upon it during World War II to keep their prisoners docile, and that its use in city drinking water will cause a slow poisoning which will gradually reduce us to robots. The great concern of conservatives [sic] over this poisoning, which they declare results in stiff backs, paralyzed legs, arthritis, intestinal disorders, stunted growth, kidney stones, loss of fertility, and slow death is in startling contrast to their absolute conviction that the effects of nuclear fallout are negligible. It is also pointed out that many Russians, and people known to be associated with Communist organizations, have positions in the Public Health Service, and on the state Boards of Public Health.[48]

[47] Charles R. Adrian, *State and Local Governments* (New York: McGraw-Hill, 1960), 437.

[48] Ralph E. Ellsworth and Sarah M. Harris, *The American Right Wing* (Washington, D.C.: Public Affairs Press, 1962), 15. See this same source for some comments on right-wing opposition to use of the Salk polio vaccine.

Many communities have experienced acrimonious political conflicts over water fluoridation.

At the national level the major health agency is the Public Health Service in the Department of Health, Education and Welfare. The Public Health Service, originally established in 1798 as the Marine Hospital Service, is now responsible for a wide range of health and medical programs and has an annual budget of more than a billion and a half dollars. The Public Health Service provides hospital and medical care for merchant seamen (its original clientele), Coast Guard personnel, Indians, inmates of federal prisons, drug addicts, and lepers. The Service also enforces foreign quarantine regulations to prevent the "importation" of diseases from abroad, advises and assists the states in preventing the spread of diseases through interstate commerce, and licenses the manufacture and interstate sale of such biological products as vaccines, serums, and toxins to ensure their potency and purity. Through the National Institutes of Health, the Service engages in or sponsors research in hospitals, universities, and other institutions on the causes, treatment, and cure of heart disease, cancer, arthritis, mental illness, and other specified diseases. NIH funds constitute 40 per cent of the annual expenditure on biomedical research in the United States.[49] The Bureau of State Services administers a number of grant-in-aid programs to help the states carry on research and disease control programs (e.g., for venereal disease and cancer) and to construct hospitals, nursing homes, rehabilitation and diagnostic centers, and other medical facilities.

In addition to the Public Health Service, two dozen other federal agencies are also involved in the health and medical field. The Veterans Administration provides complete medical care free of charge to veterans for service-connected injuries and illnesses. Veterans with nonservice connected illnesses and injuries are also eligible for free care if they are willing to state that they cannot provide for themselves. Challenges of such statements are prohibited by law and about 60 per cent of the veterans receiving care come under this category. In all, twenty-two million veterans are eligible for VA medical care and some 700,000 receive it annually.[50] Here is "socialized medicine" in the truest sense of the word—care for persons in government owned and operated facilities staffed by hired doctors. However, the American

[49] Department of Health, Education and Welfare, *Annual Report 1963,* 185.

[50] These data on the care of veterans are from Administrator of Veterans Affairs, *Annual Report, 1964* (Washington, D.C.: Government Printing Office, 1964), 13–24.

Medical Association, arch-foe of "socialized medicine" generally, has not chosen to oppose the veterans on this matter, perhaps because the veterans have high status and are a numerous, well-organized, and powerful political group. Health and medical activities are also carried on by the Defense Department for military personnel, the Welfare Administration, and the Food and Drug Administration.

Notwithstanding the many governmental health and medical programs in the United States, the provision of medical care and services for most persons has remained a private responsibility. The programs to provide for particular groups which we have referred to cover about 30 million people out of a total population of 190 million. There is no program which protects people generally against the costs of illness. The American experience presents a distinct contrast to that of Western Europe, where practically all nations have general public health insurance or government-provided medical care programs which apply either to all residents or to all employed persons.[51] Perhaps the best-known example is the British National Health Service, which provides all British citizens and foreign visitors with complete medical care. This program, in which more than 95 per cent of the British doctors participate on a fixed fee basis, is financed primarily from general government revenues. The NHS, established in 1948, represents the culmination of a series of legislative enactments which began with the approval of a national health insurance law by Parliament in 1911.

There are a number of major alternative ways by which a person's medical care expenses could be handled. First, the individual can be left with the responsibility to provide for himself out of his own income and savings, through some kind of private health insurance (such as Blue Cross-Blue Shield), or a combination thereof. Second, the government could provide for the care of needy individuals by grants from general revenue funds, as it now does for the needy aged receiving public assistance benefits. The money could be paid either to the individuals being aided or it could go directly to the doctors, hospitals, and others providing services. Third, the government could establish a compulsory health insurance program to provide people with prepaid protection against medical expenses. This program might cover all persons or it might be limited to some categories of people, such as those over 65 years of age. Finally, medical care and services could be directly

[51] A good survey and summary of government medical care and health insurance programs throughout the world can be found in J. F. Follman, Jr., *Medical Care and Health Insurance: A Study in Social Progress* (Homewood, Ill.: Richard D. Irwin, 1963), chs. 2–3.

provided for people by government-staffed and operated facilities, as is presently done for veterans. To date, the first alternative has been the general rule in the United States, with the other three alternatives being followed only in limited instances.

Efforts to secure some kind of a public health insurance program began in the United States before World War I but nothing came of them. An effort to include a medical care program in the Social Security Act of 1935 failed because of inadequate preparation by its supporters and the active opposition of the American Medical Association. Then, in 1943, the first of the Murray-Wagner-Dingell bills was introduced in Congress; similar bills were reintroduced in 1945 and 1947. These bills would have established a full-scale system of national health insurance. President Truman was a strong supporter of public health insurance and, in 1949, he proposed that the social security program (OASDI) be expanded to include a payroll tax supported program of compulsory health insurance.

Under the proposed Truman program, complete medical, dental, hospital, and nursing care would have been prepaid for all except the destitute, who would have been protected under another program. Doctors and hospitals would have been free to join or stay out of the plan. Patients would have been free to choose their doctor and doctors were permitted to reject undesired patients. Participating doctors were to be paid on a fixed-fee, per capita, or salary basis, as determined by the majority of doctors in a health service area. Alternative methods of payment were provided for minority doctors. The proposed program thus attempted to combine freedom of choice for doctors and patients within a compulsory coverage framework.

The reaction of the American Medical Association to this proposal was sharp, vigorous, and in total opposition. With the aid of a well-known public relations firm, Whitaker and Baxter, the AMA launched an extensive, well-financed campaign against the proposal and was successful in labeling and stigmatizing the proposal as involving "socialized medicine."[52] The proposal failed to get out of committee in Congress. Since this time, little real effort has been made to secure a general health insurance program; rather, attention has been focused on the medical needs and problems of the aged. The case for a general public health insurance program is less strong today than it was in the late 1940's because of the great increase in private health insurance coverage since then. This development, "in part stimulated by the

[52] The AMA campaign is well discussed in Stanley Kelley, Jr., *Professional Public Relations and Political Power* (Baltimore: Johns Hopkins Press, 1956), ch. 3.

threat of [National Health Insurance], has greatly reduced the need of compulsory health insurance for the whole population."[53] Also, per capita disposable income has risen about three times as much as the costs of medical care and, consequently, the public's capacity to finance medical care has improved.[54]

In the late 1950's and early 1960's, attention and controversy centered on proposals to establish compulsory health insurance for the aged, financed through social security. Although most people agreed that the aged often needed aid in meeting medical expenses, there was no agreement as to the form such aid should take, who should provide it, or how extensive it should be. The Forand bill, which received major consideration from 1957 to 1960, proposed to increase social security taxes in order to pay hospital and surgical care benefits to social security beneficiaries over age 65. No floor action was taken in Congress on this bill. However, in 1960, a more modest medical care for the aged bill sponsored by Senator John F. Kennedy was defeated by a 51–44 vote in the Senate. The Kennedy bill provided only for limited hospital and nursing care benefits. The Congress then went on to pass the Kerr-Mills Act, which had the support of the Eisenhower administration, the American Medical Association, and most conservatives and Republicans in Congress.

The Kerr-Mills Act provides for federal grants to the states to help them expand their payments for medical care benefits to the needy aged receiving public assistance and, second, to institute a new program to help those over 65 who are not receiving public assistance but who are unable to meet heavy medical expenses. (These persons are referred to as "medically indigent.") This program was designed to weaken the case for broader medical care legislation by providing for the obviously needy. However, many states were slow in taking advantage of the Kerr-Mills Act to help the medically indigent and by the spring of 1965, ten states still had not done so. Many of the participating states have been quite restrictive in determining standards of eligibility and amounts of benefits to be paid.

The Kerr-Mills Act did not quell or quiet the supporters of social security financed medical care for the aged (medicare) and both Presidents Kennedy and Johnson advocated the enactment of such legislation. Although an attempt by Senate liberals to pass a medicare bill was defeated in 1962, in 1964 they succeeded in attaching medicare to

[53] Seymour E. Harris, *The Economics of American Medicine* (New York: Macmillan, 1964), 301.
[54] *Idem.*

358

a House-passed bill which provided for increased social security benefits and taxes. The whole package died, however, in a deadlocked House-Senate conference committee. Seven years of work for medicare had produced no positive legislative results but in 1965 the situation changed. Before considering this matter, brief attention will be given to the contending sides in the medicare struggle.

The proponents of medicare contend that it is necessary because, generally, the aged have lower incomes than the rest of the population, they are ill more often for longer periods of time, and thus they incur greater medical expenses.[55] The coverage of private insurance plans, the argument runs, often is inadequate, or their expense is too great for many retired persons, or the aged are denied coverage. The Kerr-Mills programs are considered financially inadequate and morally objectionable because of the means test used for determining eligibility for benefits under them. Medicare is advanced as the best way of relieving the aged and their families of burdensome medical expenses and, further, of eliminating the degrading means tests by paying benefits as a matter of right. The supporters of medicare have included the AFL-CIO, the National Farmers Union, liberal groups like Americans for Democratic Action, social workers, organizations of the elderly, and most Northern Democrats in Congress.

Leading the opposition to medicare has been the American Medical Association, which claims to speak for three-fourths of the nation's medical doctors. The AMA has found compulsory health insurance no less objectionable merely because it is limited to the aged. Arguments put forward by the AMA include: it is unnecessary because of the Kerr-Mills Act and broader private health insurance coverage; it is an "entering wedge" and would eventually be expanded to cover all medical expenses for everyone, thus leading to "socialized medicine for every man, woman, and child in this country"; it will interfere with the traditional doctor-patient relationship (a strong if diffuse symbol); and its compulsory character will lead to a decline in individual freedom.[56] Although it is not articulated, AMA opposition to medicare seems based in considerable part on the fear that it would eventually lead to limitations on the earning capacity of doctors, who are the highest paid

[55] See *The New York Times,* Jan. 10, 1965, p. 6E; and Wilbur J. Cohen, "Medical Care for the Aged," *Current History*, XXXIII (August, 1963), 98.

[56] For example, see Edward R. Annis, "Medicare: Bad Medicine for Everyone," in Francis M. Carney and H. Frank Way, Jr., eds., *Politics 1964* (Belmont, Calif.: Wadsworth Publishing Co., 1964), 174–178. Annis is a former president of the American Medical Association.

professional group in the country. Joining the AMA in opposition to medicare are such groups as the Chamber of Commerce, the National Association of Manufacturers, the Farm Bureau, the National Grange, and the private insurance industry. Most Republicans and many Southern Democrats in Congress have also been among the opponents.

In the spring of 1965, the House passed a medicare bill for the first time since the campaign for legislation began. As initially proposed by the Johnson administration, the bill provided only for hospitalization, nursing home, and nursing care benefits for those over sixty-five financed by social security taxes. The administration's proposal was criticized by the AMA and Congressional Republicans on various grounds, including that it did not provide any coverage of doctors' fees. To counter this criticism, and also undoubtedly because many people believed medicare covered doctors' fees,[57] the Democrats on the House Ways and Means Committee broadened the bill to cover doctors' fees and some other medical expenses under a voluntary plan. The bill was reported out of committee and passed in the House by a 313–115 vote after a Republican substitute providing for an entirely voluntary insurance program financed jointly by individual and federal government contributions was rejected by a vote of 236–191. The medicare bill was passed rather handily in the Senate and, after conference committee action, was signed into law by the President in late July, 1965.

Before turning to a summary of the medicare program created by the 1965 statute, an attempt to account for the favorable House action will provide some insight into the policy process. Until 1965 a medicare bill had never been reported out of the House Ways and Means Committee, which has jurisdiction over such bills because of their tax provisions. In 1961 there had been a hostile majority (16–9) toward medicare on the committee. But, by 1965, new appointments to Ways and Means to replace members leaving the committee by way of electoral defeat and retirement had produced a majority favorable to medicare.[58] This alteration in the composition of the Committee paralleled growing Democratic and liberal strength in the House as a whole. Further, during the 1960's public opinion appeared to have shifted strongly in favor of medicare, and the Johnson landslide in 1964 was viewed by many as a clear mandate for medicare. After having opposed medicare for years on the grounds that it would endanger the social security program, Chairman Wilbur Mills (Dem., Ark.) of the Ways and Means Committee now became a supporter of medicare. Mills' decision to

[57] *The New York Times,* Jan. 10, 1965, p. 6E.
[58] *Ibid.,* March 25, 1965, p. 49.

back medicare apparently was strongly influenced by his belief that it was supported by a majority of both his committee and the House. Few committee chairmen want to risk losing prestige by being over-turned by either their committee or the House. At base, a shift in broad political forces—public opinion and liberal-conservative alignment in Congress—appears to have been the major factor leading to the medi-care victory. Although the alignment of interest groups on medicare was relatively unchanged from that of previous years, a change in the context of the struggle gave the advantage to the proponents of medi-care.

The 1965 medicare legislation represents the broadest expansion of the Social Security system since its inception in 1935. Financed by a 0.35 per cent increase in social security taxes (to increase to 0.80 per cent by 1987), the medicare program lightens the medical burdens of aging in two basic ways: nearly all Americans 65 or over are provided with low cost protection against hospitalization and nursing home costs and, second, against most doctor bills. Some of the major benefits for covered persons include: (1) Sixty days of hospitalization at a total cost of $40 and an additional thirty days at $10 per day. (2) One hundred days of care in a nursing home at a cost of $5 per day for each day over twenty. (3) One hundred visits at home from nurses or medi-cal technicians. (4) Twenty days of outpatient hospital diagnostic ser-vices for $20 and 20 per cent of the costs above that amount. (5) For voluntary payment of $3 a month the individual will be included in a federally matched and supervised insurance system which will provide coverage for 80 per cent of most doctor bills, after the patient pays the first $50 of fees. Though much more modest in scope and benefits than the national health insurance scheme proposed by the Truman ad-ministration, the medicare program nevertheless is a landmark in American welfare legislation.

GOVERNMENT AND THE CONSUMER

Government efforts to protect both the health and the pocketbook of the individual consumer stem from the fact that, though he is "sover-eign" and well-informed in the theoretical world of classical economics, in actuality the consumer is often rather gullible, poorly informed, somewhat manipulable, or easily deceived. The old rule of *caveat emptor,* "Let the buyer beware," in practice frequently amounts to little more than a declaration of open season on consumers for those who would take advantage of them by unfair, deceptive, or fraudulent means. As a result, demands for consumer protection have led to the legislative abrogation of the *caveat emptor* rule although, it must be said, the modern consumer is still largely on his own in many commercial situations. In this section our concern is with national action to protect and promote consumer interests.[59] The consumer is benefited by most economic legislation such as laws intended to maintain competition or providing for the regulation of public utilities, but our interest here is centered on efforts by the national government to help the consumer directly as an individual buyer satisfying personal needs in the marketplace.

In general, government strives to protect the consumer in two ways, which can be easily distinguished analytically if not always in practice. First, there are efforts to provide the consumer with accurate or meaningful information on goods and commodities so that he can, if he desires, equip himself to make better informed choices and decisions. Second, government seeks to protect the consumer against the sale of unhealthy or dangerous products, deceptive practices, and the like. The first type of action is positive, in that the government is trying to strengthen the bargaining ability of the consumer. In the second instance the government action is negative, being intended to prevent the sale of particular items or the use of particular sales practices which may be detrimental to the consumer. This is well illustrated by food, drug, and cosmetic legislation.

Though everyone is a consumer, it remains a truism in American politics that the consumer interest is notoriously unorganized. "Of all the basic economic interests, that of the ultimate consumer is the broadest, the most akin to a general interest, and yet the least organized, the least articulate, and therefore the least recognized in the dynamics of policy formation."[60] Most of the pressure groups operating in the political arena are concerned with the interests of people as producers: farmers, workers, small businessmen, oil men, and so on. Most economic legislation is enacted at the insistence of producer interests, but, as we will note further on, it does not necessarily conflict with the interests of the consumers.

Organized consumer groups are relatively few, but various other

[59] A discussion of state action in the consumer field can be found in David Hamilton, *The Consumer in Our Economy* (Boston: Houghton Mifflin, 1962), ch. 12.

[60] Merle Fainsod, Lincoln Gordon, and Joseph C. Palamountain, Jr., *Government and the American Economy* (New York: W. W. Norton, 1959), 212.

groups often speak for consumer interests. Labor organizations, farm groups, cooperatives, organized womens' groups like the League of Women Voters, may at one time or another be found as part of the "consumers' lobby." In 1962 groups supporting the new drug legislation included the AFL-CIO, the Cooperative League, the American Public Health Association, the National Consumers' League, and the National Retired Teachers' Association. However, the lack of sustained, organized group support for consumers has given rise to various efforts to provide direct representation for consumers in the government through administrative arrangements. During the 1930's consumer representation was explicitly provided in the National Recovery Administration, the Agricultural Adjustment Administration, and the National Bituminous Coal Commission. These did not prove overly effective in the face of strong producer interests involved with these agencies. Proposals by Senator Kefauver and others from the mid-1950's onward for the establishment of a Department of Consumers to include the various governmental bureaus and agencies which assist or protect consumers have come to nothing. Increased attention to consumer interests has been manifested, however, in the creation of a Consumer Advisory Council (1961) by President Kennedy and the addition of a Special Assistant for Consumer Affairs to the White House staff in 1964 by President Johnson. Whether these will have more than symbolic effect remains to be seen.

The poorly organized condition of the consumer interest, for several reasons, has not prevented the enactment of a fair amount of consumer legislation in the twentieth century. In some cases legislation has come in response to obvious public needs or strong threats to the public health or safety, such as legislation directed against quackery in medicine at the state level. Second, some sort of "crisis" situation has occasionally demonstrated or emphasized the need for action. This has especially been significant in food and drug legislation. Third, continued efforts by dedicated individuals or groups may be significant. The activity of Senator Kefauver in connection with the Drug Amendments of 1962 comes to mind here. Fourth, legislation of value to consumers may result from efforts of producer groups, as when some producers seek to legislatively prevent other producers from gaining an unfair advantage over them by unfair or deceptive practices. Reputable businessmen have frequently led or joined battles against fraud and misrepresentation. In 1962 some drug companies favored moderate legislation to restrain their less scrupulous competitors and, probably, as a means of warding off harsher legislation.

363

Legislation on Foods, Drugs, and Cosmetics

The need to protect consumers began to be strongly felt with the industrialization of the American economy subsequent to the Civil War, along with the development of mass-production and mass-marketing techniques. Canning, baking, and other methods of food processing gradually shifted from home to factory and commercial drugs and medicines replaced home remedies for illnesses. As these developments occurred, opportunities for gain by charlatans, quacks, frauds, the dishonest, and the unscrupulous multiplied. Although some of the states enacted legislation regulating the manufacture and sale of foods and drugs in the second half of the nineteenth century, it was often ineffective because interstate competition helped keep legislative standards low. And, of course, the states could not deal with goods moving in interstate commerce.

Efforts to secure national legislation began in the 1880's but not until 1906 was any general legislation enacted, and then over the strong opposition of food and drug interests and conservative groups. The influence of such interests and groups was finally overcome by public concern and indignation, fed from a number of sources. Upton Sinclair's novel *The Jungle* (1906), graphically depicted the unsanitary and loathsome practices prevalent in the meat-packing industry. Public knowledge of evils in the food and drug industries was increased by exposés published in popular magazines by muckraking journalists. These actions capped an educational program led for more than two decades by Dr. Harvey Wiley, head of the Bureau of Chemistry in the Department of Agriculture. Wiley had a voluntary "poison squad" which tested and publicized the health effects of food preparations, many of which contained poisons.

The Food and Drug Act of 1906 prohibited interstate commerce in misbranded or adulterated foods and drugs. Items were misbranded if their labels were false or misleading or if they imitated another article. Adulteration of food included removal of valuable constituents or substitution of less valuable ones, addition of poisonous or deleterious substances, and inclusion of decomposed or diseased matter. Fines and jail sentences were provided for violators along with seizure of misbranded or adulterated articles. An administrative agency, now the Food and Drug Administration in the Department of Health, Education and Welfare, was established to enforce the law. Also in 1906, Congress enacted a separate Meat Inspection Act to prevent the shipment and sale of diseased and unwholesome meat in interstate commerce. Inspection and approval by Department of Agriculture officials of all meat moving in such commerce was required. Previous meat inspection legislation had been applicable only to meat exported for sale abroad, having been enacted to meet European complaints about the quality and condition of American meat exports. In the late 1950's the inspection requirement was expanded to include poultry sold in interstate commerce.

The Food and Drug Act appears to have been fairly effective in preventing some of the more extreme forms of adulteration and misbranding. However, shortcomings in the law for consumer protection had become quite obvious by the 1930's. Various products were not covered by the labeling requirements; there was no regulation of the advertising, as distinct from labeling, of foods and drugs; new drugs and medicines did not have to be proven safe for human use before marketing. Moreover, cosmetics had come into wide use during the 1920's because of a "sociological revolution" which enabled women to so beautify themselves without being called "painted ladies" and the like. Cosmetics sometimes contained harmful or poisonous substances.

The Great Depression brought a resurgence of interest in consumer protection and, in 1933, a move to strengthen the food and drug laws got under way. Not surprisingly, it met strong resistance from manufacturing groups and advertising interests, both of which viewed such legislation as "bad for business." Just when it seemed the move to secure legislation would fail, a crisis situation dramatically portrayed the need for additional consumer protection. A patent medicine known as Elixir Sulfanilamide was held responsible for the deaths of nearly a hundred persons. Although containing a deadly poison, it had been put on the market without testing of its toxicity for humans. The lesson was clear.

The Food, Drug and Cosmetic Act of 1938 amended the earlier legislation in several ways. The definitions of adulteration and misbranding were broadened and penalties for violations were increased. The coverage of the law was expanded to include cosmetics (except soap) and therapeutic devices. The marketing of new drugs required the approval of the Food and Drug Administration, which was authorized to deny approval to drugs which had not been tested or had been proved unsafe. The agency was also empowered to inspect sanitary conditions in factories, warehouses, and other establishments handling foods and drugs. Regulatory power over the advertising of foods, drugs, cosmetics, and curative (or therapeutic) devices was vested in the Federal Trade Commission by the Wheeler-Lea Act (see Chapter 5).

A third major statute in the food and drug field was enacted in 1962. Some of the events leading to the law merit attention here. In 1958 a Senate subcommittee headed by Senator Estes Kefauver started an investigation of drug marketing. It was especially concerned with the high prices charged for many drugs and the large profits earned on them by drug manufacturers.[61] In the course of its proceedings the subcommittee found that drugs were sometimes put on the market without adequate testing and knowledge concerning their effectiveness and side effects. An omnibus bill designed to deal with both the economic and medical aspects of drug marketing was introduced by Senator Kefauver in 1961. Although it received the support of the Kennedy administration, the bill quickly became bogged down in controversy. The drug interests and their legislative supporters were especially adamant in opposing legislation involving the prices charged for drugs.

The balance of legislative power tilted in favor of the bill's proponents in the summer of 1962 because of the public concern created by a drug called Thalidomide. A sedative given to pregnant women, Thalidomide apparently caused deformities in babies when taken by women in the early stages of pregnancy. Although the drug had been distributed for testing purposes in the United States, it had not been commercially marketed because an employee of the Food and Drug Administration had repeatedly delayed approving the drug. Existing law permitted withholding of approval for only sixty days but this period had been extended by requests for more information on the drug, which had not been proved conclusively unsafe. This incident convinced many people that further legislation was needed.

The Drug Amendments of 1962 strengthened the drug laws in a number of ways. Drug companies were required to register with the government, to operate under quality manufacturing controls, and to submit to regular factory inspection. New drugs had to be proved "effective" as well as safe before they could be marketed, the government was given more time to approve or reject marketing requests, and a drug could be removed immediately from the market if it pre-

[61] For a highly interesting and lengthy account of the enactment of the 1962 legislation and the events leading up to it, see Richard Harris, "Annals of Legislation," *The New Yorker,* XL (March 14, 1964), 48 ff.; (March 21), 75 ff.; (March 28), 46 ff.

sented an imminent hazard to public health. Also, drug advertisements were required to include more information on the drug, including its generic name and any possible side effects which its use might produce. As passed, however, the law contained no provisions on the economic aspects of drug marketing. The drug interests won that part of the struggle.

At present, the problems in federal food and drug protection no longer seem to be statutory, since existing laws are fairly strong and inclusive. Nor are finances the inhibiting factor they once were because, in recent years, Congress has become more generous in its appropriations for the Food and Drug Administration. Whereas the agency's appropriations were around $5 million annually in the mid-1950's, it now receives more than $25 million annually. This does not mean that the agency is overendowed with funds, however, as its duties have expanded with the enactment of new legislation and the rapid growth in the size and scope of the food, drug, and cosmetic industries.

The Food and Drug Administration is hampered in its enforcement activities by the difficulty of obtaining sufficient evidence to convince a jury that a patent medicine is harmful or that fraud was involved in the sale of a curative device. As a form of "white-collar crime," violations of the food and drug laws are not considered as serious or as morally reprehensible as other forms of crime. Moreover, the attitudes of some of those whom the laws are designed to protect complicate enforcement in another way. Some of the gullible or ill-informed users of questionable devices or "medicines" become "loyal victims" who are willing to testify in defense of violators and who may even say that they have been "cured" of some malady. Barnum, one can conclude, was not a hundred per cent wrong!

Because of its lack of a strong clientele from which it can draw political support, the Food and Drug Administration may seek to reduce opposition from those whom it regulates by not enforcing the laws as actively as possible. Thus, critics of the agency both inside and outside of Congress contend that the agency is being administered too loosely and that many officials fraternize too much with representatives of the commercial firms they are supposed to regulate. In 1960 the chief of the administration's Antibiotics Division was removed from his job for accepting $287,000 in honorariums over a seven-year period for "editing" two antibiotics magazines published by regulated interests.[62] It is noteworthy that a large share of the criticism of the FDA

[62] Morton Mintz, "New Drugs: Is Government Supervision Adequate?" *The Reporter,* XXVIII (March 28, 1963), 46–52.

now stems from those who want it to be more vigorous and to "earn" its increased appropriations. This is a far cry from the situation in past decades, when it was the supporters of "offended" regulated interests who were most vocal and active. "One congressman once brought about severe cuts in its budget because the agency had stopped one of his constituents from making little, round balls from big, tough beets and passing them off as baby beets."[63] The Food and Drug Administration is finding that it is often no easier to please one's friends than it is to accommodate one's detractors.

Standards and Disclosure of Information

The subject here is legislation and governmental action designed to provide the consumer with information which will help him to make informed, or at least better informed, decisions in his role as a buyer. The burden of choice still rests with the consumer, however.

Official standards have long been used for weights and measures. The national government is responsible for establishing and maintaining standards but the actual regulation of weighing and measuring devices is handled almost entirely by the state and local governments. Because of their often desultory enforcement activities, much depends upon voluntary adherence to the set standards.

Voluntary standard grades have been developed by the Department of Agriculture for meat, many fruits and vegetables, and eggs. The Bureau of Standards develops quality standards for many industrial products. The use of such standards has remained voluntary because of the resistance of producer groups. Mandatory grade labeling or standardization of products, which would be of benefit to consumers, has been opposed by many "brand name" companies. These companies, through years of heavy advertising, have been able to convince many consumers that good merchandise can be obtained only under their brand labels. They have thus obtained a modicum of monopoly for themselves. This advantage would be lost if consumers, by means of grade labels, could readily determine that lesser known and less expensive brands were of similar quality. The "brand name" advertisers are joined in their opposition by advertising agencies and media which perceive compulsory grade labeling as a threat to their interests because it might reduce the value of advertising.[64]

[63] *The New York Times,* Oct. 14, 1962, p. 82.
[64] Hamilton, *op. cit.,* 190–193.

368

Disclosure legislation requires that the prospective buyer be provided with information which may be useful in making a decision or whose concealment might be detrimental to him. A series of laws require the accurate labeling of products and are enforced by the Federal Trade Commission. The Wool Products Labeling Act of 1939 requires labels on wool products showing the amounts of new, reused, and reprocessed wool and other fibers which they contain. Wool interests thought such information would increase the market for wool products. The Fur Products Labeling Act of 1951 requires that fur products have labels stating the English names of the furs used in them. The Textile Fiber Products Identification Act of 1958 states that products made from natural or synthetic fibers must have labels specifying the percentages of each fiber they contain.

The Automobile Information Disclosure Act of 1958 directs manufacturers to put tags on new cars showing the suggested retail price of the car, the cost of each optional accessory, and the cost of transportation to the dealer. This is designed to help the prospective purchaser bargain more knowledgeably with his "friendly car dealer." The legislation does not set prices nor does it protect the buyer against his own folly. In a similar vein is the "truth in lending" legislation currently before Congress. If enacted it would require full disclosure of the true interest rate and fees charged to instalment buyers so that they could protect themselves against excessively high interest rates if, it must be added, they desire to do so.

When all is said, however, government action helps protect the consumer against only a few of the many situations in which he may fall victim to fraud, deceit, chicanery, or his own ignorance. Because of his lack of organization and influence when contesting with producer groups in the political marketplace, the consumer must often depend upon his own wit rather than the government to protect his interests in the economic marketplace. So it will be until consumer interests become more politically conscious, articulate, and organized.

Chapter Nine

SOME CONCLUDING OBSERVATIONS

Public economic policies now play an exceedingly important role in shaping the structure and operation of the American economy. Although the government has always been involved in the economy, a major change in the scope and extent of its intervention separate the years since 1933 from the preceding era. Whether one views the New Deal as a cause, an effect, or both, of a changed economic role for government, the New Deal does clearly mark the passing of the old order and the laying to rest of most beliefs in the laissez faire state and the self-regulating economy.

The American economy today can best be described as a mixed economy, an amalgam of private and public enterprise, public control and subsidy of private activity, private performance of public activity (as in defense contracting and scientific research), and some cooperative enterprise. Enterprises often designated as "mixed enterprises" are emerging from the government's efforts to meet its national defense and domestic commitments in an environment compounded by rapid and far-reaching scientific and technological developments. These industries, as the word "mixed" indicates, are neither entirely private nor public. Thus, as in the aerospace industry, many companies principally operate under government contracts to produce government-prescribed products for the use of the government. In somewhat different fashion, other industries function as extensions of the government to carry out public policies. Most of the national government's research and development effort is handled, under contracts and grants, by private companies, state universities, and other institutions. Here are relationships which cannot be adequately comprehended or categorized in the old dichotomies of public and private, socialism and free enterprise.

The government's modern day economic role constitutes a rejection of both laissez faire capitalism and socialism (in the customary sense of government ownership and operation of the principal means of production, distribution, and exchange). Government regulation and promotional activity have become the accepted forms of action for meeting economic problems, public enterprise being peripheral and limited. Regulation and promotion have been viewed as moderate in nature, as avoiding the extremes of laissez faire and socialism. Indeed, regulation can realistically be viewed as a barrier against and not a step toward socialism, despite the claims and alarums of some on the right-wing side of the political spectrum. There is little if any evidence in American history to indicate that regulation of private enterprise is but a "rest station" along the road to socialism. But, this aside, the question of the wisdom or necessity of particular regulatory or promotional programs is quite another matter and one on which there is much honest disagreement.

Further, the American experience has revealed that there are many alternative forms of economic control between the poles of government enterprise and private enterprise. Imagine them as marking the ends of a continuum which indicates the amount or degree of control of private activity involved in a particular governmental control technique. Between the two poles, running from lesser to greater control, one can mark such control techniques as common-law regulation, control through corporate charters and other general business regulation (e.g., labor and securities legislation), government subsidization of a regulated corporation, antitrust legislation, the public utility type of regulation, and Atomic Energy Commission contracts (which involve extensive prescription of private activity).[1] Although sometimes bound by traditional forms, there has been much social invention in control techniques.

A wide range of government economic activities, encompassing a great diversity of control techniques, objectives, and degrees of restraint, now are part of the American economy. Included in the present structure of government controls, in no particular order, are: maintenance of competition through antitrust legislation; direct fixing of rates for public utilities; licensing of radio and television broadcasting and air transportation companies; inspection of food and drug establishments; operation of public enterprises such as the Post Office, power production facilities, and credit agencies; use of fiscal and monetary policies to maintain economic stability; welfare programs to help guar-

[1] See Robert A. Dahl and Charles E. Lindblom, *Politics, Economics, and Welfare* (New York: Harper & Row, 1953), 6–18.

antee individual security; programs to control farm production and support farm prices; prescription of minimum wages and maximum hours for workers; subsidies for the operation of merchant ships and feeder airlines; use of government purchasing to help end racial discrimination in employment and to improve wages and working conditions; education and training programs to increase economic opportunities for the poor; and demonstration programs to persuade farmers to use better farming methods. This list is by no means complete.

Notwithstanding the broad range and extent of government economic intervention, private business and enterprise still remain the basic feature of the American economic system. Within the existing structure of controls, most property, most income, most business decisions are privately controlled or determined. The amount of competition in the economy, the rate of economic growth, the development of new products, the location of industry, the evolution of new productive techniques, the level of wages, the volume of jobs, the adequacy of transportation services—these and many more matters depend substantially upon private action. Although government programs control, promote, facilitate, and supplement private action, in only a small number of situations has government action replaced private action entirely. Nor is there any trend in this direction at present.

In many instances the real choice confronting government decision makers and the public is not one between government control and no control of economic activity but rather between government control and private control. In the absence of government regulation (and labor unions) minimum wage levels will be determined by employers in many fields. In the absence of public rate regulation the rates for services will be determined by the utility companies. However, where the choice is one of control by competition or control by the government, the American people have generally preferred the former as more conducive to individual action and freedom. Efforts to eliminate competition or to engage in competitive abuses have resulted in policies to maintain competition and to prevent undesired forms of competition. Competition is an alternative to government control, but it often cannot exist unaided by government.

Government regulatory programs are negative in the sense that they restrict individual freedom by limiting the choices or courses of action which are permissible. But this is only one side of the matter because public economic policies also have functioned to help maintain freedom, diversity, and pluralism. Policies involve the balancing of interests and, in most cases, they will have the effect of decreasing the power of some groups while increasing the power of other groups. By improving the position of some groups vis-a-vis other groups, by helping some groups to survive and perhaps to prosper, the government has acted to diversify political and economic power among many competing power centers and groupings in our society—big business, small business, farmers, retailers, organized labor, professional groups, trade associations, and so on. This pluralism has helped to insulate the individual from the government while giving him a better opportunity, through group processes, to influence public policy. Moreover, because they possess power, the various groups in society are better able to protect their freedom against the actions of others. A group with little or no power is likely to be a group with little if any freedom.

Turning now to some comments on the formation of policy, the present system of public economic controls is best depicted as a pragmatic and piecemeal response to particular demands and problems. The American approach to regulation has been empirical and experimental rather than dogmatic and doctrinaire. It has been further characterized by a lack of planning for future needs and problems, as in the case of inadequate planning in the past to cope with economic fluctuations. The practical, piecemeal approach to policy has often led to conflicts in policies enacted at different times in response to different needs and interests. Thus the effect of antitrust policies is reduced by conflicting efforts to protect small retailers against price competition and incorporation laws which facilitate the growth of economic bigness. Policies to restrict agricultural production in order to raise farm prices exist side by side with scientific and educational programs designed to increase farm productivity. But if the pragmatic approach has produced policy conflicts and a lack of planning, it has also facilitated, through an open-minded attitude toward regulation, innovation in techniques and methods and the devising of forms of control best suited to particular needs and situations.

One of the factors which complicates the policy process is the absence of accepted criteria for making policy choices among conflicting interests and alternatives. Pluralism and pragmatism have certainly contributed to this situation. If, for example, it were generally agreed that policy decisions should be made according to their impact on economic efficiency, decision making would be simplified (but not necessarily simple!) and more amenable to "scientific" determination. Policies and programs would be approved or disapproved as they did or did not contribute to economic efficiency. To wit: If economic bigness contributed to economic efficiency it would be accepted and welcomed. If resale price maintenance lowered distributive efficiency it would be rejected. However, because such generally accepted criteria do not exist, because there are many competing groups with diverse interests and values seeking to influence policy making, a variety of political, social, and ethical as well as economic considerations enter into the making of public economic policy. And, consequently, the policy process involves negotiation and bargaining, the striking of balances and the making of compromises, not the finding of "correct" policies or the choice between "right" and "wrong" in any absolute sense. Although most decisions are justified as being in the "public interest," there is no universally accepted definition of that entity.[2]

A large measure of truth is capsuled in the comment that public economic policies come into being and persist because someone wants them and supports them. If there are no group demands or interests in a given area there is unlikely to be any public policy pertaining thereto (except, to be a bit vacuous, a "policy" of having no policy). With respect to group demands, the American experience indicates that the initial rejection of a group's claims does not lead to their withdrawal. Rather, claims so rejected are apt to be put forth again but in modified or more modest form. Thus railroad regulation replaced the demand for nationalization of the railroads and medicare for the aged was substituted for national health insurance. Second, the satisfaction of a group's initial demands does not necessarily end their activity. Initial success may produce further demands for the strengthening or expansion of a program, as in the extension of minimum wage coverage and the elaboration of antitrust policy since 1890. There is, in sum, extensive persistence in group demands for political action.

With regard to the institutional context of the policy process, several important developments in the twentieth century should be remarked. First, the Constitution has been interpreted by the Supreme Court, particularly since 1937, in such fashion as to give the President and Congress broad scope in economic policy making. Congress is now the judge of what it can or should do, subject to political and cultural but not much judicial limitation. Second, the courts no longer sit in judgment on the goodness or badness, the desirability or undesirability of economic legislation. Under present doctrine this is held to be a matter for the "political" branches of the government. Where once the judges acted to implement a policy of economic laissez faire, they now follow a policy of judicial laissez faire. Third, as economic

[2] Glendon A. Schubert, *The Public Interest* (New York: The Free Press, 1960).

problems have been broader in scope, assuming national or international importance, regulatory activity has shifted in dominant locus from the state to the national level. Fourth, as governmental economic activity has expanded, it has been accompanied by an increase in administrative activity. More and more control by administrative agencies acting under general statutes has become the practice as legislators, pressed for time, confronted with complex problems, and lacking technical knowledge, have delegated to the agencies the task of filling in the details of the law and making precise settlements among the affected interests. Very seldom now, in the economic policy area, does Congress employ the method of judicial enforcement of a general or particular statute.

Fifth, as administrative agencies have faced ever-growing workloads they have increasingly resorted to informal techniques—conferences, negotiation, reference to technical data—rather than formal procedures in disposing of their business. These developments in the administration of policy have created a need for judicial and other safeguards to ensure that agencies act fairly and within the bounds of their legal authority. Administrative due process has replaced substantive due process as the central concern of the courts in economic policy.

To conclude, with the passage of time, economic policies in some areas become established and generally accepted, if not universally applauded. Illustrative are antitrust, public utility control, labor-management relations, old age insurance, and soil conservation policies. Although controversy and conflict do occur in these areas, they are focused primarily on policy details and the application of policy. Whether the Sherman Act, the Taft-Hartley Act, or the Social Security Act should be retained are not open questions. But, because of dynamism in our socio-economic system, new problems are created by urbanization, technological growth, scientific developments, and changing group relationships. Where once government decision makers were primarily concerned with problems of monopoly, tariff protection, coinage of silver, railroad regulation, and the desirability of labor unions, they now must deal with automation and unemployment, poverty, air and water pollution, urban transportation, and slum clearance, urban renewal, and public housing. A decade or two hence some of these problems will seem fairly settled and still newer problems will have arisen to take their place. As long as our society remains dynamic, and as long as government is looked upon as a means for meeting social and economic problems, there will be no dearth of matters for which governmentally determined solutions and settlements are sought by the affected interest groups.

SUGGESTED READINGS

Chapter One

Allen, Frederick Lewis. *The Big Change*. New York: Harper & Row, 1952.
Hartz, Louis. *Economic Policy and Democratic Thought: Pennsylvania 1776–1860*. Cambridge, Mass.: Harvard University Press, 1948.
Heath, Milton Sydney. *Constructive Liberalism: The Role of the State in Economic Development in Georgia to 1860*. Cambridge, Mass.: Harvard University Press, 1954.
Heilbroner, Robert L. *The Making of Economic Society*. Englewood Cliffs, N.J.: Prentice-Hall, 1962.
Hofstadter, Richard. *The Age of Reform*. New York: Alfred A. Knopf, 1956.
Mason, Edward S., ed. *The Corporation in Modern Society*. Cambridge, Mass.: Harvard University Press, 1959.
Parkes, Henry Bamford. *The American Experience*. New York: Alfred A. Knopf, 1955.
Primm, James Neal. *Economic Policy in the Development of a Western State: Missouri, 1820–1860,* Cambridge, Mass.: Harvard University Press, 1954.
Reagan, Michael. *The Managed Economy*. New York: Oxford University Press, 1963.
Schlesinger, Arthur M., Jr. *The Crisis of the Old Order*. Boston: Houghton Mifflin, 1956.
Steiner, George A. *Government's Role in Economic Life*. New York: McGraw-Hill, 1953.

Chapter Two

Dahl, Robert A., and Lindblom, Charles E. *Politics, Economics, and Welfare*. New York: Harper & Row, 1953.
Edelman, Murray. *The Symbolic Uses of Politics*. Urbana: The University of Illinois Press, 1964.

Froman, Lewis A., Jr. *People and Politics: An Analysis of the American Political System*. Englewood Cliffs, N.J.: Prentice-Hall, 1962.

Key, V. O., Jr. *Parties, Politics, and Pressure Groups*, 5th ed. New York: Thomas Y. Crowell, 1963.

Latham, Earl. *The Group Basis of Politics*. Ithaca: Cornell University Press, 1952.

Lindblom, Charles E. *The Intelligence of Democracy: Decision Making through Mutual Adjustment*. New York: The Free Press, 1965.

Macmahon, Arthur W., ed. *Federalism: Mature and Emergent*. New York: Columbia University Press, 1955.

McCloskey, Robert G. *The American Supreme Court*. Chicago: University of Chicago Press, 1960.

Mendelson, Wallace. *Capitalism, Democracy, and the Supreme Court*. New York: Appleton-Century-Crofts, 1960.

Milbrath, Lester W. *The Washington Lobbyists*. Chicago: Rand McNally, 1963.

Pritchett, C. Herman. *The American Constitution*. New York: McGraw-Hill, 1959.

Schattschneider, E. E. *The Semisovereign People: A Realist's View of Democracy in America*. New York: Holt, Rinehart and Winston, 1960.

Truman, David B. *The Governmental Process*. New York: Alfred A. Knopf, 1951.

Vile, M. J. C. *The Structure of American Federalism*. London: Oxford University Press, 1961.

William, Robin M., Jr. *American Society: A Sociological Interpretation*, 2nd ed. New York: Alfred A. Knopf, 1961.

Zeigler, Harmon. *Interest Groups in American Society*. Englewood Cliffs, N.J.: Prentice-Hall, 1964.

Chapter Three

Bernstein, Marver H. *Regulating Business by Independent Commission*. Princeton: Princeton University Press, 1955.

Boyer, William W. *Bureaucracy on Trial: Policy Making by Government Agencies*. Indianapolis Bobbs-Merrill, 1964.

Freeman, J. Leiper. *The Political Process: Executive Bureau-Legislative Committee Relations,* rev. ed. New York: Random House, 1965.

Friendly, Henry J. *The Federal Administrative Agencies: The Need for Better Definition of Standards*. Cambridge, Mass.: Harvard University Press, 1962.

Hyneman, Charles S. *Bureaucracy in a Democracy*. New York: Harper & Row, 1950.

Krislov, Samuel, and Lloyd D. Musolf, eds. *The Politics of Regulation: A Reader*. Boston: Houghton Mifflin, 1964.

Lane, Robert E. *The Regulation of Businessmen*. New Haven: Yale University Press, 1954.

Millett, John D. *Government and Public Administration*. New York: McGraw-Hill, 1959.

Redford, Emmette S. *Administration of National Economic Control*. New York: Macmillan, 1952.

Woll, Peter. *American Bureaucracy*. New York: W. W. Norton, 1963.

Chapter Four

Bailey, Stephen K. *Congress Makes a Law: The Story Behind the Employment Act of 1946*. New York: Columbia University Press, 1950.

Bator, Francis M. *The Question of Government Spending*. New York: Collier Books, 1962.

Blough, Roy. *The Federal Taxing Process*. Englewood Cliffs, N.J.: Prentice-Hall, 1952.

Due, John F. *Government and Finance,* 3rd ed. Homewood, Ill.: Richard D. Irwin, 1963.

Eisenstein, Louis. *The Ideologies of Taxation*. New York: The Ronald Press, 1961.

Groves, Harold M. *Financing Government,* 5th ed. New York: Holt, Rinehart and Winston, 1958.

Jacoby, Neil H. *United States Monetary Policy,* rev. ed. New York: Frederick A. Praeger, 1964.

Lewis, Wilfred, Jr. *Federal Fiscal Policy in the Postwar Recessions*. Washington: The Brookings Institution, 1962.

Strayer, Paul J. *Fiscal Policy and Politics*. New York: Harper & Row, 1958.

Wallace, Robert A. *Congressional Control of Federal Spending*. Detroit: Wayne State University Press, 1960.

Wildavsky, Aaron. *The Politics of the Budgetary Process*. Boston: Little, Brown, 1964.

Chapter Five

Adams, Walter, and Horace M. Gray. *Monopoly in America*. New York: Macmillan, 1955.

Arnold, Thurman W. *The Folklore of Capitalism*. New Haven: Yale University Press, 1937.

Bain, Joe S. *Industrial Organization*. New York: John Wiley, 1959.

Bunzel, John H. *The American Small Businessman*. New York: Alfred A. Knopf, 1962.

Cochran, Thomas C. *The American Business System: A Historical Perspective, 1900–1955*. New York: Harper & Row, 1957.

Galbraith, John K. *American Capitalism: The Concept of Countervailing Power,* rev. ed. Boston: Houghton Mifflin, 1956.

Glaeser, Martin G. *Public Utilities in American Capitalism*. New York: Macmillan, 1957.

Mason, Edward S. *Economic Concentration and the Monopoly Problem*. Cambridge, Mass.: Harvard University Press, 1957.

Massel, Mark S. *Competition and Monopoly: Legal and Economic Issues.* Washington, D.C.: The Brookings Institution, 1962.

Palamountain, Joseph C., Jr. *The Politics of Distribution.* Cambridge, Mass.: Harvard University Press, 1955.

Phillips, Charles F., Jr. *The Economics of Regulation: Theory and Practice in the Transportation and Public Utility Industries.* Homewood, Ill.: Richard D. Irwin, 1965.

Redford, Emmette S. *American Government and the Economy.* New York: Macmillan, 1965.

Stocking, George W., and Myron W. Watkins. *Monopoly and Free Enterprise.* New York: The Twentieth Century Fund, 1951.

Whitney, Simon N. *Antitrust Policies,* 2 vols. New York: The Twentieth Century Fund, 1958.

Wilcox, Clair. *Public Policies Toward Business,* rev. ed. Homewood, Ill.: Richard D. Irwin, 1960.

Zeigler, Harmon. *The Politics of Small Business.* Washington, D.C. The Public Affairs Press, 1961.

Chapter Six

Barbash, Jack. *The Practice of Unionism.* New York: Harper & Row, 1956.

Derber, Milton, and Edwin Young, eds. *Labor and the New Deal.* Madison: The University of Wisconsin Press, 1957.

Dulles, Foster Rhea. *Labor in America.* New York: Thomas Y. Crowell, 1955.

Evans, Robert, Jr. *Public Policy Toward Labor.* New York: Harper & Row, 1965.

Gregory, Charles O. *Labor and the Law.* New York: W. W. Norton, 1958.

Leek, John H. *Government and Labor in the United States.* New York: Holt, Rinehart and Winston, Inc., 1952.

McAdam, Alan K. *Power and Politics in Labor Legislation.* New York: Columbia University Press, 1964.

Millis, H. M., and E. Brown. *From the Wagner Act to Taft Hartley: A Study of National Labor Policy and Labor Relations.* Chicago: University of Chicago Press, 1950.

Northrup, Herbert R., and Gordon F. Bloom. *Government and Labor.* Homewood, Ill.: Richard D. Irwin, 1963.

Reynolds, Lloyd G. *Labor Economics and Labor Relations,* 4th ed. Englewood Cliffs, N.J.: Prentice-Hall, 1964.

Taft, Philip. *Organized Labor in American History.* New York: Harper & Row, 1964.

Chapter Seven

Benedict, Murray R. *Farm Policies of the United States, 1790–1950.* New York: The Twentieth Century Fund, 1953.

Blaisdell, Donald C. *Government and Agriculture*. New York: Farrar and Rinehart, 1940.

Christenson, Reo M. *The Brannan Plan: A Study in Farm Politics and Policy*. Ann Arbor: University of Michigan Press, 1959.

Congressional Quarterly. *U.S. Agricultural Policy in the Postwar Years, 1945–1963*. Washington, D.C.: Congressional Quarterly, Inc., 1963.

Hardin, Charles M. *The Politics of Agriculture*. New York: The Free Press, 1952.

Hathaway, Dale E. *Government and Agriculture: Economic Policy in a Democratic Society*. New York: Macmillan, 1962.

Higbee, Edward. *Farms and Farmers in an Urban Age*. New York: The Twentieth Century Fund, 1963.

McConnell, Grant. *The Decline of Agrarian Democracy*. Berkeley: University of California Press, 1959.

Shepard, Geoffrey. *Farm Policy: New Directions*. Ames: Iowa State University Press, 1964.

Soth, Lauren K. *Farm Trouble*. Princeton: Princeton University Press, 1957.

Chapter Eight

Bornet, Vaughn Davis. *Welfare in America*. Norman: University of Oklahoma Press, 1960.

Bremmer, Robert R. *From the Depths: The Discovery of Poverty in the United States*. New York: New York University Press, 1956.

Coyle, David Cushman. *Breakthrough to the Great Society*. Dobbs Ferry, N.Y.: Oceana Publications, 1965.

Galbraith, John K. *The Affluent Society*. Boston: Houghton Mifflin, 1958.

Hamilton, David. *The Consumer in Our Economy*. Boston: Houghton Mifflin, 1962.

Harrington, Michael. *The Other America*. Baltimore: Penguin Books, 1963.

Levitan, Sar A. *Federal Aid to Depressed Areas*. Baltimore: The Johns Hopkins Press, 1964.

Leyendecker, Hilary M. *Problems and Policy in Public Assistance*. New York: Harper & Row, 1955.

Munger, Frank J., and Richard F. Fenno, Jr. *National Politics and Federal Aid to Education*. Syracuse: Syracuse University Press, 1962.

Somers, Herman M., and Anne R. Somers. *Doctors, Patients, and Health Insurance*. Washington, D.C.: The Brookings Institution, 1961.

Vasey, Wayne. *Government and Social Welfare: Roles of Federal, State, and Local Governments in Administering Welfare Services*. New York: Holt, Rinehart and Winston, 1958.

INDEX

Individualism, 32, 212, 315
Institution, defined, 34
Interstate Commerce Act, 13
Interstate Commerce Commission, 75, 76, 84

Johnson, Lyndon B., 115, 122, 126–27, 259, 340, 343, 352, 360, 363
Johnson administration, 118, 292, 309, 313, 344
Judicial attitudes:
antitrust policy, 171–72
labor unions, 235–37
Judicial self-restraint, 45–46

Kerr-Mills Act, 358–59
Kefauver, Estes, 363, 366
Kennedy, John F., 79, 107, 117, 120, 122, 139, 141, 259, 282, 285, 339, 358, 363
Kennedy administration, 78–79, 92, 115, 139, 141, 230, 253, 261, 273, 281, 283, 286, 292, 298, 337, 352, 366
Key, V. O., Jr., 146, 149, 269, 272
Keynes, John Maynard, 105

Labor injunctions, 236–37, 246
Labor legislation:
Constitution, 223–24
growth, 220
labor disputes, 255–61
minimum labor standards, 223–33
objectives, 221–22
unions, 234–55
Labor unions, 206
attitudes toward, 211–13, 217, 235
Clayton Act, 237
membership, 208–11
political activity, 213–20
political goals, 214–15
Sherman Act, 236
Laissez faire, 10, 33
Landrum-Griffin Act, 252–55
Lane, Robert E., 97, 98, 241
Lochner v. New York, 224

McAdam, Alan K., 219
McClellan Committee, 252
McGuire Fair Trade Enabling Act, 191
MacIver, Robert, 20
McMahon Act, 205
McNary-Haugen Bills, 287–88
Madison, James, 1, 39, 55
Manpower development, 341–42
Mason, Edward S., 171
Maternal and child welfare programs, 335–36
Meat inspection, 364–65
Mediation and conciliation, 257–59
Medicare, 360–61
Milbrath, Lester W., 53
Miller-Tydings Act, 191
Mills, Wilbur, 60–61
Minow, Newton W., 79
Mixed economy, 25–29, 370
Monetary policy, 108ff.
Monopoly, definitions, 161–62
Morrill Act, 303
Mosher, Frederick C., 123–24
Munn v. Illinois, 194

National Association of Manufacturers, 148–49, 243, 251–52
National Association of Retail Druggists, 191–92
National Defense Education Act, 349
National Farmers Organization, 275–76
National Farmers Union, 274–75
National Grange, 275
National Industrial Recovery Act, 238–39
National Labor Relations Board, 81–82, 240, 242, 246, 251–52
Natural Gas Act, 60, 61, 62
Natural gas regulation, 59–64
Nebbia v. New York, 195
Neighborhood Youth Corps, 343–44
New Deal, 16–19, 105–106, 175, 326

Nixon, Richard, 258–59
Nonpartisan League, 270
Norris-LaGuardia Act, 237–38

Office of Economic Opportunity, 343–44
Old Age Assistance, 331
Old Age, Survivors, and Disability Insurance, 327–29
Olds, Leland, 61
Oleomargarine, taxation, 41–42
Olney, Richard R., 168–69
Owen-Keating Act, 226

Packers and Stockyards Act, 310
Parity, 277, 293–94
Perishable Commodities Act, 310–11
Phillips Petroleum Company v. State of Wisconsin, 62
Policy formation, 49–51, 373–74
Political culture, 30–34, 54
Political parties, 55, 87
  agricultural policy, 281–82
  stability policy, 121
  welfare policy, 322–23
Poverty, 337–39
President, 86
  the budget, 125–27
  Congress, 44, 90–91, 120
  departments, 70
  Economic Report, 107
  independent regulatory commissions, 76–77
Pressure groups and policy-making, 55–59
Primm, James, 10–11
Protective tariff, 9, 11, 287
Public assistance programs, 329–31
Public enterprise, 26, 29
  causes, 203–204
  characteristics, 201
  future, 204–205
  role in economy, 202
  Western Europe, 202

Public Health Service, 355
Public Law 480, 299–300
Public utilities:
  characteristics, 193
  evaluation of regulation, 199–201
  legal concept, 194–95
  pattern of regulation, 196–97
  rate-making, 197
  regulatory commissions, 198
Public Welfare Amendments of 1962, 337

"Quality Stabilization" bill, 192

Railway Labor Act, 15, 260
Reagan, Michael D., 109
Reconstruction Finance Corporation, 16, 155
Resale price maintenance, 191–92
Resettlement Administration, 305–306
Revenue Act (1964), 115
Reynolds, Lloyd G., 235
Right-to-work laws, 247–49
Robinson-Patman Act, 189–90
Roosevelt, Franklin D., 326, 329
Roosevelt, Theodore, 13
Rostow, Walt W., 3
Rural Electrification Administration, 306–307

Samuelson, Paul A., 122
Schlicter, Sumner, 317
Selective disobedience of the law, 97
Separation of powers, 43–45, 120
Sherman Antitrust Act:
  background, 162–64
  effectiveness, 179, 192–93
  judicial interpretation, 168–75
  means of enforcement, 165–68
  politics of enforcement, 175–79
  provisions, 164
Small businessmen, 187–88, 192
Smith-Hughes Act, 303
Social Security Act, 325–27

385